FREEDOM'S BATTLE VOLUME I
THE WAR AT SEA
1939–1945

John Winton joined the Royal Navy in 1949 as a cadet and retired in 1963 as a Lieutenant-Commander. He is widely known as a novelist and historian of the sea. His books include the novels *A Drowning War* and *Aircraft Carrier*, and works of non-fiction such as *Find, Fix and Strike: The Fleet Air Arm at War 1939–45*, *War in the Pacific: Pearl Harbor to Tokyo Bay*, *Air Power at Sea 1939–1945*, *The Death of the 'Scharnhorst'*, *Ultra at Sea* and *Ultra in the Pacific*. He died in 2001.

JOHN WINTON

Freedom's Battle Volume I

The War at Sea 1939–1945

An Anthology of Personal Experience Selected and Edited by John Winton

WITH INTRODUCTIONS BY
The Earl Mountbatten of Burma and
Peter Padfield

'For Freedom's battle once begun,
Bequeathed by bleeding Sire to Son,
Though baffled oft is ever won.'
Lord Byron, *The Giaour*

VINTAGE BOOKS
London

Published by Vintage 2007

4 6 8 10 9 7 5 3

First published in Great Britain in 1967 by Hutchinson
Random House, 20 Vauxhall Bridge Road,
London SW1V 2SA

First Pimlico edition published in 1994

www.vintage-books.co.uk

Addresses for companies within The Random House Group Limited can be found at:
www.randomhouse.co.uk/offices.htm

The Random House Group Limited Reg. No. 954009

A CIP catalogue record for this book
is available from the British Library

ISBN 9781845950828

The Random House Group Limited supports The Forest Stewardship Council® (FSC®), the leading international forest certification organisation. All our titles that are printed on Greenpeace approved FSC® certified paper carry the FSC® logo. Our paper procurement policy can be found at
www.randomhouse.co.uk/environment

Printed in the UK by CPI Bookmarque Croydon CR0 4TD

Contents

Illustrations

Acknowledgements

My grateful thanks are due to Mr Roger Ashley Leonard; to Miss Rose Coombs and Mr V. Rigby, of the Imperial War Museum Library, and to Mr R. Squires of the Photographic Library; to Mr H. C. Caistor and Miss Gertrude Hennin, of St Helens Public Library (North Western Regional Reserve Library for World War Two Books); and to Commander Peter Kemp, of the Admiralty Library.

Acknowledgements are also due to Cassell & Co. Ltd, for extracts from *The Second World War*, by the Rt Hon. Winston S. Churchill, and for an extract from *Convoy Escort Commander*, by Admiral Sir Peter Gretton; to A. D. Peters & Co., for an extract from *The Fleet Air Arm* (Chapman & Hall), the poem 'Carrier Off Norway', and an extract from *Escort Carrier* (Hutchinson), all by John Moore; to Batsford Ltd, for an extract from *Sub-Lieutenant*, by Ludovic Kennedy; to the Amalgamated Press Ltd, for extracts from *War Illustrated*; to H. F. & G. Witherby Ltd, for an extract from *A Space for Delight*, by Rear-Admiral Cosmo Graham; to Purnell & Sons Ltd, for an extract from *Purnell's History of the Second World War*; to Admiral of the Fleet Sir Philip Vian, for an extract from *Action This Day* (Muller); to Ian Cameron, for an extract from *Wings of the Morning* (Hodder & Stoughton); to Collins, for extracts from *The Sands of Dunkirk*, by Richard Collier, *HMS Warspite*, by Captain S. W. Roskill, and *Saints, Devils and Ordinary Seamen*, by William H. Pugsley; to Frederick Muller Ltd, for extracts from *Adventure Glorious*, by Ronald Healiss, from *HMS Electra*, by Lieutenant-Commander T. J. Cain, and from *Unbroken*, by Lieutenant-Commander Alastair Mars; to The Society of Authors, for two poems by John Masefield, from *The Nine Days Wonder* (Heinemann); to David Paton and Admiral Sir William James, for extracts from the *Journal of the Royal United Services Institution*; to William Kimber & Co. Ltd, for extracts from *One Man Band*, by Rear Admiral Ben Bryant, *Illustrious*, by Kenneth Poolman, *Submariner*, by Charles Anscomb and from *Relentless Pursuit*, by Commander Wemyss; to Hutchinson & Co. Ltd, for two extracts from *The Stick and the Stars*, by Commander William King; to *The Times*, for 'The Gallant Little Campeador', and for an extract from the leader of 14th February 1942; to Mr. J. Piekarski, for his letter to *The Times*; to David Higham Associates, for a poem by Dorothy L. Sayers, from *The Times Literary Supplement*; Sir Ralph Furse, for a poem from *Best Poems of 1940* (Cape); to the Controller of Her Majesty's Stationery Office, for extracts from *The War at Sea 1939–1945*, by Captain S. W. Roskill, from *The Mediterranean Fleet: Greece to Tripoli*, from *His Majesty's Minesweepers*, and for an extract from the Supplement to the *London Gazette* of 5th April 1951; to John Davies, for an extract from *The Stone Frigate* (Macmillan); to Peter Davies Ltd, for two extracts from *To Sea in a Sieve*, by Peter Bull; to *Punch*, for a poem by Justin Richardson; to Souvenir Press Ltd, for an extract from *Thank You, Nelson*, by Nancy Spain; to George G. Harrap & Co. Ltd, for extracts by Peter Dawlish and Jack Easton and poem by Alan Jenkins from *Wavy Navy*, from *Before The Tide Turned*, by Lieutenant-Commander Hugh Hodgkinson, and from *A Girl Called Johnnie*, by John Frayn Turner; to Rear-Admiral Angus Nicholl and the officers and ship's company of HMS *Penelope*, for an extract from *Our Penelope* (Harrap); to Nicholas Monsarrat, for extracts from *HM Corvette* (Cassell) and from *The Cruel Sea* (Cassell); to Chatto & Windus Ltd, for an extract from *Atlantic Ordeal: Mary Cornish*, by Elspeth Huxley, and from *Men Dressed as Seamen* (Christopher), by S. Gorley Putt; to Angus & Robertson Ltd, for an extract from *San*

Demetrio, by Calum MacNeil, and from *Frogman VC*, by Ian Fraser; to William Blackwood & Sons Ltd, for extracts from *A Taranto Diary*, by Lieutenant M. R. Maund, from *One Year of Life: Prince of Wales*, by A. and G. Franklin, from *Enemy in Sight*, by Esmond Knight, from *End of a Tribal*, by Commander Scurfield, and from *The Sinking of Scharnhorst*, by Lieutenant B. B. Ramsden; to Captain Donald MacIntyre, for an extract from *U-Boat Killer* (Weidenfeld & Nicolson); to Hodder & Stoughton Ltd, for an extract from *The Eye of the Wind*, by Peter Scott; to Viscountess Cunningham of Hyndhope and Hutchinson & Co. Ltd, for an extract from *A Sailor's Odyssey*, by Admiral of the Fleet Viscount Cunningham of Hyndhope; to George Allen & Unwin Ltd, for 'Kelly' from *Louise Mountbatten: Queen of Sweden* (to be published early 1968), by Margit Fjellman, and for extracts from *Bless Our Ship* by Captain Eric Bush, and *Nice To Have You Aboard* by Captain Harold Hopkins; to Faber & Faber Ltd, for extracts from *The Bismarck Episode*, by Captain Russell Grenfell and *In Good Company*, by Commander Thomas Woodrooffe; to John Farquharson Ltd, for an extract from *Ark Royal 1939–1941* (Hart Davis) by Rear-Admiral Sir William Jameson; to the Australian War Memorial, Canberra, for an extract from *Royal Australian Navy 1939–1942*, by G. Hermon Gill; to W. H. Allen & Co, for an extract from *The Lonely Battle*, by Desmond Wettern; to London Express News & Feature Services, for an extract from the *Daily Express* of 12th December 1941; to Fred Smewin, for a poem from *More Poems from the Forces* (Routledge & Kegal Paul); to The Bodley Head, for extracts from *Blue Tapestry* (Hollis & Carter), by Dame Vera Laughton Mathews; to Evans Bros Ltd, for extracts from *Channel Dash*, by Terence Robertson, and *The Man Who Never Was*, by Ewen Montagu; to Routledge & Kegan Paul Ltd, for poems by Norman Hampson, John Wedge and Richard B. Wright, from *More Poems from the Forces*: to Alan Ross, for poems from *Something of the Sea* (Derek Verschoyle) and from *To Whom It May Concern* (Hamish Hamilton); to Commander Cherry, for an extract from *Yankee RN* (Jarrolds); to Godfrey Winn, for an extract from *PQ-17* (Hutchinson); to Andre Deutsch, for two poems by Roy Fuller from *Collected Poems*; to the Hogarth Press Ltd, for extracts from *Out of the Smoke* and *Into the Smother*, both by Ray Parkin; to John Murray, for an extract from *The Attack on St Nazaire*, by Captain Robert Ryder; to Associated Newspapers Ltd, for a report from the *Daily Mail*; to A. D. Peters & Co., for an extract from *The Ship* (Michael Joseph Ltd) by C. S. Forester; to Gerald Pawle, for an extract from *The Secret War* (Harrap); to Hugh Popham, for extracts from *Sea Flight* (Kimber) and *Against the Lightning* (John Lane The Bodley Head); to Captain Jack Broome, for his account of PQ-17; to John Pudney, for a poem from *Collected Poems* (Putnam); to Exchange Telegraph Co. Ltd, for an extract from the despatches of Arthur Thorpe; to Commander Anthony Kimmins, for an extract from *The Listener* and from *Half Time* (Heinemann); to Commander Maitland-Makgill-Crichton and Ted Cutler, for extracts from *The Listener*; to Michael Joseph Ltd, for an extract from *We Fought Them in Gunboats*, by Robert Hichens; to F. H. Guest, for an extract from *The Awkward Marine* (Longmans Green), by James Spencer; to Captain W. R. Fell, for an extract from *The Sea Our Shield* (Cassell); to F. D. Ommanney, for an extract from *Flat Top* (Longmans Green); to Crosby Lockwood & Son Ltd, for an extract from *Only Ghosts Can Live*, by Guy Morgan; to Cornelius Ryan, for an extract from *The Longest Day* (Gollancz); to Penguin Books Ltd, for *Now I Know*, by Humphrey Knight, and poems by Richard Goodman and R. C. M. Howard, all from Penguin New Writing; to Denis Glover, for *It Was D-Day*, from Penguin New Writing; to Edward Young, for an extract from *One of our Submarines* (Hart Davis); to Rear-Admiral Chalmers, for an extract from *Max Horton and the Western Approaches* (Hodder & Stoughton); to Charles Causley and Rupert Hart Davis Ltd, for poems from *Union Street* and *Survivor's Leave*; to the Wardroom Officers of HMS *Formidable*, for an extract from *A Formidable Commission* (Seeley Services & Co. Ltd); to Putnams and Captain Jack Broome for signals from *Make a Signal*; to Commander Denis

Calnan for his account of the sinking of *Haguro*; to A. C. Hardy, for an extract from *Everyman's History of the Sea War* (Nicholson & Watson); to A. P. Watt & Son, for an extract from *Instead of Tears*, by Marie Stopes; to Arthur Barker Ltd, for an extract from *Hong Kong Escape*, by R. B. Goodwin.

Great efforts have been made to trace copyright holders, but not, I am afraid, with success in every case. Sources of extracts are given in more detail under the author's names in the Index. While writing the introductions and footnotes for the items in this anthology I relied very heavily on Captain Roskill's superb history of *The War At Sea 1939–1945*, Volumes I–III (HMSO). However, any errors of fact or interpretation are mine.

J. W.

Introduction

by Peter Padfield

John Winton burst on my consciousness many years ago with *We Joined the Navy*, one of the funniest books I had read. Subsequently I have followed his prolific writing career with great interest. He is a natural stylist, although one cannot know how much sheer hard grind goes into anyone's composition, joining wit with forthright observation – in the best traditions of the service. In this present work he has confined himself to picking out good writing in others; he freely acknowledges in the Preface that some events have been omitted because he could not find 'sufficiently entertaining accounts of them'. The result is justification enough. The book can be dipped into at random in the knowledge that there is scarcely a dull passage, hardly a page without authentic insights; and it can be viewed as a social as much as a naval resource.

In this respect it makes a perfect foil for such works as Captain Stephen Roskill's histories of the Second World War at sea. Roskill marshals the facts and provides analysis; Winton, who deliberately forgoes interpretation, offers subjective human impressions. Take, for instance, the Fleet Air Arm attack on the Italian battlefleet at Taranto in November 1940: a cousin of mine, Lieutenant Commander John Hale, led the second wave of near obsolescent Swordfish aircraft in this brilliant action which altered the balance of naval power in the Mediterranean; he said little about it of course. Roskill records the heavy aircraft fire, the balloon barrage over the ships and all relevant details of that incandescent night; Winton, by contrast, has a narrative describing, minute by minute, just what it *felt like* to be one of the pilots: 'Six thousand feet. God, how cold it is here! The sort of cold that fills you until all else is drowned save perhaps fear and loneliness.'

Besides 'what it was like' there is plenty of 'how it was done'. Warships frequently had to weave a snaking path with extreme helm between bombs or torpedoes dropped from aircraft. There is a vivid description here by the Quartermaster of HMAS *Perth* that shows the strength and athleticism required of the man at the wheel as he applied a stream of helm orders from the bridge with 'a concerted swing of both shoulders: bending from the waist and carrying the movement down with the knees bent, then thrusting up again at the other side on tensed toes . . . like the weaving of a fighter around a punching bag'. At the height of the action he describes in the Far Eastern war the stifling heat made it 'impossible for a man to last more than five minutes' at the wheel.

As that piece illustrates, this is far from a top-down view of the war at sea: ordinary sailors and Marines are represented along with officers, and display equal literary ability. A Marine survivor from the aircraft carrier *Glorious*, sunk in the early stages of the war by gunfire from two German battlecruisers, recalls looking 'up the cliff face of the wall of steel forward of the bridge', seeing it shatter, and some moments later 'another salvo hit, and the whole side of the *Glorious* seemed to cave in, leaving a choking cloud of smoke and a thunderous roar that echoed away to the darkening sky'. Winton comments that the *Glorious* was caught unawares because she was not flying air-search patrols, but it is rarely he permits himself such a judgement. The Marine author of this piece pays tribute to the conduct of the ship's officers as the carrier went down: the major of Marines and two other officers were standing by the quarterdeck hatchway:

> 'Come on, lads. Don't panic now. Get into line . . . '
>
> It was nothing they said, really. But the way they stood there and said it. They could have buggered off and left us.

A leading seaman from one of the carrier's escorting destroyers, which was sunk as she launched a torpedo attack on the enemy, provides a poignant vignette:

> . . . when I was in the water I saw the captain leaning over the bridge, take a cigarette from a case and light it. We shouted

to him to come on our raft, he waved 'Goodbye and good luck' – the end of a gallant man.

A sense of shared pride and the continuity of Royal Naval tradition pervades the anthology. It is captured well in a piece by Second Officer Nancy Spain WRNS as she finds herself in the magnificent surroundings of the Royal Naval College, Greenwich; all English history seemed to be spread before her: 'The history of England, of which Nelson was a part and which I, like so many others like me, had taken for granted. And I knew that I, too, should in future feel a sense of responsibility'.

John Winton does not draw attention to the way the material strength of the Royal Navy had been reduced during the inter-war years, insisting 'This book is not intended as a serious work of naval history'! However, Treasury parsimony, the clamour for disarmament after the terrible losses of the First World War and international naval limitation treaties, had left the service with an ageing fleet much under strength in relation to its obligations; and it is the contrast between this materiél deficit and the way the ships were fought and the spirit of the ships' companies, which shines out from the pages of this book, that heightens the achievements of the British and Commonwealth navies in the war.

Most of the epic engagements are here: the River Plate, where three British cruisers harried the 'pocket battleship', *Admiral Graf Spee,* to her death, the loss of the armed merchant cruiser *Rawalpindi* while tackling two German battlecruisers – this takes the form of a moving memoir of her captain by his son, Ludovic Kennedy – the loss of another converted merchantman, *Jervis Bay,* while protecting her convoy from a pocket battleship, the rescue of the British army from Dunkirk, the loss of the great battlecruiser, HMS *Hood*, followed by the vengeance taken on her antagonist, *Bismarck*; the triumphs of Taranto and Matapan, the stunning loss of both *Prince of Wales* and *Repulse* to mass Japanese air attack, the midget submarine strike on the *Tirpitz* in Altenfjord, the sinking of the *Scharnhorst,* together with a host of virtually unknown actions and incidents.

Famous chroniclers of aspects of the war are represented:

Nicholas Monsarrat of *The Cruel Sea*, C. S. Forester, Peter Scott and, indeed, Captain Stephen Roskill in best descriptive mode; the U-boat hunters, Captain Donald MacIntyre and Vice Admiral Sir Peter Gretton and the submarine skipper/authors, Commanders Edward Young and William King. The latter's heart-stopping description of lying in wait at periscope depth for a Japanese submarine approaching on the surface – 'It was so still I could see flies on the water' – helps explain the diagnosis of the flotilla doctor he encountered in port, who asked to see his fingernails:

> Each one showed a series of concentric half-moon ridges from base to tip. 'Interesting stigmata', he said. 'If you break off patrols for a refit you'll find a gap corresponding to the time spent in harbour. Each ridge is a patrol. They occur in *all* commanding officers of submarines . . .

For my money, King's memoir, *The Stick and the Stars*, is the classic account of British submarine command.

Winton has included much poetry, and has chosen well from known and unknown poets; there is a particularly intriguing piece in the latter category by a Petty Officer:

> You must take off your clothes for the doctor
> And stand as straight as a pin
> His hand of stone on your white breast-bone
> Where the bullets all go in . . .

One poem particularly captures the spirit of Britain fighting the lone battle for freedom as she had done so many times in her history, against Philip of Spain, the Bourbon kings of France, Napoleon, the Kaiser, Wilhelm II, and now Hitler; it is Dorothy Sayers' 'The English War':

> Send us, O God, the will and power
> To do as we have done before;
> The men who ride the sea and air
> Are the same men their fathers were
> To fight the English war

It was to be, although no one knew it, the last great 'English war'. Since then British freedoms have been carelessly surrendered to others; it is good to read these splendid accounts by men and women who knew exactly what they were fighting for.

Peter Padfield
Woodbridge, 2007

Introduction

BY

ADMIRAL OF THE FLEET

THE EARL MOUNTBATTEN OF BURMA

KG, OM, DSO, FRS, ETC

I joined HMS *Lion*, Admiral Beatty's famous flagship of the Battle Cruiser Fleet, in July 1916. I missed the Battle of Jutland by six weeks in World War I, but managed to be almost sunk three times and completely sunk once in the first two years of World War II. So I have some vivid recollections of how unpleasant the War at Sea can be.

I have served in every type of ship: battle cruisers, battleships, a submarine, an anti-submarine P-boat, destroyers and cruisers. I was captain of the aircraft carrier *Illustrious* for some three months, but to my great regret was pulled out of her to go to Combined Operations before she had completed her action repairs and was ready for sea. So I can claim to have had a fairly wide experience of naval life and naval activities over the years.

I am therefore very glad to see that a compendious anthology of writing about the Royal Navy is now being published and that it is being edited by John Winton. I have read and enjoyed most of his books and this collection is superb.

I am convinced that the standards of professionalism in the Royal Navy definitely improved during the inter-war years. Certainly the record of the Navy in World War II could hardly be a finer one.

There were many sad occasions—as there must be in war—which meant the loss of personal friends and the destruction of beloved ships, but the Navy maintained the highest standards.

In World War I the public only really remembered the names of about half a dozen admirals. In World War II they will surely have remembered many more great admirals; among them names such as Sir Dudley Pound, Lord Cunningham, Lord Tovey, Lord Fraser, Sir James Somerville, Sir Max Horton, Sir Philip Vian and Sir Arthur John Power, who served under me in South East Asia during the last year of the war and under whom I subsequently served when he was Commander-in-Chief, Mediterranean.

There is no room to mention all the brilliant captains who distinguished themselves, but I am delighted to see that John Winton has included in his book the sinking of the large 15,000-ton Japanese cruiser *Haguro* by the 26th Destroyer Flotilla under Captain 'Lofty' Power (later Admiral Sir Manley Power). I was naturally eager to see my own service distinguish itself in my South East Asia Command and this surely is the perfect example of how a night destroyer attack should be carried out.

It is impossible to think of the fine record of the Navy during World War II without thinking of the Commonwealth navies who played their part in it. The Royal Canadian Navy took a big share of the vital Battle of the Atlantic; the Royal Australian and Royal New Zealand navies sent their ships to all parts of the oceans until the Japanese threat to their own countries caused them to concentrate in the Eastern theatre of war; the young Royal Indian Navy did excellent work with me on the Arakan coast of Burma. But everywhere the ships of the Commonwealth played their full part in a very exacting and arduous naval effort.

I would like to pay tribute to the RNVR—whose performances I am glad to see are well recognised by John Winton in this book. The expansion of the Navy in World War II could never have been carried out without them and I personally have every reason to remember with gratitude and affection their keenness and efficiency.

At the end of my time as Chief of Combined Operations at least 80 per cent of the 3,000 naval officers I had in my command were not regulars. When I took over at the end of 1941 Combined Ops were unpopular and we got practically no volunteers from newly fledged RNVR officers, so I went to HMS *King Alfred*, the RNVR Training Establishment, to appeal for volunteers. I was warned I should be wasting my time.

I addressed a couple of hundred young RNVR officers and for half an hour told them of the war at sea in destroyers; how thrilling it was; what a great service the destroyer service was; and I urged them, one and all, to put their names down for destroyers.

I told them that if they couldn't get into destroyers the next best thing was to volunteer for Combined Ops; here they would get command of landing craft as very junior officers; this was the proper use of sea power—to put the Army and Air Forces ashore to fight on enemy coasts of our own choosing; they were guaranteed close action.

I believe all the young officers put down two choices: (1) Destroyers; (2) Combined Ops. I knew that there were only about ten vacancies at that time for destroyers, so I pretty well scooped the lot. I hope that none of them ever regretted their second choice. They made all the difference to my command.

I cannot omit a tribute to the WRNS. They really were splendid. My elder daughter, Patricia, was thrilled when she joined them in 1943. In the great variety of jobs, some of them highly secret and of great operational responsibility, which the Wrens did they played an invaluable and unforgettable part.

It was the Fleet Air Arm that made the greatest advance in World War II. Of the *Illustrious*' attack on Taranto Lord Cunningham said:

'Taranto and the night of November 11th/12th, 1940, should be remembered for ever as having shown once and for all times that in the Fleet Air Arm the Navy has its most devastating weapon. In a total flying time of about six and a half hours twenty aircraft inflicted more damage on the Italian Fleet than was inflicted on the German High Sea Fleet in daylight action of the Battle of Jutland.'

But it was in the later years of the war that the aircraft carriers really came into their own and proved themselves to be the main unit around which the strength of a first-class navy must be built.

Finally I would say that so long as this country remains an island the Navy is certain to have an important future; whatever that future may hold, those who serve in the Navy cannot fail to draw inspiration from the spirit revealed in this book.

Mountbatten of Burma

Editor's Preface

This book is not intended as a serious work of naval history. I was asked to compile an anthology of the best writing on the war at sea from 1939 to 1945, from the British and Commonwealth points of view. I have collected together all the pieces, fact and fiction, prose or poetry, which I found most moving, or witty, or informative, but, above all, most entertaining. I have not concerned myself with whether a particular eyewitness or survivor has all his facts, dates, times and places exactly right, nor whether his opinions are justified in the light of later knowledge. It was enough for me that he was there and wrote vividly of what he saw and heard. Certain events and operations have been omitted because I did not come across, in my opinion, sufficiently entertaining accounts of them. Similarly, I have not included what I thought was a tedious piece merely because the event it described was historically important. No doubt readers will be able to suggest plenty of worth-while passages which I should have included. I apologise for any obvious omissions.

I have laid out the anthology in chronological order, because the progress of the war at sea from initial set-backs to final victory forms a dramatic framework of its own. But this method does have one disadvantage. Disasters always seem to make better reading than successes; the story of one torpedoed ship is more valuable—to an anthologist—than an account of a huge eighty-ship convoy crossing the Atlantic without loss. Thus this anthology is slightly lop-sided; about two-thirds of its contents relate to events which happened before the end of 1942, the time of Second Alamein and the landings in North Africa, which may be taken as the turning point of the war against Germany.

Any anthology which does not include contributions from the United States Navy is bound to present a somewhat unbalanced picture of the Allies' effort in the war at sea. The exploits of the Royal and Commonwealth navies described here should be seen in perspective against the massive effort of the United States Navy—and particularly their achievements in the Far East, against a skilful and fanatically determined Imperial Japanese Navy who were always ready to attack and who were still dangerous to the bitter end.

The great majority of the items in this collection are eyewitness accounts, written by a variety of people—survivors, seamen, captains of ships, Wrens, pilots, poets, admirals, war correspondents. Comparatively few of them are professional writers, but their accounts of their experiences have a vitality and an impact upon the reader's imagination which most of the carefully and painstakingly researched post-war histories lack. Therefore I hope that anyone who served in the war at sea will recognise some familiar name here, or perhaps a description of his old ship and how she behaved, and will be able to say to himself, 'Yes, by God, I remember now. It was just like that.'

JOHN WINTON

1939

On 3rd September 1939 the Admiralty sent two general signals to the Fleet. One was: 'Immediate. Special telegram TOTAL *Germany.' The other was*

WINSTON IS BACK

Nothing had been said about when I should formally receive my office from the King, and in fact I did not kiss hands till the 5th. But the opening hours of war may be vital with navies. I therefore sent word to the Admiralty that I would take charge forthwith and arrive at six o'clock. On this the Board was kind enough to signal to the Fleet, 'Winston is back'. So it was that I came again to the room I had quitted in pain and sorrow almost exactly a quarter of a century before, when Lord Fisher's resignation had led to my removal from my post as First Lord and ruined irretrievably, as it proved, the important conception of forcing the Dardanelles. A few feet behind me, as I sat in my old chair, was the wooden map-case I had had fixed in 1911, and inside it still remained the chart of the North Sea on which each day, in order to focus attention on the supreme objective, I had made the Naval Intelligence Branch record the movements and dispositions of the German High Seas Fleet. Since 1911 much more than a quarter of a century had passed, and still mortal peril threatened us at the hands of the same nation. Once again defence of the right of a weak state, outraged and invaded by unprovoked aggression, forced us to draw the sword. Once again we must fight for life and honour against all the might and fury of the valiant, disciplined, and ruthless German race. Once again! So be it.

I felt it my duty to visit Scapa at the earliest moment. I had not met the Commander-in-Chief, Sir Charles Forbes, since Lord Chatfield had taken me to the Anti-Submarine School at Portland in 1938. I therefore obtained leave from our daily Cabinets, and started for Wick with a small personal staff on the night of September 14th. I spent most of the next two days inspecting the harbour and the entrances, with their booms and nets. I was assured that they were as good as in the last war, and that important additions and improvements were being made or were on the way. I stayed with the Commander-in-Chief in his flagship *Nelson*, and discussed not only

Scapa but the whole naval problem with him and his principal officers. The rest of the Fleet was hiding in Loch Ewe, and on the 17th the admiral took me to them in the *Nelson*. As we came out through the gateway into the open sea I was surprised to see no escort of destroyers for this great ship. 'I thought,' I remarked, 'you never went to sea without at least two, even for a single battleship.' But the admiral replied, 'Of course, that is what we should like; but we haven't got the destroyers to carry out any such rule. There are a lot of patrolling craft about, and we shall be into the Minches in a few hours.'

It was, like the others, a lovely day. All went well, and in the evening we anchored in Loch Ewe, where the four or five other great ships of the Home Fleet were assembled. The narrow entry into the loch was closed by several lines of indicator nets, and patrolling craft with Asdics and depth-charges, as well as picket boats, were numerous and busy. On every side rose the purple hills of Scotland in all their splendour. My thoughts went back a quarter of a century to that other September when I had last visited Sir John Jellicoe and his captains in this very bay, and had found them with their long lines of battleships and cruisers drawn out at anchor, a prey to the same uncertainties as now afflicted us. Most of the captains and admirals of those days were dead, or had long passed into retirement. The responsible senior officers who were now presented to me as I visited the various ships had been young lieutenants or even midshipmen in those far-off days. Before the former war I had had three years' preparation in which to make the acquaintance and approve the appointments of most of the high personnel, but now all these were new figures and new faces. The perfect discipline, style, and bearing, the ceremonial routine—all were unchanged. But an entirely different generation filled the uniforms and the posts. Only the ships had most of them been laid down in my tenure. None of them was new. It was a strange experience, like suddenly resuming a previous incarnation. It seemed that I was all that survived in the same position I had held so long ago. But no: the dangers had survived too. Danger from beneath the waves, more serious with more powerful U-boats; danger from the air, not merely of being spotted in your hiding place, but of heavy and perhaps destructive attack!

Having inspected two more ships on the morning of the 18th, and formed during my visit a strong feeling of confidence in the Commander-in-Chief, I motored from Loch Ewe to Inverness, where our train awaited us. We had a picnic lunch on the way by a stream sparkling in hot sunshine. I felt oddly oppressed with my memories

For God's sake, let us sit upon the ground
And tell sad stories of the death of kings.

No one had ever been over the same terrible course twice with such an interval between. No one had felt its dangers and responsibilities from the summit as I had, or, to descend to a small point, understood how First Lords of the Admiralty are treated when great ships are sunk and things go wrong. If we were in fact going over the same cycle a second time should I have once again to endure the pangs of dismissal? Fisher, Wilson, Battenberg, Jellicoe, Beatty, Pakenham, Sturdee, all gone!

I feel like one
Who treads alone
Some banquet-hall deserted,
Whose lights are fled,
Whose garlands dead,
And all but he departed.

And what of the supreme, measureless ordeal in which we were again irrevocably plunged? Poland in its agony; France but a pale reflection of her former warlike ardour; the Russian Colossus no longer an ally, not even neutral, possibly to become a foe. Italy no friend. Japan no ally. Would America ever come in again? The British Empire remained intact and gloriously united, but ill-prepared, unready. We still had command of the sea. We were woefully outmatched in numbers in this new mortal weapon of the air. Somehow the light faded out of the landscape.

Right Honourable WINSTON S. CHURCHILL

★

The war at sea began violently, and at once. At 9 p.m. on the first day of the war the 13,500-ton Donaldson liner Athenia *was torpedoed without warning off Ireland by U-30 (Lieutenant-Commander Lemp) with the loss*

of 112 lives, including twenty-eight American citizens. At 6 p.m. on the 17th September the aircraft carrier HMS Courageous *(Captain W. T. Makeig-Jones RN) was torpedoed by U-29 (Lieutenant-Commander Schuhardt) and sank south-west of Ireland with her captain and 518 of her ship's company. Meanwhile,* Ark Royal *narrowly survived a torpedo attack by U-39 (afterwards sunk) on the 14th September, and a bombing attack on 26th.* Ark *had already entered upon her two years of charmed life —although German propaganda was already asking*

WHERE IS *ARK ROYAL*?

The bomb came down, painfully visible to everybody on deck, and exploded in the sea only thirty yards from the ship's port bow. Her bow heaved up, then fell away again, she listed five degrees to starboard, cascades of water flowed over her, and then she rocked and slowly righted herself as she turned back on to her course. The only damage was some broken china.

The pilot of the Heinkel flew back to his base and made, it seems, a perfectly honest report. He 'believed' he had scored a hit. Seeing the carrier listing to starboard, the water and spray half covering her, he might well have thought so. The German Ministry of Propaganda, with what reason we do not know, thought so too. They issued a special bulletin to the effect that the *Ark Royal* was sunk, and next morning repeated the statement in enormous red headlines in the newspapers.

The *Volkischer Beobachter* covered its whole front page with an 'artist's impression' of the *Ark* going down by the head, while flames, smoke and pieces of wreckage were hurled high in the sky above her. The weekly magazines, going one better, printed coloured pictures of *Der Flugzengtrager* variously sinking, burning or in violent dissolution. Every paper displayed photographs of the not-very-intelligent features of Leutnant Adolf Francke, who was now promoted Oberleutnant, decorated with the Iron Cross first and second class, and sent a telegram of congratulation from Field Marshal Goering himself. He was also commissioned to write an illustrated booklet for children entitled *How I Sank the* Ark Royal.

The German broadcasting stations, in every language, continued for weeks to assert that the *Ark* was at the bottom of the sea; and Lord Haw-Haw, who was already very popular in Britain, made himself still more so by asking every night, and indeed many times every night: 'Where is the *Ark Royal?* Britain, ask your Admiralty. *Where is the "Ark Royal"* ?' This question gave the greatest delight to the members of the *Ark*'s lower deck, who would chant in unison, 'We're here! We're here!' and who never grew tired of the simple joke.

Lieutenant-Commander JOHN MOORE RNVR

*

At home the early days of the war were marked by a curious atmosphere of unreality which, as the months passed, became known as 'The Phoney War'. At a time when the RAF were busying themselves with Kingsley-Wood's 'Truth Raids' the following occurred on the bridge of a destroyer in the North Sea:

First Lieutenant: 'We're stopping, sir.'
Captain: 'I know. There's a submarine somewhere about here.'
First Lieutenant: 'Are we going to depth-charge him, sir?'
Captain: 'No. I'm sending down a diver with leaflets.'

ANON

*

In those very early days, even the Admiralty suffered some understandable confusion:

Autumn 1939 From Admiralty to Destroyer:
PROCEED WITH ALL DESPATCH
From Destroyer to Admiralty:
REQUEST DESTINATION
From Admiralty to Destroyer:
ADEN REPEAT ADEN
From Destroyer to Admiralty:
AM AT ADEN

From *Make a Signal*

*

At the outbreak of war the Admiralty re-established what was known in the 1914–18 War as the Northern Patrol—an extended line of warships patrolling a vast area of the North Atlantic from Norway to Greenland. Their purpose was to intercept German shipping returning to Germany, and to report the presence of German warships breaking out into the Atlantic. Many of the patrol ships were armed merchant cruisers: ex-passenger liners fitted with guns, flying the White Ensign and commanded by retired naval officers who had been recalled to service (some of them after being on the beach since the Geddes Act of 1921). One of these officers, and very typical of them all, was Captain Edward Coverley Kennedy RN,

CAPTAIN OF *RAWALPINDI*

I spent most of my time that summer with my father. In spite of the fact that our views on most matters seldom coincided, we had a profound understanding of one another. He came of the old school of naval officers which has learnt to acknowledge discipline and self-control as the first qualities in a man. He had a code of honour, a fixed belief in what was right and wrong, and a predetermined view-point on every matter which no power on earth could change. Fresh from Oxford, where few people hold the same view on any subject for more than a few weeks, I would propound the most exaggerated theories to him. But to argue with my father was like arguing with a brick wall; there was no matter on which he did not hold a precise and definite opinion. As he had held the same opinions for the past forty years there was no likelihood that my immature convictions would alter them.

. . . I shall never forget, one wet evening, sitting alone with him in the house. He pulled an envelope out of his pocket which bore the crown of the Admiralty. 'I haven't shown you this before,' he said, 'because when I first received it there didn't seem any likelihood of it happening. It's the best news I've had for some time.'

I unfolded the letter and began to read. It contained several long paragraphs written in official language, but I soon had the gist of it. In the event of hostilities, would my father be prepared to take command of an armed merchant cruiser? I knew my father, and understood his excitement.

There is a school of naval officers (I have met some of them during this war) who are embittered at an institution which has no use for their services as senior officers. Their bitterness is understandable. When you have devoted the best years of your life to a service which equips you for no other calling, and flings you out when it has done with you, you are entitled to a complaint.

Shortly after the end of the last war the Government, for reasons of economy, decided to reduce drastically the number of senior naval officers. The 'Geddes Axe' fell, and my father was placed on the retired list. He was bitterly disappointed, but at no time embittered. He accepted the measure as a necessity for the good of his country, put the matter out of his head, and turned to politics.[1]

But he could never altogether escape the weight of the blow. Meeting old navy friends, hearing navy talk from past shipmates, any incident which brought him in touch with the Navy during the post-war years reminded him with a pang of his yearning for the sea. The thrill of conning a big ship, of ordering her ways, of influencing the lives of her crew, were memories which he could not easily forget. When he received this letter from the Admiralty he saw himself in an instant once more on the bridge of his own ship.

I finished reading the letter and handed it back to him. He turned to me with an almost youthful exuberance.

'I shall be sixty next week, old boy,' he said, 'and they still have enough faith in me to offer me a ship. Eighteen years on the beach, and they offer me a ship! Gosh, what a chance! *What* a chance!'

It was to come sooner than he, or any of us, expected.

A fortnight later I saw my father on board *Rawalpindi*.

I have never seen him so happy; he was like a child who has been given a new toy. During tea in his cabin, a luxurious room behind the bridge, he kept jumping up to discuss with dockyard officials alterations they were making to the ship's structure; or one of his officers would come to him with a batch of papers for scrutiny and signature. Afterwards he took me around the ship. We visited each cabin, each compartment, from the boat-deck to the engine-room, while he explained the alterations the ship was undergoing, many of which he had himself authorised. We would often stop while he straightened out some problem raised by one of the workmen.

His enthusiasm was unbounded, his pride immense. I knew then that the disappointments which had been rankling for the past

1. Captain Kennedy was Conservative Party agent for South Buckinghamshire.

eighteen years had vanished. They were forgotten in his passionate interest and pride in his new command.

Before I left he showed me the guns lying on the jetty, waiting to be fitted. Big, powerful creatures they looked, their snouts pointing threateningly to the sky. Across the shield of each gun was scribbled in thick white letters RAWALPINDI.

These were the guns about which my father wrote later to a friend: 'They have given me some guns, good guns, and I am going to use them.'

That was the last time I saw my father. But he used his guns all right.

'. . . The Secretary of the Admiralty,' came the impassive voice of the announcer, 'regrets to announce the loss of the armed merchant cruiser *Rawalpindi*. HMS *Rawalpindi* was an ex-P and O liner of seventeen thousand tons. . . .'

The voice drifted on, but I did not listen. For I knew then that my father was dead. . . .

My father came of the old and noble breed of naval officers who hold honour dearer than life. To them, the achievements of a ship are due to the resource of her captain. If a captain should hazard his ship, whether the blame is attributable to him or not, it is his duty to go down with her.

Today a younger school decries this theory. It recognises that the captain should be the last to leave his ship, but insists that while there is an opportunity for him to get away he should take it, and thus be of further service to his country. That is a reasonable view, of course, but one cannot well criticise such men as Captain Makeig-Jones, of the *Courageous*, who remained alone on the bridge of his ship saluting the flag as she went down.

I went over to the telephone, and eventually was put through to the Admiralty. A long pause, then a voice said:

'The captain? No, I'm afraid he's gone. . . .'

Lieutenant LUDOVIC KENNEDY RNVR

HMS Rawalpindi *was on patrol between the Faeroes and Iceland when, at 3.51 p.m., 23rd November, she sent an enemy-sighting report and a few minutes later identified the enemy as* Deutschland *(although, it was established later, it was* Scharnhorst *with* Gneisenau *in company).*

Kennedy ignored signals to heave to and to abandon his ship. Rawalpindi *was outranged, outmanœuvred and outstripped.* Gneisenau *picked up twenty-one survivors,* Scharnhorst *six, and HMS* Chitral *eleven more the next day.*

*

As winter approached, it became clear that the enemy were laying a type of mine which was immune to normal sweeping methods. In November 1939 twenty-seven merchant ships and the destroyer Blanche *were sunk by mines; many more were damaged, including the cruiser* Belfast, *and for a time the enemy almost succeeded in closing the Port of London. Then, on the night of 22nd, a German aircraft jettisoned a large object attached to a parachute into the sea off Shoeburyness. At low tide the next day a party from HMS* Vernon *went out on to the mudflats. Here is the bald, unemotional account by the officer leading the team who first dismantled the*

MAGNETIC MINE

We decided that Chief Petty Officer Baldwin and I should endeavour to remove the vital fittings; Lieutenant-Commander Lewis and Able Seaman Vearncombe to watch from what was considered to be a safe distance and make detailed notes of our actions and progress—for reference in case of accidents. There was a possibility that the mine had devices other than the magnetic one, which added to the hazard. If we were unlucky the notes which the two watchers had taken would be available for those who would have to deal with the next available specimen.

I first tackled an aluminium fitting sealed with tallow. In order to use one of the special spanners which had been rushed through (by Commander Maton) in the local workshops for us, it was necessary to bend clear a small strip of copper. That done, we were able to extract this first fitting. Screwed into its base when we drew it clear we found a small cylinder—obviously a detonator, for in the recess from which the fitting had been withdrawn were disks of explosive. These I removed. This mysterious fitting proved to be a delay-action bomb fuse; it was necessary for the airman to tear off the copper strip referred to (before releasing his load) if bomb, not mine, was the requirement.

Before we could proceed further we had to call on Lieutenant-Commander Lewis and Able Seaman Vearncombe for assistance to roll the mine over, this being firmly embedded in the hard sand and held fast by tubular horns. The fact that the mine did not, and was not intended to, float explains the non-success of our minesweepers in their efforts to secure a specimen. Lieutenant-Commander Lewis and Able Seaman Vearncombe from then onwards lent a hand with the stripping down. Dr Wood, chief scientist of the Mine Design Department, HMS *Vernon*, arrived in time to witness the later stages. We were somewhat startled to discover yet another detonator and priming charge. Having removed all the external fittings, we signalled for the caterpillar tractor and soon had the mine ashore.

We had a shock—and a laugh when the shock wore off—before we had stowed away all the removed gadgets. We stopped for a breather on the foreshore, and one of the helpers carrying a rather heavy fitting put it down on a stone. It immediately began to tick noisily. The company dispersed like lightning! That most disturbing ticking, we presently discovered, came from clockwork mechanism within the heavy fitting; actuated by pressure, it happened to rest on its starting spindle. This proved to be a delay-action device, designed to keep the mine safe until the clock setting had run off.

Lieutenant-Commander JOHN G. D. OUVRY RN
of HMS *Vernon*

Lieutenant-Commander J. G. D. Ouvry and Lieutenant-Commander R. C. Lewis were both awarded the DSO. Chief Petty Officer Baldwin and Able Seaman Vearncombe were awarded the DSM.

★

The German pocket battleship Graf Spee *(Kapitan zur See Hans Langsdorff) left Wilhelmshaven on 23rd August 1939, and for nearly four months ranged the Atlantic and Indian oceans, sinking nine ships in positions as far apart as Pernambuco* (Clement, *sunk 30th September) and Mozambique* (Africa Shell, *sunk 5th November). Meanwhile, the Admiralty disposed forces around the world to trap her; Force 'G', the South America Division, was under the command of Commodore Henry Harwood, flying his flag in HMS* Ajax *(Captain C. H. L. Woodhouse RN), with HMS* Exeter *(Captain F. S. Bell, RN) and HMNZS* Achilles *(Captain W. E. Parry*

RN)—a fourth cruiser, Cumberland, *was refitting. Two of* Graf Spee*'s last victims ss* Doric Star *(2nd December) and ss* Tairoa *(3rd December) succeeded in transmitting wireless signals before being sunk. Receiving the report of the attack on* Tairoa *on 3rd, Commodore Harwood decided that of the three likeliest next destinations—Rio de Janeiro, the Falklands, the River Plate—Langsdorff would go for the Plate. At dawn on the 13th December* Graf Spee *sighted* Exeter *and closed her at full speed, believing her to be part of a convoy escort. At 0617* Graf Spee *opened fire on* Exeter, *beginning*

THE BATTLE OF THE RIVER PLATE

'My God, it's a pocket battleship!'

I expect you have seen accounts of the scrap *ad nauseam.* I trust that Their Lordships in their wisdom have found fit to publish our prolix narratives, but nothing has yet reached us at this distance.

From the personal point of view it was a tremendous moment when we suddenly realised that we had bumped up against her, and that *this* time it was the real thing. I was PCO at the time. I would be. The captain was on the bridge, and we turned to each other and said simultaneously, 'My God, it's a pocket battleship!' I legged it as hard as I could go for my box of tricks, and just had time to wonder if there was anything in this gunnery business after all, and where I should be in half an hour's time, before all my lamps lit up and I was able to say 'SHOOT' for the first time in anger. Four minutes only, though most of the sailors were enjoying their very necessary beauty sleep at the time and we were only at cruising stations. We were rather proud of that, even though *Exeter* did beat us to it.

After that my impressions are rather confused. There were a lot of splashes growing up around that target and it wasn't a bit easy picking out my own. I can remember feeling a quite illogical resentment every time he put his great eleven-inch cannon on us, when I saw those damn great pieces belching their unpleasantnesses at myself and I can remember feeling unspeakably grateful to poor old *Exeter* every time I saw them blazing in her direction.

He came at us for about a quarter of an hour, very obligingly thinking that we were a couple of destroyers in company with *Exeter.* That covered the rather unpleasant stretch of water in which he could outrange us.

He scored a pretty little straddle after twenty minutes and his HE burst on the surface of the water and the pieces peppered us. There weren't as many casualties as one would expect. Our captain acquired a sizish hole in both legs and the chief yeoman on the bridge had a leg smashed up. In my DCT we had rather more than our share. Six pieces came inside. With my usual fantastic luck three pieces impinged on my ample anatomy (and I regret that it grows even ampler as the years go on despite my efforts to Squash it out), but caused me little inconvenience, apart from a certain mental vagueness of the ensuing minute or two. Three died quite quickly and definitely, two of whom were actually in physical contact with me, and three were wounded. I don't expect that names mean anything to you at this distance of time, but one of the casualties was an old '*Diomede*', Archibald Cooper Hirst Shaw. E. V. Shirley, another old '*Diomede*', was one of the very severely wounded. The others had the common misfortune of being imperial ratings (NZ).

The survivors behaved just as one expected and hoped. They took no notice of the shambles (and it looked more like a slaughterhouse on a busy day than a Director Control Tower) and took over the jobs of those who had been put out as if nothing had happened. One youngster had to seat himself on the unpleasantness that very shortly before had been a very efficient GO's writer and carry out his job. He was a little wide-eyed after we had disengaged but otherwise unmoved. A splinter had jammed the door and prevented the medical parties from reaching us. The wounded never murmured. Shirley quietly applied a tourniquet to himself and saved his life thereby. A sergeant of Marines who was sitting right alongside me never let on that he was wounded. I didn't discover it until the first lull, an hour later, when he nearly fainted from loss of blood.

I learnt this lesson—though it's a difficult one to put into words—that one can wish for nothing better than these troops of ours. They may be a bit of a nuisance in the easy times of peace, but one can't improve on them when things get a bit hot. A spot of trouble of this sort completely changes one's attitude to the troops. I felt very proud of my fellow countrymen. (Washbourn is a New Zealander.)

Exeter, as you know, bore the brunt. We had the attentions of the 5.8s all the time, but they weren't very effective. I think that we shot up their control fairly early on, and put at least two of the starboard battery out of action.

Tactically my only criticism is that we should have gone in earlier, but that certainly would have meant more damage and casualties than we actually received, and we did achieve the object of the exercise without it.

It was a plain straightforward scrap, with none of the 'hit-and-run' tactics which the Yellow Press credited us with. We hammered away for an hour and a half, and then hauled off under smoke. I must admit to a certain feeling of being baulked of my prey when we were ordered to turn away, because the last twenty minutes at really effective range had been most enjoyable. It turned out to be the psychologically correct moment. We had damn little ammunition left and, as it proved, the job was done. It didn't seem like it at the time. I was very depressed. We had expended most of our bricks and our enemy looked disappointingly undamaged. The after turret was temporarily out of action, and we had seen one fire on board, and he was running like a frightened rabbit, but his fire was distressingly accurate, and his speed was the same as ever, and there was no sign of structural damage.

We shadowed all day. Once or twice we ventured a bit too close and he swung round and let us have it, but he was out of our range and we didn't reply.

In the evening we gave the Uruguayans the thrill of their lives by another little brush just at sunset when we were closing the range to keep him in sight as the visibility lessened. Four times later, during the advancing twilight, he took exception to our presence, but these last Parthian shots were merely gestures.

The morale was magnificent while we were waiting for him to emerge from his hole. The fantastic fleets that Winston, ably aided and abetted by the BBC, built up outside Montevideo gave us great pleasure. We were pleased to see *Cumberland*, not for any great confidence in her fighting abilities, but from the point of view that she would again provide the first target for *Graf Spee*'s attentions.

We stayed at action stations all night, with the usual 'Hula' parties keeping us amused and awake with their Maori songs. Do you remember Gould, with his guitar and his indiarubber hips?

On the Sunday evening we three went in to finish the job off.

Graf Spee was just visible at sunset when *Ajax*'s aircraft reported that she had blown herself up. Another big moment. We steamed up close past *Ajax*, who was leading us in. Both ships had ordered 'All hands on deck', and were black with bodies who had emerged to see the last of the old enemy. Another big moment. We shouted ourselves hoarse, both ships. The 'Diggers' did their 'Hakas', and sang their songs, and the *Ajax* cheered in reply.

And that was that.

Extract from a letter written to Rear-Admiral Cosmo Graham by Lieutenant-Commander R. E. WASHBOURN RN of HMNZS *Achilles*.)

*

'I SAW THREE SHIPS'

A Fantasy

(Legend has it that the Wandering Albatross of the southern oceans harbours the soul of a Greek seaman, a survivor of the Trojan War.)

South steamed *Ajax*, *Exeter*, *Achilles*—
  Devon, New Zealand—spawn of the sea:
South steered Harwood, combing the Atlantic,
  Hunting a raider, the great *Graf Spee*.

South sailed *Exeter*, *Ajax*, *Achilles*;
  Scanned all horizons; nought could they see
But one white albatross, ghost of Odysseus
  The exiled raider—and still no *Spee*.

In the dark of a dawning the watch heard the white bird
  Return from the uttermost edge of the sea—
'I was a seaman and sailed with Achilles:
  I honoured Ajax. Come! Follow me!'

Round swung the squadron, after Ulysses
  (Fine was the morning, roomy the sea)
Ajax, *Exeter*, fleet-foot *Achilles*—
  Out of the ocean up loomed *Spee*!

Her great guns thunder searching for *Exeter:*
  On sweeps *Exeter*, silent is she.
'Down depth-charges!' signalled Odysseus.
  Foiling the enemy, up spouts the sea!

We close the range; now open our 'eight-inch'—
  Well laid our gunners! But we're hit too:
Fore turret splintered, into a mad clinch
  Drives wounded *Exeter*, bridge shot through.

Our captain shouted, 'She shall not escape us;
  Sooner I'll ram her!' Answered his crew—
'Roll out the barrel and reload our last gun;
  We'll teach Adolf a thing or two.'

Ah! But we're done for; motionless, *Exeter*
  Rolls on the ocean, gasping for breath.
Smoke from their funnels like horsehair from helmet—
  See—the Achaeans rush in upon Death!

Then prayed Odysseus to grey-eyed Athene—
  'Grant, O Goddess, yet one prayer more:
Save me these heroes who charged on Hector,
  Charging again as they charged of yore!'

From high Olympus Athene slanted
  Down to the *Spee*'s deck—snatching from Fate
Ajax, *Achilles*—blinded her gunners;
  Whispered her captain; he runs for the Plate.

Then turned Odysseus out of the sunset
  On tireless pinion over the sea
To the cave of Poseidon, where sit the old sea-dogs,
  Each with a mermaid rocked on his knee.

The heroes hailed him—'How fares the world now?
  Still sail the long ships? What of their crew?'
'Still sail the swift ships?'—answered Odysseus—
  'Aye—and their seamen are worthy of you.'

Major Sir RALPH FURSE KCMG DSO and Bar

(The theory that Captain Langsdorff's indecision and misjudgement during the battle of the River Plate were due to the goddess Athene's intervention is so far not supported by naval historians.)

*

At 6.15 pm, with battle ensigns flying on both masts, *Graf Spee* started to work cable, turned under her own power, and steamed through the breakwater, followed closely by *Tacoma*. We believed at the time that she would make for Argentine waters, but then about three miles out she turned west, stopped, and some boat activity took place between her and the *Tacoma*, which had also stopped. Two large tugs belonging to a German-owned company in Buenos Aires then appeared from the River Plate, and there was more boat activity around the pocket battleship.

Something extraordinary was about to take place. The great crowd immediately below us, denied their sight of a battle, was quite hushed. What was going to happen? Time passed in considerable speculation and suspense, but the truth, unlikely though it appeared, was beginning to dawn on some of us.

Exactly as the sun set behind her, a great volume of smoke billowed up—and an enormous flash was followed in due course by the boom of a large explosion. So the *Graf Spee* met her end.

Darkness comes quickly in those latitudes, and as we watched the sky darkened into a black background against which huge flames licked up against the underside of dense rolling clouds from the burning fuel-oil. The rumour spread that Captain Langsdorff had remained aboard and that some of his crew were trapped—and to the great crowd below us, which waited on and on through the night, this added a sense of tension and almost a sense of loss. He had made such an impression, even in those three short days.

Next morning *Graf Spee* was still burning fiercely, and indeed it was not until four days later that all traces of fire had vanished. Gradually we pieced together what had happened. Having turned his ship off the main channel, Captain Langsdorff had put her in shallow water and opened the sea-cocks. Torpedo heads had then been suspended by ropes over open ammunition hatches which led straight down to the main magazines and petrol had been sluiced over the surrounding decks and set alight as the last of the party left the ship. In the fore part of the ship the flames burned through the hemp rope, the torpedo head fell, exploded in the fore magazine, and blew it up. Ironically enough, the enormous wave of seawater sent up flooded over the aft part of the ship and put out the flame; some weeks later Lieutenant-Commander Kilroy, a torpedo and electrical specialist, went aboard and found the aft torpedo head still hanging from a badly charred rope. (The British Admiralty had bought the wreck of the *Graf Spee* from Uruguay for, I believe, £14,000.)

Admiral Sir HENRY MCCALL KCVO KBE CB DSO
(Then Naval Attaché in Buenos Aires)
From Purnell's *History of The Second World War*

1940

THE *ALTMARK*

There occurred in February 1940 the *Altmark* incident, which, partly because the land war in Europe at that time hung fire, attracted much notice in the Press.

A force led by Captain (D) 4th Flotilla in *Cossack*, with the cruiser *Arethusa* and four Fleet destroyers (*Intrepid*, *Ivanhoe*, *Maori* and *Sikh*), sailed from Rosyth at midnight on 14th February with orders to sweep the Skagerrak for German iron-ore ships on the Narvik run. The operation was unproductive, but on the evening of the 15th there arrived an Admiralty signal reporting that the armed German supply ship *Altmark*, with about 300 British prisoners on board, had passed Bergen at noon. There followed another from the Commander-in-Chief, Home Fleet, Sir Charles Forbes: '*Altmark* your objective. Act accordingly.'

There had been embarked in *Altmark* the crews of British merchantmen sunk by the battleship *Graf Spee* during her raiding cruise in the South Atlantic, which had been brought to an abrupt end some weeks earlier off the estuary of the River Plate. Eluding our patrols, *Altmark* had passed between Iceland and the Faeroes, arriving off Trondheim on the 14th. Her guns had been removed, and in appearance she passed, to Norwegian eyes, as a tanker.

At Trondheim, *Altmark* had to decide whether to make her way south, outside or inside Norwegian territorial waters. If she proceeded inside, her prisoners of war were entitled to release, since these were neutral waters. Inside she went.

Meanwhile *Cossack*'s force swept north through the long night, the commander more than a little *distrait*: there was an unexpected volume of shipping in the Leads, the background, black rock and snow, made visibility uncertain, and it would be easy to miss the objective.

At noon on the 16th, sighting reports from our aircraft began to arrive, but they gave widely separated positions, from which it was clear that several different ships were being reported.

Our force was divided, *Arethusa*, with *Intrepid* and *Ivanhoe*, being detached to search the northward zone, *Cossack*, *Maori* and *Sikh*, moving south. By the afternoon the command in *Cossack* was even more preoccupied: a stern chase after a supposed *Altmark* had proved us to be pursuing an innocuous Swede; and in spite of a flood of air reports, no surface ship had yet made contact with the genuine article.

We had, in fact, no firm information even about the appearance of our quarry. The best clue we could find was in a wardroom copy of an *Illustrated London News*. This showed a picture of two vessels, the caption of which read: 'German raider *Altmark* examining a neutral merchant ship in the Atlantic.' Which of the two was *Altmark* it did not say, and we assumed it was the four-masted ship in the foreground, rather than the tanker-type further away. So when a four-masted freighter was sighted making south along the coast I thought we had found our intended victim. Meanwhile, the long night approached.

Salvation was provided by a young officer in *Arethusa*. His keen eyes detected, far away, a shadow passing close to, and interrupting the black-and-white land background, and, significantly, the mast and funnels of a torpedo-boat, which must be a Norwegian escort. Identity became certain as *Arethusa* closed: the ship was wearing the German ensign, and soon the name *Altmark* was visible on her counter.

Acting on a policy signal from the Admiralty, which had said that interception might be carried out, if necessary, in neutral waters, *Arethusa*, Captain Q. D. Graham, sent the destroyers in. *Altmark*, however, disregarded their signals to stop, and was assisted by Norwegian torpedo-boats—there were now seen to be two—who ranged along either side, preventing the destroyers from boarding. Abreast Josing Fjord, *Altmark* turned hard to port, increased speed, and headed through the narrow entrance; the Norwegians closed in behind her, blocking the channel. Such was the position when *Cossack* arrived, just as darkness fell. If there were no prisoners on board, the Norwegian action had been correct: but if there were?

At this point Craven, a RNVR officer who spoke German and Swedish, came to the fore, where indeed he remained. From *Cossack* he hailed *Kjell*, the senior Norwegian, and invited the captain aboard.

To the latter I said that, whatever he might think, British prisoners were, in fact, on board *Altmark*; and I demanded the right to visit and search, asking him to come with me. In his reply he stated that the German ship had been examined three times since her entry into Norwegian waters, and that no prisoners had been found. His instructions were to resist entry by force: as I might see, his ships had their torpedo-tubes trained on *Cossack*. Deadlock. I then asked the Admiralty and Commander-in-Chief for further instructions.

Within three hours the Admiralty reply had been deciphered: it was very clear, and its phrasing suggested that the First Lord, Mr Churchill, had had a hand in its composition:

'Unless Norwegian torpedo-boat undertakes to convoy *Altmark* to Bergen with a joint Anglo-Norwegian guard on board and a joint escort, you should board *Altmark*, liberate the prisoners and take possession of the ship pending further instructions. If Norwegian torpedo-boat interferes, you should warn her to stand off. If she fires upon you, you should not reply unless attack is serious, in which case you should defend yourself using no more force than is necessary and cease fire when she desists. Suggest to Norwegian destroyer that honour is served by submitting to superior force.'

Closing *Kjell* once more, Craven gave the sense of this direction to the captain, who remained obdurate. It was then explained to him that time had become a factor of importance, since the intervention of German aircraft might be expected at daylight. Having placed *Cossack* in a position from which our pom-poms could play upon Norwegian decks, whilst their torpedo-tubes were no instant menace to us, I said we could parley no longer, and must board and search *Altmark* forthwith, whether we fought them or not. *Kjell*'s captain decided that honour was served by submitting to superior force, and withdrew. On rounding the bend in the fjord, *Altmark* at last came into view. She lays bows inshore, encased in ice, her great bulk standing black against the snow-clad mountains.

Thoughts of the six-inch guns with which the *Altmark* was said to be armed were naturally in our minds. Though our own guns were manned we were obviously an easy target, and the enemy's first shots might well immobilise us at once. There was nothing for it, however, but to go ahead and get to grips as quickly as possible.

The *Altmark* captain was determined to resist being boarded. On sighting *Cossack*, he trained his searchlight on our bridge to blind the command, and came astern at full power through the channel which his entry into the ice had made. His idea was to ram us. Unless something was done very quickly the great mass of the tanker's counter was going to crash heavily into the *Cossack*'s port bow.

There followed a period of manœuvring in which disaster, as serious collison must have entailed, was avoided by the skill of my imperturbable navigator, Maclean, and by the speed with which the main engine manœuvring valves were operated by their artificers.

Lieutenant Bradwell Turner, the leader of the boarding party, anticipated *Cossack*'s arrival alongside *Altmark* with a leap which became famous. Petty Officer Atkins, who followed him, fell short, and hung by his hands until Turner heaved him on deck. The two quickly made fast a hemp hawser from *Cossack*'s fo'c's'le, and the rest of the party scrambled across.

When Turner arrived on *Altmark*'s bridge he found the engine telegraphs set to full speed in an endeavour to force *Cossack* ashore. On Turner's appearance, the captain and others surrendered, except the third officer, who interfered with the telegraphs, which Turner had set to stop. Turner forbore to shoot him.

It was now clear that as a result of her manœuvres *Altmark* would ground by the stern, which she did, but not before *Cossack*, the boarding party all being transferred, had cast off, to avoid the same fate.

It was expected, with the surrender of the German captain, that the release of our prisoners would be a drawing-room affair. That this was not so was due to the action of a member of the armed guard which *Graf Spee* had put aboard. He gratuitously shot Gunner Smith, of the boarding party, in an alleyway. This invoked retaliation, upon which the armed guard decamped; they fled across the ice, and began to snipe the boarding party from an eminence on shore. Silhouetted against the snow they made easy targets, and their fire was quickly silenced by Turner and his men.

In the end German casualties were few, six killed and six badly wounded. The boarding party had none, save unlucky Gunner Smith, and even he was not fatally wounded.

Resistance overcome, Turner was able to turn to the business of the day. The prisoners were under locked hatches in the holds; when these had been broken open Turner hailed the men below with the words: 'Any British down there?' He was greeted with a tremendous yell of 'Yes! We're all British!' 'Come on up then,' said Turner. 'The Navy's here!'

. . . I received many letters from the public after this affair: a number wrote to say that, as I had failed to shoot, or hang, the captain of *Altmark*, I ought to be shot myself.

Admiral of the Fleet Sir PHILIP VIAN GCB KBE DSO

*

During the Norwegian campaign there was one brilliantly successful but now almost forgotten exploit by the Fleet Air Arm. On 10th April 1940 Skua divebombers flying from the Orkneys sank the German cruiser Konigsberg *in Bergen harbour. Although this was the first time a major warship had been sunk by air attack, the word appeared to fall on stony ground in the Admiralty; Skuas were withdrawn from operations in early 1941 and thereafter the Fleet Air Arm had no specialist dive-bomber until the unsatisfactory Barracuda in 1943. But for the Germans and the Japanese the attack on* Konigsberg *was a textbook demonstration and later in the war both showed that they had read, marked, learned, and inwardly digested the lesson of*

DIVE-BOMB ATTACK

There were sixteen of them: seven from 800 Squadron led by Captain R. T. Partridge, Royal Marines, and nine from 803 Squadron led by Lieutenant W. P. Lucy, RN. The night was cold and starlit with 4/10 cloud and no more than a whisper of wind. The Skuas, loaded to capacity with 500 lb SAPs, were sluggish and hard to taxi. Harder still to take off. For the Hatston runways were short; and several pilots saw the airfield's perimeter rushing towards them before they got their planes into the air. Nor, when they were airborne, were their troubles at an end. For the overloaded Skuas were devils to keep in formation. Like a school of ungainly hippopotami they wallowed east, having to be nursed every yard of the 300-odd miles to the Norwegian shore. But with one exception they managed to keep together.

For nearly two hours they clawed through the darkness; then, a few minutes after seven o'clock, they made the sort of landfall that every observer dreams of, hitting the Norwegian coast slap opposite

Bergen within half a minute of ETA. And as they identified their position at the mouth of Bergen Fjord the blood-red oriflamme of the sun rose over the hills to greet them. They climbed to 8,000 feet, working their way into its path. Everything was still and very quiet. The sixteen Skuas seemed to be the only living things in a world not yet awake.

Soon they could see the *Konigsberg*: a sliver of silver aglint in the sun—apparently oblivious of the wrath to come. The two squadrons went into line astern, like a string of beads threading the path of the sun. Then Lucy tipped the leading Skua into a sixty-degree dive. He was down to 4,000 feet before the ack-ack opened up.

The Germans had been caught unawares. The crew of the *Konigsberg* were not even at action stations. Their first hint of danger was the bark of their own ack-ack guns and the whistling roar of Lucy's bombs which scythed into the sea less than a dozen feet from their stern.

The *Konigsberg* was lifted half out of the water and flung violently against Skoltegrund Mole. And before her crew could recover their wits she was hit again and again and again.

For the pilots of 800 and 803 Squadrons were pastmasters in the art of dive-bombing. This was the job for which they had been trained: this was the job for which their aircraft had been designed. And now, in spite of the curtain of ack-ack which began to stream up at them, they pressed home their attack with the speed and precision of a well-rehearsed manœuvre. Within three minutes the *Konigsberg* had been smothered in fifteen hits and near misses. No bomb landed farther away from her than fifty yards, and the average mean error in bombing was well under twenty yards.

Such accuracy would have been commendable on a defenceless target. And the *Konigsberg* was far from defenceless. For as soon as the Germans woke up to what was happening, a fair volume of fire was thrown up at the Skuas: light ack-ack from positions in the encircling hills, and pom-pom and machine-gun fire from the cruiser herself and the various ships in harbour. There was no heavy ack-ack, except from one gun in *Konigsberg*. But that one gun, to quote Partridge, was 'unpleasantly accurate. And her gunners certainly had guts. They were the first to open fire. They went on firing right through the attack. And as the last aircraft pulled out of its dive they were still blazing away at us'. Three Skuas were hit: one badly.

But the *Konigsberg* suffered a great deal more.

Five bombs landed within thirty yards of her stern, flinging her bows deep under water, collandering her after gun-turrets with splinters, and swamping her with great cataracts of spray. Another five landed on Skoltegrund Mole, blasting dust and debris on to her deck. Two more sheered through her starboard rail and exploded in the few feet of water between ship and shore. And three were direct hits: one on 'A' turret, one on the port quarter, and one amidships flush between the funnels.

The *Konigsberg* became in an instant a blazing wreck. Great flames poured out of her, a hundred feet into the air. Below-decks casualties were heavy. As the last of the Skuas disappeared to seaward, she rolled slowly on to her side. Her crew fought desperately to save her. But they hadn't a hope. Within minutes the flames got through to her magazines. There was a heavy explosion: a thin column of light-brown smoke: and the *Konigsberg* broke in half. Her screws tilted up at the sky, and in a hissing cauldron of steam she capsized and sank.

The Skuas made their getaway low, zigzagging down Bergen Fjord, machine-gunning shipping *en route.* At the end of the fjord they reformed over Lyso Island; then they set course for home. All except one. Lieutenant Smeeton and Midshipman Watkinson had been seen to pull out of their dive and head down the fjord, but they were never seen again.

At 9.45, after a flight of four hours and thirty minutes, Partridge and his Skuas touched down at Hatston. Several of them hadn't enough fuel in their tanks to cover an upended penny.

IAN CAMERON

Partridge and Lucy were awarded DSOs. Lucy was shot down and killed when flying from Ark Royal *on 14th May. Partridge was shot down, badly burned in the attack on* Scharnhorst *in Trondheim on 13th June; he was picked up and spent five years as a POW.*

*

On 9th April the 2nd Destroyer Flotilla (Captain B. A. Warburton-Lee RN, in HMS Hardy*) were detached from the Home Fleet to Narvik 'to* *make certain that no enemy troops land'. In fact the enemy were already in Narvik in far greater strength than intelligence had yet reported, but Warburton-Lee signalled, 'Intend attacking at dawn high water.' The Admiralty replied, 'You alone can judge whether in these circumstances attack should be made. We shall support whatever decision you take.' Warburton-Lee therefore signalled his plan of attack to his flotilla:*

Following orders for Operation T.N. Final approach to Narvik *Hardy* will close pilot station which is close to Steinhos Light. *Hunter* will follow in support. *Hotspur* and *Havock* are to provide anti-submarine protection to the northward. Ships are to be at action stations from 0030. When passing Skrednest Light *Hardy* will pass close to shore and order a line of bearing. Thereafter ships are to maintain narrow quarterline to starboard so that fire from all ships is effective ahead. On closing Narvik *Hardy* will steer for inner harbour with *Hunter* astern in support. Germans may have several destroyers and a submarine in vicinity. Some probably on patrol. Ships are to engage all targets immediately and keep a particular look-out for enemy who may be berthed in inlets. On approaching Narvik *Hardy*, *Hunter*, *Havock* engage enemy ships inside harbour with guns and torpedoes. *Hotspur* engage ships to north-west. *Hostile* assist on either target. Prepare to lay smoke for cover and to tow disabled ships. If opposition is silenced landing parties (less *Hotspur*) when ordered to land make for Ore Quay unless otherwise ordered. *Hardy*'s first lieutenant in charge. Additional visual signal to withdraw will be one red and one green Very light from *Hardy*. Half outfit of torpedoes is to be fired unless target warrants more. In order to relieve congestion of movements all ships when turning to fire or opening are to keep turning to port if possible. Watch adjacent ships. Keep moderate speed.

From *Make a Signal*

*

At 4.30 am on the 10th Hardy *with HMS* Hunter *(Lieutenant-Commander L. de Villiers RN) and HMS* Havock *(Lieutenant-Commander R. E. Courage RN) entered Narvik harbour, while HMS* Hotspur *(Commander H. F. H. Layman RN) and HMS* Hostile *(Commander*

J. P. Wright RN) remained outside, joining the action later. One of Hardy*'s survivors tells the story of*

THE FIRST BATTLE OF NARVIK

When we sailed up the fjord to Narvik early on the morning of 10th April we did not know what we were going to meet. All we knew was that there was a big German force up there, but we did not know how big. We soon found out.

Almost before dawn we sailed in, in line ahead. Near Narvik we saw two ships. One was a German whaling factory and the other a British ship. Behind them were some German destroyers, bigger than we were.

There were plenty of other ships, but we did not have time to count them. We opened up with our torpedoes at the enemy destroyers, the destroyers all releasing 'tin fish' one after the other.

Two German destroyers were hit the first time. When our torpedo hit we saw a flash, and it was just as if some huge hand had torn the German ship in half. It just split in two.

With all those torpedoes going into the harbour, nearly every ship there seemed to be sunk. It was like a shambles, and it will be a long time before Narvik harbour can be used properly again.

Meanwhile, on shore the Germans had opened up at us with land batteries. Then we caught sight of two more German destroyers behind the other ships.

When we had circled three parts of the way round, three German destroyers came out from the mouth of a fjord behind us, firing at a distance of about 3,000 yards.

First they shot wide, then they got on the target. Things got hot. The Germans got direct hits on us. It was then that Captain Warburton-Lee was hit. It was a bad blow. Lieutenant Cross, our signals officer was killed, and Captain Warburton-Lee was obviously in a bad condition. Our navigating officer, Lieutenant-Commander Gordon Smith, was also badly wounded.

The skipper's secretary, Lieutenant Stanning, took command. By this time we were in a worse condition than anybody else. But we had guns left and kept them working against the big German destroyers that had engaged us. Then came more shells. Our steam-pipe was burst by a shell and the main feed-pipe as well. Soon the steering wouldn't work. We ran into shallow water and grounded on the rocks about 300 to 400 yards from the shore. It was then that we got our last order on the ship. It came from Captain Warburton-Lee, and it was the last order he was ever to give. It was 'Abandon ship. Every man for himself. And good luck'.

We piled overboard as best we could and swam ashore.

It was so cold that a moment after we had got into the water there was no feeling in our hands or feet. We had 100 yards to swim and at least another 200 yards to wade before we got ashore.

And all the time we were still under fire. German shells were dropping round us. They had seen we were in trouble and they let us have it.

Our torpedo officer, Lieutenant Heppell, was a real hero. He saved at least five men by swimming backward and forward between the ship and the shore, helping those who could not swim. Finally we got ashore, about 170 of us. Seventeen of us had been killed in the fight, and another two were missing.

We were freezing cold. Most of the men had discarded clothing to swim ashore, and the remainder who had arrived with some clothes on had torn them off when they landed because they were so icy cold.

Two hundred yards away there was a house. We ploughed our way through nearly six feet of snow to it, and found it had been evacuated when the battle started. But soon the woman of the house and her daughter came back, and did all they could for us. There were eighty of us in that one house, and it only had five rooms.

Then came a report that the Germans were coming. We had no arms, and thought it best to get out, so we started on a fifteen-mile hike to Ballengen. Behind us we had left Captain Warburton-Lee. Badly wounded, he had been towed ashore by Lieutenant-Commander Mansell on a float, but when he reached the shore he died. The Norwegians buried him there, I heard.

From *Everyman's History of the Sea War*.

Hunter *was also sunk.* Hardy*'s last signal was* KEEP ON ENGAGING THE ENEMY. *Warburton-Lee was posthumously awarded the first VC of the war.* Hardy *and* Hunter *were quickly avenged. On 13th April HMS*

Warspite *and her destroyer screen entered Narvik and briskly sank U-64 and eight German destroyers in*

THE SECOND BATTLE OF NARVIK

It is one of those dark nights when men have to be very careful changing the watch, for the deck is frozen and one false move and it's over the side and nobody knows. So the guns' crews prefer to remain at their action stations and sneak a few minutes' sleep there. Hallo! The ship is stopping! What's happened? A blue light flickers just alongside, and then we are under way again. The news soon spreads—an admiral has come aboard. Next a messenger calls to tell all us gunner's mates to report to the gunnery officer. His orders are short and sweet—we are going up to Narvik tomorrow and everything must be on a split yarn. Back to our stations, and plenty to do now. Fuses to be set to non-delay (only light enemy ships believed there), first-aid gear checked, fresh-water provided and all the thousand and one other little things that can make or mar good shooting.

There is very little sleep left in us now; everyone is wondering what tomorrow will bring. At last it is daylight, and the watch is being called to day defence stations. One young seaman puts his head out of the top manhole and soon bobs down again. 'Looks as though we are in the money—you ought to see the destroyers we have with us.' So out we troop and have a look. Nine destroyers. Someone must be making a fuss of us. We have our breakfast and carry on with the usual routine, cleaning and preparing. We are passing some land now, and it looks very snow-covered and forbidding. An early dinner today, before going to action stations. My own crew are on the fo'c's'le for a smoke, some wag rolls a snowball and one of 'B' turret's crew gets it in the neck. This is the general signal for a snow fight between the two turrets, when action stations sounds. . . . Our gun-house crew is soon correct and so are the shell-room and magazine crews. We report to control and the turret officer tells me I can load. We hear the order repeated to the men down below, the cages come up with a thud, and out go the rammers. We can feel that we have increased speed as the ship has begun to vibrate. Heavy explosions shake the ship, and we hear that the destroyers are attacking a submarine. Suddenly comes the order 'Salvos', and the right gun comes to the ready. Then 'Enemy in sight' and the sight-setters chant the ranges. It is just like a practice shoot. Our guns are nearly horizontal, so the range must be short. Then the 'ding-ding' of the fire gong, the right gun moves a little, comes steady and there is a 'Woof' which rocks the turret. The left gun is now at the ready, and fires while the right gun is reloading. 'B' turret, firing over our heads, blows away our 'blast bags' and the turret fills with smoke—like London on a November night. The turret officer calls out, 'Tell the crew we have hit a destroyer and she is burning nicely.' Good work, boys, keep it going. Steady firing now. Then the trainer reports, 'Blimey, another one has got it,' and the news is passed to the men below. You can hear them cheer. Down in the machinery space the OA (Ordnance Artificer), his face covered with oil and sweat, grins and holds up his thumb. Hydraulic pressure is OK. Sixteen rounds from each gun so far. The salvos now aren't going so fast, because the different targets sink or blow up. After a while 'Check fire' is ordered and the ship seems to be stopping. 'Crews may go on top of turrets,' and up there it is a sight—burning and sinking enemy ships all around us, and our own destroyers searching into every little corner that might hide something. . . . We return to our action stations, and the turret officer and I make out our report as we steam down the fjord. Nothing special in it—just that everyone did their job from the youngest to the oldest. Thirty-two rounds fired by each gun, and no salvos missed. One of the crew in the turret cabinet had a tea-kettle on the electric radiator and every time the fire gong went he lifted it off to stop it being spilt. Wounded from the destroyers are next brought aboard; some are beyond help and are buried at sea that night. Now we *Warspites* know we shall carry on as we have started.

Petty Officer DANIEL REARDON,
gunner's mate of 'A' turret in *Warspite*

*

CARRIER OFF NORWAY

There was a snowstorm coming down from the north.
  It wasn't dark, for it never really got dark,
But a ghostly twilight fell. And we stamped back and forth
  On the bare windy flight-deck; then suddenly 'Hark!'

We heard the mutter of engines faint and far
  Above the sea's surge and the wind's slow sigh
And we stared till our eyes smarted, and 'There they are!'
  We cried, and counted the specks in the grey sky.

That was lit by the pearly gleam of the midnight sun;
  We counted seven, and tried to make them eight,
But still there were seven, and when they had landed on
  There were still seven, and we said 'Billy's late.'

A ship is a village, even a great ship,
  And news travels as swiftly as the wind,
As it does in the village street from lip to lip
  And sometimes, I think, even from mind to mind.

Men on the mess-decks, stokers, look-outs, crews
  Of the guns, all talked of Billy. 'A hell of a bloke . . .
He was always the same. How bloody awful to lose
  Billy, who always had a smile and a joke.'

For us on the deck it was worse, for still we listened;
  He'd still got petrol, a few minutes to go.
Is that an engine's murmur? No, hell, it isn't,
  Sea's surge, wind's sigh, whisper of driven snow.

And then—because a ship's like a village bereaved,
  News like postman going from door to door,
We heard that a signal from Billy had been received:
  'Delayed by three Heinkels.' Nothing more.

'Delayed by three Heinkels'. We fell silent
  Thinking the same thought, although nobody spoke
As we huddled together in the lee of the island:
  'Billy always had a smile and a joke.'

And then the steady surge of the sea faltered,
  And we felt the lurch and the list as the ship's head
Swung, helm over, hope over, course altered,
  And we shrugged our shoulders and went to bed.

Lieutenant-Commander (A) JOHN MOORE RNVR

*

During the evacuation of Allied troops from Narvik in June 1940 the aircraft carrier HMS Glorious *(Captain G. D. D'Oyly-Hughes, RN) was ordered to proceed homewards independently because she was short of fuel. She was not flying normal air-search patrols and was thus caught unaware by the German battle cruisers* Scharnhorst *and* Gneisenau *on 9th June.* Scharnhorst *opened fire at 4.30 pm at a range of 28,000 yards: an hour and a half later* Glorious *turned over and sank. One of her survivors, a member of a 4.7-inch-gun crew, describes*

GLORIOUS' LAST HOUR

I reckon we were making nearly thirty knots, and *Glorious* was shuddering with speed. But I didn't know it. I was thinking. Ugly thoughts they were. Come to think of it, there must have been a lot of a rowdy jumble going on, because there was so much thudding of machinery, and the cutting of the wind, and the shouting of brisk orders, that we hardly heard the first salvo above it. You got so used to this conglomeration of sounds in the *Glorious* you didn't notice they were going on . . . until the crash of a shell put your familiar rhythm out of tempo, and there was all this noise at once, hitting you with its stark ugliness.

The flight-deck above us was wreathed in smoke, then tongues of flame, then the staccato sounds of fire rose to a great roar, and a red wall like a living furnace rose from the hangar-well.

Then it came again, like distant thunder, culminating in a sudden wall of vicious sound, leaving the whole gun platform shuddering with the impact. Merciful God, they'd got their range right! . . .

I looked up the cliff face of the wall of steel forward of the bridge and saw the steel shattering. Plummets of smoke filled the air as I watched in horror. They'd hit the bridge. At the impact, I threw myself on the platform instinctively.

We waited on maybe a couple of minutes.

'This is bloody silly!' shouted Ginger above the roar of flames. 'There's nothing we can do here. Let's scram up and do what we can about the hangar fire.'

'But orders . . .' said Taff stolidly, shaking his head.

'There won't be any more orders. Not from there. The bridge is gone.'

The rest couldn't hear this above the roar of the inferno; but they could read Ginger's lips, and we were with him. No use staying here.

It was that instant another salvo hit, and the whole side of the *Glorious* seemed to cave in, leaving a choking cloud of smoke and a thunderous roar that echoed away to the darkening sky. The sea, so calm before the action, was now churned up and flecked with grey. God I thought we've nearly had our chips! Stupefied, we waited. And I wish we hadn't. For that's when I saw Ginger McColl. He was walking over from his post with P.5. Walking. Holding on to the crazily twisted rails of the ship and laughing at me.

'You're a lucky lot of sods, you are. You're all right. That was our gun, that was. Lifted the whole ruddy gun right out. Last I saw was that bloke Jarvis with it, looking as if he was holding the gun in his great mitt, like he holds a water-polo ball.'

Then I saw why he was walking oddly. His uniform was ragged, what was left of it. Just a torn shirt and part of his trousers. One leg was shot off, and there was the splintered bone, dripping red and black blood, and white strings of sinews. My throat was full of spittle, and I could vomit just to look at him. I thought the world of Ginger.

'I must go and get this wrapped up,' was all he said, then hobbled off guiding his way through the smoke and clutching the twisted rail.

'Let's get,' I said, and the rest of our lot followed me, clambering up towards the flight-deck. In the grey steel plating was the shell-hole. The first shell-hole I'd ever seen. Fascinated, I gazed at the jagged edge. A young sailor came screaming down the ladder from the deck, and he was clutching the rails with both hands kicking out with both feet. I could see he wasn't injured, only hysterical.

'Cut it out,' said Taff. 'Cut it out, lad.'

And he lunged out and hit the kid a welt across the face so hard it sent him staggering back against the deck. The kid stopped screaming all right.

We ran on. There was the hangar, the wall of fire still rising.

. . . There was nothing we could do here. But the lower hangar? Half a dozen of us ran to the nearest watertight door, which by wartime routine was always closed. One man alone couldn't undo the great lock. So we all clambered for a handhold.

Another swing and we've done it, boys. . . . With our combined weight we heaved, and the door gave. It gave so suddenly we were all flung on our backsides, and the flame gushed out like the very flames of hell. I thought the huge steel door of the hangar would never swing back. It was like the boiler end of an express train coming up at you.

We scrambled up, cursing the fire, cursing the door, shouting to one another for help to get it shut again, as the giant inrush of air gave new zest to the furnace. As tongues of flame shot out, I got to one side of the door with Taff, and as we began to heave it shut there was a sight on the deck such as I could never picture even in a nightmare.

The wheel-lock of that door had huge star-fish spokes. The spokes of that wheel had pinned one of the crew, running right through his body with a clear X pattern like a bruised hot-cross bun. He must have died instantly, the way the imprint of the wheel was left right through his diaphragm. And there was a bit of his shirt, squelching blood, still hanging from the wheel-lock.

I reckon we went berserk at that door. But somehow we got it shut, imprisoned the flames that by now were eating the heart out of *Glorious*. We dripped sweat with the effort and were blackened by the flames. But I still had my jacket on. That was damn silly. So I took it off, and laid it over the punctured corpse on the deck.

By now the *Glorious* was listing, and all the filth was draining that way across the slanting decks.

. . . Just then we got the order to abandon ship, and kicking our way through the stacks of empty shell-cases which we hadn't time to fling over after the live projjies, we marched off, quite orderly, to our special stations.

And then we marched back.

The abandon ship order was cancelled almost as soon as we got it, and we got the action stations again.

. . . The abandon ship order came again soon after—not in the precise metallic way of the Tannoy but with one of the officers running along the battery shouting words which on the *Glorious* sounded brutally unreal. 'Abandon ship. . . . All hands prepare to abandon ship. . . .'

And off we went like sheep, a thin file of bewildered, scorched and oil-scarred men, joining the throngs of others struggling against the sharply listing deck until we became a flood of humanity, pressing through the shell debris and the wreckage, running with the ugly current of a crowd towards our appointed stations for abandon ship.

We knew where to go. Week after week, in peacetime and in war, we'd practised it. A lot of bull, just to conform to regulations. We'd never need to know. . . .

Week after week we went through the motions, but not through the actions. That's the part of the deck you'll stand on, but for Christ's sake don't stand on it now when I've just swabbed it down. That's the guy-rope you'll hang on, but don't hang on the blamed thing now, because it's just been painted.

Now the decks were deep in dust and debris, and the new paint scorched as we were ourselves, and we stood there in flocks, sheep-like, wondering what came next after the order abandon ship. We'd never been told what came next.

One or two of the lads took the order literally and threw themselves over the rails.

'For God's sake, come back!' their pals screamed after them as they dived off the listing deck; but it was no use. The speed we'd been travelling when the action was at its height meant the *Glorious* still had way on her, and to dive into that white frothing cauldron now meant being left miles behind without a hope of rescue.

We felt perplexed because up to this awful moment we'd been obeying orders, and now there weren't any more orders to obey. What comes after abandon ship? . . .

Then it was we saw how wonderful the officers could be. There were the hordes of bruised and injured men waiting like an untidy crowd at the end of a seaside pier, and there was the major of Marines and two other officers by the hatchway leading down from the centre of the quarterdeck.

'Come on, lads. Don't panic now. Get into line. . . .'

It was nothing they said, really. But the way they stood there and said it. They could have buggered off and left us.

Orders were what we wanted, so they gave us orders. 'You and you and you. That's right lads. The three of you. Check the cutter in the storage bay. . . .'

We checked it.

In the next bay to where I was standing was storage for a motor-driven cutter, a thirty-foot clinker-built job. Now the planking was shelled and jagged. The transom was split off. The launching cradle was smashed. And, anyway we could not launch the thing because of the list of the ship. But we checked it, like we'd been told to do.

There were useful, purposeful things to do as well. There was the job of getting floatable things off that were undamaged. There was the idea of getting some rations in case any of the ship's boats had no fresh stores or water; but this was now too late and impossible. There was the matter of tending to the men who had not been injured seriously enough during the action to be taken to the first-aid posts, but who were now flagging from the strain and shock.

Next to me was a matelot suffering from gunshock, and he kept on trying to vomit until his frame was weak with retching. Somewhere in my trousers pocket I found the sticky paper of glucose sweets, and he sucked them and gave me a bit of a smile. That stopped it.

By now the quarterdeck was sloping at an angle of nearly forty-five degrees, and as each man prepared to jump, it meant a struggle to climb up for it. Little knots of men clawed each other round the waist as they clambered up the rails, laughing and swearing as they stripped off their boots and trousers and prepared to jump.

Then my turn came. I got to the top of the deck, and stood there looking down. It must have been thirty feet. And down there I saw the ship's screw on the starboard side still churning beneath me.

It was going to be one hell of a jump. I didn't want to hit that ruddy great green bronze screw, nor any of those oily black bobbing heads in the water.

'Teach you to drown, young 'un!'

A voice was driving through my brain. It was my brother Bill. We were at New Brighton again, when I was a kid and he was teaching me to swim. Swim? Well, he held me up by the chin, then yelled: 'Teach you to drown, young 'un,' and he let me go. A couple of mouthfuls, I kicked out. And I could swim. No foot on the bottom. I could really swim.

'Teach you to drown, young 'un. . . .'

That laughing voice followed me as I jumped.

Marine RONALD HEALISS

The author's nickname was 'Tubby' and he ascribed to his fatness his endurance of four days and nights in a damaged life-boat. Three officers and forty men were saved of a ship's company of more than 1,200. Forty-seven men of the RAF were also lost, including the crews of eight Gladiators and ten Hurricanes of Nos. 263 and 46 Squadrons, who had flown on board rather than abandon their aircraft in Norway.

*

Glorious' *two destroyer escorts, HMS* Acasta *(Commander C. E. Glasfurd RN) and HMS* Ardent *(Lieutenant-Commander J. F. Barker RN), fought with great bravery to save her. Both laid a defensive smoke-screen to shield the carrier and then advanced to attack the German battle cruisers with torpedoes. Both were overwhelmed and sunk, although* Acasta *hit* Scharnhorst *with one torpedo. There were two survivors from* Ardent *and one sole survivor from* Acasta.

FROM *ACASTA*, GOING TO THE WAR

On board our ship, what a deathly calm, hardly a word spoken, the ship was now steaming full speed away from the enemy, then came a host of orders, prepare all smoke-floats, hose-pipes connected up, various other jobs were prepared, we were still stealing away from the enemy, and making smoke, and all our smoke-floats had been set going. The captain then had this message passed to all positions: 'You may think we are running away from the enemy, we are not, our chummy ship (*Ardent*) has sunk, the *Glorious* is sinking, the least we can do is make a show, good luck to you all.' We then altered course into our own smoke-screen. I had the order to stand by to fire tubes six and seven, we then came out of the smoke-screen, altered course to starboard firing our torpedoes from port side. It was then I had my first glimpse of the enemy, to be honest it appeared to me a large one and a small one, and we were very close. I fired my two torpedoes from my tubes, the foremost tubes fired theirs, we were all watching results. I'll never forget that cheer that went up; on the port bow of one of the ships a yellow flash and a great column of smoke and water shot up from her. We knew we had hit, personally I could not see how we could have missed so close as we were. The enemy never fired a shot at us, I feel they must have been very surprised. After we had fired our torpedoes we went back into our own smoke-screen, altered course again to starboard. 'Stand by to fire remaining torpedoes'; and this time as soon as we poked our nose out of the smoke-screen the enemy let us have it. A shell hit the engine-room, killed my tubes' crew, I was blown to the after end of the tubes. I must have been knocked out for a while, because when I came to, my arm hurt me; the ship had stopped with a list to port. Here is something believe it or believe it not, I climbed back into the control seat, I see those two ships, I fired the remaining torpedoes, no one told me to, I guess I was raving mad. God alone knows why I fired them, but I did. The *Acasta*'s guns were firing the whole time, even firing with a list on the ship. The enemy then hit us several times, but one big explosion took place right aft. I have often wondered whether the enemy hit us with a torpedo, in any case it seemed to lift the ship out of the water. At last the captain gave orders to abandon ship, I will always remember the surgeon-lieutenant,[1] his first ship, his first action. Before I jumped over the side I saw him still attending to the wounded, a hopeless task, and when I was in the water I saw the captain leaning over the bridge, take a cigarette from a case and light it. We shouted to him to come on our raft, he waved 'Goodbye and good luck'—the end of a gallant man.

Leading Seaman C. CARTER, of *Acasta*

*

TO THE SOLDIERS

They march over the Field of Waterloo,
By Goumont and La Haie, and then fell back,
Forever facing front to the attack
Across the English bones.

Westward, by Fontenoy, their ranks withdrew;
The German many bomb-bursts beat the drum,
And many a trooper marched to kingdom come
Upon the Flanders stones.

1. Temporary Surgeon-Lieutenant H. J. Stammers, RNVR.

Westward they went, past Wipers, past the old
Fields bought and paid for by their brothers' blood.
Their feet were in the snapping of the flood
That sped to gulf them down.

They were as bridegrooms plighted to the mould
Those marching men with neither hope nor star,
The foeman in the gateways as a bar,
The sea beyond to drown.

And at the very sea, a cloud of night,
A hail of death and allies in collapse,
A foe in the perfection of his traps,
A certainty of doom.

When, lo, out of the darkness, there was light,
There in the sea were England and her ships,
They sailed with the free salt upon their lips
To sunlight from the tomb.

JOHN MASEFIELD OM

*

DUNKIRK

Now from every port the boats were moving out, bent on a crazy, incredible rescue . . . from Ramsgate and Margate . . . from Dover, Folkestone and Portsmouth . . . from Sheerness and down the tidal rivers . . . their wakes planing like a sickle through wet grass . . . frail streamers of smoke trailing to the sky . . . a fleet almost a thousand strong.

There never had been an armada like it. The destroyer *Harvester*, built to fulfil a foreign contract, with all its gun-laying instructions in Brazilian; the *Count Dracula*, launch of the German Admiral Ludwig von Reuter, scuttled at Scapa Flow in 1919 but salvaged years later; the armed yacht *Grive*, where the captain, the Hon. Lionel Lambert, took his own personal chef; the *Canterbury*, the bejewelled ferry-boat of the cross-Channel run, with memories of

Princess Paul of Yugoslavia and Delysia; Arthur Dench's *Letitia*, the little green cockle-boat from the Essex mudflats, breasting the waves like a seagull.

And still they streamed across the waters: the Thames hopper barge *Galleon's Reach*, built to pack in not men but the muddy spoil of dredgers; Tom Sopwith's yacht *Endeavour*; the Fleetwood fishing trawler *Jacinta*, reeking of cod; the Yangtse gun-boat *Mosquito* bristling with armament to ward off Chinese river-pirates; *Reiger*, a Dutch *schuit*, redolent of onions, still hung with geranium pots, with mighty bunks for mighty men; the Deal beach-boat *Dumpling*, built in Napoleon's time, with a skipper seventy years young.

As the cockle-shell armada fanned out towards Dunkirk, even seasoned naval officers felt a lump rise to their throats: absurd yet magnificent, it was without all precedent in the world's naval history. On the bridge of the destroyer *Malcolm*, the navigating officer, Lieutenant Ian Cox, was moved almost to tears to see the oncoming fleet led by, of all craft, the *Wootton*, the old Isle of Wight car-ferry, wallowing like a sawn-off landing-stage through the water. His voice shaken by emotion, Cox burst out to the seaman beside him with the classic lines of Shakespeare's *Henry V* before another assault upon the coast of France:

> And gentlemen in England now a-bed
> Shall think themselves accurs'd they were not here,
> And hold their manhoods cheap while any speaks
> That fought with us upon Saint Crispin's day.

As with the boats, so with the crews. The rich and the famous, the poor and the unknown, as motley a bunch as ever set sail made up this mercy fleet. The Earl of Craven, third engineer in the rescue tug *St Olave* . . . a Dominican monk in a reefer jersey skippering the yacht *Gulzar* . . . 'George', the salty bos'n of the contraband control vessel *Ocean Breeze*, still wearing a privateer's golden ear-rings below his steel helmet . . . Captain 'Potato' Jones, sixty-seven-year-old skipper of the *Marie Llewellyn*, famed for running Franco's blockade through the Spanish Civil War.

Age was no barrier: though skipper Charlie Alexander didn't know it yet, fourteen-year-old Ronald Pridmore, the galley-boy, was sheltering below deck in the tug *Sun IV*, determined to show there were other proofs of manhood than shaving. Lieutenant-Colonel Charles Wharton, coming down from Oulton Broad in Suffolk, felt the same: they had rejected him for re-enlistment at sixty, but still, though wearing carpet slippers for comfort, he'd show them this was an oldster's war too.

Neither race nor colour had meaning, for this was an international fleet—a true United Nations . . . Californian-born John Fernald skippering one of the twelve life-boats towed by the tug *Racia* . . . Dick Jacobus Hoogerbeets, a young shipyard plater from Ijmuiden, aboard motor-boat 74 . . . Chinese Steward Ah Fong rushing tea to Captain Lewes on the bridge of *Bideford* . . . a crew from Stornoway with their own Gaelic interpreter in the minesweeper *Fitzroy* . . . Fireman Ali Khan, shovelling as if all life depended on it in the stokehold of *Dorrien Rose*.

The mood was unique too—the grim gaiety of the gambler staking all his chips on the last spin of the wheel. Bouncing towards Dunkirk in motor-boat 67, a World War I veteran with a compass twenty degrees out, Lieutenant Courtney Anderson RN, almost carolled with joy; only a bottle of malted-milk tablets donated by his mother-in-law stood between the crew and starvation, but today it was good to be alive.

Spotting an old friend, Lieutenant Chris Dreyer, ferrying a brigadier back from Dunkirk in motor-boat 102, Anderson couldn't resist yelling: 'Excuse me, can you tell me the way to Dunkirk?'

Dreyer, playing up, jerked a thumb: 'Back there, you can't miss it. It's burning.' As the brigadier turned crimson with horror, both skippers collapsed in unholy glee.

Not all the outsiders had signed T 124—the form that made them Royal Naval volunteers for a month—for they prized their independence too much. Some in any case were there despite official qualms: Stewardess Amy Goodrich, the only woman to be awarded a Dunkirk decoration, swore that so long as the nurses sailed in the hospital ship *Dinard* she'd sail too. Most were entitled to £3 for their services, but few bothered to collect. They were sworn to one single improbable purpose: the rescue of the British Army.

Their callings were as varied as their garb. Engineer Fred Reynard, who'd talked an admiral into letting his crew take over the motor-vessel *Bee*, wore an open-necked shirt, V-necked sweater, blue dungarees. Wilfred Pym Trotter, a Bank of England clerk, wore much the same, though he'd reported as for any city stint—bowler hat, pin-stripe trousers, umbrella. Dr Basil Smith, a peppery little chartered accountant who skippered the *Constant Nymph*, wore a padded golf cap, a lounge suit and a cork life-belt so thick he had to stand a foot away from the wheel. Raphael de Sola, one of London's wealthiest stockbrokers, wore the full rig of the Royal London Yacht Club: blue gabardine raincoat lined with red flannel, yachting cap with the club's insignia.

Aboard the *Tollesbury*, Skipper Lemon Webb was garbed more prosaically: old sailcloth trousers and jersey, shapeless trilby hat still perched on his head. He wasn't dressing up for this show.

Incredibly, the old barge was as well equipped as any craft destined to make this trip. Despite Captain Wharton's efforts at Ramsgate, despite all that Rear-Admiral Alfred Taylor, *Dynamo*'s maintenance officer at Sheerness, could do, craft after craft was moving out with scarcely enough gear or provisions for a leisurely cruise up an estuary.

Aboard the motor-yacht *Constant Nymph*, Dr Basil Smith and two stoker ratings were already off Dunkirk—ferrying load after load of French troops to the Dutch *schuit Jutland*. The excitement staved off hunger, which was as well—the Navy had given them a sirloin of beef and a sack of potatoes but the little boat boasted only a two-burner Primus.

In the Clacton life-boat Wilfred Pym Trotter faced the same problem. There was just one way to make tea: wedge a kettleful of water, tea and milk in the boat's funnel and wait until the dubious brew boiled.

It was the same in boat after boat. From the Admiralty's Small Vessels Pool to Ramsay's own staff, the Navy had worked like beavers to muster the small craft at all. Boat-builders Jack Powell and his brother Pat had been two of a team working non-stop at Sheerness to make the craft serviceable—in the grim knowledge that a full forty per cent had never put to sea.

Now, *en route* for Dunkirk, both Powells saw the shape of things to come. In the motor-yacht *Reda* the engine control gave out before Dover was even lost to view; thereafter Pat Powell's petty officer had to work the old remote-control engine by hand. In the twin-engined *Cordelia* Jack Powell was at his wits' end: the cabin-cruiser was leaking at the seams and only one engine deigned to function at all.

And the small craft under naval control fared no better. Sub-Lieutenant Alfred Weaver had no sooner left Ramsgate than the *Quijijana*'s engine caught fire; dousing it with the extinguisher, Weaver ploughed on, but the minute he sighted Dunkirk the old yellow-funnelled pleasure launch began shipping water. Finding the bilge pump inoperative, Weaver and his crew had to bale desperately with their service caps.

For the first time Weaver saw the brass plate affixed to the bulwarks—'Licensed to ply between Chertsey and Teddington'—and understood. That stretch of the River Thames, he knew, measured only fourteen miles.

The armament was primitive. Aboard the yacht *Chrystobel II*, a rich man's plaything, Lieutenant Hubert Wigfull had one Lewis gun—but the only sturdier weapon was an 1890 saluting gun geared to an angle of forty-five degrees. And other ships, moving out with less protection, faced a grimmer ordeal. The cargo-boat *Roebuck*, still on the Channel Islands run, had been unloading daffodils and new potatoes in Weymouth Harbour when the order came to set out. The old ship wasn't even degaussed—her hull wound with electric cable as protection against magnetic mines—yet Captain Wilfred Larbalestier moved off without question.

In the personnel ship *St Helier* Captain Richard Pitman had no contact with the outside world at all; after several gruelling trips twenty of his crew had walked out so that now, halfway to Dunkirk, he didn't even have a wireless operator. After a despairing prowl round the wireless cabin, Pitman, sending for engineer Dick Dougal and second mate Frank Martin, experimentally touched a switch. Promptly a blue flame danced like a will o' the wisp across the cabin; the three men gave up. Without benefit of radio the *St Helier* steamed on.

The pitiful shortages might have made any man lose heart. In the tug *Sun IV* the 'ample supplies' of dressings promised to Charles Jackson's Gravesend ambulance team just hadn't been forthcoming: even the surgical scissors turned out to be nail scissors. Without more ado they stripped off their underclothes, began slicing them into bandages. Not to be outdone, skipper Charlie Alexander rummaged through cupboards and drawers. Soon all of them were shearing methodically through towels, pillow-cases, even the skipper's shirts.

Now the small craft drew nearer to the shore. The full impact of Dunkirk plunged home.

Above the scene for thirty miles loomed the black pall of the oil-tanks of St Pol, 11,000 feet high, a mile wide, two million tons of oil roaring as one. To Chief Engineer George Tooley, aboard the *Maid of Orleans*, it looked 'like doom itself'.

A few found grounds for optimism. Glancing at the inky smoke that mingled with the fog, almost blotting out the land, ambulance officer Charles Jackson, in *Sun IV*, felt his spirits soaring: 'Good old Navy, look at the smoke-screen they've put up.'

RICHARD COLLIER

*

TO THE SEAMEN

You seamen, I have eaten your hard bread
And drunken from your tin, and known your ways;
I understand the qualities I praise
Though lacking all, with only words instead.

I tell you this, that in the future time
When landsmen mention sailors, such, or such,
Someone will say, 'Those fellows were sublime
Who brought the Armies from the Germans' clutch.'

Through the long time the story will be told;
Long centuries of praise on English lips,
Of courage godlike and of hearts of gold
Off Dunquerque beaches in the little ships.

And ships will dip their colours in salute
To you, henceforth, when passing Zuydecoote.

JOHN MASEFIELD OM

*

ST VALERY—11TH JUNE 1940

Ever since the 51st Highland Division surrendered to a German armoured division at St Valery it has been widely believed that the flotilla sent from Portsmouth to evacuate the division failed to reach the pier because the coast was fog-bound. The truth is very different. I was Commander-in-Chief at Portsmouth at the time, and the full story is in two letters that I wrote shortly after the failure to embark the division.

Letter of 16th June

On the 8th Pegram and some shipping men joined my staff to help to organise a withdrawal from the Havre district and we were all night making plans. We collected an armada of vessels of all sorts and sizes. The 'Butterflies', fast passenger ships, were our best ships. Cameron at Newhaven organised three flotillas of small craft and boats, and my flag lieutenant. Fogg-Elliot, did likewise in the Hamble River.

We also had a number of Dutch schoots which we had commissioned earlier, and Coppinger, Captain of Dockyard, took command of the dockyard tugs with cutters in tow. Altogether about 200 vessels. I chose Warren of St Vincent and Armstrong of the Navigation School for the command of this armada, and gave them destroyers as senior officers' ships. We got the whole business shipshape and sailed all the squadrons for Havre hopefully expecting that the order to take off our men would soon come through, as it was obvious that the French armies were no use.

As I received no orders about evacuating by the morning of the 10th, I became restless and decided to go over and see things for myself. As we approached Havre I realised that the situation was pretty bad, as the oil tanks were blazing and we heard continual explosions, which I found out later were from demolition operations.

I called alongside our flotillas to cheer them up and then landed and made my way to our military HQ through streams of refugees. One glance at the big map was enough to show that the situation of our 51st Division was as bad as it could be, and whilst I was in the map-room despatch riders were constantly arriving with bad news. The French were giving way everywhere and the Germans were beginning to encircle the 51st Division and press them back to the coast. I telephoned to the Admiralty and told them I was going to move the flotillas at once to a position off St Valery, as it was obvious our troops would have to embark there.

I then went to see the French admiral who, by their strange organisation, was the supreme authority and the only man who could give the orders for evacuation, and found him in a very excited state, and quite unconvinced that there was any need to evacuate, and evidently still under the delusion that the French Army was conducting a fighting retreat. Then to the harbour and contacted Warren and Armstrong, and told them to prepare to embark the 51st Division at St Valery.

On arrival back at Portsmouth I at once got on to the War Office and told Haining what was really happening, but I found to my surprise that the War Office had been assured by Weygand that the French northern armies would fight back to the Somme. The War Office were in a very difficult position, as Fortune's division had been made part of a French army and were entirely under the orders of the French general. The weather was then quite clear.

You will appreciate that it was no surprise to me when we received signals on the 11th showing that the situation of the 51st Division was critical.

I had meantime been compelled to withdraw the flotillas some distance from the coast as they were having a nasty time from dive-bombers, and when at long last Ian Tower, who was senior officer in Havre, got the French admiral to agree to evacuate, the visibility had decreased due to haze and there was difficulty in communicating with all the small vessels who had no wireless.

It was 5 pm when Tower's message arrived, and when I told Warren to go ahead I still hoped for the best. But signals about fires at St Valery and gun-fire from the shore soon dashed our hopes. It gradually became clear that the order to evacuate had been given too late.

I learnt afterwards that some of our smaller vessels that approached St Valery were met with heavy fire and one has not been heard of since. One schoot got in not far from St Valery and brought off some officers and men who were sheltering behind a stone wall, and though the stories of these officers were rather disjointed, it appears certain that the Germans had captured St Valery long before the order to evacuate was given.

Are you surprised that I feel bitter about all this? The French were skedaddling or laying down their arms, our fine 51st Division was there waiting to embark, the necessary ships and boats were there ready to embark them, and yet they are now prisoners.

Letter of 4th July

On the 25th I had a surprise and most welcome visitor in the shape of Commander Elkins who went over to join the 51st Division with wireless sets. He appeared in the dress of a French fisherman. I hope the story of his escape will be published one day. He got away with an officer of the Gordon Highlanders when they had nearly reached Germany and, after many adventures, stole a boat and sailed over, landing at Hayling Island.

I was so glad to get the complete story of St Valery. He told me that he went down to the pier on the morning of the 11th and had a talk with some officers who were to act as beach masters. He then went to discuss matters with the general and returned to the harbour at about three in the afternoon. He was quite innocently walking on the beach when fire was opened at him. He ducked behind some stones and then a voice from the cliffs called out that he had better surrender as he was covered by guns. He then found to his surprise that a large number of German tanks were drawn up on the cliffs—and it was not till 5 pm that day that I got permission to evacuate!

No wonder our craft found it impossible to approach St Valery. If they had survived the enemy's fire there would have been no 51st Division to bring off. Elkin's story shows that the game was lost early in the afternoon.

Admiral Sir WILLIAM JAMES GCB

*

The Skagerrak in the summer of 1940 was a nightmare place for a submarine on patrol; the shallow sea depth, the sudden fresh-water layers, the interminable hours of daylight, and the almost continuous surveillance from the air meant that submarines could only stay in the area for short periods and were relieved every four days. In June HMS/M Sealion *was there on what her captain called*

MY WORST PATROL

Shark was going to relieve us next day and I decided that I must tell her to keep out; this meant relaying the message home because only Rugby could transmit to a submerged submarine. The skies clouded over, low cloud, but at last there was no aircraft in sight. It might only be because they were behind cloud cover, but we had to charge batteries and we had to get a signal through to *Shark*. It was a risk we had to take.

We surfaced with just enough buoyancy to bring out the conning-tower hatch and I scrambled through as it came clear. I was half out when I saw the aircraft; it came out from behind a cloud straight at us. I pressed the hooter, slammed shut the hatch and down we went; two depth-charges straddled us as we went down. Steering, hydroplanes and gyro compass went off the board, some of the lights went and more paint rained down. This time there were no surface craft to follow up, we got things under control and working again, and soon after midnight I decided to have another shot. Somehow we had got to tell *Shark* to keep out. The heavens remained black, one could not see what was behind the clouds. Unless we could charge batteries we were impotent; we could not get away from Stavanger submerged and we would have to run for it on the surface.

Once again our conning tower broke surface. This time I had hardly opened the hatch when there was a roar; a Heinkel came out of a cloud so close that she did not have time to bomb. I pulled the hatch shut and down we went again; we were clear of the position before the depth-charges came down and they did no damage.

Now we had to consider things carefully. The air was foul and we were already panting—one always did as the carbon dioxide collected. The conning tower had not been open for more than a few seconds during either of our attempts to surface and no fresh air had reached the boat. The battery was practically flat—another crash-dive would finish it; the enemy knew where we were; we could not get away submerged and equally we could not surface. The only thing was to stick it out submerged and hope that we would be able to last out till they gave up. We found a water layer to sit on; stopped the motors; switched out practically every light and settled down to wait.

From time to time we renewed the trays of soda lime which were laid out throughout the boat. They were meant to absorb the carbon dioxide, and so, after a fashion, they did, but without proper air-conditioning plant to force the foul air through the absorbent it could only be partially effective. We could still receive routine signals from Rugby and from time to time we came off our layer to have a look round, but there was always a hunter in sight. The damage was made good and everybody, except those on watch, lay down to conserve the air. The hours dragged by, everyone had headaches, sleep was impossible, one's body felt cold and clammy. I had always imagined that if one got stuck in a submarine and ran out of air one would fall into a stupefying doze and just not wake up. It would seem that this is not so, one cannot sleep. Some cold food was served out with lime juice to drink, but no one seemed interested in the food.

Then we got an enemy report: a ship was coming our way. She would have to come to us. There was still enough life in the battery to turn the boat around, but there was no question of our moving to intercept her. We brought the boat back to periscope depth; the T.I. checked over his tubes and waited. Panting was getting heavier; it was obvious that we were fairly near our limit, but still the sweeping A/S forces were in sight. They were farther off now, but too near to get away on the surface. I decided to try our small store of oxygen.

When experience of long dives indicated that air was a major problem the medicos were called in; they provided us with the carbon-dioxide absorbent, but pronounced that there was no need to provide oxygen since there was enough oxygen available to last us far longer than all the carbon-dioxide absorbent we could carry. I knew that the Germans, or at least one German U-boat, had carried oxygen in World War I. Years before during my training class I had heard a story in the mess of how a surrendered U-boat, which had no high-pressure air left had blown her tanks by connecting up the oxygen cylinders she carried. Whilst I believed the experts, I still felt that the Germans had not carried oxygen for nothing, for space and stowage is very precious in a submarine. On the principle of taking no chances, I had secured some cylinders of oxygen, and a reducing valve, just before this patrol.

Everyone was pretty sick by this time and at least it could not do any harm. It was beginning to become doubtful whether, if the reported ship did come past us, we could make much of a show of attacking her. The oxygen was switched on, a gentle hissing in the silent boat; conversation except for an occasional order had long since ceased. It is not easy to talk when panting. Some of the men said they felt better; I knew that it must be imagination, but at least it was good to think you felt better.

The long-awaited ship did not come past us; it was probably just as well, but a bit disappointing at the time. We sank back to our layer and waited. The oxygen ran out; the hours dragged past; the headaches nagged. Just before midnight on the second day the sea and sky seemed clear. Men moved to their diving stations and the tanks were blown. I went up through the conning tower; this time all was clear. Then I leaned over the side of the bridge and was sick; not having eaten for some thirty hours, this was not particularly satisfactory, but it helped. The look-outs came up and they too were sick.

Down below they were trying to start the diesels; but it was some time after the fans had been running before they would fire. Diesels are more particular about the quality of air than humans.

Some time later further investigation by the medicos established that oxygen was absolutely essential in such circumstances. My cautious, belt-and-braces philosophy had paid a dividend.

I have said that all was clear, but over towards the landward horizon something was going on. It was twilight, the nearest we ever got to darkness in those latitudes, but one could see tracer bullets and flashes. We tried again to get our signal through to *Shark*. But it was too late; we were watching *Shark* fighting her last action. The hunt had changed their foxes; she was being sunk whilst we lay sick and helpless, unable to go to her assistance.

It took three or four hours for the headaches to wear off; after everything was settled down, and we had cleared the coast, I went down below. I was feeling rather despondent; *Salmon* was overdue,

Shark had gone, two of the four boats which had formed our division before the war. The war was going badly and one felt very alone on patrol; it seemed that the war depended upon you personally and I had missed the convoy and nearly lost the boat; I felt that I had let down the crew.

I wandered for'ard where men off watch were sleeping on the deck, covered with their oilskins to catch the drips, and suddenly the atmosphere of unworried serenity passed from them to me. I realised that they would go into action on the morrow without backward thoughts, that with crews such as I was privileged to command we could not be beaten; the depression left me.

Rear-Admiral BEN BRYANT CB DSO and two bars, DSC

*

By now subconscious forces began to affect the bodies as well as the minds of submarine captains. I was sitting in the mess waiting for patrol orders when our doctor asked casually, 'Let's have a look at your fingernails.' Each one showed a series of concentric half-moon ridges from base to tip. 'Interesting stigmata,' he said. 'If you break off patrols for a refit you'll find a gap corresponding to the time spent in harbour. Each ridge is a patrol. They occur in *all* commanding officers of submarines, in most of their subordinate officers and in a small proportion of responsible ratings—purely psychological.'

Commander WILLIAM KING DSO DSC RN
(Then Captain of HMS/M *Snapper*)

*

THE GALLANT LITTLE *CAMPEADOR*

A naval officer writes:

In these days of tremendous events at sea, on land, and in the air the loss of a ship only attracts momentary attention except to those who mourn the loss of husband, son, or friend. But there was something unique about HMS *Campeador*, whose loss was recently published. *Campeador* was a steam yacht owned by Mr V. W. McAndrew She was commissioned for patrol service by Commander C. H. Davey, OBE, Master of the Dartmoor Foxhounds, and the three sub-lieutenants RNVR appointed to her were Mr McAndrew, the owner, Mr C. E. Turner, a docks superintendent, and a retired surgeon rear-admiral J. R. Muir. The youngest of these men was aged fifty-eight and the oldest sixty-seven.

The ship soon acquired a high reputation of remaining on her station and refusing to return to port to remedy defects if these could possibly be remedied at sea. She was eighty-four days at sea out of the first ninety-five days of the war and these gallant gentlemen, by their fortitude and unabated cheerfulness, were a splendid example to everyone in the Portsmouth Command. After some months Sub-Lieutenant McAndrew and Sub-Lieutenant Muir were recommended for promotion to lieutenant, and their captain felt fully justified in entering against the various qualities on the promotion form the highest marks permissible.

The stirring story of the *Campeador* came to the notice of the First Lord of the Admiralty and, characteristically, he wrote across the recommendation certificate: 'Promote them, age will be served.' Sir Muirhead Bone, who was working at Portsmouth, heard of this famous band of brothers and made a drawing of them sitting in their mess.

As they would have wished, they died together in the service of their country, but their example will long remain an inspiration to the younger generation, and the little *Campeador* will be remembered and talked about long after the war is over by those who served in the same waters.

From *The Times*, 23rd July 1940

*

After the fall of France an extraordinary feeling, almost of defiant exhilaration, swept through the service and the country as a whole. We now had no allies. On the other hand, there was no one to let us down either. This mood was exactly caught in a poem of the time:

THE ENGLISH WAR

Praise God, now, for an English war—
The grey tide and the sullen coast,

The menace of the urgent hour,
The single island, like a tower,
  Ringed with an angry host.

This is the war that England knows,
  When all the world holds but one man—
King Philip of the galleons,
Louis, whose light outshone the sun's,
  The conquering Corsican;

When Europe, like a prison door,
  Clangs; and the swift, enfranchised sea
Runs narrower than a village brook;
And men who love us not, yet look
  To us for liberty;

When no allies are left, no help
  To count upon from alien hands,
No waverers remain to woo,
No more advice to listen to,
  And only England stands.

This is the war we always knew,
  When every county keeps her own,
When Kent stands sentry in the lane,
And Fenland guards her dyke and drain,
  Cornwall, her cliffs of stone;

When from the Cinque Ports and the Wight,
  From Plymouth Sound and Bristol Town,
There comes a noise that breaks our sleep,
Of the deep calling to the deep
  Where the ships go up and down,

And near and far across the world
  Hold open wide the water-gates,
And all the tall adventurers come
Homeward to England, and Drake's drum
  Is beaten through the Straits.

This is the war that we have known
  And fought in every hundred years,
Our sword, upon the last, steep path,
Forged by the hammer of our wrath
  On the anvil of our fears.

Send us, O God, the will and power
  To do as we have done before;
The men that ride the sea and air
Are the same men their fathers were
  To fight the English war.

And send, O God, the English peace—
  Some sense, some decency, perhaps
Some justice, too, if we are able,
With no sly jackals round our table,
  Cringing for blood-stained scraps;

No dangerous dreams of wishful men
  Whose homes are safe, who never feel
The flying death that swoops and stuns,
The kissing of the curtseying guns
  Slavering their streets with steel;

No dreams, Lord God, but vigilance,
  That we may keep, by might and main,
Inviolate seas, inviolate skies;—
But, if another tyrant rise,
  Then we shall fight again.

DOROTHY L. SAYERS

*

THE RNVR

The RNVR officers brought to the Navy qualities which were peculiarly their own. Because they had not been moulded by the long education and apprenticeship of the regular officer they had less respect for the authority of rank; but they also had fewer inhibitions against indulging in novel experiments in organisation, equipment and procedure. Indeed some of their experiments were so novel that they affronted (and may have been designed to affront) their more conventional-minded superiors. Yet they quickly developed, and were astute enough to show a genuine respect for what was admirable and timeless in naval tradition; and because they were always ready to listen to the counsels of experience, they gained the confidence and the affection of the regular officers. Furthermore they brought to their new tasks an infectious enthusiasm and a boundless sense of humour. Into a service in which conservatism was not the least common characteristic they blew a strong, fresh wind of unconventionality and non-conformity; and the regulars for their part returned the respect shown to their professionalism with a sympathetic understanding of the RNVR's open-minded approach to every problem and a tolerance of their occasional idiosyncrasies. Indeed the regular and reserve officers soon found that they could each learn from the other, to the advantage of the service as a whole.

Captain S. W. ROSKILL DSC RN

*

RECRUITING DRIVE

Under the willow the willow
   I heard the butcher-bird sing,
Come out you fine young fellow
   From under your mother's wing.
I'll show you the magic garden
   That hangs in the beamy air,
The way of the lynx and the angry Sphinx
   And the fun of the freezing fair.

Lie down lie down with my daughter
   Beneath the Arabian tree,
Gaze on your face in the water
   Forget the scribbling sea.
Your pillow the bright shiners.
   Your bed the spilling sand,
But the terrible toy of my lily-white boy
   Is the gun in his innocent hand.

You must take off your clothes for the doctor
  And stand as straight as a pin
His hand of stone on your white breast-bone
  Where the bullets all go in.
They'll dress you in lawn and linen
  And fill you with Plymouth gin,
O the devil may wear a rose in his hair
  I'll wear my fine doe-skin.

My mother weeps as I leave her
  But I tell her it won't be long,
The murderers wail in Wandsworth Gaol
  But I shoot a more popular song.
Down in the enemy country
  Under the enemy tree
There lies a lad whose heart has gone bad
  Waiting for me, for me.

He says I have no culture
  And that when I've stormed the pass
I shall fall on the farm with a smoking arm
  And ravish his bonny lass.
Under the willow the willow
  Death spreads her dripping wings
And caught in the snare of the bleeding air
  The butcher-bird sings, sings, sings.

Petty Officer CHARLES CAUSLEY

*

A mist of fine rain was driving through the streets outside. The branches of the sooty limes were beaded with moisture, the pavements gleamed, and the road was greasy. The grey North London suburb was almost deserted. An ambulance and a tradesman's van passed with hissing tyres. The only pedestrian, an elderly woman, was walking towards me holding a large black umbrella against the rain.

Impulsively I approached her, so impulsively indeed that I appeared within her limited field of vision with somewhat disconcerting suddenness. She stopped and looked at me. She was an elderly grey woman. Her worn coat was grey, her hair grey, her face grey and lined.

Already the impulse had spent itself. 'I wanted to tell you I've just joined the Navy,' I said, rather foolishly. She continued to look at me. Her eyes did not change, but the lines about her mouth softened slightly.

'God 'elp yer, lad,' she said quietly. Then she set her umbrella to the rain and walked on.

Lieutenant JOHN DAVIES RNVR

*

I had better make it quite clear at the outset that the sea was not in my blood and I took jolly good care that my blood was not in the sea. But at Fulham Labour Exchange, on an autumn day in 1940, it was apparent that I had a major decision to make.

I had had plenty of time to study the choices: heights make me giddy, which immediately ruled out the RAF or the NFS; the Army would entail a lot of walking, and battledress would be unbecoming to my ample figure; I was therefore left with the Senior Service to consider.

I liked the uniform, and had once given an inspiring performance at the Coventry Repertory Theatre in a play called *England Expects*, which dealt with the life of some gentleman called Nelson, and my big moment was to come on the stage and say, 'The *Leviathan* has been sunk'. This seemed to cause a sensation, particularly when one night, for reasons best known to myself, I substituted 'The *Lusitania*' in my one line. I was paid two pounds for the week which, on enquiry, seemed in excess of what His Majesty was prepared to pay for the performance. But at Coventry I had also played one of Lady Hamilton's footmen, and the Fulham Labour Exchange seemed to think that my chances of a similar 'double' were remote.

Previous sea experience included a trip to America in the *Normandie* and some not unexciting times on the Serpentine with a friend who could 'feather'. So it seemed only natural to reply 'Navy' when the man so kindly asked me.

Lieutenant-Commander PETER BULL DSC RNVR

*

And the lorry stopped inside a courtyard, I think, where dusk was already falling and I saw nothing but a dark hall and cold grey stones, and a strip of carpet and the superintendent of the OTC reading out names from a list held in the left hand.

This moment was not altogether a shock to me. The superintendent had once taught me history at school when I was eleven years old and I was prepared for her to be there, as she for me.

She nodded at me as she called my name, and I knew that the years had not impaired her perception, nor the war her kindliness, nor circumstance her friendly interest in human nature. Just the same, I felt she knew there was a hole in my stocking.

But the moments that followed. They were like a blow between the eyes.

Like many people in England, many Wrens indeed, I was still unaware of much of the inheritance that Nelson, Drake, Frobisher, Raleigh, and the rest, fought for and held for us serenely and splendidly over five centuries.

Until the moment that I walked out into the January dusk and saw the white Palladian colonnades and domes of which Samuel Pepys wrote: 'The King (Charles II) is mightily pleased with his new building', I was almost unaware of Greenwich.

But that evening, rising from snow, like a conception of God rather than of man, all English history spread itself before my eyes.

The history of England, of which Nelson is a part and which I, and so many others like me, had taken for granted. And I knew that I, too, should in future feel a sense of responsibility.

So, with Pepys, to dinner.

A joy, the selection of a table-napkin from the pigeon-holed erection under the blind, marble stare of Nelson and St Vincent . . . and then . . . and then . . . the Painted Hall, for which no contemporary eulogy, nor nineteenth-century engraving, had wholly prepared me.

How could I know what I ate, under the lovely, silly paintings of Sir James Thornhill, from the perfect copies of Queen Anne tables . . . carved from the timbers of ships that had fought at Trafalgar . . . had sailed against the enemies of England. The lights blazing from a thousand points in silver candlesticks, again 'after' Queen Anne, seemed limelight as much as illumination. The echoing floor, the lofty grandeur of the high tables under rarer, sillier paintings recalled the cold to me.

It certainly was cold.

And what was that?

We had to sleep in the air-raid shelter?

Well . . . well.

And, sure enough, through the Painted Hall there echoed the sound of the guns from Woolwich. England's enemies, at it again.

The Blitz punctuated the whole of that fortnight. It held up our trains, it disturbed our sleep, it smashed the buildings around us, it sent us to bed at 2200 hours like a lot of gloomy, eiderdown-trailing sheep . . . but it did one good thing, for me at any rate. It made me appreciate still more the beauty and power of those buildings which mere Luftwaffes could not damage.

*

Dreaming dome and colonnade
endured the horrors that have been,
and others that may lie ahead
in other centuries unseen.
So many weary centuries
of pain the London ghosts have spent,
they look upon our agonies
as just another incident.
Although at night the heavens blaze,
the immortal River seems to burn,
in our most placid winter days
we see the peace we love return.

ENVOY

The waves with little boats will dance,
where drifts of sea-gulls white are laid,
and still the setting sun will glance
on dreaming dome and colonnade.

Second Officer NANCY SPAIN WRNS

*

RNVR

We are the Wavy Navy.
See, where our sleeves proclaim
By undulations in their golden stripes
The element unstable that we serve.
The regular RN
Shows by a straighter gilt straight discipline;
Our citizen authority
May wear its rank less rigid. And our braid
Is narrow, as befits our junior state.
Nor are we burdened with great tale
Of rings; two is our span,
Or, greatly favoured, yet another half:
The fingers of a hand will number those
Who bear the clangour of a brazen hat,
Being Commanders.
Yet does our lowly multitude outstrip
The ranks of Dartmouth, Keyham, and Britannia;
And ours the host of little ships
That, restless, bob and toss like corks
To hold the circling net of our defence.

The naval quip has dubbed us gentlemen
Essaying to be sailors. We'll not ask
A better name, not know a fairer task.

Commander JUSTIN RICHARDSON OBE RNVR

*

THOSE CHARMING OLD GENTLEMEN

I like to picture those charming old gentlemen receiving their summons to return to the Navy. They had never really left it in spirit, and now they handed over the leads of their little rough-haired dogs to their wives, said their farewells to the locals who had known them, in tolerant friendliness, as 'Commander' or 'Admiral', shook the moth-balls from their carefully preserved uniforms, ordered the village taxi in a new sort of voice that had a snap to it, dropped quite twenty years from their shoulders, and gave scarce a glance at the gardens they had disciplined or the window-frames they had painted in the years of retirement. I am sure they did not want a war any more than we civilians, but how good it was to be necessary again. What joy in that first wardroom gin and the shout from old shipmates! They had always known that a day would come when the Navy and the nation would need them, and now it had come. It was a full and satisfying sensation, and if they scowled on the sentry who brought his rifle up less smartly than it had been brought up in the old Navy, if they barked outwardly and sneered inwardly at the Jack-ashore with his cap aback and his bell-bottoms swaying, who can blame them? No one had shivered at their voice for some twenty years.

My Lords of the Admiralty, whose hind-ends our charming old gentlemen had kicked at Dartmouth, carefully kept them away from what was now the Royal Navy. They were given shore jobs, except those few who barged into the presence of senior officers they had known as scruffy-necked midshipmen and demanded a ship. Those few were soothed and given converted yachts or made commodores of convoys—and achieved miracles. The others, the majority, became any of a dozen strings of letters as SNO, PRO, and were sent forth to create naval bases in every tiny fishing port, in Highland lochs, on the upper reaches of peaceful rivers, on mountain-tops, and to take in hand the raggle-taggle in ships and men that were us—the wartime sailors—and our Fleet.

It was a herculean task. Those charming old gentlemen achieved it. They might have been cast onshore by a man named Geddes and never have commanded anything larger than a pinnace; they had gone out as lieutenants or a trifle higher and now came back after serving up to twenty years as dog-trotters or vegetable-trainers; but they possessed one tremendous quality: they were stiff with naval tradition and pride in a craft they had never forsaken in their hearts. To these charming old gentlemen theirs was a holy task. They swept aside the rights of property owners like any 'damned socialist' and claimed the fairest vistas in England; they remembered every trick of scrounging or thievery they had learned as magistrates on the

Bench; they tricked their bosom friends, lied, bullied, and blackguarded; and they raised every sort and shape of hut in every possible material from asbestos sheeting to plywood and named it HMS This or That. A square of concrete became a quarterdeck. A tin hut was a wardroom. Their bridge was a varnished chair, and, I repeat, they built a navy—our navy.

I wonder how many of these elderly gentlemen looked on their charges for the first time and sighed for their peaceful villages and their gardens? Maybe they saw a trawler enter harbour with the commanding officer in a favourite striped jersey and the crew hanging over the rail and making mating sounds at a Wren or the women dockyard workers. They saw a keen young man smack a valuable new craft slam into a sister ship or a granite quay. A cheerfully grinning youth took a cigarette from his lips and greeted them with, 'Careful, Dad, you'll fall into the ditch': he was a quartermaster of one of HM ships. They tripped over ropes left littering the decks where they had been dropped. Ensigns rose on the day a ship commissioned, and stayed up until they had been blown away thread by thread. Signal stations complained that they had been calling up a ship for hours to pass an important signal, and it was discovered that in harbour all hands came from their bunks only to eat or go onshore. Ships broke from their moorings on stormy nights, and there was no one on board but the cook because, sir, the Base Dance was on that night. How often must our charming old gentlemen have looked at those blank, wondering, bewildered faces across the defaulters' table and wanted to weep. Give them a job to do and this strange navy went forth gaily and contentedly. Inform them that ships must enter harbour with crews in some sort of naval uniform and they sulked like prima donnas.

They, those elderly gentlemen, were, of course, quite the wrong people to be running us amateur sailors. To them, anyone not a sailor was lower than the worm; and there was only one sort of sailor—that of the Royal Navy. Those of us with some experience in merchant ships were wise if we kept the fact tight under our hats, for once out and we were suspect. Lord, the stories these old gentlemen could tell of merchant service chaps! Of the fishermen now skippers RNR! No, there were no sailors but Royal Navy sailors, and even these were far from being what they had been. Our elderly gentlemen looked at us landsmen, and other sorts of sailors, and let us see just what they thought of us. Destroyers with RN officers could come into harbour with all hands in bathing suits and nothing would be said, but let us bring our ships in with everything not according to the handbook and we should be scowled upon from the quayside, and there would be outspoken remarks about what the Navy was coming to and signals demanding reasons in writing. One implacable law for us was that we were to get away with nothing. These elderly gentlemen had their moments when they were far from charming.

We learned to fool them. Word was passed that the SNO at one place had an old man's whim in discovering a ship's efficiency by the amount of dried paint on the rubber of watertight doors or the amount of fly dirt on electric bulbs. Most of these elderly gentlemen swore by boats and mess-decks and made a bee-line for these when they made an inspection. They all had their pet fads, as all old sailors do, and we learned these and saw to it that they were indulged.

We had, we told ourselves, taken these old chaps' numbers. We would play at boats and the Navy with them and give them senile pleasure. For some ports we would scrub boats and scour-mess-decks, for others clean electric bulbs, or have quartermasters with bosun's calls mounted, and meantime we would get on with the war. That these elderly gentlemen had any part in the real work of the war was something we would not consider. They were an irritation or an amusement in port, but, thank God, they stayed there. Once at sea we could take our hair down and get on with the job.

We both took a long time to learn. Both of us might be excused. We were civilians hugging tight to ourselves the illusion of freedom, and quite forgetting that as civilians we had had to push down a clock handle at certain times every day, reach an office or a schoolroom on the dot, wear a collar and tie between certain hours, and not indulge our sense of humour by throwing bricks through shop-windows. We resented this thing our elderly gentlemen kept harping on—this naval discipline. What in hell, we demanded, has bringing down an ensign exactly at a stated time or wearing a blue jean collar on entering port got to do with sweeping mines or escorting colliers up the East Coast? When we got a lecture on leaving deck hoses hanging from the signal yards all day instead of 'complying with Port Captain's Orders' to have them stowed in their racks by 0800 we hardly bothered to point out his other Standing Order about hoses being dried properly before stowing away, or to remind our critic that the day had been damp. Standing Orders were just another of these old gentlemen's toys. Roll the damned hoses up and let 'em rot. We're in the Navy now.

They, those elderly gentlemen, were hardly less foolish. They had known only one Navy, where crews were highly trained specialists before they were sent on board a ship, and they forgot or would not realise that 80 per cent of wartime sailors resented being in any sort of navy and certainly possessed no pride in being where a war had shoved them. They refused to believe that a small ex-fishing-boat or a square barge was not, in her essentials, a battleship. They, in fact, knew nothing about small ships, so they protected themselves by a colossal assumption that our faults came from heart-bone laziness and stupidity. And they were determined to make this pig's ear a silk purse of Royal Navy pattern. Inside the greater conflict another went on between us and those elderly gentlemen.

Then, slowly, somehow, things happened. Our elderly gentlemen ceased to be stiff, hidebound old so-and-so's for a moment: they ticked an officer off in a signal that was as neat a joke as we had found, they uttered a word of praise in a genial voice, they accepted a gin and sat yarning of their dogs, their vegetables, or their young days in the last war, and it was mightily interesting. Their wives asked our wives to lunch and our wives came from that lunch saying what a lovely man he was; or we began to learn that if we ran a ship to the routine the elderly gentlemen laid down, she was sweeter and neater than the ship alongside; or we picked up a buoy quicker; and that there was a strange and full satisfaction in holding a ship just a certain distance from another or bringing her into port with her decks neat. And, damme! That old man's smile of friendliness and his words of approval warmed the heart. And if the old gentleman had noticed that the crew were not in Number Threes, but all of them in jerseys and trousers only, he never mentioned the fact. Maybe he was learning too.

And those elderly gentlemen who had learned that there were other navies could smile to themselves as they remembered young men who wore wavy stripes but had become more 'pusser' than the most proud RN, whose years in the service were to be a lifelong memory and boast, whose ships had been run with an almost pathetic adoration of 'naval practices'. Did a ship do her job better with officers in uniform and not old striped jerseys? With crews who handled ropes without cigarettes sticking from their lips or tucked behind their ears? I don't know. I know we—most of us—got most damnably stiff with anyone who sneered at navy ways, and we puffed ourselves up like pigeons when one of these elderly gentlemen congratulated us on a smart ship. We even went to Base Church Parades and laughed like a drain if another ship committed some small crime against what we knew was real navy style. Our younger, dandier members started wearing a certain sort of white collar and showing an inch of white shirt cuff, and pretty soon, except for our wavy stripes, no one would have known us from the real McCoy.

Was it necessary? I don't know. It was very pleasant, and our charming elderly gentlemen went out of their way to show that they liked us. They now used *King's Regulations and Admiralty Instructions* to prop up the broken leg of a table, while we consulted ours like a bible. We had moments when we felt they weren't behaving quite in the manner of a naval officer and were letting the service down, and had they been on board our ships they'd have been brought up with a round turn. They, we felt, were almost too damned charming to be real naval officers.

And by that time we had built our little navy, and it worked.

PETER DAWLISH

*

In my capacity as Senior Medical Officer (acting, unpaid) I once had occasion to send a chit to naval sick quarters to accompany 'So and So, Stoker 1st Class, who is believed to be suffering from the complaint commonly known as crabs'. The answer came back in due course, signed by a surgeon lieutenant RNVR: 'I confirm your diagnosis, and add that your stoker is also suffering from the complaint commonly known as the Itch (scabies). For your future reference, crabs, by the way, are called "Pediculosis Pubis", or, Little Pattering Feet on the Private Parts'.

I should like to meet that man.

A commander visited the ship, to give us pleasure and the once-over; with a comet-tail of officers he toured us very thoroughly, asking innumerable questions (dear me, we thought, what an inquisitive man): for some reason he picked on H. as the weakest link in the chain, and what a good guess that turned out to be.

'What's your job?' he asked H. as soon as he got aboard.

'Barrister, sir,' answered H. cheerfully, glad to be on safe ground. 'I'd been in practice about five years when . . .'

'I meant your job in the ship,' interrupted the commander, looking rather old-fashioned at him.

'Signal officer, sir.'

'Ah . . . How many ten-inch projectors do you carry?' he asked, when we were up on the signal bridge.

H., confusing projector (a Morse lamp) with projectile, and being none too certain about either, replied: 'I'm not sure, sir. And I'm afraid the gunnery officer is on leave.'

The commander got out of this impasse by ignoring it: I suppose he thought he had been misheard, or perhaps he had already decided that H. was rather simple. We moved on, a silent, thoughtful party.

A little later on a sound of Morse coming in at high speed was heard from the W/T cabinet.

'Can you read that?' asked the commander, rounding on H. suddenly.

'No, sir.'

'Pity. You could intercept the German broadcasts.'

The picture of H., a slow mover, intercepting German broadcasts in Morse was too much for me. I turned away, and gave my attention to some nearby paintwork. H., visibly weakening, but still rashly eager to clear his yard-arm, tried to put the reasonable citizen's view-point.

'I'm afraid it's rather too fast for me, sir.'

'I thought you said you were the signal officer,' said the commander, as if he could not believe his ears.

'Well—*faute de mieux*, sir.'

'What?'

'*Faute de mieux*, sir.'

'Oh. . . .' A keen glance, suspicious of insolence. '*Faute de mal*, I should think you mean.'

The French may have been vulnerable, but the thought was clear.

Lieutenant-Commander NICHOLAS MONSARRAT RNVR

*

MY LAST MINE

The mine, a type 'C', hung suspended through a hole in the ceiling, its nose within six inches of the floor. Standing close to it, I looked up and saw that the parachute was wrapped partly round a chimney-pot and again caught on an ancient iron bedstead in the room above. The reason why the door had not opened was that several planks which had been part of the bedroom floor had been pushed down by the mine. Now they rested with their one end against the door and their other end under the round nose of the mine, so forming a prop. My first task should have been to make an easy escape route, but this would have meant disturbing the mine where it hung, and that was inviting trouble. I decided to dismantle the mine as it hung. I called my rating into the hallway and explained the position. He would remain in the passage and pass me, through the partly open doorway, whatever tools I required.

The fuse was clear of obstructions, but when I attempted to fit the misnamed safety horns I discovered that the fuse had been damaged, probably as the bomb crashed through the house. The horns would not go into their place. I handed the attachment back to the rating as useless and took the tools for unscrewing the keep ring. The damage to this had jammed it, and, although I exerted as much effort as I could, it would not turn. I had been working to detach this ring for perhaps a minute when the bomb slipped in front of me. There was a sound of falling brickwork as the chimney-pot overhead collapsed, and I heard the whirr of the bomb mechanism. Unless I got clear I had exactly twelve seconds to live.

On such work one had to plan ahead. When I discovered that the door could not be opened without disturbing the mine I had decided on a sequence of movements if the mechanism did become active. Now, to the stimulant of the whirring sound, I acted without thinking. I shouted a warning to the rating to run, grasped and pulled open the door against the weight of the planks, for now it no longer mattered if the mine was disturbed, and I ran. I was through the hall in two leaps. As I emerged from the doorway I saw the rating running down the street to what he, poor devil, thought was safety. I had no time to use distance for safety, and ran across the roadway to a surface air-raid shelter opposite where I was. It was a red brick and concrete-roofed structure. I reached it and flung myself on its far side, its bulk between me and the house I had just left. I flung myself tight against it, face down on the ground.

I heard no explosion. It has since been explained to me that if you are near enough to an explosion of such force unconsciousness is upon you before any sound it makes reaches you, which is a merciful thing. I was blinded by the flash that comes split seconds before the explosion, but that was all I experienced.

I do not know what time passed before I became conscious. When I did I knew I was buried deep beneath bricks and mortar and was being suffocated. My head was between my legs, and I guessed my back was broken, but could not move an inch. I was held, imbedded.

Men dug me out eventually. To this day I do not know how long I spent in my grave. Most of that time I was unconscious. The conscious moments are of horror and utter helplessness. Being buried alive is certainly a good example of a living hell, and in the war years to come after 1940 the brave men, women, and children of London and of all the other cities, towns and villages of Britain not only had my sympathies, but some—those who had been buried alive—had my prayers. I really knew the physical and mental torture they endured.

My rating was killed. He was beheaded by the blast. The mine destroyed six streets of working-class homes, and it was six weeks before his body was found among the rubble. He was a brave man and left behind a brave widow. I saw her receive her husband's decoration from His Majesty the King.

Lieutenant JACK M. C. EASTON GC RNVR

*

In 1940 the Children's Overseas Reception Board, under the chairmanship of Mr Geoffrey Shakespeare MP, Under Secretary for the Dominions, was formed to arrange for the evacuation of British children to Canada, Australia, New Zealand and South Africa. Despite the fate of the first 'evacuee' ship Vollendam*—torpedoed two days out, but all the children were saved—ninety children sailed for Canada in the* City of Benares *(Captain Landles Nicoll), which left Liverpool on Friday, 13th September 1940. During the voyage the children were looked after by escorts, among them a forty-one-year-old music teacher, Miss Mary Cornish. The ship was torpedoed on 17th September: there were forty-six people in Miss Cornish's life-boat, including thirty-two lascars and six small boys, the fourth officer in charge.*

CITY OF BENARES

They had been a week at sea.

The strength of the boys was ebbing fast. They had barely eaten for five days; and their thirst was becoming acute. Almost as bad was the constant pressure against other bodies, the aching of bruised muscles, and the pain of sleepless bloodshot eyes. Several of the lascars were lying semi-conscious in the bottom of the boat. Still the life-boat kept her course, under sail now, for the sea was a little calmer.

At noon the steward brought round the usual water ration, which each person poured into his empty condensed milk tin. This was the last time—although the steward did not tell them then—that they would get water at noon. Next day the ration was to be halved, and water issued only in the evening. They were nearing the bottom of the cask.

The delirious boy recovered with the coming of daylight, although he was weak, and his feet were sore. Thirsty or not, that evening the boys still wanted their bedtime instalment of Captain Drummond and Mary Cornish gave it to them. She found the effort considerable, for not only was it difficult to speak with a parched, dry throat and a swollen tongue, but a week with little food and water, and with constant anxiety over the boys, had begun to affect her mind. She had to force her thoughts with conscious effort, like squeezing hardened paint out of a tube. But she managed to think of the day's plot somehow, although her voice sounded thick and barely intelligible in her own ears.

That evening messages came down from the stern that the lascars were restive and needed to be watched. On board was a hatchet used to split open cases of canned provisions. This was kept in the bows, and the escorts, by way of precaution, put it down within easy reach.

After nightfall another of the boys became delirious. His feet were so painful that he could not bear to have them touched. As the night wore on he became obsessed with the fear of going mad. By some trick of the moonlight, shadows from the rigging were falling across him in dark bars. To his delirious mind these seemed to him to be the real bars of a prison, and he shouted to be let out, rolling from side to side in fear. Sometimes he screamed horribly, and shouted, 'I'm mad, I'm going mad, I *know* I'm going mad.'

A message came down from the stern: could the escorts for God's sake keep that boy quiet, his screams might drive the lascars over the edge. Mary Cornish tried to calm him, but if anyone touched him he shouted all the more. Father O'Sullivan said in French: 'This boy is dying of thirst.'

A message went back to the steward: could he spare an extra dipperful of water? A few drops were smuggled past the lascars by one of the seamen coming off duty. But after this no more could be done. Only one torch with a live battery was left on board, and the lascars had it. They were keeping its beam trained on the sick boy in the bows. They were not taking any chances; no one was going to cheat them of their share of water by giving an extra ration to the sick boy.

There was one service that the priest alone could perform. He took the boy in his arms and offered prayers for his soul. The others could not understand the rapid Latin phrases, but the boys trusted him, and his low-voiced words had a soothing effect.

There was a disturbance among the lascars, and then the gunner appeared. He took in the situation at a glance: the kneeling priest, the prayers for the dying, and the solemn atmosphere.

'What's going on here *now*?' he demanded. 'What's wrong with the poor little blighter?'

The boy, croaking like a frog, cried out for water.

'Water?' the gunner said. 'Is *that* all? Of course you want water; we all do. You'll get your water in the morning.'

The boy only cried out again for a drink.

'Now you forget about it,' the gunner commanded. 'You'll have plenty of water when we're picked up, and that won't be long now. Is *that* all that's wrong with you?'

'My feet are cold,' the boy answered weakly.

The gunner snorted triumphantly, and glared at the escorts. 'Huh! So your feet are cold. That's a nice way to look after a kid. . . .'

He rearranged Mary Cornish's jacket round the boy's legs. 'Are your feet warm *now*?'

The boy mumbled: 'My feet are cold.'

The cadet, who was off duty in the bows, took off his overcoat, and the gunner wrapped this also round the sick boy's feet.

'There. Any better?' he demanded.

'My feet are cold.'

'No, they're not,' the gunner said firmly. 'They're wrapped up properly now, and they'll be as warm as toast in half a jiffy. Now—are your feet warm?'

'My feet . . .' the boy began.

'Don't let me hear another sound out of you till the morning,' the gunner said fiercely. 'No more of this yelling out. Now—*are your feet warm?*'

'Yes,' the boy whispered feebly.

'Then you'll be all right till the morning.'

He went off, muttering under his breath about boys with cold feet, women who didn't know how to look after kids, and the respective merits of saying prayers and keeping children warm. His methods were effective; the atmosphere was changed. The boy did not scream any more, and when his companion, who had been delirious the night before, offered to lie down beside him, he gradually quietened down. . . . . It was a boy who first saw the flying-boat. With a cry of 'Sunderland', he pointed to the west. A speck in the sky was growing larger. Nobody believed it at first. A dozen Sunderlands had already been sighted, only to resolve themselves into gulls. But this time it was real. By a freak of chance the path of a flying-boat patrolling far out into the Atlantic had crossed their own.

ELSPETH HUXLEY

The survivors were picked up on the eighth day by the destroyer HMS Anthony. *Only thirteen children had survived from the* City of Benares *and there were no more 'evacuee' ships. Miss Cornish, Fourth Officer Cooper and the steward Purvis were each awarded the BEM.*

*

HMS *ECLIPSE* APPROACHES FREETOWN

September 1940

I sing of the keen destroyer
Banging on the silken doors of the morning,
Cutting through the panels of the South Atlantic:
Strands of light streaming in the steel rigging.
And the warning:
The yellow stammer from the lighthouse of white sugar
Pales as the African sun unfolds her tail of golden peacock
Over the fevered harbour.

Borne on the lusty tide
Past mountains deep and green as Victorian postcards,
My iron mistress, my rusty virgin
Carries me into Sierra Leone, under the lion mountain:
The land of violet lightning and the thunderstorms of sheet iron,
The hills, rich and bursting with the brown and orange of
  Gauguin.
And, in the distance, the blue Sugar Loaf
Wears decently her conventional mists.

Petty Officer CHARLES CAUSLEY

*

On the evening of 5th November 1940, in mid Atlantic, the homeward-bound Halifax convoy HX 84, escorted by the armed merchant cruiser Jervis Bay (*Captain E. S. F. Fegen RN*), *was attacked by the German pocket battleship* Admiral Scheer (*Kapitan zur See Theodor Krancke*). *Though hopelessly outgunned,* Jervis Bay *advanced towards* Admiral Scheer, *whilst behind her the convoy scattered under cover of smoke.* Jervis Bay *was inevitably sunk, her captain being awarded a posthumous*

Victoria Cross, but all except five of the thirty-seven ships in the convoy escaped. During the action the Eagle Oil tanker San Demetrio *(Captain Waite OBE), with 12,000 tons of high-octane petrol on board, was set on fire and was abandoned by her crew, who took to the life-boats.*

SAN DEMETRIO

Later that afternoon a second ship was sighted to windward and we all started to pull once more, arguing about her identity, wondering whether she was one of the convoy or another enemy ship.

A ship at sea is very deceiving. The farther away she is the more she seems to stand out of the water and the bigger she looks. What may look like a big liner may prove to be quite a small vessel. As we drew nearer two things were noticeable: it was obvious that this ship was on fire and that she was drifting with the tide and abandoned.

Then something about her seemed more familiar to us. The bos'n, who before the attack was making *San Demetrio* shipshape and painted up ready for our homecoming, noticed that the masts and funnels were red-leaded—the same as those the Yank[1] had been working on for days before we left Halifax. As if he had seen a ghost he addressed the Yank: '*San Demetrio*! You never finished chipping and painting the funnel!' For what must have been the first time in his life, the Yank was speechless. He just stared vacantly at the ship on the horizon.

'Well, I'll be goddamned,' he said at last.

It was then that we all realised we were looking at *San Demetrio*, still burning and helpless. She was drifting down towards us, and at a much faster rate than we could make. She was not only burning but sending out great columns of smoke, and was surrounded by an immense area of petrol lying on the water. Clouds of murky smoke were pouring from amidships; she was down by the head, and at every roll huge volumes of green water poured over her two well-decks.

There was a high sea running, and in the late-afternoon light patches of foam were running past the life-boat's gunwales. We would have to be very cautious about getting alongside, for our

1. Able Seaman Oswald Preston.

life-boat was made of steel and should we knock against the ship's side a spark might ignite the petrol which lay on the water. This would send the ship and our life-boat sky high. So we decided to pass around the stern and keep on her weather side in case she should come crashing down on us when darkness fell.

That night we lowered sail, set our sea-anchor, and rigged a canvas dodger round the life-boat's bows to shelter us from the cruel wind and sea. Then we had a further issue of water and biscuits, and this time we split into two watches: Mr Hawkins[1] took the first half of the night and I took the other, so that there might be some possibility of rest during the night.

We argued amongst ourselves whether to board the blazing vessel or not, provided she was still there in the morning. A helpless and burning ship with a cargo of petrol is a sorry refuge, and so is a ship's small boat in a storm in the middle of the North Atlantic.

The weather became worse, and torrential rain added to our discomfort. Most of the men were now suffering from cold and exposure and weakened by perpetual seasickness. Darkness closed around us, clouds hid the moon, and again we had to row and pull hard to keep the boat's head into the wind and sea.

Suddenly a light shone overhead and a shout of 'A plane, a plane' went up. We burnt a flare, we signalled with a torch, and all was hustle and scurry. Then from the stern we heard young Jones's feeble voice saying, 'That is no plane, that's bloody Jupiter.' He was right. Bloody Jupiter it was.

The night passed slowly, and somehow dawn broke at last, but the sea was bare. Not even a gull glided over it. *San Demetrio* was lost. True, she was on fire and might have blown up at any moment, but it was rotten luck to have lost her.

There was no argument now as to whether we should board her. After a while someone said he thought he saw her, and was accused of dreaming. But sure enough there she was still blazing and smoking and still slipping away from us. This time we meant business, and, despite the Atlantic gale, sail was hoisted and we soon began to close down on her. Hopes ran high through the boat's company. It would not be long now before we could get aboard a blazing vessel with a cargo of oil. She was the only thing we could see in all

1. Second officer.

the wide circle of ocean and she looked good. At least very warm. She might blow up at any time, but that was a quick and painless death compared with this slow freezing and sickness, this forced labour of failing muscles. And, besides, she was our own ship, still floating in spite of what she had suffered. She meant home to us, she was ours and had not failed us. She had looked for us and by some miracle had found us. We would not fail her.

Once again I took charge of the sailing and had to nurse the boat and manœuvre her very carefully in the strong gale, and purposefully, instead of with the jerky progress of tired rowers, she leant over and made for our parent vessel.

A little before noon we drew to her and once more passed round her stern, this time to get to leeward of her. We approached her from the starboard side where the remains of a boat-ladder were hanging over her quarter. We put the boat's blankets over the gunwale to prevent any sparks striking from the possible clash of steel, then the Yank was up the ladder and on board making our painter fast. I unshipped the rudder while the rest climbed on board.

It was about twenty-four feet from the water to the boat-deck, and a rope ladder is a horrible contrivance to climb at the best of times, even when a man is in good health. So it was a task to manage when men were suffering from exposure and frost-bite. Everyone was drenched to the skin and everyone had been unremittingly seasick.

The third engineer's feet had turned black from exposure; both Davies and Boyle suffered great pain from broken ribs, and young Jones's lips were swollen and he suffered severely from piles. But there was too much to be done to stop and think of things like these.

A half-full bottle of rum was found in the second engineer's cabin and was equally divided into small tots and shared amongst us. It was certainly a help, and we soon got to work.

Our first concern was the life-boat, for that represented our only chance of safety were it necessary for us once more to abandon *San Demetrio*. The life-boat was banging about under the counter and might be knocked to pieces by the rudder and propeller, for the ship was well down by the head and the propeller well out of the water.

The Yank went over the side with a life-line attached to him. Had that life-line parted there would have been no possibility of saving him. We managed to work the boat alongside until we got under the starboard davits—a very difficult job, and there was a very heavy sea running. The Yank attempted to bail the boat out and square her under the falls, and then everyone on board struggled to hoist him up, and succeeded in getting the boat halfway up the ship's side. By now she was half full of water and too heavy for us to get her any farther. We had to leave her hanging in that position, and there was no way we could secure her. Unfortunately, about two o'clock in the afternoon she broke adrift and was never seen again. That left us with only the Shetland dinghy, a small boat twelve feet long, pointed at each end. These dinghies draw eighteen inches of water. This one had suffered damage from the action, but had she been whole she would have swamped in the storm in mid-Atlantic. However, it was considered possible to patch her up, so that if we succeeded in making landfall I could somehow sail inshore in search of help. The knowledge that, damaged as she was, she was still on board and could be used in an emergency was some small measure of comfort.

The next serious job was to extinguish the fires. One was still raging amidships above No. 7 port tank, and the other—in the freezer, ironically enough.

Had we not reboarded *San Demetrio* when we did in another quarter of an hour No. 7 would have wholly ignited and the whole ship would have been lost. So by the skin of our teeth we had scored another victory.

There was much to be done, for the sight which confronted us was not a heartening one. Fire had destroyed the poop and the after cabins on the port side, and the flying bridge amidships; the navigating bridge had been demolished by a direct hit, and the monkey island—the deckhead over the wheelhouse—was white-hot.

The wireless operators must have stayed a little too long at their post as the bridge was struck, for we found only their ashes where the wireless-room had been.

Young Ernest Daines, OS, who had joined us only a few days before in Halifax, was also killed, while on look-out duty on the fo'c's'le head. When the first shell struck, making a hole in our port bow, Daines's body must have been blasted overboard, for no signs of him were found.

All amidships was gutted by fire. The wireless, compasses, steering gear, charts and signalling flags were all gone. The main deck plating, which was over the main cargo decks, was buckled and crumpled like cardboard and riddled with shell-holes. The shell which had first hit the vessel on the port side of the fo'c's'le had burst the forepeak, the splinters had pierced the collision bulkhead, and the forehold was flooded. The pipeline, steam- and exhaust-lines were all destroyed. The only accommodation left on board was the starboard side aft. Elsewhere every cabin was gutted by fire and holed by splinters. Not one scrap of the interior fittings remained, and with them had gone everyone's personal property. The steward's stores were completely gutted, and the fresh-water tanks amidships were destroyed; luckily two tanks aft were undamaged.

Every time the ship rolled petrol spurted out of the holes in her decks and ran into the lee scuppers, and smouldering debris was everywhere.

The chief engineer and his team of three men, Wiley, Boyle and Davies, went down to the engine-room. As the chief put it, what a hell of a mess it was. Three or four feet of water had come up to the engineers' platform and all the fuel units were under water. But the lubricating and water-cooling systems were undamaged, and the main engines proved to be in working order, although everything was wet. A bucket and fire extinguisher party was formed on deck to deal with the fires there, and while we worked at this the engine-room team was busy down below reassembling the Paxman generator so that electricity should once more be available to start the oil-fuel pump.

Now the Paxman generator had just been overhauled ready for entering the mine danger zone, where it would have been in constant use for days, supplying current for the degaussing mains. Degaussing is necessary only in mine-infested waters nearer land, and so just before the attack the generator had been dismantled for overhaul. Before anything could be done it was necessary to have this assembled, and the engine-room team worked like Trojans to have it fixed before dark. It was necessary to replace the crankcase doors and couple up the fuel-line, and this was quickly accomplished, but difficulty was experienced in getting the engine started owing to the coldness and to the water which ran over it continually from the pierced deckhead.

At last everything was ready and electricity was available, but still the electrically driven fuel unit did not start up, and this was discovered to be because all the electric cables had been damaged by shell-fire. Next thing was to repair these cables. Damaged parts were cut out and the cables reconnected. The auxiliary starboard boiler flashed up immediately, for it had not been cooled down, and the operation of raising steam was rushed through. There was seventy pounds of pressure soon showing on the starboard boiler gauge. This was enough, and a hose soon coupled on the ballast pump. This was necessary because the deck service water-lines were all damaged, and so at last our fire-hoses were brought into service. It was impossible to get the port boiler going. Every time the feed pump was started water poured out from its furnace.

Darkness was catching up on us once again, and the chief decided to get a little fire going in the remains of the galley and boil water for tea. (He never had time to repeat this operation, and would not allow anyone else to do so, because it was so dangerous.) Some tea, which was being taken home as a present, was found in a cabin. No one as yet had had any food, and we were more than ready for something.

Where the meat-safe had been we found quantities of charred and burnt meat, and the eggs had all been burnt black. Some ventured to eat some of the meat, but unfortunately it had been soaked in oil and chemicals from the fire extinguishers. This made them violently ill in the days to follow.

Some paint was discovered in the paint locker up forward, and it was decided to paint SOS and HELP in conspicuous places all over the ship.

Although it was impossible to work in the engine-room after dark that night, because no light could be shown, pumping operations were continued. Several times during the night the hose had to be played on the meat-room aft, which was very heavily insulated and had become the focal point of damage. The cork insulation round it was nearly twelve inches thick faced with cement and covered in steel plate, and it kept burning and sparking. In the meat-room itself a fire was burning, and all along the deck were holes spouting petrol. Every time the wind blew in this direction the fire would blaze up again. It was not until daylight next morning that we were able to chisel away the cork and get a hose down behind it, so that there was no longer anything to keep on smouldering. That night also the engine-room was pumped dry of water and soundings taken of all tanks. These soundings tallied near enough to those taken before the attack, and showed we were not making water and therefore had no damage below the waterline. Not much more could be done that night, but the pumps had to be kept under supervision. Early next morning all hands were kept busy plugging the holes on deck with cotton waste and rough wooden pegs made out of whatever wood we could find.

At last, three days later, about eight o'clock on the morning of Friday, the 8th of November, the danger from fire was mastered, everything was nearly ready, and all were anxious to get under way.

Why, considering the low flash-point of our cargo, the ship had not exploded will never be known for certain. There have been many theories. One is that, owing to the intensity of the fires, heat was generated so rapidly that the tanks were converted to gasometers, thus automatically putting pressure in them which prevented the flames coming back and igniting the oil. In an oil-tanker all tanks are fitted with safety-valves which come automatically into action and prevent the tank pressure from getting dangerously high, while still keeping enough pressure to prevent the flames getting in.

Since the bridge had gone, it followed that all communication to the engine-room was out of action. So the task of inventing some method of signalling from the deck to the engine-room had to be overcome. It was decided to arrange lights, and when these were fitted they were in a fore-and-aft direction. When the forward light went on it meant 'ahead', and flickering of the light meant 'increase speed'; the centre light meant 'stop' and the after light meant 'astern'. Owing to a shortage of cable these lights had to be erected high up in the engine-room, and to attract the attention of the men below a signal was given by the simple method of knocking on the skylight with a hammer. These old-fashioned arrangements worked perfectly.

It must be remembered that all our normal steering gear had gone. Even the auxiliary emergency steering gear aft was partly destroyed.

There was a small steering wheel aft, of which all but the hub, four spokes, and a bit of the rim had been burnt away. The wooden cleat which supported this wheel had also been burnt, so we had blocks of wood cut and fitted to shore up this pedestal.

The steering standard aft operates the steering engine by means of a series of shafts and bevel wheels in the steering flat below, but owing to the intense heat of the fire the bulkheads through which the shafting passed had become distorted, and these bulkheads had to be hammered out to free the shafts for action.

The compass binnacle was found, having dropped through two decks below. It was all damaged and buckled with heat, and a big bubble of fluid was showing on the card. We erected the compass in position (but it was subsequently found to be useless).

About two o'clock in the afternoon of the 8th the chief engineer went below and tested his beloved engines ahead and astern and they turned over beautifully. They were set going again about half past two on that grey and stormy afternoon, and *San Demetrio* was once more under way.

When I laid my hands on the remains of that tiny wheel with four spokes, below in the engine-room flat the huge green-painted tiller began to swing obediently. So once again we were on our way and heading for Britain's shores—we hoped!

That was a triumphant moment for us all, when we were once again under our own power in a live vessel which had found a soul.

Able Seaman CALUM MACNEIL of *San Demetrio*

*After that masterpiece of improvised damage control, with no charts, no compass and steering 'by guess and by God', Second Officer Hawkins made a landfall at Black Sod Bay, Southern Ireland, on 13th November and—escorted, but still under her own power—*San Demetrio *reached the Clyde on the 15th. Calum MacNeil and another able seaman from* San Demetrio, *Roddie MacLennan, went home on leave to their native island of Barra in the Outer Hebrides—to find there an acute shortage of whisky. However, early in December ss* Politician, *with a cargo mostly of whisky, ran aground in thick fog to the north of Barra. The islanders went out in their small boats and there was 'Whisky Galore' for MacLennan's wedding later that month.*

*

Perhaps the best tribute to Captain Fogarty Fegen, VC and the officers and ship's company of HMS Jervis Bay *appeared in* The Times *on 2nd December 1940:*

London
26th November

Sir,

I avail myself of this opportunity to write to you after safe arrival in this country on behalf of myself and the crew of the Polish steamer *Puck*, the smallest of all which took part in the recent convoy from Canada, which was shelled by a German raider of the *Graf Spee* class on 5th November, to express our grateful thanks through the columns of *The Times* for the way in which the *Jervis Bay* defended us to the last. The fine example set to us by the British crew of this ship, who through their sacrifice saved a lot of valuable tonnage and very valuable cargo, filled us with deep admiration and made us their spiritual debtors. This fresh example of British valour on the high seas is sufficient to give renewed confidence in the British Navy and in British victory.

On behalf of my crew and myself I should like to say how much we commiserate with the relatives and friends of the courageous crew of the *Jervis Bay* who lost their lives in this historic action, but who may be proud for the role they have played in the fight for freedom.

I am, Sir, your obedient servant,

J. PIEKARSKI

As a matter of interest for the maritime historian, Puck's *cargo was listed as '329 standards of spoolwood'—whatever that may be.*

*

Operation 'Coat' was the codeword given to the passage of a reinforcement from Force H, consisting of the battleship Barham, *the cruisers* Berwick *and* Glasgow *and three destroyers, at one end of the Mediterranean, to the Mediterranean Fleet at the other end. The force was late and only arrived one day before the already planned attack on Taranto.*

From Commander-in-Chief Mediterranean to Flag Officer Force H: THANK YOU FOR MY COAT. I NEARLY CAUGHT A COLD WAITING FOR IT. I STILL HAVE NO TROUSERS BUT INTEND TAKING THOSE OFF MUSSOLINI SHORTLY.

From *Make a Signal*

*

TARANTO

The klaxon has gone and the starters are whirring as, stubbing out our cigarettes, we bundle outside into the chill evening air. It is not so dark now, with the moon well up in the sky, so that one can see rather than feel one's way past the aircraft which, with their wings folded for close packing, look more like four-poster bedsteads than front-line aeroplanes.

Parachute secured and Sutton harness pinned, the fitter bends over me, shouts 'Good luck, sir' into my speaking-tube, and is gone. I call up Bull in the back to check intercom—he tells me the rear cockpit lighting has fused—then look around the orange-lighted cockpit; gas and oil pressures O.K., full tank, selector-switches on, camber-gear set, and other such precautions; run up and test switches, tail incidence set, and I jerk my thumb up to a shadow near the port wheel. Now comes the longest wait of all. 4F rocks in the slip-stream of aircraft ahead of her as other engines run up, and a feeling of desolation is upon me, unrelieved by the company of ten other aircraft crews, who, though no doubt entertaining similar thoughts, seem merged each into his own aircraft to become part of a machine without personality; only the quiet figures on the chocks seem human, and they are miles away.

The funnel smoke, a jet-black plume against the bright-starred sky, bespeaks of an increase in speed for the take-off; the fairy lights flick on, and with a gentle shudder the ship turns into wind, whirling the plan of stars about the foretop.

A green light waves away our chocks, orders us to taxi forward; the wings are spread with a slam, and as I test the aileron controls, green waves again. We are off, gently climbing away on the port bow where the first flame-float already burns, where the letter 'K' is being flashed in black space. Here—in this black space—I discover

Kemp, and close into formation; here also Kemp eventually gains squadron formation on Wilkinson, and the first wave is upon its way, climbing towards the north-west. At first the course is by no means certain, in fact Wilkinson is weaving, and station-keeping is a succession of bursts of speed and horrible air clawings, but in five minutes we have settled down a little.

At 4,000 feet we pass through a hole in scattered cloud—dark smudges above us at one moment, and the next stray fleece beneath airwheels filled with the light of a full moon.

Six thousand feet. God, how cold it is here! The sort of cold that fills you until all else is drowned save perhaps fear and loneliness. Suspended between heaven and earth in a sort of no-man's-land—to be sure, no man was ever meant to be here—in the abyss which men of old feared to meet if they ventured to the ends of the earth. Is it surprising that my knees are knocking together? We have now passed under a sheet of alto-stratus cloud which blankets the moon, allowing only a few pools of silver where small gaps appear. And, begob, Williamson is going to climb through it! As the rusty edge is reached I feel a tugging at my port wing, and find that Kemp has edged me over into the slipstream of the leading sub-flight. I fight with hard right stick to keep the wing up, but the sub-flight has run into one of its clawing moments, and quite suddenly the wing and nose drop and we are falling out of the sky. I let her have her head, and see the shape of another aircraft flash by close overhead. Turning, I see formation lights ahead and climb up after them, following them through one of the rare holes in this cloud mass. There are two aircraft sure enough, yet when I range up alongside, the moonglow shows up the figures 5A—that is Olly. The others must be ahead. After an anxious few minutes some dim lights appear among the upper billows of the cloud, and opening the throttle we lumber away from Olly after them. Poor old engine—she will get a tanning this trip.

The sub-flight is reassembled now at 8,000 feet. We have to come to the edge of the cloud. The regular flashing of a light away down to starboard claims my attention. 'There's a flashing light to starboard, Bull, can you place it?' 'Oh, yes,' and that is all—the poor devil must be all but petrified with the cold by now.

Then the coast appears. Just a band of dull wrinkled greyness.

Bull arouses himself from his icicles enough to be able to tell me that we have roughly forty minutes to go, and I enough to remind him to close the overload tank-cock before we go in. But we make no turn to get out to seaward again; instead we shape our course parallel to the coastline, not more than five miles away, giving away in one act any chance of surprise we might have hoped for.

Years later. Some quaint-coloured twinkling flashes like liver-spots have appeared in the sky to starboard. It is some time before I realise their significance; we are approaching the harbour; and the flashes are HE shells bursting in a barrage on the target area. We turn towards the coast and drop away into line astern, engines throttled back. For ages we seem to hover without any apparent alteration; then red, white, and green flaming onions come streaming in our direction, the HE bursts get closer, and looking down to starboard I see the vague smudge of a shape I now know as well as my own hand. We are in attacking position. The next ahead disappears as I am looking for my line of approach, so down we go in a gentle pause, glide towards the north-western corner of the harbour. The master-switch is made, a notch or two back on the incidence wheel, and my fear is gone, leaving a mind as clear and unfettered as it has ever been in my life. The hail of tracer at 6,000 feet is behind now, and there is nothing here to dodge; then I see that I am wrong, it is not behind any more. They have shifted target; for now, away below to starboard, a hail of red, white, and green balls cover the harbour to a height of 2,000 feet. This thing is beyond a joke.

A burst of brilliance on the north-eastern shore, then another and another as the flare-dropper releases his load, until the harbour shows clear in the light he has made. Not too bright to dull the arc of raining colour over the harbour where tracer flies, allowing, it seems, no room to escape unscathed.

We are now at 1,000 feet over a neat residential quarter of the town where gardens in darkened squares show at the back of houses marshalled by the neat plan of streets that serve them. Here is the main road that connects the district with the main town. We follow its line and as I open the throttle to elongate the glide a Breda swings round from the shore, turning its stream of red balls in our direction. This is the beginning. Then another two guns farther north get our scent—white balls this time—so we throttle back again and make for a black mass on the shore that looks like a factory, where no balloons are likely to grow. A tall factory chimney shows ahead against the water's sheen. We must be at a hundred feet now and soon we must make our dash across that bloody water. As we come abreast the chimney I open the throttle wide and head for the mouth of the Mare Piccolo, whose position, though not visible, can be judged by the lie of the land. Then it is as though all hell comes tumbling in on top of us—it must have been the fire of the cruisers and Mare Piccolo canal batteries—leaving only two things in my mind, the line of approach to the dropping position and a wild desire to escape the effects of this deathly hailstorm.

And so we jink and swerve, an instinct of living guiding my legs and right arm; two large clear shapes on our starboard side are monstrous in the background of flares. We turn until the right-hand battleship is between the bars of the torpedo-sight, dropping down as we do so. The water is close beneath our wheels, so close I'm wondering which is to happen first—the torpedo going or our hitting the sea—then we level out, and almost without thought the button is pressed and a jerk tells me the 'fish' is gone.

We are back close to the shore we started from, darting in and out of a rank of merchant ships for protection's sake. But our troubles are by no means over; for in our dartings hither and thither we run slap into an Artigliere-class destroyer. We are on top of her fo'c's'le before I realise that she hasn't opened fire on us, and though I am ready for his starboard pompom, he was a sitting shot at something between fifty and a hundred yards. The white balls come scorching across our quarter as we turn and twist over the harbour; the cruisers have turned their fire on us again, making so close a pattern that I can smell the acrid smoke of their tracer. This is the end—we cannot get away with this maelstrom around us. Yet as a trapped animal will fight like a fury for its life, so do we redouble our efforts at evasion. I am thinking, 'Either I can kill myself or they can kill me,' and flying the machine close down on the water wing-tips all but scraping it at every turn, throttle full open and wide back.

With a shock I realise that we are clear of the worst of it, anyway. Ahead is the island that lies between the horns of the outer harbour, a low black mass that, at our speed of 120 knots, is suddenly upon us.

We blithely sail by its western foot, oblivious of what it may contain, when comes the tearing sound of shell as red balls spurt from a position no more than a hundred yards away, passing close ahead of us. Away we turn to starboard, then, as the stream grows, round to port again, and so we zigzag out into the open sea.

Now it seems we are clear enough to start climbing, but no sooner do we get to a hundred feet than another shower of unpleasantness chases up our tail, and we are forced to return to sea-level.

Turning to look back at last, my nearly hysterical mind is amazed. 'Bull! Just look at that bloody awful mess—look at it! Just look at it!' and more of that tempo. A huge weeping willow of coloured fire showers over the harbour area; above it still the bursting HE shells and sprays of tadpole-like fire, whilst every now and then a brilliant flame bursts in the sky and drifts lazily down.

At last we are free to climb. At 3,000 feet it is cool and peaceful, a few shining clouds casting their dark shadows on the sea, the warm orange cockpit light showing up the instruments that tell me all is well. All we have to do now is to get back and land on, thoughts that worry me not at all.

Near the heel of Italy we come upon a small vessel which on our approach burns a flare—an air look-out perhaps. Then the clouds begin to thicken; even at 4,000 feet they tower above us, and for ten unhappy minutes we fly blind. Bull in the back is listening eagerly for the beacon note. Just before coming out of this murk a voice announces that we have picked up the beacon, and we adjust our course to close the ship. A light bursts out on our port side, then another ahead—some of the others are about, anyway, releasing their unwanted flares.

One thousand feet. The all-round signal is coming through now, but there is no sign of the ship on the cloud-darkened sea, so we fly on until another bearing comes through. And so, casting back, two flame-floats appear to port, then a third. A destroyer's wake shines dimly below. We are home.

My God, I am hungry! I feel as though we had not eaten, drunk or slept for days.

We circle once before the raised deck-lights go on. The three bright lights ahead are the deck landing-control officer telling us 'steady approach'—the flying-deck is suddenly underneath us. Back throttle stick—a pause—the gentle brush of wheels on the deck, and the wires have got us.

A crowd of people in the glaring AIO, jabbering like men possessed—as indeed they are. I am giving my evidence. A Littorio battleship, I think. Yes, good clear run of 1,000 yards. A good drop. Oh—about thirty feet.

The wardroom warm and sane. Three rapid whiskies-and-soda, followed by some eggs-and-bacon I can scarcely taste. A camp-bed on the quarterdeck in the grey light of dawn. A jumble of scattered pictures chases through my mind. Unconsciousness.

Lieutenant M. R. MAUND, RN, of 824 Squadron

The author was killed flying from Malta on 11th January 1943.

The aircraft which attacked Taranto were from Nos. 813, 815, 819 and 824 Squadrons, Fleet Air Arm. Although the aircraft were actually flown from HMS Illustrious, *they included some aircraft from HMS* Eagle.

The strike was launched in two parts: the first, of twelve Swordfish, taking off at 8.40 pm on the 11th November and the second, of nine Swordfish, at 9.30 pm. Taranto was, from all aspects, a brilliant victory. It conclusively demonstrated, even to the most sceptical, the effectiveness of air power at sea. The balance of capital ship power in the Mediterranean was dramatically altered; for the loss of two Swordfish and their crews, the Mediterranean Fleet had sunk one battleship (Conte di Cavour) *and damaged two others* (Littorio *and* Caio Duilio) *so badly that they were out of the war for a year, besides other damage to cruisers and shore installations. Furthermore, Taranto had important psychological effects on the enemy. It is true to say the Italian Admiralty were on the defensive from then onwards.*

After Taranto:

From Commander-in-Chief (Mediterranean) to *Illustrious*:

MANOEUVRE WELL EXECUTED.

From Flag Officer Force H (Admiral Somerville) to Commander-in-Chief Mediterranean:

CONGRATULATIONS ON SUCCESSFUL DE-BAGGING. IF THIS GOES ON UNCLE BENITO WILL SOON BE SINGING ALTO IN THE CHOIR.

From *Make a Signal*

1941

One of the immediate results of Taranto was the transfer of the 10th Air Corps (General Geissler's 'Fliegerkorps X', the Luftwaffe's anti-shipping specialists) from Norway to Sicily. They caught Illustrious *off Pantellaria on 10th January 1941, in the early afternoon.*

ILLUSTRIOUS' FIGHT FOR LIFE

The Stukas came in from three bearings, port and starboard bows and starboard quarter, all at the same time. Bill Banham watched them, diving in groups of three from each direction, dove-tailed neatly together, clover-leaf fashion. Down they hurled through the 4.5 barrage and into the pompom screen.

Nothing could stop them. In a terrifying crescendo of crashing sound *Illustrious* disappeared in spray and smoke. All was bursting bombs, bursting shells, the racket of the guns and the roar and scream of aircraft.

They knocked the broadcasting system out of action and shattered the radar. A bomb hit P1 pompom on the port side for'ard, smashing the gun, killing two of its crew as it passed through the gun platform and exploded on hitting the water, sending jagged pieces flying upwards to kill and wound more men.

The bombers that came in from the starboard bow hit S2 pompom and destroyed it and all its crew. The same bomb killed three men at S1 pompom below and injured many in the ammunition supply parties.

Another heavy bomb fell directly into the after-lift well when the after lift was halfway down. On the lift was a Fulmar with its young midshipman pilot in the cockpit.

Jago, in the hangar, heard a great crash aft. The Fulmar on the lift had been obliterated and the lift itself thrown up end on.

Aircraft at that end of the hangar started to burn. Heavy chunks of metal from the bomb flew in all directions through the walls of the lift well and into the gun-bays of the after turrets. All eight 4.5-inch guns located after were knocked out and their crews killed or injured.

In the hangar fire started to get a hold among the aircraft. Janvrin, climbing on to a Swordfish to get a first-aid kit out of the machine, suddenly felt the whole aircraft jump into the air and hurl sideways.

He felt nothing himself, but when his feet touched the deck his legs gave under him and he realised he had been hit.

Tuck was down on the main deck with the central damage control parties when he felt the heavy shock aft. He immediately ran with Guttridge, the shipwright, and the bosun along the main deck to the scene of the explosion. There he found the lift well shattered and men fighting the fires which had developed. Then the bomb burst for'ard on P1 pompom. Damage Control HQ reported all the damage to Captain Boyd on the bridge, who was taking avoiding action with his eye on the diving Stukas.

Pilots and observers were helping to fight the fires. Going had been rubbernecking up on the starboard catwalk when blast blew his cap off. Hastening below to see what he could do, he found the after flat in darkness. He went to his cabin, collected his torch and on making his way further aft discovered that the after damage control officer had been killed. He decided to remain below and take his place.

Up on the flight-deck a few of the hands were rigging fire hoses. Bill Acworth and Bill Banham lent them a hand. Through the flames and smoke shooting up from the after lift they saw a stoker petty officer staggering under the weight of an officer's body.

'Well done,' said Acworth quietly.

S2 pompom was a blackened, twisted wreck. Poor old Annie. All that remained was a heap of smouldering clothes and a leg in a seaboot. Men at S1 pompom were removing the remains of their oppos. In the middle of the flight-deck lay the torso of a man. Captain Boyd noticed it from the bridge, caught the eye of the chief bosun's mate, who was heaving on a hose with Bill Banham, and nodded. The petty officer picked up the bloody object and heaved it overboard.

The padre came up. 'Have a biscuit,' he said, calmly holding out a big paper bag. Then the screech of the warning telephones started again as another wave of bombers screamed down at the ship.

High-level bombers came over this time as well. Once again the ship lurched and staggered as bombs fell all around her. Noise between decks was terrifying, like a thousand Tube trains roaring out of the tunnel. A bomb smashed through the flight-deck and through the boys' mess-deck. Passing out of the ship's side it hit the water and exploded. White-hot metal shot in all directions, holing the ship in many places above and below the waterline and causing bad flooding in the unarmoured for'ard section. Blast from the same bomb smashed aircraft in the hangar and punched the for'ard lift upwards into an arch. Wind rushed immediately into the hangar through this arch, and fanned the fires there into a great blaze. Flame and smoke poured from the after-lift well.

Jago had dashed into a spraying room at the side of the hangar to get the sprayers working. When he got back into the hangar it was a ghastly shambles. Dead and badly wounded men lay on the deck, some hit by pieces of steel from the hangar fire-screens which had shattered to pieces and flung sharp slivers like scythe blades through the hangar. He saw an officer he knew looking straight at him. The man had no top to his head. He immediately had all access doors to the hangar closed and got the sprayers going. Ammunition was exploding all over the hangar and planes were burning. Down one side of the hangar were six swordfish with depth-charges attached, and another six armed with torpedoes.

'Don't worry,' said the Gunner (T), 'they won't cook off.'

Streamline Robertson appeared in the hangar. He saw four Fulmars, one in each corner of the after sub-hangar, on fire, and noticed that although many of the Swordfish were shattered and burning, their torpedoes were still intact. More than anything else he felt furiously angry that the Nazis were spoiling the ship.

The flight-deck became in places laminated with the heat and too hot to walk on. When water was turned on from the hoses, clouds of steam arose to mingle with the smoke and flames pouring up from the lift wells and the holes in the deck. Those guns still intact kept firing.

Then there was a blinding, staggering crash and a great thousand-pounder struck the flight-deck right on the centre-line. It burst through the armoured deck and the hangar-deck below, hit the after ammunition conveyor and exploded, killing and badly wounding everybody in the wardroom flat. All the officers taking a hasty meal in the wardroom were wiped out. The whole after part of the ship went dark and dead. The fire took hold everywhere and raged through the torn and shattered compartments where men lay trapped. A smashed petrol-pipe sprayed streams of liquid flame through the dark, smoke-filled passages.

Bill Banham found that the after bulkhead door was partially open. Peering into the wardroom flat through the thick, acrid haze, he saw the flare from a burning petrol-pipe roaring like a huge blowlamp. Ammunition near the shattered conveyor started to go up. Flame suddenly appeared through the openings in the conveyor.

Bill flashed his torch round the shattered keyboard flat. The secondary light lamps had gone, the magazine light boxes, junction and distributing boxes torn away. Electric leads and cables hung down in festoons, fire-hydrants lay smashed, hoses ripped to shreds, paintwork scorched, blackened and blistered.

Just then Commander Tuck and his party arrived upon the scene and joined the men from the ammunition parties. Tuck decided to open the bulkhead door. Slowly he opened the door and he and Guttridge crawled into the flat wearing long-tubed smoke helmets. Tuck could see fire burning in the hangar above but none in the flat below. Water from the hangar spray system poured through the shattered deck. There seemed to be no serious danger of fire below threatening the magazines—thanks to the prompt action of the hangar spray party—and nothing more could be done.

Bill made his way along to the fore magazines. Here the after magazine crews, their own guns out of action, had joined up to give a hand. Still at it! Good old Gunner's Party!

Tuck came up and said that ammunition was wanted at the guns. With power gone, Bill and his men began to pass the heavy boxes up hand to hand.

Then he went back to the top of the fore magazine. All round the next flat he found rows of badly wounded men on stretchers.

'I'll never be an angel now, sir, I've got to lose me arm,' said one as he passed by. He watched one man being laid gently down. The man carrying him said to the doctor, 'Something went crack as I picked him up, sir.'

'Yes,' said the doctor, 'I'm afraid his back is broken.'

All the time the yammer and thump of the guns, the roar and scream of diving planes, the crump and terrible clangour of bombs, went on above.

During brief lulls everything possible was done to clear the debris away from the guns and keep them firing. At one stage it was reported to Captain Boyd that fire was dangerously near one of the magazines. Would he give permission to flood it? He thought of the Stukas and fresh attacks to come. Better the devil you know than the devil you don't, he thought, and refused permission.

Down aft Going and his party worked feverishly, putting out fires, opening compartment after compartment looking for dead and wounded. They worked in a terrible and macabre setting. Flames illuminating the water cascading down the lift well made a beautiful and eerie spectacle. Sitting in the reflected glare were the remains of a man with no arms or legs.

By now it looked to Going as if the fires down there were under control, and he ordered everybody out. A warrant officer, Mr Howe, came up and volunteered his help.

'I am not in the habit of giving orders to warrant officers,' said Going, 'but I'm giving you one now. Get to hell out of here!'

He was just about to go himself when there came a terrible shock and roar and he was thrown down. In a great void of blackness he was aware of staggering up and dragging himself up a vertical ladder. Then he passed out.

Another thousand-pound bomb had plunged into the after-lift well. This bomb burst the deck of the lift well and put the steering gear in the compartment below out of action. The ship began to swing crazily round in circles. She remained out of control until Captain Boyd began steering her on main engines alone and headed for Malta.

It was then that her captain, who loved *Illustrious* so well, went down off the bridge, 'to see,' as he said, 'what they had done to my lovely ship'.

He found *Illustrious* terribly, grievously hurt, her between-decks torn and blackened, with fires still raging, and a very great number of her men dead or seriously injured. He moved among the wounded and badly burned men, trying to cheer them with a personal word here and there.

'But,' he said, 'I could not tell one from the other.'

Slowly they fought the ship to Malta, through several more heavy attacks, her stokers maintaining steam in a temperature of 140 degrees, with the air vents sucking in thick, acrid smoke, her gunners keeping up a fierce barrage with the fury and blind anger of men who were watching their shipmates die and agonise all around them, and their beloved, beautiful ship smashed into punch-drunk helplessness.

Bill Banham went aft again, back to the desolation and the stench. Standing by the wrecked keyboard, he saw, undamaged, the Royal Marines' big drum. He passed the American lieutenant-commander, who had fought the fires with a damage control party throughout the battle, and was now going coolly round checking on the damage.

Back on the flight-deck Bill met the captain, looking unperturbed as ever and puffing at his old pipe.

'Poor Mr Anstice,' he said, looking at the blackened, twisted wreck of S2 pompom, 'still, never mind, you're still here, you old so-and-so.'

The run-about crane, old Jumbo, looked drunk, hunched black and gaunt, useless. The first lieutenant was worrying that he had given too much morphia to a badly wounded man. *Never mind, Number One, he'll sleep twice as sound.*

Something was smouldering still at S2 pompom. Bill kicked it away. . . . The flight-deck was hot to the feet, the after end still obscured by smoke and steam. The stench of burning flesh lay everywhere. At gun quarters great piles of empty brass cordite cylinders sprawled.

It was nearly dark now and the list on the ship seemed to be growing worse. Fire still raged in the hangar. Bill was soaked with sea water from the hoses and white with foamite. He was beginning to feel very tired.

More firing? Yes, the pompoms had started again. It was the last attack of the day. One long continuous roar of gun-fire began again. The firing stopped and they began replenishing empty ready-use lockers once more.

Wearily Bill climbed up through the ladderways and hatchways in the dark on to the flight-deck. In the darkness the fires at the after end still glowed. Over on the beam a ship was flashing a message.

The carrier moved slowly forward, uncannily quiet now, except for the hissing of steam.

Somebody broke the silence by saying, 'I can smell the goats in Malta.'

Someone else said, 'Where shall we go tonight, the Vernon or the White Ensign—or Jimmy Bung's bar?'

Everywhere tense nerves quivered in worn-out bodies.

A man suddenly screamed with delayed shock. His oppos took hold of him and quietened him down.

The magazine parties came up, grimy and puffy-eyed, from the stinking darkness that had imprisoned them all day, and asked for news.

The air was brittle. Every noise, every movement now, seemed magnified, an agony. White faces jerked up at every tremor. The ship shuddered as a tug bumped alongside. Word went round that they were entering Grand Harbour.

At last—'Secure from action stations.'

Everyone came up into the fresh air, clambering stiffly up to the flight-deck and gaping dully at the shambles there. As the ship slowly passed the harbour mouth, cheering rose up on either hand. Slowly *Illustrious* came alongside the dockyard wall, then stopped, as if with head bowed.

KENNETH POOLMAN

*

The three great U-boat aces of the early part of the Battle of the Atlantic were Gunther Prien (U-47), Joachim Schepke (U-100), and Otto Kretschmer (U-99). Each was credited with sinking more than 250,000 tons of Allied shipping. Ironically, all three were themselves sunk in the same month of March 1941. U-47 was sunk by HMS Wolverine *(Commander J. M. Rowland) whilst attacking Convoy OB 293 on 8th. U-99 and U-100 both attacked Convoy HX 112 on*

ST PATRICK'S DAY, 1941

In the next hour five ships were torpedoed. I was near to despair and I racked my brains to find some way to stop the holocaust. While the convoy stayed in impeccable formation, we escorts raced about in the exasperating business of searching in vain for the almost invisible enemy. Our one hope was to sight a U-boat's telltale white wake, give chase to force her to dive, and so give the Asdics a chance to bring our depth-charges into action. Everything had to be subordinated to that end and so, with binoculars firmly wedged on a steady bearing, I put *Walker* into a gently curving course, thereby putting every point of the compass under a penetrating prove. It worked.

As her bows swung, a thin line of white water came into the lens of my glasses, a thin line which could only be the wake of a ship. There were none of ours in that direction; it had to be a U-boat! I shouted orders increasing speed to thirty knots and altered course towards the target. Suddenly, the U-boat spotted us and in a cloud of spray he crash-dived. A swirl of phosphorescent water still lingered as we passed over the spot and sent a pattern of ten depth-charges crashing down. We could hardly have missed; it had been so quick we must have dropped them smack on top of him. Then the depth-charges exploded with great cracking explosions and giant water-spouts rose to masthead height astern of us. Two and a half minutes later another explosion followed and an orange flash spread momentarily across the surface. We had every reason to hope that this was our first 'kill'.

Though we learned that this was not so, for our charges had exploded too deeply to do him fatal damage, we felt almost certain at the time when our Asdic search showed no trace of a contact. *Vanoc* came racing past to rejoin the convoy and offered assistance. I refused this, convinced as I was that we could safely leave the scene with a 'probable' marked down in the log-book, and ordered her back to her station.

However, no U-boat was officially recorded as destroyed without tangible evidence and I continued the Asdic search until such time as wreckage should come to the surface.

It was just as well. For half an hour later we gained contact with a certain U-boat. Our prey had not been 'killed'; he was, in fact, sneaking back towards the convoy, still bent on attack.

Recalling *Vanoc* to assist in the hunt, we set about our target with a series of carefully aimed patterns of depth-charges.

Taking it in turns to run in to the attack, pattern after pattern of depth-charges went down as we tried to get one to within the lethal range of about twenty feet of our target. But he was a wily opponent and, dodging and twisting in the depths, he managed to escape destruction though heavily damaged.

Soon the waters became so disturbed by the repeated explosions, each one of which sent back an echo to the Asdic's sound beam, that we could no longer distinguish our target from the other echoes and a lull in the fight was forced upon us.

I had for some time past noticed in the distance the bobbing lights from the lifeboats of one of our sunken ships, but with an enemy to engage there was nothing for it but to harden my heart and hope that the time might come later when I could rescue the crews. This lull seemed a good opportunity and perhaps if we left the area temporarily the U-boat commander might think he had shaken us off and be tempted into some indiscretion. So, the *Vanoc* steaming round us in protection, we stopped and picked up the master and thirty-seven of the crew of the ss *J. B. White*.

This completed, the time was ripe to head quietly back to where the U-boat had last been located and perhaps catch him licking his wounds on the surface.

We had hardly got under way when I noticed that *Vanoc* was drawing ahead fast and thought perhaps she had misread the signal ordering the speed to be maintained. As I ordered a signal to be made to her, Yeoman of Signals Gerrard said, 'She's signalling to us, sir, but I can't read it as her light is flickering so badly.' I realised that *Vanoc* must be going ahead at her full speed and being, like *Walker*, an old veteran, her bridge would be shaking and rattling as her 30,000 hp drove her forward through the Atlantic swell.

Rupert Bray, on the bridge beside me, said, 'She must have sighted the U-boat.' Even as he spoke, *Vanoc* came on the air with his radio telephone, with the laconic signal: 'Have rammed and sunk U-boat.'

What a blissful moment that was for us, the successful culmination of a long and arduous fight. Something in the way of revenge for our losses in the convoy had been achieved.

There was grim joy on board *Walker*, and not least amongst the merchant seamen from the *J. B. White*, who felt they had a personal score to settle. But for the moment our part was confined to circling *Vanoc* in protection, while she picked up the few survivors from the U-boat and examined herself for damage. We were glad of this breathing space, as, with all the depth-charges carried on the upper deck expended, the depth-charge party, led by Leading Seaman

Prout, were struggling to hoist up more of these awkward heavy loads from the magazine, with the ship rolling in the Atlantic swell, and often with water swirling round their waists. They were not a moment too soon, for, as we circled *Vanoc*, I was electrified to hear the Asdic operator Able Seaman Backhouse excitedly reporting, 'Contact, contact.' But I could hardly credit it, for not only was it unbelievable that in all the wide wastes of the Atlantic a second U-boat should turn up just where another had gone to the bottom, but I knew that there were sure to be areas of disturbed water persisting in the vicinity from our own and *Vanoc*'s wakes. The echo was not very clear and I expressed my doubts to John Langton, but Backhouse was not to be disheartened. 'Contact definitely submarine,' he reported, and as I listened to the ping the echo sharpened and there could be no further doubt. With a warning to the men aft to get any charges ready that they had managed to hoist into the throwers and rails, we ran into the attack. It was a great test for John Langton, for, with the maddening habit of the beautiful instruments of precision provided for us, they all elected to break down at the crucial moment. But much patient drill against just such an emergency now brought its reward. Timing his attack by the most primitive methods Langton gave the order to fire. A pattern of six depth-charges—all that could be got ready in time—went down. As they exploded, *Walker* ran on to get sea-room to turn for further attacks, but as we turned came the thrilling signal from *Vanoc*—'U-boat surfaced astern of me.'

A searchlight beam stabbed into the night from *Vanoc*, illuminating the submarine U-99 which lay stopped. The guns' crews in both ships sprang into action and the blinding flashes from the four-inch guns and tracers from the smaller weapons made a great display, though I fear their accuracy was not remarkable. Destroyer night gunnery in such a mêlée is apt to be pretty wild and in those days, when flashless cordite was not issued to us, each salvo left one temporarily blinded. In *Walker* confusion soon reigned around the guns, for the enthusiasm of our guests from *J. B. White* knew no bounds. Joining up with the ammunition supply parties, shells came up at such a phenomenal rate that the decks were piled high with them till the guns' crews were hardly able to work their guns. But fortunately we were able very soon to cease fire as a signal lamp flashing from the U-boat, 'We are sunking' [*sic*], made it clear that the action was over. Keeping end on to the U-boat in case he still had some fight left, we prepared to lower a boat in case there was a chance of a capture, but even as we did so the crew of the U-boat abandoned ship and she plunged to the bottom.

I manœuvred *Walker* to windward of the swimming Germans and as we drifted down on to them, they were hauled on board. Some of them were in the last stages of exhaustion from the cold of those icy northern waters by the time we got them on board. Some indeed would never have made safety had not Leading Seaman Prout gone over the side fully clothed to aid them.

The last to come over the side was obviously the captain, as he swam to *Walker* still wearing his brass-bound cap. We were soon to find out that we had made indeed a notable capture, for the captain was Otto Kretschmer, leading ace of the U-boat arm, holder of the Knight's Cross with oak leaves and top scorer in terms of tonnage sunk.

Captain DONALD MACINTYRE DSO and two bars, DSC RN
Captain of *Walker*

The other U-boat, rammed and sunk by Vanoc, *was Joachim Schepke's U-100.*

*

Early on the morning of Sunday, 6th April 1941, the destroyer HMS Broke *(Commander B. G. Scurfield RN) passed the armed merchant cruiser HMS* Comorin *and her escort destroyer HMS* Lincoln *in the Atlantic. At 1600 the same day the following signal was received in* Broke: 'HMS COMORIN SERIOUSLY ON FIRE IN POSITION 54°39'N 21°13'W JOIN US IF POSSIBLE'.

When we drew near the scene was awe-inspiring. The great liner lay beam on to the seas, drifting very rapidly. A red glow showed in the smoke which belched from her funnel and below that amidships the fire had a strong hold. Clouds of smoke streamed away from her lee side. The crew were assembled aft and we were in communication by lamp and later by semaphore. From the weather quarter the *Lincoln*'s Carley rafts were being loaded up—a dozen men at a time and hauled across to the destroyer lying about two cables away.

It was a desperately slow affair and we went in close to see if we could not go alongside.

Various objects were falling from time to time from the *Comorin* into the sea. Each time one looked carefully to see if it was a man, but it was not. Some of the things may have been oil-drums, in an attempt to make the sea's surface calmer. We looked at the weather side first and passed between *Lincoln* and *Comorin*, only discovering that they were connected by line after we were through. But the line did not part, it had sunk deep enough for us to cross. We turned and tried to lay some oil between the two ships. This meant that we nearly got sandwiched. There were two raft-loads going across at the time and the sailors in them waved us to go back. They seemed incredibly tiny and ant-like in their rafts on those angry slopes of grey sea.

The *Lincoln* was rolling wildly and once when her propellers came clear of the water we could see that she had a rope round the starboard one. Her starboard side was black, which we thought at first was burnt paintwork, but discovered afterwards was oil which they had tried to pump out on the weather side and which had blown back all over their side and upper deck.

To go alongside *Comorin* seemed an impossibility. The waves were fifty to sixty feet from trough to crest and the liner's cruiser stern lifted high out of the water at one moment showing rudder and screws and crashed downward in a cloud of spray the next. I thought a destroyer could not possibly survive such an impact.

Round on the leeward side we got our grass line out on to the fo'c's'le and dropped a Carley raft into the water attached to it. The liner drifted to leeward and so did we, but the raft with less wind surface did not drift so fast. So it appeared to float away up wind towards the other ship, and in a very short time was against the liner's lee side. There was a Jacob's ladder over the side and one rating went down and eventually got into the raft. We started to haul in on the grass, but we had allowed too much grass to go out, the bight of it had sunk, the great stern had lifted on a wave and come down on the near side of the rope; the bight was round the rudder. When we hauled on the grass it pulled the raft towards the liner and under her. Each time the ship lifted it pounded down on the man in the raft, who began to cry out. At this time we drifted round the stern and could not see him any more. I am not certain if he was drowned, but it can only have been a miracle that saved him.

We were close to the stern now and we fired our Coston line-throwing gun. We fired it well to windward, but a little too high and the wind blew it horizontally clear of the ship like straw. But we were close enough to get a heaving line across—after many had missed—and we connected the Coston line to the departing heaving line as we drew astern and finally pulled an end of the grass rope to it and passed it over to the other ship. Then we put another Carley raft in the water so that they could haul it in to windward, but for some time they made no effort to do this and finally their captain made a signal that he thought the only chance was for *Broke* to go alongside and let the men jump. This was at 9.50 pm.

I had various discussions with my captain as to which side it should be. I must confess that I did not believe we could survive such a venture. By this time it was almost dark and the *Lincoln*'s raft ferry had failed owing to the parting of their grass line. I do not know how many people they had rescued by this ferry, but it cannot have been very many as it was desperately slow. Not that it wasn't enormously worth doing, for at the time it seemed to be the only way at all.

I saw one body floating away and wondered if it was the chap from our raft. Indeed I felt sure it was, though I heard a rumour afterwards that he had managed to climb back on board, and I know that several men were drowned embarking in the *Lincoln*'s ferry service. Obviously a raft secured to the upper deck of a heavily rolling ship cannot be secured close alongside. If it were it would be hauled out of the water by its end whenever the ship rolled away and all those already embarked would be pitched out. The rafts therefore had to remain ten or fifteen yards from the *Comorin*'s side and men had to go down the rope to them. It was here that several men were drowned.

As it gradually got dark the glow from the fire shone redly and eventually became the chief source of light. As soon as we knew we were going alongside I went down to the fo'c's'le, got all the fenders over to the port side, and had all the locker cushions brought up from the mess-decks.

I suggested that hammocks should be brought up, but Angus

Letty, our navigating officer, said that since it was still doubtful if we should get alongside he thought it would be a pity to get them all wet. I wish I had pressed the point, but I didn't. Letty had been doing excellent work on the fo'c's'le all the time, but I think his judgement was at fault in this and so was mine in not seeing at once that he was wrong. What are a few wet hammocks by comparison with broken limbs?

So we closed the starboard (leeward) quarter of the *Comorin* and in a few minutes we had scraped alongside.

The absolutely bewildering thing was the relative speed that the ships passed each other in a vertical direction. The men waiting on the after promenade deck were forty feet above our fo'c's'le at one moment and at the next they were ten feet below. As they passed our fo'c's'le they had to jump as if jumping from an express lift.

The first chance was easy. About nine jumped and landed mostly on the fo'c's'le, some on 'B' gun-deck. They were all safe and uninjured. As they came doubling aft I asked them how they got on and they were cheerful enough.

One petty officer came with this lot—Petty Officer Fitzgerald—and I immediately detailed him to help with the organisation of survivors as they embarked.

There was little, if any, damage to the ship from this first encounter and we backed away to get into position for the next. As we closed in for the second attempt the terrific speed of the rise and fall of the other ship in relation to our own fo'c's'le was again the main difficulty for the jumpers, added to which the ships were rolling in opposite directions, so that at one minute they touched, at the next they were ten yards apart. This very heavy rolling made it almost impossible for us to keep our feet on the fo'c's'le. We had to hold on tightly nearly all the time. I remember I had started the operation wearing a cap, as I thought I should be easier to recognise that way, but I so nearly lost it in the gale that I left it in the wireless office for safe keeping.

The second jump was much more difficult than the first. Only about six men came and three of them were injured. From then on I do not remember the chronology of events, as one jump followed another with varying pauses for manœuvring. Our policy was not to remain alongside for any length of time as this would have been very dangerous and might well have damaged us to the point of foundering in these monstrous seas. Instead we quickly withdrew after each brief contact in order to assess the damage and decide upon the seaworthiness of the ship before closing in again for another attempt.

The scene was lit chiefly by the fire, as it was not pitch dark. Occasionally the *Lincoln*'s searchlight swept across us as they searched the sea for the last Carley raft which had somehow broken adrift. At each successive jump a few more men were injured.

We decided to rig floodlights to light the fo'c's'le so that the men could judge the height of the jump. These were held by Leading Telegraphist Davies and Ordinary Seaman Timperson all the time. The pool of light which they formed gave the whole scene an extraordinary artificiality, as if this were some ghastly film scene, and I can remember, as I stood impotently waiting for the next jump, feeling suddenly remote as if watching through the wrong end of a telescope.

As soon as the jumping men had begun to injure themselves I sent aft for the doctor who was in bed with a temperature. He came for'ard at once and started to work. At the third jump we drew ahead too far and the whaler at its davits was crushed, but several men jumped into it and were saved that way. Another time the captain changed his mind and decided to get clear by going ahead instead of astern. The ship was struck a heavy blow aft on the port for'ard depth-charge thrower.

At this jump there had been a good many injured and as we went ahead into the sea again to circle *Comorin* for another approach the decks began to wash down with great seas. This was awkward for the disposal of the injured and I went up and asked the captain if in future we could have a little longer to clear away and prepare for the next jump—to which he readily agreed.

My routine was to be down by A gun for the jump. There was a strut to the gun-cover frame which was the best handhold. Here I saw that the padding was properly distributed, the light properly held, the stretcher parties in readiness and hands all ready to receive the survivors.

Then we would crash alongside for a few breathtaking seconds whilst the opportunity did or did not arise for a few to jump.

Sometimes there would be two opportunities—first while we still went ahead, and then again as we came astern. The great thing was to get the injured away before the next people jumped on to them. As soon as this had been done I went with the shipwright to survey the damage and then up to report to the captain. This was a rather exhausting round trip and before the end I got cramp in my right arm through over-exercise of the muscles.

The damage to the ship was at first superficial, consisting of dents in the fo'c's'le flare and bent guard-rails and splinter shields. But at length one bad blow struck us near the now crushed whaler on the upper-deck level. I ran aft and found a large rent in the ship's side *out* of which water was pouring. I did not think the boiler-room could have filled quickly enough for this to be sea-water coming out again, and came to the conclusion that it was a fresh-water tank. This was later confirmed by the shipwright. As I had thought, it was the port 'peace' tank. This was an incredible stroke of good fortune, as a hole of that size in the boiler-room would have been very serious indeed in that sea.

Several of *Comorin*'s officers had now arrived and we began to get estimates of the numbers still to come. There seemed always to be an awful lot more. I detailed Lieutenant Loftus to go down to the mess-decks as chief receptionist and went back to my usual round—fo'c's'le for a jump, clear the injured, view the damage, report to the captain and back to the fo'c's'le.

By now some of the injuries appeared to be pretty bad. There were a good many broken legs and arms and one chap fell across the guard-rail from about twenty-five feet. Letty came aft to me and said, 'That fellow's finished—cut his guts to bits.' It appears that Able Seaman George, a young Gibraltar seaman who was doing excellent work on the fo'c's'le, had put a hand on his back—felt what he took to be broken ribs and withdrawn his hand covered with blood. No such case ever reached the doctor and although there is a possibility that an injured man could have gone over the side owing to the heavy rolling, I am inclined to think that the account was an exaggerated one.

It filled me with gloom, and since at least one-third of the survivors landing on the fo'c's'le had to be carried off it, I became desperately worried by the high percentage of casualties. True, they had improved lately since we had ranged all available hammocks in rows, like sausages. They made very soft padding, but a few ankles still slipped between them and got twisted.

On one of my round trips I met an RNVR sub-lieutenant survivor trying to get some photos of the burning ship (I never heard whether they came out). There were a good many officers on board by this time, mostly RNR. Of course they did not recognise me, hatless in duffle-coat, grey flannel trousers and sea-boots, and it took a few moments to persuade them to answer my searching questions.

Still the estimated number remaining did not seem to dwindle. Sometimes there were longish pauses while we manœuvred into position. Twice we went alongside without getting any men at all. Once the ship came in head on and the stem was stove in, for about eight feet down from the bull-ring, and we got no survivors that time either.

Somewhere around 11.30 pm the fire reached the rockets on the *Comorin*, which went off splendidly, together with various other fireworks such as red Very lights and so on. Later the small-arms ammunition began to explode, at first in ones and twos and then in sharp rattles and finally in a continuous crackling roar.

The sea was as bad as ever and at each withdrawal we had to go full astern into it. This meant that very heavy waves were sweeping the quarterdeck, often as high as the blast shield of 'X' gun (about eight feet). When these waves broke over the ship she shuddered and set up a vibration which carried on often for twenty or thirty seconds. All this time the hull was clearly under great strain. As we got more used to going alongside some of my particular fears grew less, but the apparent inevitability of casualties was a constant source of worry and there was also the continual speculation upon how much the ship would stand up to.

Once on the first approach there seemed to be a chance for a jump. Two men jumped, but it was too far and they missed. I was at the break of the fo'c's'le at the time, and looked down into the steaming, boiling abyss. With the two ships grinding together as they were there did not seem the slightest chance of rescuing them. More men were jumping now and theirs was the prior claim. The ship came ahead, men jumped on to the flag-deck and the pompom deck amidships was demolished: then as we went astern I ran again to the side to see if there was any sign of the two in the water, but there was none that I could see.

Lieutenant-Commander PETER SCOTT CBE DSC RNVR
of *Broke*

Broke *approached* Comorin *again and again for survivors to jump down on to her fo'c's'le. By brilliant seamanship (and 685 engine-room telegraph orders in three hours) 180 of* Comorin*'s people were saved. Commander Scurfield was awarded the OBE.*

*

In March 1941 the Mediterranean Fleet were fully engaged in Operation 'Lustre': convoying troop reinforcements and supplies for the campaign in Greece. The enemy were well aware of these movements and, under pressure from the Germans, the Italians at last prepared to interrupt the flow of convoys by major surface-ship action. By 27th March it was confirmed that an Italian fleet, including the battleship Vittorio Veneto, *was at sea. Admiral Cunningham, flying his flag in* Warspite, *sailed from Alexandria that evening. The next day Vice-Admiral Pridham-Wippell and his cruiser force made contact with the enemy and aircraft from the carrier* Formidable *scored a torpedo hit on* Vittorio Veneto *and also crippled the heavy cruiser* Pola. *In the evening the Italian Admiral Angelo Iachino detached the cruisers* Zara *and* Fiume *to assist* Pola. *Whilst pursuing the enemy, first Pridham-Wippell's force and then* Valiant *reported a radar contact—a large unknown ship lying, apparently stopped, to port of the battle fleet. This contact led to*

THE BATTLE OF MATAPAN

Our hopes ran high. This might be the *Vittorio Veneto*. The course of the battle fleet was altered forty degrees to port together to close. We were already at action stations with our main armament ready. Our guns were trained on the correct bearing.

Rear-Admiral Willis was not out with us. Commodore Edelsten, the new Chief of Staff, had come to gain experience. And a quarter of an hour later, at 10.25, when he was searching the horizon on the starboard bow with his glasses, he calmly reported that he saw two large cruisers with a smaller one ahead of them crossing the bows of the battle fleet from starboard to port. I looked through my glasses, and there they were. Commander Power, an ex-submarine officer and an abnormal expert at recognising the silhouettes of enemy warships at a glance, pronounced them to be two 'Zara'-class eight-inch-gun cruisers with a smaller cruiser ahead.

Using short-range wireless the battle fleet was turned back into line ahead. With Edelsten and the staff I had gone to the upper bridge, the captain's, where I had a clear all-round view. I shall never forget the next few minutes. In the dead silence, a silence that could almost be felt, one heard only the voices of the gun-control personnel putting the guns on to the new target. One heard the orders repeated in the director tower behind and above the bridge. Looking forward, one saw the turrets swing and steady when the fifteen-inch guns pointed at the enemy cruisers. Never in the whole of my life have I experienced a more thrilling moment than when I heard a calm voice from the director tower—'Director layer sees the target', sure sign that the guns were ready and that his finger was itching on the trigger. The enemy was at a range of no more than 3,800 yards—point-blank.

It must have been the Fleet gunnery officer, Commander Geoffrey Barnard, who gave the final order to open fire. One heard the 'ting-ting-ting' of the firing gongs. Then came the great orange flash and the violent shudder as the six big guns bearing were fired simultaneously. At the very same instant the destroyer *Greyhound*, on the screen, switched her searchlight on to one of the enemy cruisers, showing her momentarily up as a silvery-blue shape in the darkness. Our searchlights shone out with the first salvo, and provided full illumination for what was a ghastly sight. Full in the beam I saw our six great projectiles flying through the air. Five out of the six hit a few feet below the level of the cruiser's upper deck and burst with splashes of brilliant flame. The Italians were quite unprepared. The guns were trained fore and aft. They were helplessly shattered before they could put up any resistance. In the midst of all this there was one milder diversion. Captain Douglas Fisher, the captain of the *Warspite*, was a gunnery officer of note. When he saw the first salvo hit he was heard to say in a voice of wondering surprise: 'Good Lord! We've hit her!'

The *Valiant*, astern of us, had opened fire at the same time. She also had found her target, and when the *Warspite* shifted to the other cruiser I watched the *Valiant* pounding her ship to bits. Her rapidity of fire astonished me. Never would I have believed it possible with these heavy guns. The *Formidable* had hauled out of the line to starboard; but astern of the *Valiant* the *Barham* was also heavily engaged.

The plight of the Italian cruisers was indescribable. One saw whole turrets and masses of other heavy debris whirling through the air and splashing into the sea, and in a short time the ships themselves were nothing but glowing torches and on fire from stem to stern.

Our searchlights were still on, and just after 10.30 three Italian destroyers, which had apparently been following their cruisers, were seen coming in on our port bow. They turned, and one was seen to fire torpedoes, so the battle fleet was turned ninety degrees together to starboard to avoid them. Our destroyers were engaging, and the whole party was inextricably mixed up. The *Warspite* fired both fifteen-inch and six-inch at the enemy. To my horror I saw one of our destroyers, the *Havock*, straddled by our fire, and in my mind wrote her off as a loss. The *Formidable* also had an escape. When action was joined she hauled out to starboard at full speed, a night battle being no place for a carrier. When she was about five miles away she was caught in the beam of the *Warspite*'s searchlight sweeping on the disengaged side in case further enemy ships were present. We heard the six-inch control officer of the starboard battery get his guns on to her, and were only just in time to stop him from opening fire.

The four destroyers, *Stuart*, Captain H. M. L. Waller, Royal Australian Navy; *Greyhound*, Commander W. R. Marshall-A'Deane; *Havock*, Lieutenant G. R. G. Watkins; and *Griffin*, Lieutenant-Commander J. Lee-Barber, in company with the battle fleet, were then ordered to finish off the enemy cruisers, while the battle fleet collected the *Formidable* and withdrew to the northward to keep out of their way. According to their own reports the destroyers' movements were difficult to follow; but they had a wild night and sank at least one other enemy destroyer.

At 10.45 we saw very heavy gun-fire, with star-shell and tracer, to the south-westward. Since none of our ships was on that bearing it seemed to us that either the Italians were engaging each other, or that the destroyers of our striking force might be going in to attack. Just after 11 pm I made a signal ordering all forces not engaged in sinking the enemy to withdraw to the north-eastward. The objects of what I now consider to have been an ill-considered signal were to give our destroyers who were mopping up a free hand to attack any sizable ship they saw, and to facilitate the assembly of the fleet next morning. The message was qualified by an order to Captain Mack and his eight destroyers of the striking force, now some twenty miles ahead, not to withdraw until he had attacked. However it had the unfortunate effect of causing Vice-Admiral Pridham-Wippell to cease his efforts to gain touch with the *Vittorio Veneto*.

Just after midnight the *Havock*, after torpedoing a destroyer and finishing her off by gun-fire, reported herself in contact with a battleship near the position where we had been in action. The battleship was Captain Mack's main objective, and the *Havock*'s report brought Mack's destroyer striking force back hot-foot from their position nearly sixty miles to the westward. An hour later, however, the *Havock* amended her report to say that it was not a battleship she had sighted but an eight-inch cruiser. Soon after 3 am she sent a further message reporting herself close to the *Pola*, and, as all her torpedoes had been fired, Watkins asked whether 'to board or blow off her stern with depth-charges'.

The *Havock* had already been joined by the *Greyhound* and *Griffin*, and when Captain Mack arrived he took the *Jervis* alongside the *Pola*. That ship was in a state of indescribable confusion. Panic-stricken men were leaping over the side. On the crowded quarter-deck, littered with clothing, personal belongings and bottles, many of the sailors were drunk. There was no order or discipline of any sort, and the officers were powerless to enforce it. Having taken off the crew, Mack sank the ship with torpedoes. The *Pola*, of course, was the vessel reported by Pridham-Wippell and the *Valiant* between nine and ten the night before as lying stopped on the port side of our fleet's line of advance. She had not been under gun-fire or fired a gun, but had been torpedoed and completely crippled by one of the aircraft from the *Formidable* during the dusk attack.

Her sinking at 4.10 am was the final act of the night's proceedings.

Reconnaissance at dawn by the *Formidable*'s aircraft, with others from Greece and Crete, failed to discover any trace of the enemy to the westward. As we discovered afterwards, the *Vittorio Veneto* had been able to increase speed and get clear away during the night.

As daylight came on 29th March our cruisers and destroyers were in sight making for the rendezvous with the battle fleet. Feeling fairly certain in our minds that the *Warspite* had sunk a destroyer in the mêlée the night before, we eagerly counted them. To our inexpressible relief all twelve destroyers were present. My heart was glad again.

It was a fine morning. We steamed back to the scene of the battle to find the calm sea covered with a film of oil, and strewn with boats, rafts and wreckage, with many floating corpses. All the destroyers we could spare were detached to save what life was possible. In all, counting the men from the *Pola*, British ships rescued 900, though some died later. In the midst of this work of mercy, however, the attentions of some German Ju. 88s pointed the fact that it was unwise to dally in an area where we were exposed to heavy air attack. So we were compelled to proceed to the eastward, leaving some hundreds of Italians unrescued. We did the best we could for them by signalling their exact position to the Italian Admiralty. They sent out the hospital ship *Gradisca*, which eventually saved another 160.

Admiral of the Fleet Viscount
CUNNINGHAM OF HYNDHOPE KT GCB OM DSO
Commander-in-Chief at Matapan

After the Battle of Matapan:

From Captain of Destroyer Flotilla to Commander-in-Chief Mediterranean:

HAVE ITALIAN SURVIVORS INCLUDING THE ADMIRAL. HE HAS PILES.

From Commander-in-Chief:

I AM NOT SURPRISED.

From *Make a Signal*

*

During the Battle of Crete the Mediterranean Fleet's task was to prevent any German attempt at a sea-borne invasion from the north. Such an attempt was indeed defeated on the night of 21/22nd May. At dawn on the 22nd HMS Warspite, *flying the flag of Rear-Admiral H. B. Rawlings in command of the 1st Battle Squadron, steamed to the Kithera Channel to give support to the cruisers* Naiad *and* Perth *who had been under heavy air attack. Just after lunch (a favourite time for the Luftwaffe)* Warspite *was herself attacked. Admiral Sir Charles Madden, who was then* Warspite*'s executive officer, describes*

THE BOMBING OF *WARSPITE*

In the early afternoon we were standing in to the north-west of Crete to provide anti-aircraft support for the cruisers. It was a clear, blue Mediterranean day. The ship was at action stations and I was stationed in the upper conning tower, listening through the voice-pipe to what went on on the bridge. I heard the report: 'Hit starboard side amidships', and left the UCT to investigate. As I reached the back of the bridge I saw dense smoke coming from the starboard four-inch battery. On reaching the upper-deck level it was apparent that one four-inch mounting had gone overboard completely, and that the other was at an angle. There was a huge hole in the deck between the two mountings from which smoke and flame were pouring out.

I then went down to the port six-inch battery to see if fire parties were ready, and to try to get at the seat of the fire through the armoured door that connected the port and starboard six-inch battery decks. I found the fire party lined up ready by this door, asked two ratings to enter with me, and told the fire parties to open the door and follow us in. We had great difficulty in opening this door and had to use a sledge-hammer. Finally it gave, to display a gruesome scene. The starboard battery was full of flames and smoke, in among which the cries of burned and wounded men could be heard. These were very unnerving and I remember thinking how accurate were the descriptions in C. S. Forester's books of the carnage on the gun-decks in Nelson's day. The flames seemed pretty fierce and I was doubtful if we would make headway against them. However, my two volunteers came either side of me with their hoses and we walked into the battery. To my surprise the flames, which I suppose were dying down, seemed to subside before us, and soon we had the fire parties following us and were putting out the flames as we advanced.

I was soon joined by more fire parties coming from the after end of the starboard battery, and felt confident that I could get the fires out, but was hampered by the continued cries of the burned men, which distracted the fire parties, who wanted to leave their hoses to assist their comrades. I therefore concentrated on administering morphia.

About this time the smoke cleared in the hole in the deckhead, and I could converse with those on the deck above. I sent for all officers with morphia, and soon had several on the job, which became the main task as soon as the flames were out. As it was dark and wounded men were thrown in all directions amidst piles of ironwork and rubbish this was not easy.

The hole in the upper deck was now clear of smoke, and through it we could see the deep blue sky and the next wave of attacking aircraft coming at us. The four-inch battery being out of action made it seem unpleasantly quiet, until the pompoms started up, which caused a lot of the broken ironwork to fall about. I can remember the pompom bursts filling up the area of sky we could see and the aircraft still coming on, and some of the fire parties dropping their hoses to shake their fists at them.

I now had plenty of officers to take charge in the battery and we were moving the wounded out, so I went down to the mess-decks under the battery. The port side was cleared for casualties, which were being laid out in rows. A surprising number of men had trickled along to look after their friends, and I had some trouble in reducing their number, as they were all being kind and helpful.

I then went to the starboard mess-decks, where a fresh and unexpected scene of carnage greeted me. The armoured deck overhead, that of the starboard six-inch battery, had been pierced by the explosion, the force of which had descended into a mess-deck where communication ratings off watch were resting. These, contrary to instructions, and because of the heat, were lightly clad, and there were heavy casualties from burns. The great amount of water we had pumped into the battery above to put out the fires had poured into the mess-deck, which was in parts knee-deep in water, thus adding to the confusion of scattered mess tables, lockers and bodies.

When all was under control I went to the bridge to report. The calm, blue afternoon seemed unreal after the dark and smelly carnage below.

I then busied myself with removing the dead. I made as I thought sensible arrangements for laying them out in one of the after flats, but had not counted on the strong feelings of the men, who insisted that they should all be taken to the chapel—a tortuous journey through the armoured 'dips'. Sorting the dead out and identifying them occupied most of the dog watches, and they were then sewn up in hammocks for burial. The stout corporal of Marines who served so cheerfully in the wardroom bar volunteered for and personally led this operation throughout the next two days till we returned to harbour.

Admiral SIR CHARLES MADDEN, BART., GCB

*

KELLY

On 23rd May I understand that the German radio announced that the *Kelly* had been sunk with all hands, which included her captain. I hope this did not worry you and that you realised it was German propaganda. Edwina was very worried at first, but as soon as the news came through that we had been picked up the Admiralty told her and put her out of her misery. Patricia and Pammy were worst hit because their stupid governess brought them out of school to tell them that I was missing because she believed the German propaganda, and so they were pretty worried children for twenty-four hours.

As a matter of fact it was a bit of a miracle that we were picked up, at least those of us who survived, which in the case of the *Kelly* was less than half the officers and men.

The *Kelly* and some of the destroyers of my flotilla had been stationed in Malta and when we were not out on sweeps were subjected to a lot of air attack in the harbour which was unpleasant and frightening. However, except for the *Jersey*, who was sunk just after passing the breakwaters into Grand Harbour by a magnetic mine, none of the rest of my flotilla were damaged.

When news came to Malta of the beginning of the Battle of Crete I realised that we should soon be sent for to take part. I went and called on the admiral, Ford, and I gave him a suitcase which contained a suit of blue uniform, a suit of white uniform, pyjamas, underclothes, a sponge, and a toothbrush, and I told him that if the *Kelly* was sunk as seemed quite probable in the Battle of Crete and if I were picked up as I hoped I would be I would presumably be taken to Alexandria and I would be grateful if the admiral could put my suitcase into the next RAF aircraft flying from Malta to Alexandria. He promised he would do so. I got the suitcase ready because as we were the latest and finest destroyers I was sure we would be used for rear-guard action in the most dangerous exposed positions and we would be the most likely to be sunk. In any case after twenty-one months' intense activity in the war it was unlikely that the *Kelly* could go on having lucky escapes.

Shortly after this I got the signal to join the Fleet and we sailed. We joined the Mediterranean Fleet at the same moment as a medium-level bombing attack took place and a number of the bombs were aimed at us, but luckily we were able to dodge them.

Later that evening on 22nd May I was ordered to proceed into Canea Bay to bombard Maleme airstrip which the Germans had just captured and which the New Zealand Brigade were waiting to counter-attack as soon as our bombardment lifted.

Having lost the *Jersey*, I only had three ships of my own division instead of four, and they were the *Kelly*, *Kashmir*, and *Kipling*. We set off around the North-Eastern Cape of Crete and quite early on the *Kipling*'s steering gear became defective and as I couldn't risk having a ship whose steering wasn't perfect following me on such a hazardous night operation I told her to rejoin Rear-Admiral Rawlings, having first steered to the westwards for at least three hours not to betray the presence of this force. The little cherub who sits up aloft and looks after us poor sailormen must have put the *Kipling*'s steering gear out of action, for it was due to this incident that we owe our lives.

As we entered Canea Bay a large caique was sighted loaded with German troops steering towards Crete. Both ships opened fire and sank her very quickly, the wretched Germans jumping into the water in full marching order. In any other circumstances we would have stopped to pick them up, but even at thirty knots it was doubtful if I could get into position to carry out the bombardment in time, so I had to push on.

We hadn't got the exact position of the aerodrome, but worked out from a contour map where the airstrip must be. After having completed our bombardment we withdrew at high speed and came across another caique carrying ammunition. Shortly after we started firing at her she blew up in a very spectacular way.

Dawn broke as we rounded the North-Eastern Cape and we steamed at thirty knots down the Kithera Channel to rejoin Rawlings' force. As the sun rose a German Dornier 215 appeared out of the east and was engaged before she dropped five bombs which missed *Kelly* astern; forty minutes later three more Do. 215s made a high-level bombing attack on *Kelly* and *Kashmir* in the face of good 4.7-inch controlled fire. Both ships avoided the bombs. I sent for my breakfast on the bridge and I continued reading C. S. Forester's book about my favourite hero Hornblower called *Ship of the Line*.

Just before 8 am we sighted a mast above the horizon and I hoped it belonged to the *Kipling* though I couldn't think why she had waited for us.

By now the sun was well up, the sea was calm and it was a lovely Mediterranean day. Just about 8 am we suddenly saw twenty-four ominous black objects. Their distinctive shape soon revealed them as the dreaded Stukas, the Ju. 87s. They had a reputation for diving almost vertically on ships and only releasing their bombs when they were so low that they couldn't miss. They were hard to distinguish against the rising sun, but presently we could see that they broke up into two parties of about twelve in each.

I pressed the alarm rattlers, for this required full action stations, and I hoisted the signal to the *Kashmir* to 'act independently'.

The first party made for the *Kashmir* and they started diving in waves of three. I could see the bombs dropping round her and all her guns were firing. Then a wave of three peeled off from our lot and started to dive. I put the telegraphs at 'full ahead'. I gave the order 'hard-a-starboard' to bring the ship under the dive-bomber to force it to dive ever steeper in the hopes they would finally be pushed beyond the vertical and lose control. This happened and the bomber hit the sea close by sending up an enormous splash. I reversed the wheel 'hard-a-port'. The next dive-bomber was also forced to dive steeper and steeper and this one we actually shot down into the sea. The next one also missed.

But now to my horror I saw that the third or fourth wave had hit the *Kashmir* somewhere amidships and she was finished. I remember thinking, 'Oh God, even if we are not hit now we shall have to stay and pick up the survivors and they will get us then!'

I think it was about the fourth wave of the three where one of the Stukas suddenly came lower than the others and although I had the wheel over to 'hard-a-starboard' and we were turning at over thirty knots under full helm the bomb was released so close to the ship that it couldn't miss. It hit square on 'X' gun-deck and killed the crew of the twin 4.7-inch gun mounting, including that nice young boy Michael Sturdee, who was in command.

The next wave were coming in and I gave the order to the navigator 'midships' and then 'hard-a-port', but we only listed over more heavily to port. All ships list outwards under full helm at full speed, but this list was getting worse. I gave the order 'stop engines' and then heard the coxswain shout up the voice-pipe, 'Ship won't answer the helm. No reply to the engine-room telegraphs!' Then I realised we were for it.

The next wave of Stukas had started their dive towards us and I remember shouting out, 'Keep all guns firing', an unnecessary order, for all guns continued to fire until the guns crews were actually washed away from their guns. I realised the bomb must have torn a gaping hole down near 'X' magazine, as we had lost our stability and were rolling right over. I suddenly saw the water rise on our port side in a raging torrent of over thirty knots and thinking, 'Whatever happens I must stay with the ship as long as I can. I must be the last to leave her alive.' We were over beyond ninety degrees now and I climbed up on to the distance-correction indicator of my station-keeping gear which I had invented and was fitted in the flotilla. With my arms I clung round the gyro compass pedestal. And then the sea came in a roaring maelstrom. I saw officers and men struggling to get out of the bridge and then I took an enormously deep breath as the water closed over my head. The awful part was that even after we were upside down we continued to race through the water, though, of course, at a rapidly decreasing rate. Somehow I managed to flounder and work my way across the upside-down bridge until I got to the bullet-proof bridge screens. Here I had to pull myself under them and up to this moment it was horribly dark. A faint glimmer of daylight appeared on the other side of the bridge screens, but the water was churning round and I could distinguish nothing.

I suddenly felt my lungs were going to burst and that I would have to open my mouth unless I could somehow keep it shut. With my right hand I gripped my mouth in a vice-like grip and with my left hand I held my nostrils shut. It was a fight of willpower. Would my hands obey me and keep my mouth and nose shut longer than the reflex action which would force me to open them and swallow a lot of sea-water?

I had my Gieve waistcoat on, but had not blown up the rubber ring which is fitted in the waistcoat. This was lucky because it had made it easier for me to get out from under the bridge, but now I had to kick hard to fight my way to the surface. Slowly, infinitely slowly, the water got brighter and lighter and then suddenly with lungs bursting I broke surface. I gasped for breath, but the next moment I saw the stern of the ship approaching us with both our great propellers still revolving in the air. They looked as though they were going to come right over us and hit us. I saw the navigator, Lieutenant Maurice Butler-Bowdon, with his back to the ship. I yelled to him to 'Swim like hell' because I was afraid that the propellers would hit him. We both managed to get clear, but only by a matter of six or seven yards.

At this moment up bobbed one of our stoker petty officers, a great character and a bit of a humorist. He looked at the 'pilot' and then at me and then produced a typically cheery crack. 'Extraordinary how the scum always comes to the top, isn't it, sir?' I looked round. I could only see one Carley raft, which someone must have had time to release before the ship turned over. I saw men all round me in the water and yelled out, 'Everybody swim to the raft.'

I suddenly noticed I still had my steel helmet on, and this seemed ridiculous in the water, so I took it off and threw it away. I pulled the mouth-piece and tube out of my waistcoat and blew up the rubber ring. That made it easier to stay afloat. Then at that moment, suddenly and unexpectedly, a row of splashes appeared between us and the Carley raft, then with a roar one of the Stukas shot overhead with her machine-guns firing at us. I bitterly regretted throwing away my tin hat; you have no idea how naked one feels in the water without one when one is being machine-gunned.

By now I had reached the raft and gave orders that only the wounded were to be allowed inside the raft, those who were not wounded were to hold on outside and those for whom there was no room would hold on to the men who were holding on to the raft.

The dive-bombers came again, and again a hail of machine-gun bullets swept by, this time killing some of the men around the raft. As men died or were killed I had them gently taken out of the raft and men recently wounded put in to take their place. It was a gruesome and unpleasant business, and yet the sea was calm, the sun was shining, and it reminded me of so many bathes I had had in the Mediterranean in the days before the war.

My eyes were stinging and my mouth had a bitter acrid taste and looking round I saw everybody's face smothered in heavy oil fuel looking like Negro minstrels. This added greatly to our discomfort and to the unpleasantness.

I thought it would be a good thing to start singing to keep up people's courage and so I started that popular song 'Roll Out the Barrel' and the others soon joined in, which seemed to help.

And then the miracle happened. The *Kipling* appeared from below the horizon at full speed coming to our rescue. She had seen the Ju. 87s diving on us and didn't think we would be able to survive. It was a gallant act of the captain, for he was obviously going to draw the attacks on himself now.

The *Kelly* was just afloat. One could see the bottom under the bows afloat. Suddenly she started to go as the *Kipling* approached and I called for 'Three cheers for the old ship'. It was for me the saddest moment of a sad day.

As *Kipling* approached she unfortunately grazed the sharp bow of the *Kelly* under water and was holed. Luckily the hole was in the reserve feed tank, which meant that no water actually got into the ship.

Kipling lowered scrambling nets over her side. I told everybody to swim to the scrambling nets as soon as they could. I towed a very badly wounded man who was bleeding freely, but by the time I got him as far as the *Kipling* he was obviously very dead and so I let go.

As soon as I got on board I went up to the bridge. I was still in command of my flotilla and the *Kipling* was under my orders, but naturally I did not interfere with the captain, Aubrey St-Clair-Ford, who was a brave, brilliant and very competent man. I thanked him for coming to our rescue and asked him to go over and pick up the survivors of the *Kashmir*.

This was a much more difficult job, for she went down far more slowly than the *Kelly* and there were no less than five Carley rafts and they had more survivors than the *Kelly*. Hardly had we got opposite the first Carley raft and stopped engines than some Ju. 88s appeared. Though not of the terrifying vertical dive-bomber type, they dived in a shallow dive and the captain had to go ahead with the wheel hard over to avoid being hit. Every time he came back to a raft the same thing happened. Finally I told him to lower his fast motor-boat which could then go round collecting the survivors from each raft and would be able to come alongside the *Kipling* in whatever position we were without having to try to manœuvre the whole ship alongside a Carley raft. Aubrey thought this a good idea and gave the necessary orders.

Hardly had the boat reached the water than he came to me and said, 'There's another Ju. 88 diving at us. I'm afraid I shall have to go ahead out of it.'

I shouted to the men in the waist to 'cut the falls' of the motor-boat. This was necessary because the fast motor-boat is not a 'sea-boat', it is normally only lowered in harbour. There is no quick-release hook but a big steel shackle with a screw pin which takes half a dozen turns to unscrew. There was no time to do this. That is why I told them to cut the actual rope falls which were holding the boat.

A man with a knife dashed at the foremost falls and cut them. I shouted, 'Cut the after falls, you bloody fool!' because I knew what was going to happen.

I had personally supervised a course of all the engineer officers of my flotilla at the Experimental Oil Fuel Establishment at Haslar to ensure that they should be able to increase speed at a far greater rate than had been customary. The *Kipling* was no exception. Her 40,000 horse powers were applied with such speed that the ship leaped forward and the bows of the motor-boat were driven under. My cry to cut the after falls had been heard by my own first lieutenant, Lord Hugh Beresford, and the first lieutenant of the *Kipling*, John Bushe. Together they leaped to the after falls at the moment when the ship had gathered such speed and the heavy motor-boat had sunk so deep in the water that the after davit was pulled right over and seemed to crush them as the falls tore away and the boat sank in the sea together with the two first lieutenants. Hugh was one of my oldest friends; he had been a midshipman with me in 1927 in the *Queen Elizabeth*. He was a great-nephew of Papa's great friend, Lord Charles Beresford. I think this incident hurt me more than any that day.

The captain remarked, 'This is going to take a very long time now. I only hope they don't get us before we pick up all the *Kashmir*'s.' I replied that this was my responsibility and told him to go ahead. With great skill and great courage he gradually nosed his way from one raft to another in between the persistent attacks of the Ju. 88s. But it was a long and painful business and after two hours some of my own staff officers who had been saved came to me to ask whether I would not consider allowing the *Kipling* to leave the rest of the *Kashmir*'s and proceed to Alexandria. They pointed out, with complete justification, that the *Kipling* now had on board all *Kelly* survivors, more than half of the *Kashmir*'s survivors and it was becoming more and more difficult to pick up the remainder and avoid being hit by the bombers. I decided that we should stay. After three hours there was only one more raft-load to be picked up and this proved particularly difficult because the attacks were getting worse. After consulting the captain, my staff came back and urged that the right decision was to let the *Kipling* go before she was sunk with the loss of an additional five or six hundred lives. I decided we should stay to pick up all we could. I felt it would be better for us all to be sunk together than to leave any of our flotilla mates struggling helplessly in the water without any prospect of being saved.

At last we were able to turn for Alexandria. The damage to the *Kipling* prevented her from doing more than about half-speed, so we limped home at sixteen or seventeen knots, the mess-decks and upper decks everywhere being crowded with survivors, many of them wounded and in poor shape.

I went round with a notebook and pencil which I borrowed to get particulars of the more severely wounded and to find out which of their families they wanted me to send messages to to say that they had been saved.

I found that my leading steward, Kamenzuli, had been killed and my petty officer steward, Micallef, had been injured and badly burned. I was particularly sad about this, for they were the only two of the original Maltese retinue who had volunteered to stay with the ship when the remainder were released on our not going to the Mediterranean.

I had a word with the flotilla engineer officer, Commander Mike Evans. He had been in the engine-room when we turned over. In accordance with my strong orders no one had moved at all until he gave the order to try to get out. By this time the ship was upside down and they had to jump down feet first through the water to the two little circular engine-room hatches. Somehow or other several of them managed to escape by this method, but their experience must have been a great deal worse than ours on the bridge.

When I finished going round the men I went back to the bridge. The attack was still going on. I sat in the captain's chair on the starboard side of the bridge and watched with admiration the way that Aubrey managed to dodge the bombs. Of course these were shallow-dive bombers and not the steep-dive-bombers, and so it was much easier, but even so there were a horrible lot of near misses. I counted over eighty near misses, some of them so close that everybody on the bridge was drenched with the spray. Her guns crew had been augmented by some of the best gunnery ratings from the *Kelly* and the *Kashmir*, which helped to fight off the bombers.

Finally they gave up the attempt and so we steamed on through the night. At dawn we ran out of fuel, but the *Protector* was sent out to meet us and give us some more fuel.

As we entered Alexandria harbour everyone who could still walk crowded out on to the upper decks. There must have been between four and five hundred crowding every inch.

The Mediterranean Fleet, which had only got back shortly before us from the battle, were moored close together in harbour. All the ships' companies cleared lower deck and gave us a heart-warming cheer as we steamed past.

I went ashore in the first boat that was sent for us to report to the Commander-in-Chief. At the landing stage I was met by the cheery, grinning face of our nephew Philip, who had come to meet me. He roared with laughter on seeing me and when I asked him what was up he said, 'You have no idea how funny you look. You look like a nigger minstrel!' I had forgotten how completely smothered we all were in oil fuel. The Commander-in-Chief, Admiral Sir Andrew Cunningham, sent a car to collect me and put me up in his own house and lent me some clothes. I enquired about the famous suitcase which would now be so handy, but it never turned up. Later enquiries showed that the Royal Air Force had been too clever by half. A printed label with my name and the Broadlands address on it was still attached to the suitcase, so, disregarding Admiral Ford's orders to take it to Alexandria, they flew it straight back to England, where it arrived but was not much use. So I had to go, like everybody else, to buy some ready-made clothing.

That evening the surviving officers of the *Kelly* had a dinner party at the club. We had been a very happy mess and now nine were missing and only eight of us were present. And yet the evening was a tremendous success. We reminisced about the happy times of the commission. We talked in turn about each of those who were absent in terms of warm friendship and affection. It was rather as though they were just temporarily away and not gone for good.

The next day came the painful business of saying goodbye to the survivors of the ship's company. Those who were not wounded were being drafted to other ships to carry on with the battle. I made them one of my little speeches, but without any jokes, and when the moment came to shake hands with each of them it was almost more than I could bear. I somehow felt this really was the last of the *Kelly*, for while the ship's company were gathered together her spirit appeared to survive. Yet I couldn't help feeling her spirit would survive because we had all loved the ship so much and were such a happy band of brothers. I have never known a ship with such a tremendously high ship's spirit and I don't suppose I ever will again.

Extract from an account of the sinking of HMS Kelly, *on 23rd May 1941, in the Battle of Crete, given by the captain, Lord Louis Mountbatten, (afterwards Admiral of the Fleet Earl Mountbatten of Burma) to his sister Louise, Queen of Sweden.*

★

THE LAST RALLY OF THE ROYAL MARINES: CRETE, 1941

Eventually reaching the beach at Sfakia too late for the last lift, the battalion was disbanded by Major R. Garrett, Royal Marines, on 31st May, by order of the senior army officer ashore.

Major Garrett, having carried out his instructions, then made it known that he would never allow himself to be taken prisoner, that he intended to find a boat and make his way to Africa. Having made his purpose plain to his famished and exhausted men, he set off in search of a boat, and in the bay found the landing craft abandoned by Lieutenant McDowall RNVR. Swimming off to her he found a wire foul of the port screw and the engines incapacitated. She had, however, some provisions on board and appeared to be seaworthy.

Major Garrett then went in search of an engineer. In the ruins of the bombed village he found one J. Lester, a lance-corporal of the 2/7 Australian Battalion, who had been a mechanic in civil life and was still game for anything. On their way off to the lighter they were joined by another Australian, Lieutenant K. R. Walker, and between them they got life into the engine, and finally warped the lighter inshore. Major Garrett then called for volunteers to join him on this desperate venture. It was the last rally of the Royal Marines in Crete. To his stout-hearted 'Who goes home?' five officers and 134 other ranks responded. They included Royal Marines, Australians, New Zealanders and men from the Commandos landed by the *Abdiel* on 24th and 26th May. They collected all the petrol, water containers and rations they could lay their hands on, and at 9 am on 1st June they cast off; there was a light mist drifting in from seaward and under cover of this they made their way to Gavdopula Island that had harboured the crew of the ML 1030. Here they secured in a cave.

An armed party was landed and returned with the report that they were the only inhabitants of the island. A well was found and all containers filled. The engine-room staff, consisting of four Australian corporals and a Commando sergeant, refitted the engine. The troops were 'exercised in seamanship'. The phrase is taken from

Major Garrett's report. What these exercises comprised is not known but the sentence has a brave ring.

A complete muster was made of all their resources. Then came a good dinner, the first proper meal for three days, followed by a substantial supper, a last drink at the well, and a 'top-up' of every water container. At 9.30 pm, on 1st June, off they went.

Before leaving Sfakia, Major Garrett had somehow contrived to find a map of the eastern Mediterranean in the village. Lieutenant R. R. Macartney, of the 3rd Field Regiment, AIF, had a map of North Africa. With these two aids to navigation they set a course for Tobruk, 180 miles distant, which they knew to be in our hands. They had, of course, no sextant, no knowledge of the compass deviation, no log or chronometer or means of calculating the set of currents. They estimated they had petrol for 140 miles.

They lost two hours during the night of 1st June repairing the steering gear, which broke down. An experiment with diesel fuel in one engine, in an attempt to save petrol, merely resulted in the engine packing up. The other broke down in sympathy shortly afterwards.

Undaunted by the contrariness of the machine, Major Garrett made plain sail, the canvas being furnished somewhat inadequately by the winch cover. This just enabled them to keep the lighter on her course.

The sea rose and seasickness overwhelmed them. The devoted engine-room staff continued, however, to strip down the engine and clear it of dieselite, which enabled them to get under way again until 6 pm on 2nd June, when their petrol was exhausted.

All night they wallowed in a heavy sea under their rag of sail. On 3rd June they were rationed to a sixth of a pint of water, an inch and a half cube of bully-beef and half a ship's biscuit. They burned flares at night, using the diesel oil. Two young marines, A. Harding and A. R. Booth, were inspired to improvise a distilling plant from petrol tins, using the diesel oil as fuel. In two days they produced four and a half gallons of drinking water. Rummaging among the stores, Major Garrett found a tin of petrol which he hoarded for emergencies.

At 7.45 on the morning of 4th June a Blenheim aircraft sighted them and circled them twice. This heartened everybody; they were getting very weak. The engineers busied themselves in changing the port clutch and gear-box with the starboard, which was slipping, and they ran the engine for half an hour in the evening to keep their spirits up.

Next day, unable to sight land, they used up the rest of the petrol, hoping to lift the African coast; but when the engine petered out it was still the same horizon of waves heaving against the lonely sky to the south of them. Marine Harding built a raft of diesel oil-drums, with floorboards as paddles; a raft party volunteered to go to look for Africa and fetch help, but their craft was too unstable and the project had to be abandoned. Next day they rigged a canoe, but it would only take one man and they were too weak for a single-handed task. That too was given up.

They then devoted all their energies to sailing the lighter. They contrived to make four blankets into a jib and six into a mainsail. A marine named Yeo distinguished himself as sailmaker. The lighter refused to answer her helm and yawed despairingly. To wear ship it was necessary for these exhausted men to plunge overboard in small parties and by swimming with all the energy left in them push the bows round on to the proper course again.

They had two colour-sergeants and one sergeant of the Royal Marines on board. The former were 'old-timers', the latter 'Hostilities Only'. Between them they heartened and sustained that clamjamfrey of armed scarecrows, bearded and gaunt and hollow-eyed, crowded together on the sun-grilled plates of a landing craft. The senior, Colour-Sergeant C. A. Dean, was the lighter's sergeant-major, a combination of master-at-arms and purser, issuing the meagre ration of water with stern impartiality.

His fellow, Colour-Sergeant H. C. Colwill, organised the watches on board and constituted himself a sort of sailing master, which involved leading the swimming party into the water every time it was necessary to steady the ship on her course. Sergeant Bowden helped his seniors in these various activities. As a 'Hostilities Only' he was probably not expected to be familiar with the routine of sailing the high seas in a square-nosed lighter that refused to answer her rudder and was propelled by blankets, and kept on her course by swimmers towards a coast they might never reach in time. It must be supposed that he just picked it up as he went along.

On 8th June Private H. J. Wysocky and Driver K. Watson, 155 Battery, 52nd Light AA Brigade, died from exposure and exhaustion, and were buried. At 5.45 pm land was sighted.

At 1.30 am on the 9th they ran on to a sandy beach and lowered the brow. A patrol, under Lieutenant Macartney and Sergeant Bowden, was landed with orders to move south in the hope of striking the Sollum road. Two Maori soldiers, Private Thompson and Gunner Peters, volunteered to land and find water. They found a well a quarter of a mile away within forty-five minutes.

Sergeant Bowden reappeared after some hours. He announced that they were beached seventeen miles west of Sidi Barrani, 100 miles to the eastward of Tobruk. They had made good 230 miles, but must have travelled nearer 250. Sidi Barrani was the headquarters of the 1st AA Regiment, and motor transport had been arranged for the following morning. Sergeant Bowden had found his way back across five miles of desert in the dark without a compass. The colour-sergeants must have agreed that one way and another Sergeant Bowden showed promise.

The following morning, 10th June, Major Garrett marched his force across the desert to where the lorries awaited them.

From *The Mediterranean Fleet: Greece to Tripoli*

*

BISMARCK

The most correct conclusion to draw concerning the *Bismarck*'s destruction is undoubtedly that it was the fruit of co-operative action on the part of numerous sea and air forces, the latter partly naval and partly RAF, all working in close accord for the one common end, and including all those surface vessels, submarines and aircraft which searched and patrolled without finding her. Without a Coastal Command flight, the *Bismarck* would not have been sighted in her Norwegian fjord. Without a Fleet Air Arm flight, her departure thence would not have been discovered. Without cruisers in the Denmark Strait, she would not have been sighted on her way through that passage at a time when shore-based flying was inoperative. Without heavy ships to engage her next morning, she would not have been hit and her course brought round to where the *Victorious'* aircraft could torpedo her, and other forces get at her. Without Coastal Command and Fleet Air Arm aircraft she might not have been resighted after being lost. Without the aircraft from the *Ark Royal* she would not have been decisively slowed up. Without the destroyers, it would have been difficult to keep track of her movements during the night, and her rediscovery the next day might have been too late for the battleships' critically low fuel supplies to allow them to engage her. And without the battleships she would probably not have been sunk, for the *Ark Royal*'s aircraft had torpedoes for only one more strike and the *Bismarck* could probably have withstood the likely extra torpedo hits well enough to have been towed home.

Captain RUSSELL GRENFELL RN

*

A Fleet Air Arm aircraft from Hatston (Orkney) with an experienced observer (Commander G. A. Rotherham RN) reported on 22nd May 1941, that Bismarck *and* Prinz Eugen *were no longer in Bergen. The first ship to sight them was HMS* Suffolk *(Captain R. M. Ellis RN) in the Denmark Strait on the 23rd:*

Suddenly at 7.22 in the evening one of the look-outs sighted the *Bismarck* and the cruiser *Prinz Eugen* emerging from a snow-squall between the *Suffolk* and the ice. There could be no mistaking the vastness of the battleship at the point-blank range of seven miles, though the somewhat inappropriate remark of a midshipman—'*Hood* and *Prince of Wales*, I suppose!'—subsequently became legendary. The enemy ships were moving fast in a south-westerly direction roughly parallel to our own.

This was the culminating moment of all those weary months of training and waiting. 'Action stations' was immediately piped, full speed rung down to the engine-room, and a sharp alteration of course made away into the enveloping mist. Every second was vital. In a flash the first of a long stream of sighting reports was sent out; that stream which set in motion the elaborate chase that followed.

Meanwhile the *Suffolk* had increased speed and located the enemy ships with her radar. We could tell by the tremendous vibration that she was putting all her reserves into the chase. I had never seen the needle touch thirty knots before, and it was difficult to use the ruler on the plotting table. Every moment we expected the *Bismarck* to open fire. At this stage, however, it was more important that we should maintain contact than force an action and be annihilated.

About an hour later HMS *Norfolk*, which had been due to relieve us on patrol, joined us and began to shadow too. So the pursuit continued at high speed throughout the night, moving roughly parallel to the coast of Greenland. I remember losing all sense of time, especially as in that latitude there is no true night but merely a kind of pallid twilight. Bully-beef and hot cocoa were brought round from the galley. I have memories of the hot syrupy liquid spilling and sloshing over the deck. Perhaps that is the reason I can no longer stomach it. Throughout the time we were sending out a succession of messages, reporting the enemy's position, course, and speed.

Instructor Lieutenant-Commander
DAVID PATON RN, *Suffolk*'s plotting officer

★

Suffolk *was joined by HMS* Norfolk *(Captain A. J. L. Phillips RN) flying the flag of Rear-Admiral W. F. Wake-Walker, in command of the 18th Cruiser Squadron. Both ships shadowed the enemy until the arrival of HMS* Prince of Wales *(Captain J. C. Leach RN) and HMS* Hood *(Captain R. Kerr RN) flying the flag of Vice-Admiral L. E. Holland, in command of the Battle Cruiser Squadron, on the 24th:*

After minutes of staring at the blank distance, suddenly—and one could scarcely believe one's eyes—there appeared the topmasts of two ships! Again that phrase was shouted by the first man who could find his voice—'Enemy in sight!' Silently, but as if controlled by one main switch, the director towers of the main and secondary armaments swung in that direction, immediately followed by the great fourteen-inch guns and the 5.25s on the starboard side. The minutes raced by, but time during those unendurable moments seemed to be standing still. There they were, in deep sharp silhouette on the horizon—*Bismarck* and *Prinz Eugen*, steaming in smokeless line ahead, unperturbed and sinister. 'Ye gods!—what a size!' I heard someone mutter. On we raced, keeping the same course. The range was now closing at an alarming speed, and we on the bridge began to look at each other and wonder what the next move was to be. I must say I was rather relieved at this time to see that even old George was looking a trifle—but only a trifle—paler. The two enemy ships, travelling at probably about thirty knots, were now practically crossing our bows, still on the horizon, while we were closing to a range which should be deadly. Had anything gone wrong?

Had the admiral decided to change his plan at the last moment?

Why had we not opened fire?

All those thoughts raced through one's head as the great guns of the *Hood* and *Prince of Wales* followed the enemy steadily as the relative positions changed.

At last it came—a signal flashed from *Hood*—'Open fire!' Almost immediately after there were the great orange flashes and huge clouds of black smoke belching from the for'ard turrets of the *Hood* as she fired her first salvo. This was the great moment everyone had been waiting for. A few more seconds of agonising waiting and then that ding-ding ringing up in the fourteen-inch director tower which told us that our own guns were about to open fire.

Two more moments of unendurable ecstasy, then that pulverising crashing roar, which for a second seems to knock one senseless—we had opened fire! We were blinded by a dense sheet of flame which rose before us, mixed with clouds of black, bitter-smelling smoke. For a second we closed our eyes till it dispersed: then, peering through binoculars we gazed anxiously to see where the first salvo had fallen. At this moment nothing was visible except the serene forms of the enemy ships. There was no change in what we saw; for our own shells were actually still in the air, hurtling towards the enemy, while they had not yet opened fire.

The first salvo from *Hood* fell just astern—one could see the great towering columns of water spurting into the air. Almost simultaneously we saw those brilliant flashes and the same jet-black smoke belching from *Bismarck*, as she, in turn, opened with her first returning salvo. Now followed the most exciting moments that I am likely to experience—those desperate and precious seconds racing past while guns were reloaded and the enemy's first salvo was roaring to meet us. Suddenly one became conscious of that unmistakable noise, which produced a horrid sinking feeling inside one—a noise growing in a gradual crescendo—something like the approach of an underground train, getting louder and louder and filling the air, suddenly to cease as the first great spouts of water rose just astern of *Hood*. I looked over at George—he was thinking the same as I was—just a little too close to be comfortable, wasn't it? The next moment might have taken minutes, may have taken hours; it was impossible to measure time, except that one could remember that heavy concussion as we got off salvo after salvo. I could see that our own falls of shot must have been embarrassing to the enemy, since they were certainly falling in line, but a little towards their stern. Then again that horrible rushing noise, and suddenly an enormous geyser of sea-water rising on our starboard side as a shell from *Bismarck* fell just short. This seemed to hang in the air for a second or two, then fell in a soaking cascade across the bridge. At intervals there was an ear-splitting crack as HE shells from *Prinz Eugen*, exploding practically overhead, rained showers of shrapnel on to the decks and into the sea around. The enemy had certainly got the range taped.

We were racing on, on the same course, and tearing my eyes from the great form of the *Bismarck*, which now appeared in clear detail in my glasses, I ran to the other side of the ship, where, to my horror, I saw a great fire burning on the boat-deck of the *Hood*. They would have a job to put that out. Then, as one looked . . . the incredible happened: there had been that rushing sound which had ominously ceased, and then, as I looked a great spouting explosion issued from the centre of the *Hood*, enormous reaching tongues of pale-red flame shot into the air, while dense clouds of whitish-yellow smoke burst upwards, gigantic pieces of brightly burning debris being hurled hundreds of feet in the air. I just did not believe what I saw—*Hood* had literally been blown to pieces, and just before she was totally enveloped in that ghastly pall of smoke I noticed that she was firing her last salvo. I felt quite sick inside and turned away and looked towards George, where he was standing with his hands limply to his sides, staring like a man in a dream. 'Well, that's the end of her.' 'What's that?' '*Hood*'s gone!' I turned back and looked again, with a weak feeling in my knees—the smoke had cleared and the *Hood* was no more; there was nothing to be seen of her. It was fantastic, one just couldn't grasp it.

I think that almost simultaneously our own gunnery department had registered a direct hit with at least two shells on *Bismarck*, for she altered course away, and one could see smoke issuing from her after-deck.

From this moment everything seems hazy, except that I remember again hearing that great rushing noise, like the approach of a cyclone, and having quite an irrelevant dream about listening to the band in Hyde Park, and then being conscious of a high ringing noise in my head and slowly coming to. I had the sensation that I was dying. It was a strange feeling, and one that made me feel rather sad—no more. There was a lot of water swishing about—I was lying on my side with a great weight on top of me. What on earth had happened? Things did not seem quite right somehow; then, like a wave breaking over me, it all came back. Again the deck below me was shuddering under the vibration of another salvo; there were muffled voices, and shouts of 'Stretcher-bearer!' and 'Clear the way there!' I remember being able to raise enough breath to let out a squeaky, 'Georgie, old boy, can you get me out?' Strong hands lifted the dead men off me; there was a horrible smell of blood, and the uncanny noise that men make when they are dying. Somehow or other I fumbled down those ladders I knew so well—everything feeling quite unfamiliar and dream-like. Below decks I was conscious of water rushing in the passages, the smell of the sick-bay, and the efficient bustle of the ship's doctors as they attended to that sudden, rather unnerving rush of casualties. 'Hallo! What are *you* doing here?' It was the voice of the PMO speaking. I asked him if he knew the *Hood* had gone. 'Open your eyes, old boy.' I did so with difficulty, but I could not see him. I was lying in a bed with my clothes on—sticky and hot, with rough bandages round my face—again a great roar which shook the ship as the fight was carried on—the smell of iodine and ether, the sure touch of a medical attendant when he could spare time to give one another shot of morphia, the familiar voice of the gunnery officer telling the ship's company over the broadcasting system that a hot meal would be served while men remained at action stations—at such and such a time . . . then a deep sleep, with fantastic dreams of horror and obscenity—consciousness again, and I heard someone saying we were going back to Iceland. But I should not see it—what a pity! I believe the Icelandic falcon really is seen there sometimes.

Lieutenant ESMOND KNIGHT RNVR in *Prince of Wales*
The author is now the well-known actor.

*

Destroyers, including HMS Electra *(Commander C. W. May RN), went to pick up* Hood*'s survivors.*

But where were the boats, the rafts, the floats? . . . And the men, *where* were the men? I thought of how we'd last seen *Hood*; and I thought of her impressive company. Like a small army, they'd looked, as they mustered for divisions. Then I thought of my words to Doc . . . 'We'll need everyone we've got to help the poor devils inboard.'

But almost immediately came another hail, and far over to starboard we saw three men—two of them swimming, one on a raft. But on the chilling waters around them was no other sign of life. . . .

Chiefie exclaimed incredulously as we looked again: 'But there *must* be more of them—there can't be only *three* of them! Where the hell are all the others?'

The first man we got inboard, an able seaman, had belonged to the crew of one of *Hood*'s four-inch anti-aircraft guns. Positioned on the boat-deck during the opening of the action, he could tell us very little—the exchange of fire had lasted for eight minutes, he'd been unconscious for three of them.

When the enemy ships were first sighted he and his mates were so keen to get at them that they had almost broken into a cheer, then they'd waited tensely for *Hood*'s opening thunder, which followed a quarter of an hour later. But even as the battle cruiser rolled from the blast of her big fifteen-inch guns, the *Bismarck* too had fired—hitting home and hitting hard, at fifteen miles range and with her very first salvo!

In a flash it seemed to the able seaman that the vast well-ordered world that had been the *Hood* had turned upside down and was falling about his ears. One of the German shells had ripped through the deck beside him, hurling the smooth and spotless surface into a jagged confusion of upturned and twisted steel; deluging him beneath a hail of splinters. He hardly knew what was happening, he was deaf from the noise, and still dazed from the shock wave. Only one thing was clear to him—the *Hood* had taken a mortal blow. Then, as he scrambled to his feet, a cloud of dense black smoke poured suffocatingly from the hole that the hit had made and was followed almost immediately by a sheet of roaring flame. On one side was a furnace, on the other the broad Atlantic. So what to do? He hesitated, then looking upward saw an ammunition locker come hurtling from the sky towards him, and, quite instinctively, he chose the sea.

No, he told us, he hadn't a clue what had happened after he hit the water. In fact, considering the speed at which *Hood* was travelling, and considering the height from which he'd jumped, it was a wonder he hadn't broken his neck. All that he did know—and he couldn't get over the horror of it—was that when he came to the surface and looked round for the ship he found that she had gone. Then he'd had to duck again as *Prince of Wales*, her guns blazing, came charging up from astern. . . .

The second survivor was a signalman, who said that *Bismarck* and *Prinz Eugen* had opened fire together, and had evidently concentrated upon the *Hood*. He couldn't remember much more, except that there had been a terrific explosion behind the funnel and that he'd woken up in the drink.

But Snottie[1] had the strangest adventure. On duty in the spotting top, about 140 feet above the sea, he had actually been washed out of one of its windows as the battle cruiser plunged into her grave. He told us—if I remember rightly—that he had been carrying a cup of cocoa to his betters when the ship received her first blow; then other shells arrived. He had been 'flung about a bit', and didn't know what the hell was happening, save that the compartment was filled mysteriously with water. But he had no time to wonder, for a moment later he was struggling for his life against the suction that followed *Hood*'s death-throes.

I said rather weakly, at the end of his story: 'Well, what an extraordinary escape.'

To which he replied, very simply: 'Yes . . . I *was* rather lucky.'

Lieutenant-Commander T. J. CAIN RN, of HMS *Electra*

[1]Midshipman W. Dundas: he was killed after the war in a car accident.

Prince of Wales *broke off the action, but she had indeed scored two hits, and Admiral Lutjens in* Bismarck *decided to make for St Nazaire. Thereafter the shadows closed in upon* Bismarck. *On the 25th, 825 Squadron Swordfish from* Victorious *scored one torpedo hit; and on the 26th aircraft from* Ark Royal *obtained two hits—one of them vital, aft on her rudder. She was attacked with torpedoes by the 4th Destroyer Flotilla (Captain P. Vian RN in HMS* Cossack) *throughout the night of 26th/27th May. In the morning the Commander-in-Chief Home Fleet, Admiral Sir John Tovey, flying his flag in HMS* King George V, *with HMS* Rodney, *arrived and opened fire on* Bismarck *just before 9 am. By 10.15* Bismarck *was a burning shambles—but still afloat.*

1044 From Commander-in-Chief
ANY SHIPS WITH TORPEDOES ARE TO USE THEM ON BISMARCK.

1045 Commander-in-Chief to Force H:
CANNOT SINK HER WITH GUNS.

Signals from HMS *Dorsetshire* (Captain B. C. S. Martin RN):
GERMAN BATTLESHIP BISMARCK IS SINKING
ENEMY IS SUNK
AM TRYING TO PICK UP SURVIVORS
AM PICKING UP SURVIVORS. TOO ROUGH TO LOWER BOAT. HUNDREDS OF MEN IN WATER.

1107 From *Dorsetshire:*
I TORPEDOED BISMARCK BOTH SIDES BEFORE SHE SANK. SHE HAD CEASED FIRING BUT HER COLOURS WERE STILL FLYING.

From *Make a Signal*

*

At eleven o'clock I had to report to the House of Commons meeting in the Church House, both about the battle in Crete and the drama of the *Bismarck*. 'This morning,' I said, 'shortly after daylight the *Bismarck*, virtually at a standstill, far from help, was attacked by the British pursuing battleships. I do not know what were the results of the bombardment. It appears, however, that the *Bismarck* was not sunk by gun-fire, and she will now be dispatched by torpedo. It is thought that this is now proceeding, and it is also thought that there cannot be any lengthy delay in disposing of this vessel. Great as is our loss in the *Hood*, the *Bismarck* must be regarded as the most powerful, as she is the newest battleship in the world.' I had just sat down when a slip of paper was passed to me which led me to rise again. I asked the indulgence of the House, and said, 'I have just received news that the *Bismarck* is sunk.' They seemed content.

Rt. Hon. WINSTON CHURCHILL

*

In August 1941 Winston Churchill crossed the Atlantic in HMS Prince of Wales *to meet President Roosevelt in USS* Augusta *at Placentia Bay, Newfoundland. On the voyage home from this meeting the Prime Minister was told that there was a huge convoy ahead of* Prince of Wales, *and only just off her course. He insisted on seeing it:*

It was the high spot of the voyage home. In the evening we overtook them. The *Prince of Wales* went straight through the middle of the convoy, our escort taking the outer lanes. The merchantmen were doing eight knots to our twenty-two. So relatively we sped by at fourteen knots. From her signal halliards flew the signal in international code, 'Good luck—Churchill'.

Those seventy-two ships went mad. It was a great moment for everyone both in the convoy and the *Prince of Wales*, but for none more than for the Prime Minister. Quickly every ship was flying the 'V' flag; some tried a dot-dot-dot-dash salute on their sirens. In the nearest ships men could be seen waving, laughing and—we guessed though could not hear—cheering. On the bridge the Prime Minister was waving back to them, as was every man on our own decks, cheering with them, two fingers on his right hand making the famous V-sign.

Soon we were through them and well ahead, when to everyone's surprise we did an eight-point turn, and shortly after another. Mr Churchill wanted an encore. He just could not see enough of those incomparable officers and men of the Merchant Navy, perpetually in the front line of the Battle of the Atlantic.

So, on the flank of the convoy, we dropped astern of it, did a further sixteen-point turn, and then steamed through its ranks once more. If dusk had not been approaching I believe we should have done it again and again.

A. and G. FRANKLIN

CONVOY

This friendly feeling towards the ships of our convoy was quite remarkably strong. As we changed station with our other escorts, steaming ahead or astern, to port or to starboard of the flock, I came to know each one, and there was something sharply individual, even personal, about them all. What was the history, for instance, of that prim little Norwegian spinster over there? Riding high, her propellers churning air as well as sea, she seemed hardly to be moving at all, and her thin tall funnel looked as full of conscious rectitude as a poke-bonnet. What courteous discipline could ever restrain that long low modern monster tanker, just beyond her, to keep an equal speed? No doubt about *his* identity—he was a slightly raffish young Dutch businessman, and the dark-grey paintwork was set off by a glimpse of a buff underbelly just as spats will set off a natty business suit. One could go on inventing a character for them all, for ships are at least as well distinguished as people. What is even that anti-submarine trawler but a new conscript, rather self-conscious in battledress, with a little stern gun cocked up over the shoulder like a new rifle?

When the sun came out and the air was clear and salty there was a most cheerful sense of colour in these assorted ships. War had certainly veiled the genial paintwork of peacetime: there were no longer funnels of every hue—bright vermilion, cornflower blue, yellow with black tops, or funnels with the gay house-flag of their line painted on the sides. But there was always a *sense* of colour in all these ships, even when they were wearing sober Atlantic suits of grey-and-black, and the Red Ensign was agreeably varied, often enough, with the red, white and blue of Holland, the pale-blue cross and blue and white stripes of Greece, or the most elegant flag of Norway—a blue cross on a white cross on a red field.

The names, too, were a constant pleasure, reminding me of the pleasure schoolboys take in 'collecting' names of engines or motor-cars, of the pleasant haphazard list of names of horses on race-cards, or of the jumbled titles of books dumped for salvage—or ship's libraries! There are grand names and odd names, ports and adjectives and emperors and rivers and goddesses and the names of the owners' wives. You might have in your convoy—at a random invention—*Trajan, Elizabeth P. Harris, Hippodrome, Versatility, New South Wales, Portland Cement, Hjalfjiord, Tresillian* and *Fanny Winkworth.*

Ordinary Seaman S. GORLEY PUTT

*

INSTEAD OF TEARS

In Memoriam for Officers and Men
Who went down on HMS Cossack— *'The Navy is Here'*
—and especially for Lieutenant H. William Rose RN

You have no foothold now on solid earth
The sky, the sea, the beating sea of tides
Sway with your multitudinous appeal,
And you escape the earth-bound common rule
Of earth to earth playing an earth-warmed part.
No flowers will spring from any clay you've used,
The dark sea holds what her cold fires have fused.
Earth burial means flowers spring from the heart
But the sea pastures are more strange and cool
Her phosphorescent ripples in life's wheel
Show beauty's iridescent changing sides
Darting from death to sensuous new birth.

In a wild moment all was wrenched in twain
The *Cossack* murdered, with a broken back,
Your strength destroyed by instantaneous speed,
That severed elements, re-crashed and rolled
Like booming thunder over rearing waves.
You, our Bill Rose, sucked this vortex down,
Wearing for ever a rosemary crown.
Are you now laughing in Nerina's caves
Herding sleek porpoises to Neptune's fold?
Or did the impact make your warm heart bleed
Upon the fringes of the seaweed track
To citadels whence you'll not come again.

So swiftly, swiftly, swiftly, all was shed
Disruptive water with its myriad powers
Of transformation swept you into lives
Manifold, cool, remote, concealed, and strange.
The body nurtured by ten myriad lives
Returned their gifts, speeding along their ways
Carrying the torch of life through ocean's maze,
Molecular enravishment that strives
Through all life's facets eagerly to range.
Having received, generous, your body gives
And scatters in its giving like the flowers.
Yet you, Bill Rose, Bill Rose, you are not dead.

From an Elegy by MARIE CARMICHAEL STOPES
(HMS *Cossack* was torpedoed in the Atlantic on 23rd October 1941.)

*

The exchange of somewhat ribald signals between Admirals Somerville and Cunningham was a feature of the war in the Mediterranean. For example, Admiral Somerville was flying his flag as Flag Officer Force H in HMS Nelson, *escorting the Malta convoy 'Halberd' in September, 1941, when* Nelson *was hit by a torpedo:*

From Commander-in-Chief Mediterranean (Cunningham) to Flag Officer, Force H (Somerville):
I HOPE THAT THESE MY CONGRATULATIONS WILL COMPENSATE FOR A SLAP IN THE BELLY WITH A WET FISH.

From Flag Officer Force H to Commander-in-Chief Mediterranean:
THANK YOU. AT MY AGE KICKS BELOW THE BELT HAVE LITTLE SIGNIFICANCE.

And again, when Admiral Somerville, already a KBE, received the KCB:

From Commander-in-Chief Mediterranean to Flag Officer Force H:
FANCY, TWICE A KNIGHT AND AT YOUR AGE.
CONGRATULATIONS.

From *Make a Signal*

*

The cruisers HMS Aurora *(Captain W. G. Agnew RN) and* Penelope *(Captain A. D. Nicholl RN) arrived in Malta on 21st October, 1941, and with the destroyers HMS* Lance *and* Lively *formed a small squadron known as Force K. For some reason Force K always seemed to go to sea on Saturdays. On 8th November they sailed on yet another*

'SATURDAY CLUB RUN'

It started as before—just another 'club run'. A Maryland aircraft had sighted six enemy merchant vessels escorted by four destroyers in a position forty miles east of Cape Spartivento at 1400 that afternoon. We were more hopeful than usual when we started, as we had been promised an aircraft to shadow the enemy and guide us to them: unfortunately, the aircraft's wireless broke down, and we went dashing on into the night without much hope of success. We had, indeed, almost given up hopes of finding them, and were getting very near the time for turning homeward, when, at 0039, we suddenly received a signal from *Aurora* reporting the enemy on a bearing of 030°. Our Bridge Record shows that someone said: 'My God! There they are—bloody great haystacks!' This remark is ascribed to the captain, but he says he has no recollection of saying any such thing.

The methods to be employed in attacking a convoy had often been discussed between the captains of our four ships of Force K: after the first general alarm bearing, Senior Officer K had only to make two more signals during the whole action—one to reduce speed, and one to warn against wasting ammunition. Everyone knew what to do, and it only remained for them to do it. The first thing that was done—an example of brilliant judgement by Captain Agnew—was to 'stalk' the enemy. *Aurora* led round to the northward to silhouette the enemy against the moon. Light conditions were ideal; and our light camouflage (we had spent the previous week painting ship to the accompaniment of the usual growls about 'peacetime' routine) was so effective that we got to within 6,000 yards of the enemy, apparently without having been sighted, before *Aurora* opened fire on the left-hand destroyer astern of the convoy.

We opened fire thirty seconds later on the right-hand destroyer, and continued to shoot her up for four minutes. *Aurora* then led round and passed up the western side of the convoy, and the 'party' started, as the merchant ships were deliberately and in turn engaged by the whole force. The ships seemed to make no effort to escape, and it was all too easy; they burst into flames as soon as we hit them. A large tanker was like a wall of flame, and an ammunition ship gave a superb display of fireworks before she blew up with a tremendous explosion. We could soon see about eight burning ships, and a great pall of smoke where the ammunition ship had been.

One destroyer was a bit of a nuisance firing at us from astern, and she straddled us several times. We engaged her with our starboard four-inch guns, and saw what looked like an enormous Christmas tree of sparks in the position from which she had been firing. Anyway, she gave us no more trouble. We got no chance to use torpedoes, though *Aurora* and *Lance* did so with good effect. *Lively* was missed astern by enemy torpedoes at one time. Two destroyers made off to the north-east, but *Aurora* rightly refused to be drawn off after them. We fired a few salvos at them, and think we obtained some hits. It turned out that this was the end of the engagement.

We steamed round the convoy and passed close to a fiercely burning ship which was obviously loaded with motor-vehicles: someone described her as being 'lousy with charabancs'. A rating on the bridge remarked at 0130 that his twenty-first birthday had been quite exciting so far. The captain sent a signal to S.O. K: 'Congratulations to *Aurora* on her magnificent Borealis.'

Thus ended our first action—a memorable night. The 'bag' was ten supply ships, two destroyers sunk and three damaged. Of course, we were lucky. We were lucky in finding the enemy; we were lucky in that they allowed us to get so close to them, and even then made little attempt to scatter. We in *Penelope* were particularly lucky in having a task that was so successful for our first taste of action. We had, up to this moment, never fired a gun 'in anger' and it was, in fact, the first time the six-inch guns had been fired since practice firing on 29th August. No ship could ask for a more perfect routine for 'working up'.

From *Our Penelope*

No one was killed in Force K and Penelope*'s only casualties were six canaries who died of heart failure when the guns fired. This was regrettable,* *'but', wrote the author (anonymous), 'it is interesting to note that the ship's canaries seemed to toughen up after this, and later on a number of them would sing on deck during the most violent actions'.*

From Vice-Admiral (Malta) (Vice-Admiral W. T. R. Ford) to Force K after this action:

IT IS WITH GREAT REGRET THAT I SEE IN THE ITALIAN BROADCAST THAT ONE OF THE CRUISERS RECEIVED TWO HITS AND A DESTROYER ONE HIT DURING TORPEDO BOMBING. I CAN ONLY THINK THAT IN VIEW OF THE LACK OF DAMAGE I SAW TODAY THE DOCKYARD IS MORE EFFICIENT THAN I THOUGHT OR YOUR CAMOUFLAGE EXCELLENT.

To which Captain Nicholl replied:

THERE WAS AN AIR-WOP FROM TARANTO
WHO SET OUT FOR AN EXPLOIT GALLANTO.
HE SINKA DA CRUISE
AND GET INTO DA NOOZE,
TO MAKE UP FOR DA KICK IN DA PANTO.

Penelope *were very good at limericks. For instance, when General 'Electric Whiskers' Bergonzoli was captured:*

Electrico B. of Benghazi
Tried hard to look tough like a Nazi
At his foes he would glare
Through a jungle of hair,
But they only guffawed and looked blasé.

*

In November 1941 HMS Ark Royal *(Captain L. E. H. Maund RN) took part in Operation 'Perpetual'—to strengthen Malta's air defences by transporting aircraft to within flying distance of the island. On 13th November she and* Argus *had successfully flown off thirty-seven Hurricanes and seven Blenheims to Malta and were returning to Gibraltar when, at 3.41 pm,* Ark *was hit by one of three torpedoes fired by U-81 (Lieutenant-Commander Guggenberger).*

THE LOSS OF *ARK ROYAL*

Captain Maund was on the flight-deck when he felt his ship shudder violently and saw smoke pouring from the bomb-lift doors. As he made for the bridge he thought at first there might have been an internal explosion, as none of the seven screening destroyers had reported a contact. In the very short time it took him to reach the bridge the ship had already listed some ten degrees to starboard, or rather more than the heel of a particularly heavy roll. His first thought was to take the way off the ship (she was steaming at twenty-two knots), so as to avoid spreading the damage unnecessarily, and to send his crew to action stations; but all communications between the bridge and the rest of the ship were severed—no telephone would work, the broadcaster was silent and the engine-toom telegraphs jammed. Action stations were soon ordered by bugle and word of mouth, but some minutes elapsed before a verbal order passed to the machinery control-room reversed the engines and brought the ship to rest.

It was now about a quarter of an hour since the *Ark Royal* had been torpedoed. She had heeled over to starboard until the horizontal wireless masts were almost touching the water, and the list seemed to be increasing. Without any telephones and with much of the ship below decks in semi-darkness, it was impossible immediately to ascertain the full extent of the damage. There were 1,600 men aboard, many of whom would certainly be lost if the *Ark Royal* capsized—as the *Courageous* had done earlier in the war, with the loss of nearly half her crew, and as the *Eagle* was to do a few months later. Captain Maund decided to evacuate all surplus men and ordered the destroyer *Legion* to come alongside.

As soon as the *Legion* had nosed her way into position on the port quarter the evacuation began. Most of the Ark Royals were in the clothes they stood up in, but some had seized particularly treasured possessions. The pockets of a petty officer were bulging with silk stockings—presents for his wife. One of the ship's cats, a large ginger tom, arrived in the arms of a Royal Marine. Paymaster-Commander Steele had two suitcases full of money—£10,000 in each, it was said—and his appearance was greeted with a cheer.

'Schooly' Jenkin strolled up immaculately dressed, a folded raincoat over his arm and carrying a neat attaché case. In half an hour 1,487 officers and men had been transferred, many of them jumping on to a 'bed' of hammocks piled on the destroyers fo'c's'le. At 16.48 the *Legion*, carrying nearly ten times her normal complement, returned to her place in the screen.

When the torpedo struck most of the ship's company were below decks, working in the hangars, or on watch in the machinery spaces and other compartments. Men off duty were in their messes having tea. Everything was as it had been hundreds of times before.

Without any warning the ship was shaken by a violent convulsion. Decks seemed to whip like springboards. Some of the lights went out and in places near the seat of the explosion smoke gushed from the ventilating trunks. After a very short pause the ship began to heel to starboard, so quickly that at first she seemed to be turning right over. The torpedo had exploded abreast of the bridge on the starboard side. Here, many decks down and below the waterline, four men were on watch in the lower steering position, main switchboard room and main telephone exchange. The concussion was extremely violent. The lights went out, oil gushed in, and fumes half choked them as they groped in pitch darkness, up to their waists in a mixture of fuel and water, for the hatch leading to the compartment above. Three men escaped, but Able Seaman E. Mitchell was never seen again.

Lieutenant-Commander (E) A. G. Oliver, the senior engineer, had just come up from below and was still in dungarees. He was beginning to think of having tea, but in the meantime had spread some of his stamp collection on his little desk. He now ran to the machinery control-room, where he joined the engineer officer, Commander (E) H. Dixon. The ship was already listed heavily to starboard and still going over. Clearly some large compartments on the starboard side had been flooded, but with every telephone out of action it was impossible to know which. Dixon sent Oliver to investigate. He found all well in the starboard engine-room and hurried forward to the starboard boiler-room. In this part of the ship, near where the torpedo had struck, all main lighting had failed. Oliver stumbled forward through the half-darkness over the already steeply sloping decks and found the men from the starboard boiler-room mustering near the hatch. A stoker said, 'I think there is a stoker petty officer still down there,' and he and the senior engineer climbed down to investigate. In the light of their torches they saw black water, covered with oily scum, rising rapidly around the tops of the boilers. There was no one there. Hatches and fan intakes were closed, and Oliver moved to the neighbouring compartment—the centre boiler-room. Here water was rising rapidly from below and splashing noisily from above as it poured through the uptake casing vents. Already the level had risen several feet above the floor, and this boiler-room also had to be abandoned. The third or port boiler-room was well away from the explosion on the 'high' side of the listing ship, and was steaming normally.

Things could have been a good deal worse. As Oliver made his way back to the machinery control-room he heard the loudspeakers, which were now in action again, broadcasting orders for evacuation. He continued to organise the closing of the hatches and doors. The captain's order to reduce the list by flooding compartments on the port side was also being carried out; oil fuel was pumped from starboard to port and at 1700 the list had steadied at about seventeen degrees.

The disembarkation of surplus members of the crew had been completed in half an hour in circumstances which made it very difficult to separate those who should go from those who must remain. Open deck-spaces below the flight-deck were small, access to them restricted and the men were crowded together on the sloping, slippery deck. Under these conditions some men needed on board found themselves ordered out of the ship and some remained who had not the technical knowledge for the work in hand. But now, at about five o'clock, a much more serious difficulty arose.

In the port boiler-room Warrant Engineer S. A. Woodriffe, Chief Stoker H. Walley, Mechanician J. Hall and Stoker H. D. Scott were trying to keep steam in the boilers, but the level of water in the gauge-glasses had dropped dangerously low. Water was not coming to them from the main feed-pumps in the engine-room, and an attempt to draw on the auxiliary tanks was unsuccessful. There was nothing for it but to shut off the oil-burners. All machinery, including the dynamos, now stopped; the remaining main lighting went out, and the ventilation fans came to rest. In the weird and unaccustomed silence you could hear men cursing as they stumbled in the semi-darkness. Most serious was the stopping of the pumps which were keeping the flooding at bay elsewhere in the ship.

The bridge, still without any communications with the rest of the ship, had been abandoned and an emergency conning position set up on the flight-deck, with a field telephone to the engine-rooms. The destroyer *Laforey* was now ordered alongside; leads were connected from her dynamos to provide lighting and power, and a hose was run out to pump more feed-water into the *Ark Royal*'s tanks. *Laforey* (Captain R. M. J. Hutton) was handled exceedingly well, but all this took time.

Conditions on board had become most difficult. Counter-flooding and pumping had temporarily arrested the list, but it was difficult to move around over decks smeared with oil and water. The auxiliary lamps, designed to last for only a short time, were becoming dim; often only torchlight was available. Without ventilation, temperature in the engine-rooms rose rapidly—the ladders were almost too hot to hold and no one could remain below for more than a few minutes at a stretch. Without telephones all communications had to be passed by messenger, entailing much delay—it took an active man ten or fifteen minutes to do the round trip between the engine-room and boiler-room. On deck darkness was falling, increasing the possibility of a further submarine attack when the moon rose. Destroyers and motor-launches were patrolling all around, but the great ship, stopped and helpless, was a tempting target.

But gradually, with feed-water pumped over from the *Laforey*, it was possible once again to raise steam.

The tug *Thames* had arrived from Gibraltar, and the seamen on the cable deck, under Lieutenant-Commander Larken, soon had the ship in tow, moving slowly towards safety. At 2200 two dynamos were running; lighting had been partly restored, power was available for the pumps and steam steering engine, and would soon be put on the port shaft as well. Nowhere was the water gaining, and in the starboard engine-room, which had started to flood at one time, it was falling quite steadily. At 2230, when Admiral Somerville, who had left the *Malaya* at Gibraltar and hurried back in a destroyer, arrived on the scene, hopes were high.

For four hours, until shortly after 0200 on 14th November, *Ark*

Royal crept slowly westward, guarded by destroyers and motor-launches. There was a slight current against her, but Gibraltar was now only thirty miles away. At 0200 the tug *St Day* appeared out of the darkness, was secured alongside and joined in the tow.

But all this time, out of sight, the damage was slowly spreading. Under the pressure of water, joints weakened by the shock were giving way. Water was gradually spreading into hitherto undamaged places. The list had not increased, but the *Ark Royal* was lower in the water. As she settled a new and terrible difficulty arose.

For over eight hours Mr Woodriffe and his men had been working in the port boiler-room. The bulkhead separating them from the flooded centre boiler-room was bulging ominously and spurting water from some of its joints, but there was not much water in the bilges and a pump was available. Occasionally it was possible to give some of the men a short spell on a higher deck—somewhere above the waterline and nearer the open air—somewhere where there was a chance of escape if another torpedo struck or the straining bulkhead collapsed.

The flat immediately above the boiler-rooms ran across the ship. In it were the uptakes leading from the boilers to the funnel, crossing the ship from port to starboard before turning upwards well over on the starboard side. The lower (starboard) side of this flat was full of water, the level of which was gradually rising as the *Ark Royal* settled lower. As the water rose, the clear space above it, through which the funnel gases must pass, became less and less. Somewhere about the middle of the night (they had long ago lost all count of time) the senior engineer and Mr Woodriffe noticed that the gap remaining above the encroaching water was only a matter of inches, and still the ship was settling. In the engine-rooms the steam pressure, which had slowly risen to nearly 200 lb per square inch, began to go back—196—195—194—190—185. In the boiler-room the furnaces, their outlet partially choked, were becoming less effective. Extra oil-fuel sprayers were put on to keep up the steam pressure, but suddenly it was noticed that flames were issuing from a crack high up on the boiler casings. This fire was extinguished but another took its place. The temperature in the boiler-room rose rapidly. Fumes filled the stokehold, half blinding and half choking the men, who somehow worked on. Two of the stokers collapsed and with great difficulty were helped up on deck up steep ladders and through the steel air-lock doors, which could only just be moved against the list of the ship. Lieutenant (E) M. A. Clark, one of the youngest officers on board, had only been at sea for a few months, but was proving invaluable. Clark now took over, when Mr Woodriffe, gasping and retching, had to go up into fresher air. Three times great fires blazed up in the boiler-casings. Three times they were extinguished. Parts of the boiler-casings were literally red-hot. The place was an inferno. Oliver, who had for some time been in the boiler-room, now had to admit that the boilers could no longer be steamed. The water-level in the uptake flat was so high that the port boilers had no outlet to the funnel. The men could scarcely see or breathe. Steam pressure was dropping back. They could do no more. He ordered the boiler-room to be evacuated. Shortly afterwards he himself collapsed. Stoker Petty Officer Winscott, just leaving the boiler-room, luckily heard him fall, went back and helped the senior engineer up to safety.

Without steam there were again no lights. Worse still, the pumps had stopped. The *Laforey*, ordered alongside, supplied electric power with very little delay, but it was now impossible to keep the list under control. Steadily it increased: slowly at first, then more rapidly. As the ship heeled over, water made its way into compartment hitherto dry. Aircraft and other bulky objects broke loose and slid into the lee scuppers, their weight heeling the ship still further. Down below you could hear them going. Rumble, rumble, crash—then a few minutes later another—and another.

The pumps were running again, and the *Laforey* was helping with the tow, but the list went on steadily increasing. The navigating officer, Lieutenant-Commander Maclean, reported that he and his party must leave the conning position on the flight-deck, as they had nothing adequate to hold on to. At about this time, when the list was twenty-seven degrees, Commander (E) Dixon reported that there was little more that could be done. It was 0400. Captain Maund gave orders that everyone was to come up from below. Ropes were hung over the side ready for the final evacuation of the 250 men left on board.

Quite rapidly now the list increased. Decks sloped to the angle of a steep roof. Men were standing not on the sills, but half on the sides of the watertight doors. More gear broke loose below, crashing over to starboard. Lockers on the mess-decks spilled their contents, which slid down into the water gradually rising in the lee scuppers —clothes, letters, photographs; carefully wrapped Christmas gifts. Everyone was up from below, including Leading Stoker Thomas and Stoker Mortimer, who had worked cheerfully and courageously throughout. With the ship apparently about to capsize, men were ordered into the tug *St Day*. The wires joining the tug to the ship were tightening rapidly as the cliff-like side of the *Ark Royal* tilted over. Some of them parted before they could be slacked off.

The list was now thirty-five degrees and the *Ark Royal* was gradually raising her weed-coated bilge clear of the sea. It was a long way down to the tug far below, and ropes' ends that had been adequate a few minutes before were now too short. Several men dropped into the water, though all were picked up by MLs following astern. At 0430 Captain Maund, his uniform covered with green weed from the bottom of his ship, slid down into the tug, to be greeted with a cheer. The *Laforey* and the *St Day* shoved off, though the *Thames* continued to tow for about an hour longer, as the *Ark Royal* turned very slowly over. At 0600 the flight-deck was vertical and the island lying flat upon the sea. In the dim light before dawn all the screening destroyers could see was a dark smudge lying in the water.

At 0613 on 14th November came the end. 'She's gone,' said one of the watchers, and no one spoke for a while.

Quietly and gently, without any fuss, the fine old ship slid below the surface on her last journey, 1,000 fathoms down.

When the sun came up there was nothing left except a great patch of oil and some floating debris. The sea was so absolutely calm that rats, which successive first lieutenants had tried vainly to dislodge, could be seen swimming around, each one leaving a little 'v' as it parted the water. A careful check accounted for all but one of her company (Able Seaman Mitchell). An ML nosing amongst the debris found one of the ship's cats clinging to a piece of wood, angry but quite unharmed. Sadly the tugs and escorts turned for home. There was quite a concourse of ships west of Gibraltar, but the sea looked strangely bare. Patrolling flying-boats had gone, and the sky was quite empty.

Rear-Admiral SIR WILLIAM JAMESON KBE CB

The loss of this splendid ship, so often attacked and so repeatedly claimed sunk by the enemy, to only one torpedo hit was, of course, the cause of great disappointment and the subject of searching inquiry. The general conclusions were that the list taken by a damaged ship may appear more dangerous than it is, and that correction of a list by admitting sea-water to compartments on the other side should be undertaken as quickly as possible. But for a fire in the port boiler-room, which was caused by flooding of the funnel uptake resulting from the list on the ship, the *Ark Royal* would probably have been saved.

Captain S. W. ROSKILL DSC RN

*

THE TRAGEDY OF HMAS *SYDNEY*

Just before 4 pm on Wednesday, 19th November 1941, the German raider *Kormoran* was off the Western Australian coast, approximately 150 miles south-west of Carnarvon. There was a gentle SSE wind and slight sea, a medium SW swell. The day was very clear, and visibility extreme. Nightfall was some three hours distant. *Kormoran*, with a complement of 393 officers and men, was steering NNE at eleven knots. At 3.55 pm the look-out reported a sighting fine on the port bow. It was at first thought to be a sail, but was soon identified as a warship. At 4 pm Detmers—*Kormoran*'s captain—sent his crew to action stations, altered course WSW into the sun, and ordered full speed—about fifteen knots, which the temporary breakdown of one engine limited to fourteen knots for about half an hour. The warship, now identified as a 'Perth'-class cruiser, steering southwards and some ten miles distant, altered towards and overhauled on a slightly converging course on *Kormoran*'s starboard quarter. She made the letters NNJ continuously on her searchlight. To this *Kormoran* made no reply. When about seven miles distant, *Sydney* signalled to *Kormoran* by searchlight to hoist her signal letters.

Detmers hoped to avoid action by passing *Kormoran* off as a Dutch vessel. He therefore showed Dutch colours, and hoisted the flag signal PKQI for *Straat Malakka* on the triatic stay between the foremast and the funnel. So placed it was difficult to read, and *Sydney* repeatedly signalled: 'Hoist your signal letters clear'.

Ahlback, *Kormoran*'s yeoman of signals, drew the halliards to the starboard side to make the flags more visible to *Sydney*. In the early stages *Kormoran* ranged *Sydney* on a three-metre rangefinder, but when the cruiser, overhauling on the starboard quarter and showing a narrow silhouette, had approached to within five miles, this was discontinued for reasons of disguise, and a small rangefinder was used.

At 5 pm, to further the deception, *Kormoran* broadcast a 'suspicious ship' message in the name of *Straat Malakka*. This was picked up, faint and in a mutilated form, by the tug *Uco*, and by Geraldton wireless station at 6 pm Western Australian time (eight hours ahead of Greenwich, so that sending and receiving times tally, *Kormoran*'s time being only seven hours ahead). In the mutilated portion read by Geraldton only the time and part of a position were readable, and there was no indication that it was a distress message. When, after ten minutes, there was no repetition, Geraldton broadcast all ships asking if there was anything to report. No reply was received. Apparently no significance was therefore attached to the original message, of which the Naval Board did not learn until the 27th November.

Soon after 5.15 pm *Sydney* had drawn almost abeam of *Kormoran* to starboard, less than a mile distant. Both ships were steering approximately WSW at about fifteen knots. The cruiser was at action stations with all guns and torpedo tubes bearing. Her aircraft was on the catapult with, apparently, the engine running. She signalled, both by flags and light: 'Where bound?' *Kormoran* replied: 'Batavia.' The crucial moment was approaching. *Sydney* made a two-flag hoist, the letters IK which the raider could not interpret. They were in fact (and their being quoted correctly under interrogation is corroboration of the German story) the centre letters of *Straat Malakka*'s secret identification signal, which was unknown to the Germans. They made no reply.

Sydney then made by light the fateful signal: 'Show your secret sign.' It told Detmers that he would have to fight. He answered immediately by dropping all disguise, striking the Dutch colours and hoisting the German, and giving the order to open fire with guns and torpedoes. It was then 5.30 pm.

Simultaneously with opening gun-fire, *Kormoran* fired two torpedoes. Lieutenant Fritz Skeries, the raider's gunnery officer, directed the gunnery from the control position above the bridge in this last engagement. According to his and corroborative evidence, *Kormoran*'s initial single-gun-ranging salvo at just over 1,400 yards was short. A second at 1,750 yards was over. Hits were scored, within about four seconds of opening fire, on *Sydney*'s bridge and director tower, at a range of 1,640 yards. These were followed immediately by a full salvo from *Sydney* which went over and failed to hit. *Kormoran* again scored quickly with two salvos which hit *Sydney* on the bridge and amidships: 'Fifth shot the cruiser's aeroplane (burnt) —motor ran and then shut off—shots fired systematically—lucky shot that aeroplane was hit.'

The range was so short that *Kormoran* used her anti-aircraft machine guns and starboard 3.7-inch guns effectively against *Sydney*'s bridge, torpedo tubes, and anti-aircraft batteries. For a few seconds after initial salvo *Sydney* did not reply. It would seem that her 'A' and 'B' (forward) turrets were put out of action (according to Skeries by *Kormoran*'s third and fourth salvos; but after the raider's fifth or sixth salvo the cruiser's 'X' turret (foremost of the two after turrets) opened fast and accurate fire, hitting *Kormoran* in the funnel and engine-room. 'Y' turret fired only two or three salvos, all of which went over. At about this time one of the raider's two torpedoes struck *Sydney* under 'A' and 'B' turrets. The other passed close ahead of the stricken ship, which was being repeatedly hit by shells.

Her stem low in the water, *Sydney* now turned sharply towards *Kormoran* as though attempting to ram. As she did so, the top of 'B' turret flew overboard, blown up, Skeries said, by the raider's tenth salvo. The cruiser passed under *Kormoran*'s stern, heading to the southward and losing way. *Kormoran*, maintaining her course and speed, was now on fire in the engine-room, where the hits by *Sydney*'s 'X' turret had caused severe damage. Smoke from the fire hid *Sydney* from *Kormoran*'s bridge, but the raider continued to engage with her after guns at a range lengthening to approximately 4,400 yards.

At about 5.45 pm *Sydney* fired four torpedoes. Detmers was then turning to port to bring his broadside to bear and as he did so *Kormoran*'s engines began to fail. The torpedo tracks were sighted but *Kormoran* just cleared them and they passed close astern. Simultaneously the raider's engines broke down completely. *Sydney*, crippled and on fire from the bridge to the after funnel, steamed slowly to the southward. Apparently her turrets were now out of action, but she continued to fire with her secondary armament, and Skeries stated: 'Shots from one-inch guns of cruiser mostly short.' She was constantly hit by gun-fire from the raider, whose forward control position was working with the port broadside in action at 5.50 pm, when the range was about 6,600 yards. Ten minutes later, at a range of 7,700 yards, *Kormoran* fired one torpedo, which missed *Sydney* astern.

The action had then lasted half an hour. Both ships were crippled and on fire, the raider in the engine-room, now untenable; the *Sydney* far more extensively. *Kormoran* fired her last shot at 6.25 pm, at a range of about 11,000 yards. In all she fired 450 rounds from her main armament, and probably some hundreds from her anti-aircraft batteries. She was now in a bad way, her engines wrecked and her engine-room ablaze, and with her full equipment of mines, some 200, still on board. Dusk was creeping from the eastward over a sea that was rising with a freshening breeze. At 6.25 pm Detmers ordered abandon ship, and lowered all boats and life-saving equipment. With the gathering gloom the form of *Sydney* disappeared from view, last seen about ten miles off, heading approximately SSE. Thereafter, until about 10 pm, a distant glare in the darkness betokened her presence. Then occasional flickerings. Before midnight they too had gone.

By 9 pm most of *Kormoran*'s boats and rafts were lowered, filled and cast off. Almost all the officers, and enough ratings to man the guns, remained on board while the final scuttling arrangements were made. At midnight, with smoke increasing heavily on the mining-deck, the scuttling charge was fired, and the last boat cast off. Half an hour later the mines exploded, and *Kormoran* sank rapidly stern first. Of her complement seventy-eight lost their lives, about twenty killed in action on board and the remainder drowned through the capsizing of an overloaded raft. Of *Sydney*'s total complement of forty-two officers and 603 ratings, not one survived.

The story of how *Sydney* was lost would appear to be straightforward. What induced Captain Burnett to place her in the position where her loss in such a way was possible must remain conjecture.

Burnett had the usual peacetime sea experience of an RAN officer on the permanent list both in ships of the RAN and on exchange with the Royal Navy; but by reason of his wartime appointment at Navy Office, and the employment of his first wartime command in routine duties in an area which for nearly twelve months had known no enemy action, he lacked that experience which, gained in a recognised war zone, sharpens suspicion and counsels caution on all chance meetings. Yet, as Deputy Chief of the Naval Staff at Navy Office, he had participated as a behind-the-scenes operator in the early raider attacks on or near the Australia Station. He would have realised that a repetition was always possible. From the fact that he went to action stations and approached *Kormoran* with his main armament and torpedo tubes bearing, it would seem that he had suspicions of her *bona fides*. If it were just a routine measure, other routine measures of greater importance in such a situation were neglected.

Why Burnett did not use his aircraft, did not keep his distance and use his superior speed and armament, did not confirm his suspicions by asking Navy Office by wireless if *Straat Malakka* was in the area, are questions that can never be answered. From *Sydney* herself no word was ever received, and only one small shell-torn float was found as tangible evidence of her loss, in spite of wide and thorough searching. The story of her last action was pieced together through exhaustive interrogation of *Kormoran*'s survivors.

Lieutenant-Commander G. HERMON GILL RANVR

The loss of Sydney, *with all hands, was a particularly cruel blow for the Royal Australian Navy. She had played a distinguished part in the war and, in a model action, sank the Italian cruiser* Bartolomeo Colleoni *off Cape Spada, Crete, on 19th July 1940.*

*

Mediterranean, 4.29 pm, 25th November 1941:

'GOD, SHE'S GOING!'

A great tower of water had leaped up amidships on the *Barham*, so that only her bows and stern were in sight. I yelled to the captain, who was just below in his sea-cabin, and we swung round and increased speed to try to find the attacker by tell-tale torpedo tracks. We were 'outside left' on the screen, and at the time I imagined that a torpedo had been fired from long range. I had only seen one plume of water, so I thought she would be fairly safe, as battleships can stand more than one torpedo, and reach port with ease. I could not watch her much myself, for I was searching for tracks to starboard as we raced towards her. Then to my amazement I heard someone say, 'God, she's going!' I took a quick look at her, and she was listing heavily. Actually the submarine had dived clear under the screen, and surfaced to periscope-depth to find himself within a few hundred yards of the *Barham*. He immediately fired at least three torpedoes, and they had struck almost simultaneously and so close together that only a single splash had gone up from the three of them. His skill and courage were above praise, for the greatest luck and special conditions are needed to dive under a modern screen and torpedo a battleship.

It was an agony not to watch her every second, but I still kept my eyes glued to starboard. Meanwhile the submarine had been blown to the surface by the explosion, and passed down close to the *Valiant* —so close, in fact, that even the pompoms could not depress their guns on to her. The *Valiant* hoisted 'Submarine astern' by signal, but by that time she was in the smoke of *Barham*'s explosion, and few saw her signal.

After three minutes the captain turned in towards her, and I could then watch her. The *Jervis* had turned in also from the centre of the screen and was racing to the spot of her agonies.

Suddenly she started heeling over quickly, but before she had gone far she was rent by a colossal explosion, and completely disappeared in a vast puff of smoke, which reared its head a thousand feet into the air like a cobra about to strike. As we were nearest, Captain (D) told us to rescue survivors. This I had anticipated. Already the crew were cutting the stowage lines of the rescue nets. All rafts were being manhandled to the side. The whaler was manned, and I sent down the young midshipman to cox her. The captain had slowed down, and we were nosing into what looked like a London fog, and smelled worse.

I ran up on to the fo'c's'le to ascertain the best moment to slip the whaler. All was ready. I had a few seconds to think. I looked into the murk ahead. She had gone down in four minutes, blowing up at the last moment before plunging. How many of that crew of eleven hundred could have survived the blinding speed of that misfortune? Mighty few, I thought.

We passed into and through the thick fog, which had by now drifted to leeward, and suddenly it cleared. There around and ahead of us was the living aftermath of that tragedy. Dozens of heads bobbed in the water. Far more than I had ever hoped for. The captain steered up for a large clump, who were clinging to the *Barham*'s mast. I shouted final instructions to the midshipman: 'Go for the far and solitary ones, or those in distress. Leave the rest for us.' Then I lowered the whaler to the waterline, and slipped her.

As soon as we stopped the little bobbing heads moved slowly in towards us and the men were heaved on board. At the same time all our own Carley rafts were slipped, and two men from our own crew dived over the side, and clambered on board each of the rafts to paddle them out to more distant groups.

Great episodes always bring latent greatness to the surface where one never expected it. Young ODs were over the side manning those rafts whom I had hardly noticed before. A stoker saw a raft on our windward side with no paddles to propel it towards us. Grabbing one end of a heaving line, he was over the side and swimming towards it before anyone knew he could swim. Others paid out the line from aft, until he reached his objective and secured his end to the raft. Then the whole outfit was heaved up to the rope rescue ladders. Each one of our own rafts had a grass line paid out behind it, so that as soon as it was full we could heave it back at high speed to the ship. The remainder of those on deck hurled lifebuoys on lines, and heaved dripping individuals back to life. Lines I had specially prepared for rescue in Greece and Crete came out of their safe hiding place, and now added to the speed of the rescue.

Each man, as he came over the side, was black with oil. Bales of waste were brought up from the store to clean them off. The whole upper deck became layered with oil, so that one could hardly stand up. Sick-bay was filling up with oil-smeared wounded. The whaler came alongside with men too badly wounded to climb out. Neil Robertson stretchers were lowered, and the men hoisted out, groaning, by tackles slung over the torpedo davit. A Maltese steward came up grinning, with half his backside blown away.

Winston talked of blood and toil. This was blood and oil. You couldn't tell which. The captain moved the ship slowly up towards the group clinging to the mast. Here the oil was thickest. It was solid, and the men could hardly swim, or hardly cling to the great spar. It touched alongside, just by our foremost net, and men started clambering limply up. There was a Carley raft there, too, from which men were climbing. One seemed to be in charge, and was exhorting each to make his utmost effort. He was too thickly covered with oil to recognise, and he was swimming by the raft and holding on, to give the weaker ones a chance to lie in the raft. When all were up he started too. He put an arm up to a helping hand. It seemed to be nothing but gold stripe, and I realised who it was. I never expected to receive an admiral on board in such circumstances, but this was Vice-Admiral Pridham-Wippell.[1]

Lieutenant-Commander HUGH HODGKINSON DSC RN
First Lieutenant of HMS *Hotspur*

Tactically, the significant point of this attack was the range at which U-331 (Lieutenant-Commander Freiherr von Thiesenhausen) detected Barham *and her escorts by hydrophone.* Barham *was hit at tea-time, but the U-boat had been in sonar contact since the morning and, though she headed for the target at once, her first actual sighting was not until 2.30 pm. Eight hundred and sixty-two of* Barham's *people were lost, including her commanding officer Captain G. C. Cooke RN.*

*

When Japan attacked Pearl Harbour, the gunboat HMS Peterel *(Lieutenant Stephen Polkinghorn RNR) was lying in the Whangpoo River at Shanghai, acting as a floating W/T station for the British Consulate.* Peterel's *total armament was a few Lewis machine-guns but when the Japanese demanded her surrender Polkinghorn replied:*

'GET OFF MY BLOODY SHIP'

The *Peterel* lay off the French Bund, or landing stage. Downstream on the usual British buoys lay the American gunboat *Wake*, doing a

1. Commanding the 1st Battle Squadron, flying his flag in *Barham*.

similar job for the American Consulate as that done by *Peterel* for the British authorities. Further downstream lay the Japanese cruiser guardship *Izumo*, as well as a Japanese destroyer and a gunboat. The Italian gunboat *Lepanto* lay nearly abreast the *Izumo*. Leading Seaman Ted Munn had recently caused considerable confusion amongst the Italians by blowing up a surgical glove, tying the wrist with string and painting Hitler's face on it. It was then launched from the *Peterel*'s motor-sampan so that it drifted down on to the bows of the Italian ship. The Italians, seeing the fingers of the glove sticking out of the water, thought they were a mine's horns and at once started lowering boats and trying to move their ship away. Lieutenant Polkinghorn heard of this and told Munn with no uncertainty that he would have won the VC in European waters but 'out here all you'll get will be an able seaman's rating again if you're not careful'.

In the early hours of 8th December . . . from downstream came the sound of a motor-boat's engines. Soon a launch flying the Japanese flag came in view. In the stern were several senior naval officers and the boat was crammed full of armed marines.

. . Up on the fo'c's'le Able Seaman Tipping handed Able Seaman Mariner the quartermaster's pistol and belt. Mariner watched the Japanese launch come alongside and saw a senior Japanese naval officer come on board. He heard the officer say, 'We want to keep the peace of Shanghai.' 'Come into the wardroom,' Polkinghorn replied. Mariner gripped the pistol more tightly. The rest of the conversation was lost to him.

The next thing both Munn and Mariner heard was Polkinghorn saying, 'Get off my bloody ship.' The Japanese officer, who they later heard was chief of staff to the flag officer in the port, climbed back into the launch after handing a copy of the surrender demand to Polkinghorn. The launch turned and started to move back downstream.

. . . Polkinghorn and Munn watched the Japanese launch move away from the ship. It had not gone more than a few yards when two red Very lights were fired from it.

. . . After the Japanese launch had left the ship the Japanese guns on the French Bund and across the river on the Pootung side had joined with the *Izumo*, a destroyer and a gunboat, in firing on the *Peterel*. As soon as he saw the Very lights go up from the launch

Polkinghorn gave the order for the ship's two manned Lewis-guns to open fire. From 'A' gun-deck Petty Officer Linkhorn poured a steady stream of fire into the Japanese launch. Mariner manned the other gun and joined with Linkhorn, firing on the launch. Several of the men in it were hit. Neither had time to realise they were the first Englishmen to fire on the Japanese in the war.

The fire from the Japanese ships was murderous. One destroyer only 200 yards away was pumping shells into the tiny gunboat. Fortunately one shell in the action parted the forward cable and the ship swung across the river, leaving one side comparatively safe from the enemy's fire.

... Telegraphist Honywill planned to make his way to the signals office to give a hand in destroying the confidential books. But the gangway had been reduced to a shambles. He was unable to get through and there were no lifebelts in sight. As he had trodden on broken glass from the mess-deck fanlights, he stopped for a moment and sat on the mess-deck stool to pick the glass splinters from his bare feet. Several people were on the mess-deck, though he could not distinguish them in the darkness. He heard Lieutenant Polkinghorn shout, 'Bring the launch round to the starboard side.' This side was sheltered from the heavy fire. Then a tremendous explosion shook the mess-deck and the stove disappeared. He saw someone lying face downwards and felt a heavy blow on his right knee. Then he heard Polkinghorn shout 'Abandon ship' several times. He and Polkinghorn appeared to be the only people left alive on board. He tried to walk but found his right leg was broken at the knee. He crawled to a ladder and down the steps to the guardrail. He managed to ease himself over the guardrail and flopped into the water.

DESMOND WETTERN

*

THE DESTRUCTION OF FORCE Z: SOUTH CHINA SEA
10TH DECEMBER 1941

At 11 am a twin-masted single-funnel ship is sighted on the starboard bow. The force goes to investigate her. She carries no flag.

I was looking at her through my telescope when the shock of an explosion made me jump so that I nearly poked my right eye out. It was 11.15 am. The explosion came from the *Prince of Wales*'s port-side secondary armament. She was firing at a single aircraft.

We open fire. There are about six aircraft.

A three-quarter-inch screw falls on my tin hat from the bridge deck above from the shock of explosion of the guns. 'The old tub's falling to bits,' observes the yeoman of signals.

That was the beginning of a superb air attack by the Japanese, whose air force was an unknown quantity.

Officers in the *Prince of Wales* whom I met in their wardroom when she arrived here last week said they expected some unorthodox flying from the Japs. 'The great danger will be the possibility of these chaps flying their whole aircraft into a ship and committing hara-kiri.'

It was nothing like that. It was most orthodox. They even came at us in formation, flying low and close.

Aboard the *Repulse* I found observers as qualified as anyone to estimate Jap flying abilities. They know from first-hand experience what the RAF and the Luftwaffe are like. Their verdict was: 'The Germans have never done anything like this in the North Sea, Atlantic or anywhere else we have been.'

They concentrated on the two capital ships, taking the *Prince of Wales* first and the *Repulse* second. The destroyer screen they left completely alone except for damaged planes forced to fly low over them when they dropped bombs defensively.

At 11.18 the *Prince of Wales* opened a shattering barrage with all her multiple pompoms or 'Chicago Pianos' as they call them. Red and blue flames poured from the eight-gun muzzles of each battery.

I saw glowing tracer shells describe shallow curves as they went soaring skyward surrounding the enemy planes. Our 'Chicago Pianos' opened fire; also our triple-gun four-inch high-angle turrets. The uproar was so tremendous I seemed to feel it.

From the starboard side of the flag-deck I can see two torpedo planes. No, they're bombers. Flying straight at us.

All our guns pour high explosives at them, including shells so delicately fused that they explode if they merely graze cloth fabric.

But they swing away, carrying out a high-powered evasive action without dropping anything at all. I realise now what the purpose of the action was. It was a diversion to occupy all our guns and observers on the air-defence platform at the summit of the mainmast.

There is a heavy explosion and the *Repulse* rocks. Great patches of paint fall from the funnel on to the flag-deck. We all gaze above our heads to see planes which during the action against the low fliers were unnoticed.

They are high-level bombers. Seventeen thousand feet. The first bomb, the one that rocked us a moment ago, scored a direct hit on the catapult-deck through the one hangar on the port side.

I am standing behind a multiple Vickers gun, one which fires 2,000 half-inch bullets per minute. It is at the after end of the flag-deck.

I see a cloud of smoke rising from the place where the first bomb hit. Another comes down bang again from 17,000 feet. It explodes in the sea, making a creamy blue-and-green patch ten feet across. The *Repulse* rocks again. It was three fathoms from the port side. It was a miss, so no one bothers.

Cooling fluid is spurting from one of the barrels of a 'Chicago Piano'. I can see black paint on the funnel-shaped covers at the muzzles of eight barrels actually rising in blisters big as fists.

The boys manning them—there are ten to each—are sweating, saturating their asbestos anti-flash helmets. The whole gun swings this way and that as spotters pick planes to be fired at.

Two planes can be seen coming at us. A spotter sees another at a different angle, but much closer.

He leans forward, his face tight with excitement, urgently pounding the back of the gun swiveller in front of him. He hits that back with his right hand and points with the left a stabbing forefinger at a single sneaker plane. Still blazing two-pounders, the whole gun platform turns in a hail of death at the single plane. It is some 1,000 yards away.

I saw tracers rip into its fuselage dead in the centre. Its fabric opened up like a rapidly spreading sore with red edges. Fire. . . .

It swept to the tail, and in a moment stabiliser and rudder became a framework skeleton. Her nose dipped down and she went waterward.

We cheered like madmen. I felt the larynx tearing in the effort to make myself heard above the hellish uproar of guns.

A plane smacked the sea on its belly and was immediately transformed into a gigantic shapeless mass of fire which shot over the waves fast as a snake's tongue. The *Repulse* had got the first raider.

For the first time since the action began we can hear a sound from the loudspeakers, which are on every deck at every action station. It is the sound of a bugle.

Its first notes are somewhat tortured. The young bugler's lips and throat are obviously dry with excitement. It is that most sinister alarm of all for seamen: 'Fire!'

Smoke from our catapult-deck is thick now. Men in overalls, their faces hidden by a coat of soot, manhandle hoses along decks. Water fountains delicately from a rough patch made in one section by binding it with a white shirt.

It sprays on the Vickers gunners, who, in a momentary lull, lift faces, open mouths and put out tongues to catch the cool-looking jets. They quickly avert faces to spit—the water is salt and it is warm. It is sea-water.

The 'Chicago Pianos' open up again with a suddenness that I am unable to refrain from flinching at, though once they get going with their erratic shell-pumping it is most reassuring.

All aboard have said the safest place in any battleship or cruiser or destroyer is behind a 'Chicago Piano'. I believe them.

Empty brass cordite cases are tumbling out of the gun's scuttle-like exit so fast and so excitedly it reminds me of the forbidden fruit machine in Gibraltar on which I once played. It went amok on one occasion and ejected eight pounds in shillings in a frantic rush.

The cases bounce off the steel 'C' deck, roll and dance down the sloping base into a channel for easy picking up later.

At 11.25 we see an enormous splash on the very edge of the horizon. The splash vanishes and a whitish cloud takes its place.

A damaged enemy plane jettisoning its bombs or another enemy destroyed? A rapid Gallup poll on the flag-deck says: 'Another duck down.' Duck is a word they have rapidly taken from the Aussie Navy. It means enemy plane.

Hopping about the flag-deck from port to starboard, whichever side is being attacked, is the plump figure of a naval photographer named Tubby Abrahams.

He was a Fleet-Street agency pictureman, now in the Navy. But all his pictures are lost. He had to throw them into the sea with his camera. He was saved. So was United States broadcaster Cecil Brown, of Columbia System.

Fire parties are still fighting the hangar outbreak, oblivious of any air attacks so far. Bomb splinters have torn three holes in the starboard side of the funnel on our flag-deck.

Gazing impotently with no more than fountain pen and notebook in my hands while gunners, signallers, surgeons, and rangefinders worked, I found emotional release in shouting rather stupidly, I suppose, at the Japanese.

I discovered depths of obscenity previously unknown, even to me.

One young signaller keeps passing me pieces of information in between running up flags. He has just said: 'A couple of blokes are caught in the lift from galley to servery. They're trying to get them out.'

The yeoman of signals interjected: 'How the bloody hell they got there, God knows.'

There is a short lull. The boys dig inside their overalls and pull out cigarettes. Then the loudspeaker voice: 'Enemy aircraft ahead.' Lighted ends are nipped off cigarettes. The ship's company goes into action again. 'Twelve of them.' The flag-deck boys whistle. Someone counts them aloud: 'One, two, three, four, five, six, seven, eight, nine—yes, nine.' The flag-deck wag, as he levels a signalling lamp at the *Prince of Wales*: 'Any advance on nine? Anybody? No? Well, here they come.'

It is 12.10 pm. They are all concentrating on the *Prince of Wales*. They are after the big ships, all right. A mass of water and smoke rises in a tree-like column from the *Prince of Wales*'s stern. They've got her with a torpedo.

A ragged-edge mass of flame from her 'Chicago Piano' does not stop them, nor the heavy instant flashes from her high-angle secondary armament.

She is listing to port—a bad list. We are about six cables from her.

A snottie, or midshipman, runs past, calls as he goes: '*Prince of Wales*'s steering gear gone.' It doesn't seem possible that those slight-looking planes could do that to her.

The planes leave us, having apparently dropped all their bombs and torpedoes. I don't believe it is over, though. 'Look, look!' shouts someone, 'there's a line in the water right under our bows, growing longer on the starboard side. A torpedo that missed us. Wonder where it'll stop.'

The *Prince of Wales* signals us again, asking if we've been torpedoed. Our Captain Tennant replies: 'Not yet. We've dodged nineteen.'

Six stokers arrive on the flag-deck. They are black with smoke and oil and in need of first aid. They are ushered down to the armoured citadel at the base of the mainmast.

The *Prince of Wales*'s list is increasing. There is a great rattle of empty two-pounder cordite cases as 'Chicago Piano' boys gather up the empties to stow them away and clear for further action.

12.20 pm . . . The end is near, although I didn't know it.

A new wave of planes appears, flying around us in formation and gradually coming nearer. The *Prince of Wales* lies about ten cables astern of our port side. She is helpless.

They are making for her. I don't know how many. They are splitting up our guns as we realise they are after her, knowing she can't dodge their torpedoes. So we fire at them to defend the *Prince of Wales* rather than attend to our own safety.

The only analogy I can think of to give an impression of the *Prince of Wales* in those last moments is of a mortally wounded tiger trying to beat off the *coup de grâce.*

Her outline is hardly distinguishable in smoke and flame from all her guns except the fourteen-inchers. I can see one plane release a torpedo. It drops nose heavy into the sea and churns up a small wake as it drives straight at the *Prince of Wales*. It explodes against her bows.

A couple of seconds later another explodes amidships and another astern. Gazing at her turning over on the port side with her stern going under and with dots of men leaping from her, I am thrown against the bulkhead by a tremendous shock as the *Repulse* takes a torpedo on her port-side astern.

With all others on the flag-deck I am wondering where it came from when the *Repulse* shudders gigantically. Another torpedo.

Now men cheering with more abandon than at a Cup Final. What the heck is this? I wonder. Then see it is another plane down. It hits the sea in flames also. There have been six so far as I know.

My notebook, which I have got before me, is stained with oil and is ink-blurred. It says: 'Third torp.'

The *Repulse* now listing badly to starboard. The loudspeakers speak for the last time: 'Everybody on main-deck.'

We all troop down ladders, most orderly except for one lad who climbs the rail and is about to jump when an officer says: 'Now then—come back—we are all going your way.' The boy came back and joined the line.

It seemed slow going. Like all the others, I suppose I was tempted to leap to the lower deck, but the calmness was catching. When we got to the main-deck the list was so bad our shoed feet could not grip the steel deck. I kicked off mine, and my damp stockinged feet made for sure movement.

Nervously opening my cigarette case, I found I hadn't a match. I offered a cigarette to a man beside me. He said: 'Ta. Want a match?' We both lit up and puffed once or twice. He said: 'We'll be seeing you, mate.' To which I replied: 'Hope so. Cheerio.'

We were all able to walk down the ship's starboard side, she lay so much over to port.

We all formed a line along a big protruding anti-torpedo blister, from where we had to jump some twelve feet into a sea which was black—I discovered it was oil.

I remember jamming my cap on my head, drawing a breath and leaping.

Oh, I forgot—the last entry in my notebook was: 'Sank about 12.20 pm.' I made it before leaving the flag-deck. In the water I glimpsed the *Prince of Wales*'s bows disappearing.

Kicking with all my strength, I with hundreds of others tried to get away from the *Repulse* before she went under, being afraid of getting drawn under in the whirlpool.

I went in the wrong direction, straight into the still-spreading oil patch, which felt almost as thick as velvet. A wave hit me and swung me round so that I saw the last of the *Repulse*.

Her underwater plates were painted a bright, light red. Her bows rose high as the air trapped inside tried to escape from underwater forward regions; and there she hung for a second or two and easily slid out of sight.

I had a tremendous feeling of loneliness, and could see nothing capable of carrying me. I kicked, lying on my back, and felt my eyes burning as the oil crept over me, in mouth, nostrils and hair.

When swamped by the waves I remember seeing the water I spurted from my mouth was black. I came across two men hanging on to a round lifebelt. They were black, and I told them they looked like a couple of Al Jolsons. They said: 'Well, we must be a trio, 'cos you're the same.'

We were joined by another, so we had an Al Jolson quartet on one lifebelt. It was too much for it, and in the struggle to keep it lying flat on the sea we lost it.

We broke up, with the possibility of meeting again, but none of us would know the other, owing to the complete mask of oil.

I kicked, I must confess somewhat panicky, to escape from the oil, but all I achieved was a bumping into a floating paravane. Once again there were four black faces with red eyes gathered together in the sea.

Then we saw a small motor-boat with two men in it. The engine was broken. I tried to organise our individual strengths into a concerted drive to reach the idly floating boat. We tried to push or pull ourselves by hanging on the paravane, kicking our legs, but it was too awkward, and it overturned.

I lost my grip and went under. My underwater struggles happily took me nearer to the boat.

After about two hours in the water, two hours of oil-fuel poisoning, I reached a thin wire rope which hung from the boat's bows.

My fingers were numb, and I was generally weak as the result of the poisoning, but I managed to hold on to the wire by clamping my arms around it. I called to the men aboard to help me climb the four feet to the deck.

They tried with a boat-hook, but finally said: 'You know, we are pretty done in, too. You've got to try to help yourself. We can't do it alone.'

I said I could not hold anything. They put the boat-hook in my shirt collar, but it tore, and finally they said: 'Sorry, pal, we can't lift you. Have you got that wire?'

'Yes,' I said. They let me go, and there I hung. Another man arrived and caught the wire. He was smaller than I was. I am thirteen stone. The men aboard said they would try to get him up. 'He's lighter than you,' they said.

They got him aboard, during which operation I went under again when he put his foot on my shoulder. The mouth of one black face aboard opened and showed black-slimed teeth, red gums and tongue. It said: 'To hell with this.'

He dived through the oil into the sea, popped up beside me with a round lifebelt, which he put over my head, saying: 'Okay. Now let go the wire.'

But I'm sorry to say I couldn't. I couldn't bear to part with it. It had kept me on the surface about fifteen minutes.

They separated us, however, and the next thing I was draped through the lifebelt like a dummy being hauled aboard at a rope's end, which they could grip as it was not oily or slimy.

Another oil casualty was dragged aboard, and later thirty of us were lifted aboard a destroyer. We were stripped, bathed and left naked on the fo'c's'le benches and tables to sweat the oil out of the pores in the great heat.

Admiral Sir Tom Phillips was last seen close beside Captain Leach. They were in the armoured bridge, and were seen slipping as the *Prince of Wales* heeled over, and the bridge got to water-level.

So it is probable that Britain loses yet another brilliant naval officer, because of the time-honoured tradition that captains must be the last to leave their ships.

Captain William Tennant, of *Repulse*, and his commander leaped at the last minute into the sea together, with a senior petty officer, both officers being dressed in long white trousers and tunics. Tennant's head hit a piece of floating wood, but he managed to keep swimming till rescued.

A remarkable feature of the Japanese attack is that their bombers did not have any fighter escort. Once the *Prince of Wales* and the *Repulse* sank, the planes left without bothering the destroyers.

O'DOWD GALLAGHER of the *Daily Express* in *Repulse:*
From *Daily Express*, 12th December 1941

*

I was opening my boxes on the 10th when the telephone at my

bedside rang. It was the First Sea Lord. His voice sounded odd. He gave a sort of cough and gulp, and at first I could not hear quite clearly. 'Prime Minister, I have to report to you that the *Prince of Wales* and the *Repulse* have both been sunk by the Japanese—we think by aircraft. Tom Phillips is drowned.' 'Are you sure it's true?' 'There is no doubt at all.' So I put the telephone down. I was thankful to be alone. In all the war I never received a more direct shock.

Rt Hon WINSTON CHURCHILL

It was some time—possibly some years—before the Navy appreciated the true meaning and full magnitude of this disaster. It was not just the loss of two splendid capital ships—though this was grave enough in the Far East in 1941. Nor was it just the final eclipse of the battleship era—which indeed it was. More important still, it was the first time for hundreds of years that the Royal Navy lost its supremacy in any theatre of a war at sea and failed eventually to regain it; after the loss of Prince of Wales *and* Repulse *the Royal Navy became, and has remained ever since, very much the junior boy in the Far East. It could be said that the mantle of the RN began to pass to the USN from 1.20 pm on the afternoon of 10th December 1941.*

After Admiral Phillip's death, Admiral Sir Geoffrey Layton, Commander-in-Chief China Station, took over as Commander-in-Chief of what was left of the Eastern Fleet and was responsible for one of the most misunderstood signals of the war:

WITH YOUR HEADS HELD HIGH AND YOUR HEARTS BEATING PROUDLY, I LEAVE THE DEFENCE OF SINGAPORE IN YOUR STRONG AND CAPABLE HANDS. I AM OFF TO COLOMBO TO COLLECT A NEW FLEET.

Undoubtedly the Admiral meant his signal to be encouraging and his move to Colombo was certainly in the best tactical interest, but the phrasing of the last sentence could only have one interpretation on the lower deck: 'Up ladder, Jack—I'm inboard!'

1942

DOCKYARD: JANUARY 1942

Red glow the braziers and light
Luminous men who stamp dead feet
And beat their frozen hands for warmth.
Sharp ring the hammers, and sound
Renaissance to the ships that come again
To port, their torn and twisted decks—
Spattered with blood.

Pale grows the day, and wintry sun
Warms not the wind which tosses stark twigs
In spiritless dance against grey skies.
But somewhere there the dandy thrush
Rides his slight bough and scatters
His gay song upon the unpromising day—
Touching it with warmth.

Oh! homely, dirty dockyard—
Your ringing hammer's aching din, and lonely singing bird

Sing welcome on our coming safely in
And sound us curious fanfare, when
We sail again the cold, unwarming wave.
In lonely hours we dwell in thought again
On your remembered sounds.

Able Seaman FRED SMEWIN

*

As the war progressed, the Navy came to rely more and more upon the marvellous contribution of the WRNS. Their strength increased from nil in June 1939 to 72,000 by June 1945. By the end of the war, there were few facets of the Service which the Wrens had not stamped with their own individual flavour. They brought a touch of colour and an element of intuitive feminine logic into an otherwise austere scene. For instance, no one who served in the Navy is likely to forget

THE HAT

At the beginning of 1942 the Navy was shaken to the depths of its being by a change in the Wren hat. Whatever may be the popular idea that men do not notice women's clothes, my experience is all to the contrary. At a much later date, when the fighting was over and important matters concerning demobilisation were before the House of Commons, I remember that the one thing which really roused the gentlemen who govern us to enthusiasm was the announcement that the WAAF were to be allowed to wear silk stockings.

The first Wren hat, rudely referred to by senior naval officers as the 'pudding basin', was a modernised version of the original 1918 hat. It was actually a copy of a Bond Street yachting hat, and I still think that most of its unpopularity was due to the shocking material supplied for the early hats. We were told that if we insisted on gabardine we would have to go short for raincoats, which were obviously even more essential. With later experience we would have known that the impossible can always be achieved if one is determined enough, but as it was we allowed ourselves to be fobbed off with unsuitable material which was the doom of the first hat.

Perhaps it all worked out for the best, because the sailor cap became such a rage and such a hallmark of the modern Wren. It was the First Lord of the Admiralty, Mr A. V. Alexander, who (backed by the Admirals) insisted on a change being made. I have heard him asking Wrens at inspections if they liked their hat and being acutely disappointed if they said they did.

Both the King and Queen evinced the greatest interest and I was summoned to the Palace twice, once to see the King and Queen together and once the Queen alone. The Queen made no secret of the fact that she had tried on the cap herself and that this had been greeted by 'the children' in a manner representative of the best family tradition.

Even Wren ratings were afraid that they were going to appear as Mr Cochran's young ladies. However, the cap, when adopted, was an immediate success; it became the latest civilian fashion and filled the shops in a variety of colours and materials so that the best a senior WRNS officer could do if she wanted to cut a dash in plain clothes was to appear in a glorified Wren rating's cap.

When I went for my CBE early in 1942 the first thing the King said to me was, 'How's the hat?'

I was able to reply, 'All's well, sire.'

Dame VERA LAUGHTON MATHEWS DBE,
Director WRNS

In winter 1940 when Wrens were buying up all available serge to make trousers, one Commander-in-Chief made the following signal:
WRENS CLOTHING IS TO BE HELD UP UNTIL THE NEEDS OF SEAGOING PERSONNEL HAVE BEEN SATISFIED.

From *Make a Signal*

*

Vice-Admiral Ciliax has succeeded where the Duke of Medina Sidonia failed: with trifling losses he has sailed a hostile fleet from an Atlantic harbour up the English Channel, and through the Straits of Dover to safe anchorage in a North Sea port. Nothing more mortifying to the pride of sea-power has happened in home waters since the seventeenth century.

From *The Times*

The news that Scharnhorst, Gneisenau *and* Prinz Eugen *had escaped from Brest back to Germany through the Straits of Dover on 12th February 1942, sent an electric tremor of indignation and outrage through the country. It was the first time since 1690, when the French admiral Tourville defeated an Anglo-Dutch force off the Isle of Wight, that major enemy warships had approached so close to the English coast. In the Commons the episode was called 'The war's greatest blunder' and the Prime Minister set up a board of inquiry under Mr Justice Bucknill.*

However, if Scharnhorst *and* Gneisenau *escaped, it was not from want of trying to stop them. But the attempts were disjointed and not properly co-ordinated. The bravest, and probably the most hopeless of all, was*

THE GALLANT SORTIE OF 825 SQUADRON

Three thousand yards to go.

The light flak slackened as more fighters closed in around the leading flight. Esmonde began weaving again to shake the aim of fighters attacking on his tail. A new menace struck Brian Rose, FW 190s, fast and more manœuvrable than the Messerschmitts, and armed with cannon, concentrated their waves of attacks on his Swordfish.

His guns stopped their clamour and Edgar Lee glanced round to see Johnson slumped over the machine-guns. He stood up, turned and reached back, trying to lift the gunner's body clear of the guns. This proved impossible, but a sudden idea made him call into the intercom:

'I'll keep watch astern, Brian, and let you know when the bastards are coming.'

In the middle of a suicidal battle, he stood upright staring into the noses of attacking FW 190s; and at his urgent shouts of 'Now, Brian, now . . .' the pilot swerved violently towards either beam attackers, causing them to climb on their tails to avoid collisions, while the stern attacker would invariably overshoot.

In this manner, and in a way which repudiates gallantry as an apt description, the young sub-lieutenant from Ipswich stood half in and half out of his cockpit to gaze at the enemy guns, forcing himself to guess the moment they would fire so that he could shout warnings to his pilot.

He could see in the third Swordfish of the sub-flight, behind and slightly below, Samples and Bunce brandishing their arms and shouting insults at the enemy, although their words were lost in the din.

Facing astern, he missed another incredible act of courage by Esmonde's gunner, Clinton. But Flight-Lieutenant Michael Crombie, flying in a Spitfire overhead, nearly collided with an enemy fighter as he gazed down at the leading Swordfish, fascinated at the sight of the gunner out of his rear cockpit and sitting astraddle the body, beating with gloved hands at tiny flames licking from the fabric. It is likely that the fire was caused by tracer bullets passing through the fuselage and threatened either to engulf the gunner's cockpit or had blinded him when he most wanted to fire his guns. He had climbed out, extinguished the fire with his hands and then returned to his guns.

Esmonde was over the inner screen now, and wide holes in his fuselage showed where heavy shells had hit and passed on through. It was the turn of the main eleven-inch armament of the battle cruisers to come into action. Belching smoke and flame, they laid down a thick carpet barrage ahead of him, sending up a wall of water which crashed down on the limping Swordfish. No attempt was made to hit him. At almost nought feet even a slight fall of water would send him down into the sea. The next broadside hit the water fifty feet in front of Brian Rose, and the aircraft waggled wildly as the plumes of water cascaded down into the cockpits drenching the engine.

Edgar Lee turned on wobbly, nerveless legs to identify the targets just as the rear of Rose's cockpit blew to pieces in front of him. A cannon-shell had whipped through the aircraft, passed between his own body and the fuselage and exploded against the thin steel plating on the pilot's backrest. The full force of shrapnel and splinters plunged deep into Rose's back. Lee heard the pilot groan; the aircraft's nose dipped dangerously. He leaned forward, shouting hoarse urgent warnings to pull up.

The pilot's hunched body moved and the Swordfish came under control again. Breathing heavily with exertion, Lee looked ahead again, and to his astonishment they had cleared the inner screen. Over the engine cowling loomed the massive targets.

In front, close enough for Lee to see the crew, was Esmonde's Swordfish, and in that instant its lower port wing vanished, shot clean away by a shell designed to make a water-splash, but which ricocheted instead and hit W-5984. Lee saw the nose point down towards the water and the jerky movements in the front cockpit as Esmonde fought to bring the plane under control. Gradually the nose came up again and steadied.

It seemed to Lee that his leader was heading for the *Scharnhorst*, so he called out to Rose to alter course slightly to bring *Gneisenau* directly ahead. As they moved slowly across, a burst of tracer bullets whined past and tore into Esmonde's cockpit.

Fifteen hundred yards to go.

The flak barrage fell off again as more Luftwaffe fighters drove down on the Swordfish, which, miraculously, were not only still flying, but looked as if they might succeed in their attack.

Desperately wounded in the head and back, Esmonde held his course for *Scharnhorst*. In the cockpits behind him slumped the figures of Williams and the brave Clinton, both killed. With no defences, his guns silent, he had crossed two screens and dodged milling flights of enemy fighters.

The cost of duty was being paid; life was quickly draining from his body when he took a last look through a film of blood covering his eyes, pulled the aircraft's nose up into the wind for the last time and released the torpedo.

A dozen fighters fell upon his mortally crippled Swordfish, pumping bullets into his already lifeless body. Still standing in his cockpit, Lee watched his leader crash into the sea while the torpedo ran towards the target.

The entire scene flashed across his mind in seconds, then he was absorbed by the urgent need to keep shouting at Rose to prevent the pilot lapsing into unconsciousness. Somehow Rose kept the swimming blessedness of oblivion at bay and with nearly sightless eyes automatically obeyed his observer's instructions.

'Keep the nose up, Brian. For God's sake keep it up. Now a little to starboard. Christ, we've been hit!'

A heavy thump in the nose startled Rose from his lethargy and put strength back into his arms as he hauled painfully at the controls. Leaning over his shoulder, Lee shouted:

'Look, the fuel gauge. It's falling down.'

Rose nodded and Lee leant out over the side. The fuselage was streaming with petrol. A shell had exploded in the main tank. He touched Rose's head and gestured to the gauge and then over the side. The pilot's head jerked in acknowledgement and his fingers flipped over the switch to the emergency tank holding a reserve of fifteen gallons. The engine coughed, faltered and spluttered to life again; the Swordfish skimmed the water as it caught speed and pointed at *Gneisenau*.

A thousand yards to go.

'Now, Brian. Fire the torpedo!'

Lee's urgent scream snapped the pilot alive, and with obvious effort he grasped the release lever, pulling it down. The Swordfish leapt upwards with the loss of weight. Lee glanced down to see the torpedo bounce on the water and then run towards the target. His eyes flickered ahead, automatically registering that they had fired not at *Gneisenau* but at *Prinz Eugen*.

A feeble voice reached Lee through the intercom:

'I think we might try making it to the outer screen. You shout directions.'

Lee looked down at Rose's head, and just the faintest gleam of hope sparked suddenly in his eyes. The incidental thought crossed his mind that Esmonde's torpedo must have missed. Certainly by now theirs should have hit. Another miss. He could see the white faces of the German gunners behind the sparking muzzles of their guns as the seemingly huge ship altered course towards the aircraft to evade the torpedo.

'Up, Brian. Up fast. We're going into him.'

The nose jumped upwards and the Swordfish passed over the German cruiser—close. Sweat poured down Lee's face, drenching his eyes. They were in the middle of the battle formation now and it was on him that their chances rested for getting out.

The enemy fighters were leaving them alone; they were torpedoless and presented no further threat to the ships. To starboard Lee saw Kingsmill's Swordfish limping over the destroyer screen, taking tremendous punishment from the flak. Once inside, fighters pounced again.

The two top cylinders of the single engine were shot away, the engine itself burst into flames and the port wing caught fire. All three of the crew were severely wounded, but Kingsmill was fighting with what strength he had left to keep the Swordfish under control. At 2,000 yards he released his torpedo at *Prinz Eugen* and turned away, heading down towards the stern of the battle fleet.

In his overwrought condition Lee felt the joy of seeing at least one of his squadron retire. Kingsmill's engine went dead as he reached the wake of the last E-boat and the aircraft flopped, rather than crashed, into the sea. Each of the crew painfully clambered from their cockpits, and fell exhausted into the water. Their dinghy had been destroyed in the burning wing.

The E-boat continued on its course, but an MTB leaving the scene saw the aircraft land and raced over to rescue the survivors.

Meanwhile, Lieutenant Saunders in MTB 44, had seen the plight of the Swordfish piloted by Brian Rose. It came erratically out over the inner screen with only ineffectual flak half-heartedly put up to stop it. Rose had summoned his waning strength again for the next emergency.

'I'll have to try and ditch her in a minute,' he called out in his strongest voice since the attack.

Lee nodded and settled down in his cockpit in readiness for the bump. The Swordfish crossed the outer screen, coughed; Rose held the controls firmly. The aircraft lost height slowly and belly-landed perfectly in the rising sea.

Above them Thompson's sub-flight were weaving their way into the attack, still in Vic formation. The flak eased off while the fighters leapt in again. Three FW 190s, with undercarriages lowered and flaps fully down to reduce speed, were on the tails of the Vic, spewing cannon-fire into each Swordfish in turn.

They crossed the outer screen, approached the inner, losing height. Struggling to fly, bodies in ribbons, wings like skeletons with the struts showing bare and crews who must not only be wounded but dead or dying, they crossed the line of destroyers and met the smoke spumes of water thrown up by the heavy ships' 'water-spout' barrage.

For a brief instant the Luftwaffe drew off, and quite alone but still maintaining a steady course the three Swordfish vanished into the spray of the 'water-spout'. What happened behind the wall of that dreadful barrage remains a mystery. It is officially presumed that they dropped their torpedoes before the end. In this event it must also be assumed that they came out from that horrible cascade of cordite and water with the mask of death already set on their faces as they followed Eugene Esmonde into the Narrow Sea.

Neither the three Swordfish nor the nine youngsters who manned them were ever seen again.

Lieutenant TERENCE ROBERTSON RNR

No torpedo hits were scored on any German ship. There were five survivors from the eighteen members of the Swordfish aircrews. Lieutenant-Commander Eugene Esmonde DSO RN, Commanding Officer of 825 Squadron, was awarded a posthumous Victoria Cross. His body was recovered from the Medway on 29th April.

From Admiral Ramsay to Admiralty:

IN MY OPINION THE GALLANT SORTIE OF THESE SIX SWORDFISH CONSTITUTES ONE OF THE FINEST EXHIBITIONS OF SELF-SACRIFICE AND DEVOTION TO DUTY THAT THE WAR HAS YET WITNESSED.

★

THE BATTLE OF THE ATLANTIC

"A WAR OF GROPING AND DROWNING, OF AMBUSCADE AND STRATAGEM, OF SCIENCE AND SEAMANSHIP."

The only thing that ever really frightened me during the war was the U-boat peril.

Rt Hon. WINSTON CHURCHILL

*

CORVETTE

Dully she shudders at the solid water
A pause, and spray stings angrily over.
She plunges, and the noisy foam leaps widely
Marbling the moon-grey sea. Loud in the shrouds
Untrammelled winds roar songs of liberty.
Free as the petrels hovering astern
Her long lithe body answers to the swell.

Pardon if all the cleanness and the beauty
Brave rhythm and the immemorial sea
Ensnare us sometimes with their siren song,
Forgetful of our murderous intentions.
Through our uneasy peacetime carnival
Cold sweat of death rained on us like a dew;
Even this grey machinery of murder
Holds beauty and the promise of a future.

Sub-Lieutenant NORMAN HAMPSON RNVR, HMS *Carnation*

*

THE DEAD HELMSMAN

For *Compass Rose* there were special times which stuck in the memory, like insects of some unusually disgusting shape or colour, transfixed for ever in a dirty web no cleansing element could reach.

There was the time of the Dead Helmsman (all these occasions had distinctive labels, given them either when they happened, or on later recollection. It simplified the pleasure of reminiscence.) This particular incident had a touch of operatic fantasy about it which prompted Morell to say, at the end: 'I think we must have strayed into the Flying Dutchman country': it was a cold-blooded dismissal, but that was the way that all their thoughts and feelings were moving now.

The ship's life-boat was first seen by Baker during the forenoon watch: it was sailing boldly through the convoy, giving way to no man, and pursued by a formidable chorus of sirens as, one after another, the ships had to alter course to avoid collision, The captain. summoned to the bridge, stared at it through his glasses: he could see that it must have been adrift for many days—the hull was blistered, and the sail, tattered and discoloured, had been strained out of shape and spilled half the wind. But in the stern the single figure of the helmsman hunched over the tiller, held his course confidently: according to the strict rule of the road he had, as a sailing-ship, the right of way, though it took a brave man to put the matter to the test without, at least, paying some attention to the result.

It seemed that he was steering for *Compass Rose*, which was a sensible thing to do, even if it did give several ships' captains heart failure in the process: the escorts were better equipped for dealing with survivors, and he probably realised it. Ericson stopped his ship, and waited for the small boat to approach: it held its course steadily, and then, at the last moment, veered with a gust of wind and passed close under *Compass Rose*'s stern. A seaman standing on the depth-charge rails threw a heaving-line, and they all shouted: the man, so far from making any effort to reach them, did not even look up, and the boat sailed past and began to draw away.

'He must be deaf,' said Baker, in a puzzled voice. 'But he can't be blind as well. . . .'

'He's the deafest man you'll ever meet,' said Ericson, suddenly grim. He put *Compass Rose* to 'slow ahead' again, and brought her round on the same course as the boat was taking. Slowly they overhauled it, stealing the wind so that presently it came to a stop: someone in the waist of the ship threw a grappling-hook across, and the boat was drawn alongside.

The man still sat there patiently, seeming unaware of them.

The boat rocked gently as Leading Seaman Phillips jumped down into it. He smiled at the helmsman: 'Now then, chum!' he called out encouragingly—and then, puzzled by some curious air of vacancy in the face opposite, he bent closer, and put out his hand. When he straightened up again he was grey with shock and disgust.

He looked up at Lockhart, waiting above him in the waist of the ship.

'Sir,' he began. Then he flung himself across and vomited over the side of the boat.

It was as Ericson had guessed. The man must have been dead for many days: the bare feet splayed on the floorboards were paper-thin, the hand gripping the tiller was not much more than a claw. The eyes that had seemed to stare so boldly ahead were empty sockets—some sea-bird's plunder: the face was burnt black by a hundred suns, pinched and shrivelled by a hundred bitter nights.

The boat had no compass, and no chart: the water-barrel was empty, and yawning at the seams. It was impossible to guess how long he had been sailing on that senseless voyage alone, hopeful in death as in life, but steering directly away from the land, which was already a thousand miles astern.

Lieutenant-Commander NICHOLAS MONSARRAT RNVR

*

ACTION STATIONS

'Action stations'. Tin hats and apprehension;
Rush to guns and hoses, engine room
And wireless office. Air of tension.
Eyes uplifted and some seawards gazing.
Ears are straining for a distant 'boom',
Or roar of engines. Lips are phrasing
Prayers, maybe, or curse upon the Hun.
Friendly aircraft in the distance loom
And are gone. Minutes pass . . . 'Carry On'.

Midshipman JOHN WEDGE RNVR

*

THE BURNT MAN

There was a time, a personal time for Lockhart, which he knew as the time of the Burnt Man.

Ordinarily, he did not concern himself a great deal with looking after survivors: Crowther, the sick-berth attendant, had proved himself sensible and competent, and unless there were more cases than one man could cope with, Lockhart left him to get on with his work alone. But now and again, as the bad year progressed, there was an overflow of injured or exhausted men who needed immediate attention; and it was on one of these occasions, when the night had yielded nearly forty survivors from two ships, that Lockhart found himself back again at his old job of ship's doctor.

The small, two-berth sick-bay was already filled: the work to be done was, as in the old days, waiting for him in the fo'c's'le. As he stepped into the crowded, badly lit space, he no longer felt the primitive revulsion of two years ago, when all this was new and harassing; but there was nothing changed in the dismal picture, nothing was any the less crude or moving or repellent. There were the same rows of survivors—wet through, dirt-streaked, shivering: the same reek of oil and sea-water; the same relief on one face, the same remembered terror on another. There were the same people drinking tea or retching their stomachs up or telling their story to anyone who would listen. Crowther had marshalled the men needing attention in one corner, and here again the picture was the same: wounded men, exhausted men, men in pain afraid to die, men in a worse agony hoping not to live.

Crowther was bending over one of these last, a seaman whose filthy overalls had been cut away to reveal a splintered knee-cap: as soon as he looked the rest of the casualties over, Lockhart knew at once which one of them had the first priority.

He picked his way across the fo'c's'le and stood over the man, who was being gently held by two of his shipmates. It seemed incredible that he was still conscious, still able to advertise his agony: by rights he should have been dead—not moaning, not trying to pluck something from his breast. . . . He had sustained deep and cruel first-degree burns, from his throat to his waist: the whole raw surface had been flayed and roasted, as if he had been caught too long on a spit that had stopped turning; he now gave out, appropriately, a kitchen smell indescribably horrible. What the first touch of salt-water on his body must have felt like, passed imagination.

'He got copped by a flash-back from the boiler,' said one of the men holding him. 'Burning oil. Can you fix him?'

Fix him, thought Lockhart: I wish I could fix him in his coffin right now. . . . He forced himself to bend down and draw close to this sickening object: above the scored and shrivelled flesh the man's face bereft of eyelashes, eyebrows, and the front portion of his scalp, looked expressionless and foolish. But there was no lack of expression in his eyes, which were liquid with pain and surprise. If the man could have bent his head and looked at his own chest, thought Lockhart, he would give up worrying and ask for a revolver straight away. . . . He turned and called across to Crowther:

'What have you got for burns?'

Crowther rummaged in his first-aid satchel. 'This, sir,' he said, and passed something across. A dozen willing hands relayed it to Lockhart, as if it were the elixir of life itself. It was in fact a small tube of ointment, about the size of a toothpaste tube. On the label was the picture of a smiling child and the inscription: 'For the Relief of Burns. Use, Sparingly.'

Use sparingly, thought Lockhart: if I used it as if it were platinum dust, I'd still need about two tons of it. He held the small tube in his hand and looked down again at the survivor. One of the men holding him said: 'Here's the doctor. He'll fix you up right away,' and the fringeless eyes came slowly round and settled on Lockhart's face as if he were the ministering Christ himself.

Lockhart took a swab of cotton wool, put some of the ointment on it, swallowed a deep revulsion, and started to stroke, very gently, the area of the burnt chest. Just before he began he said: 'It's a soothing ointment.'

I suppose it's natural that he should scream, thought Lockhart presently, shutting his ears: all the old-fashioned pictures showed a man screaming as soon as the barber-surgeon started to operate, while his friends plied the patient with rum or knocked him out with a mallet. . . . The trouble was the man was still so horrifyingly alive; he pulled and wrenched at the two men holding him, while

Lockhart, stroking and swabbing with a mother's tenderness, removed layer after layer of his flesh. For the other trouble was that, however gently he was touched, the raw tissue went on and on coming away with the cotton wool.

Lockhart was aware that the ring of men who were watching had fallen silent: he felt rather than saw their faces contract with pity and disgust as he swabbed the ointment deeper and deeper and the flesh still flaked off like blistered paintwork. I wonder how long this can go on, he thought, as he saw, without surprise, that at one point he had laid bare a rib which gleamed with an astonishing cleanness and astringency. I don't think this is any good, he thought again, as the man fainted at last, and the two sailors holding him turned their eyes towards Lockhart in question and disbelief. The ointment was almost finished: the raw chest now gaped at him like the foundation of some rotten building. 'Die!' he thought, almost aloud, as he sponged once more, near the throat, and a new layer of sinew came into view, laid bare like a lecturer's diagram. 'Please give up, and die. I can't go on doing this, and I can't stop while you're still alive.'

He heard a dozen men behind him draw in their breath sharply as a fresh area of skin suddenly crumbled under his most gentle hand and adhered to the cotton wool. Crowther, attracted by the focus of interest and now kneeling by his side, said: 'Any good, sir?' and he shook his head. I'm doing wonders, he thought: they'll give me a job in a canning-factory. . . . Some blood flowed over the rib he had laid bare, and he swabbed it off almost apologetically. Sorry, he thought: that was probably my fault—and then again: Die! Please die! I'm making a fool of myself, and certainly of you. You'll never be any use now. And we'll give you a lovely funeral, well out of sight. . . .

Suddenly and momentarily, the man opened his eyes and looked up at Lockhart with a deeper, more fundamental surprise, as if he had intercepted the thought and was now aware that a traitor and not a friend was touching him. He twisted his body, and a rippling spasm ran across the scorched flesh. 'Steady, Jock!' said one of his friends, and Die! thought Lockhart yet again, squeezing the last smear of ointment from the tube and touching with it a shoulder muscle which immediately gave way and parted from its ligament. Die. Do us all a favour. Die!

Aloud, he repeated, with the utmost foolishness: 'It's a soothing ointment.' But: Die now! his lips formed the words. Don't be obstinate. No one wants you. You wouldn't want yourself if you could take a look. Please die!

Presently, obediently, but far too late, the man died.

Lieutenant-Commander NICHOLAS MONSARRAT RNVR

*

SURVIVORS

With the ship burning in their eyes
The white faces float like refuse
In the darkness—the water screwing
Oily circles where the hot steel lies.

They clutch with fingers frozen into claws
The lifebelts thrown from a destroyer,
And see, between the future's doors,
The gasping entrance of the sea.

Taken on board as many as lived, who
Had a mind left for living and the ocean,
They open eyes running with surf,
Heavy with the grey ghosts of explosion.

The meaning is not yet clear,
Where daybreak died in the smile—
And the mouth remained stiff
And grinning, stupid for a little while.

But soon they joke, easy and warm,
As men will who have died once
Yet somehow were able to find their way—
Muttering this was not included in their pay.

Later, sleepless at night, the brain spinning
With cracked images, they won't forget
The confusion and the oily dead,
Nor yet the casual knack of living.

Lieutenant ALAN ROSS RNVR

*

THE SKELETONS

There was the time of the Skeletons.

It happened when *Compass Rose* was in a hurry, late one summer afternoon when she had been delayed for nearly half a day by a search for an aircraft which was reported down in the sea, a long way south of the convoy. She had not found the aircraft, nor any trace of it: *Viperous* had wirelessed: 'Rejoin forthwith', and she was now hurrying to catch up before nightfall. The sea was glassy smooth, the sky a pale and perfect blue: the hands lounging on the upper deck were mostly stripped to the waist, enjoying the last hour of hot sunshine. It was a day for doing nothing elegantly, for going nowhere at half-speed: it seemed a pity that they had to force the pace, and even more a pity when the radar operator got a 'suspicious contact' several miles off their course and they had to turn aside to investigate.

'It's a very small echo,' said the operator apologetically. 'Sort of muzzy, too.'

'Better take a look,' said Ericson to Morell, who had called him to the bridge. 'You never know. . . .' He grinned. 'What does small and muzzy suggest to you?'

To Morell it suggested an undersized man tacking up Regent Street after a thick night, but he glossed over the thought, and said instead:

'It might be wreckage, sir. Or a submarine, just awash.'

'Or porpoises,' said Ericson, who seemed in a better humour than he usually was after being woken up. 'Or seaweed with very big sand-fleas hopping about on top. . . . It's a damned nuisance, anyway: I didn't want to waste time.'

In the event, it wasted very little of their time, for *Compass Rose* ran the distance swiftly, and what they found did not delay them. It was Wells—the best pair of eyes in the ship—who first sighted the specks on the surface, specks which gradually grew until, a mile or so away, they had become heads and shoulders—a cluster of men floating in the water.

'Survivors, by God!' exclaimed Ericson. 'I wonder how long they've been there.'

They were soon to know. *Compass Rose* ran on, the hands crowding to the rail to look at the men ahead of them. Momentarily Ericson recalled that other occasion when they had sped towards men in the water, only to destroy them out of hand. Not this time, he thought, as he reduced speed: now he could make amends.

He need not have bothered to slow down: he might well have ploughed through, the same as last time. He had thought it odd that the men did not wave or shout to *Compass Rose*, as they usually did: he had thought it odd that they did not swim even a little way towards the ship, to close the gap between death and life. Now he saw, through his glasses, that there was no gap to be closed: for the men, riding high out of the water, held upright by their life-jackets, were featureless, bony images—skeletons now for many a long day and night.

There was something infinitely obscene in the collection of lolling corpses, with bleached faces and white hairless heads, clustered together like men waiting for a bus which had gone by twenty years before. There were nine of them in that close corporation; they rode the water not more than four or five yards from each other: here and there a couple had come together as if embracing. *Compass Rose* circled, starting a wash which set the dead men bobbing and bowing to each other, like performers in some infernal dance. Nine of them, thought Morell in horror: what is the correct noun of association? A school of skeletons? A corps?

Then he saw—they all saw—that the men were roped together. A frayed and slimy strand of rope linked each one of them, tied round the waist and trailing languidly in the water: when the ripples of the ship's wash drove two of the men apart, the rope between them tightened with a jerk and a splash. The other men swayed and bowed as if approving this evidence of comradeship. . . . But this is crazy, thought Ericson: this is the sort of thing you hope not to dream about. *Compass Rose* still circled, as he looked down at the company of dead men. They must have been there for months. There was not an ounce of flesh under the yellow skins, not a single reminder of warmth or manhood. They had perished, and they had gone on perishing, beyond the grave, beyond the moment when the last man alive found rest.

He was hesitating about picking them up, but he knew that he would not. *Compass Rose* was in a hurry. There was nothing to be gained by fishing them out, sewing them up, and putting them back again. And anyway. . . .

'But why roped together?' asked Morell, puzzled, as the ship completed her last circle, and drew away, and left the men behind. 'It doesn't make sense.'

Ericson had been thinking. 'It might,' he said, in a voice infinitely subdued. 'If they were in a life-boat, and the boat was being swamped, they might tie themselves together so as not to lose touch during the night. It would give them a better chance of being picked up.'

'And they weren't,' said Morell after a pause.

'And they weren't. I wonder how long . . .' But he did not finish that sentence, except in his thoughts.

He was wondering how long it had taken the nine men to die: and what it was like for the others when the first man died: and what it was like when half of them had gone: and what it was like for the last man left alive, roped to his tail of eight dead shipmates, still hopeful, but surely feeling himself doomed by their company.

Perhaps, thought Ericson, he went mad in the end, and started to swim away, and towed them all after him, shouting, until he lost his strength as well as his wits, and gave up, and turned back to join the majority.

Quite a story.

Lieutenant-Commander NICHOLAS MONSARRAT RNVR

*

DEATH

I had not thought of death
Until that naked body floated past,
Sea-swollen and obscene
That once had been so supple.
Even then I did not think of it as that,
Or being torn in bloody gobbets
By mine or burnt by swift torpedo flash
Or sucked down by the sea in that last moment
Of drowning, longer than all the centuries of time:

I suddenly thought of it as never again delighting in
Small things that had no great significance before
But now seemed very dear—
Listening to fellows talk about their homes,
Of fields they'd ploughed or factories
They'd clocked in at;
Or talking with men about the dignity of their craft,
Shepherds or carpenters with names older than
Many a nobleman's;

Or reading books by a winter-eager fire,
Or watching bullfinches slip through dark pines
Like shards from the setting sun;
Or hearing music through quiet windows
Hemmed in with peonies and elegant hydrangeas;
Or seeing wild duck hurtle above the loamy trees,
Swift for life, swift for the waiting gun:
And foremost I thought of it as meaning that
Never again would I be with you
Or sit with you at the theatre we both loved,
Or stroll in controversial picture galleries
Airing our ignorance with enthusiasm,
Or know your silence
That tells far more than others' tongues.

Reader, you weary of this catalogue?
If you had seen that pallid, sodden corpse
Turning a shoulder in his haggard dream
You'd clutch the things you knew would vanish:
If death meant merely becoming
A comic corpse that Goya might have drawn,
I would not be afraid: but though
His mouth with sea-water was stopped,
He told me many things I had not known before.

Lieutenant (S) ALAN C. JENKINS RNVR

*

THE BURNING TANKER

There was the time that was the worst time of all, the time that seemed to synthesise the whole corpse-ridden ocean; the time of the Burning Tanker.

Aboard *Compass Rose*, as in every escort that crossed the Atlantic, there had developed an unstinting admiration of the men who sailed in oil-tankers. They lived, for an entire voyage of three or four weeks, as a man living on top of a keg of gunpowder: the stuff they carried—the life-blood of the whole war—was the most treacherous cargo of all; a single torpedo, a single small bomb, even a stray shot from a machine-gun, could transform their ship into a torch. Many times this had happened in *Compass Rose*'s convoys: many times they had had to watch these men die, or pick up the tiny remnants of a tanker's crew—men who seemed to display not the slightest hesitation at the prospect of signing on again, for the same job, as soon as they reached harbour. It was these expendable seamen who were the real 'petrol-coupons'—the things one could wangle from the garage on the corner: and whenever sailors saw or read of petrol being wasted or stolen they saw the cost in lives as well, peeping from behind the headline or the music-hall joke, feeding their anger and disgust.

Appropriately, it was an oil-tanker which gave the men in *Compass Rose*, as spectators, the most hideous hour of the whole war.

She was an oil-tanker they had grown rather fond of: she was the only tanker in a homeward-bound convoy of fifty ships which had run into trouble, and they had been cherishing her, as they sometimes cherished ships they recognised from former convoys, or ships with queer funnels, or ships that told lies about their capacity to keep up with the rest of the fleet. On this occasion she had won their affection by being obviously the number one target of the attacking U-boats; on three successive nights they had sunk the ship ahead of her, the ship astern, and the corresponding ship in the next column; and as the shelter of land approached it became of supreme importance to see her through to the end of the voyage. But her luck did not hold: on their last day of the open sea, with the Scottish hills only just over the horizon, the attackers found their mark, and she was mortally struck.

She was torpedoed in broad daylight on a lovely sunny afternoon: there had been the usual scare, the usual waiting, the usual noise of an underwater explosion, and then, from this ship they had been trying to guard, a colossal pillar of smoke and flame came billowing out, and in a minute the long shapely hull was on fire almost from end to end.

The ships on either side of her, and the ships astern, fanned outwards, like men stepping past a hole in the road: *Compass Rose* cut in towards her, intent on bringing help. But no help had yet been devised that could be any use to a ship so stricken. Already the oil that had been thrown skywards by the explosion had bathed the ship in flame: and now, as more and more oil came gushing out of the hull and spread over the water all round her, she became the centre-piece of a huge conflagration. There was still one gap in the solid wall of fire, near her bows, and above this, on the fo'c's'le, her crew began to collect—small figures, running and stumbling in furious haste towards the only chance they had for their lives. They could be seen waving, shouting, hesitating before they jumped; and *Compass Rose* crept in a little closer, as much as she dared, and called back to them to take the chance. It was dangerously, unbearably hot, even at this distance: and the shouting, and the men waving their arms, backed by the flaming roaring ship with her curtain of smoke and burning oil closing round her, completed an authentic picture of hell.

There were about twenty men on the fo'c's'le: if they were going to jump, they would have to jump soon. . . . And then, in ones and twos, hesitating, changing their minds, they did begin to jump: successive splashes showed suddenly white against the dark grey of the hull, and soon all twenty of them were down, and on their way across. From the bridge of *Compass Rose* and from the men thronging her rail came encouraging shouts as the gap of water between them narrowed.

Then they noticed that the oil, spreading over the surface of the water and catching fire as it spread, was moving faster than any of the men could swim. They noticed it before the swimmers, but soon the swimmers noticed it too. They began to scream as they swam, and to look back over their shoulders, and thrash and claw their way through the water as if suddenly insane.

But one by one they were caught. The older ones went first, and then the men who couldn't swim fast because of their life-jackets, and then the strong swimmers, without life-jackets, last of all. But perhaps it was better not to be a strong swimmer on that day, because none of them was strong enough: one by one they were overtaken, and licked by flame, and fried, and left behind.

Compass Rose could not lessen the gap, even for the last few who nearly made it. Black and filthy clouds of smoke were now coursing across the sky overhead, darkening the sun: the men on the upper deck were pouring with sweat. With their own load of fuel-oil and their ammunition, they could go no closer even for these frying men whose faces were inhumanly ugly with fear and who screamed at them for help; soon, indeed, they had to give ground to the stifling heat, and back away, and desert the few that were left, defeated by the mortal risk to themselves.

Waiting a little way off, they were entirely helpless; they stood on the bridge, and did nothing, and said nothing. One of the lookouts, a young seaman of not more than seventeen, was crying as he looked towards the fire; he made no sound, but the tears were streaming down his face. It was not easy to say what sort of tears they were—of rage, of pity, of the bitterness of watching the men dying so cruelly, and not being able to do a thing about it.

Compass Rose stayed till they were all gone, and the area of sea with the ship and the men inside it was burning steadily and remorselessly, and then she sailed on. Looking back, as they did quite often, they could see the pillar of smoke from nearly fifty miles away: at nightfall there was still a glow and sometimes a flicker on the far horizon. But the men, of course, were not there any more: only the monstrous funeral pyre remained.

Lieutenant-Commander NICHOLAS MONSARRAT RNVR

*

HURRICANE

After midnight a rending crash tore the sleep from my eyes. I awakened in a destroyer that was bucking up and down with the fury of a wild horse trying to throw a rider. And my bunk was lunging upwards at the bulkhead so that the mattress and I were almost standing one moment and lying down again the next. The ship quivered and shook as though in convulsions and would spit us out. Groans of protest shrieked from her thousand and more aged joints. Chairs, drawers of desks and wardrobes, books, dishes, pillows, blankets, bags, duffle-coats, boots and the water on the deck, everything not thoroughly secured hurled themselves about. It was a frightening awakening. And all of us thought it was all over but for the agony of dying. That's how it happens, that's how it comes. In those seconds of suspended animation the words of the hymn 'For those in peril on the sea' flashed in my mind and took on real significance. I recalled vividly an occasion when 'C' class had sung that hymn in the chapel in the Naval College, Greenwich, for shipmates of a ship that had gone down, and we had contributed to a fund for their orphans. Strange, it had never occurred to me that one day they might sing the same hymn for my ship. Water rushed down the passageways, down the ladders and poured into the lower decks. By this time all of us off duty were on our feet. I saw Number One's back as he dashed, swayed and sloshed through water down the officer's passage and out of the wardroom with the duty bridge messenger in his wake.

I hurriedly pulled on my wet boots and fumbled into a sou'-wester. Dazed by the rough shaking up and swaying drunkenly with the shifting deck, I made for topsides. My breathing was coming fast and shallow, and as I came into the open the wind gagged me, and the terrifying noises numbed my brain. And then I froze with fright at what I saw. *Reading*, tiny and forlorn, clung precariously to a spot on a mountainous wave in a violent world in black darkness. And a full-grown hurricane was raging about us. *Reading* was turning helplessly before it, as though her fighting heart had given out. If the hurricane caught the ship broadside I knew we were lost, we would be rolled over. But where was the captain? What's happened?

I flung myself against the screaming wind, grasped the ladder to the bridge with both hands and hurled myself up the iron steps. My eyes blinked with disbelief! The bridge was in chaos. The super-structure of the starboard section was smashed like a tin can and the bridge was bent and jarred backwards. Shatter-proof bridge glass lay scattered and slid about the lurching deck. Just below the bridge, the heavy steel fo'c's'le storm door, that had been bolted, was buckled and ripped from its lock and hinges. It was this door that protected our passageways, the open decks and lower decks from the onrushing heavy seas that tore down on the fo'c's'le. And as I swung my eyes to the wheel, a sigh of relief escaped me. The captain and the men hadn't been washed overboard. Though dazed and shaken the captain was fighting the force of the hurricane with man-made power, the ship's engines. The sailors stood at their posts, port side, obeying orders in the hellish darkness. *Reading* writhed, shuddered and tugged like a fish hooked by the hurricane, and the hurricane was playing her with a crafty hand, teasing her more and more to a position broadside to the watery mountain when it could tear her hold on the surface of the water and roll her over.

But too much engine power and *Reading* would gain speed and bury herself in the trough and the wave would break her back. The captain was *Reading*'s brain and he was not breaking one hold only to find *Reading* locked in another.

Our fate hung on moments so tense it seemed the ship's clock held its beat. A tug-of-war was going on before our eyes—the hurricane and seas against *Reading* and her men. The suspense seemed to rob us of our breath. The port propeller churned and pushed and the hurricane blew and raged and held *Reading* in its grip. Something had to give. The captain ordered more power, 'Half ahead port,' the Chiefie's men below responded. *Reading* quivered under the jolt. The dazed quartermaster stood by the large cumbersome wheel gripping it, waiting for the moment when *Reading* would begin to respond to the rudder when he would have to hold the ship's head in the continuing struggle. With a desperate quiver *Reading* leaned to the command of the churning propeller. She broke the hurricane's hold and fought her way into the teeth of the wind, exposing only her bow where *Reading* was least vulnerable to the hurricane's brute force.

But this wasn't the only struggle for life going on in *Reading*. The fo'c's'le storm-door that had been bashed in left a gaping hole that had to be sealed off. Unless this was done quickly the breaking seas would rush through the opening, flood the lower decks and if perchance the engine rooms were flooded, the cold water, mixing with

The German pocket battleship *Graf Spee*, scuttled and burning off Montevideo. Admiral Sir Henry McCall, an eyewitness, describes the scene on p. 18.

The destroyer HMS *Grenville* (Captain G. E. Creasey RN) mined and sunk off the Thames Estuary on 19th January 1940. There were 118 survivors, among them A.B. Bromfield, shown here clinging to a scuttle. According to the original 1940 caption Bromfield (a non-swimmer) maintained this precarious position for 1½ hours.

Dunkirk, June 1940. Picture taken from a Coastal Command aircraft. See p. 43.

The Luftwaffe's revenge on HMS *Illustrious*. A 1000 lb. bomb has pierced the flight deck and the explosion has blown out the after lift. See p. 95.

Bismarck firing at HMS *Hood*. This picture was taken by Yeoman 1st Class Fritz Bunsert in *Prinz Eugen* and it came to light in America after the war was over, when *Prinz Eugen* was on her way to act as a 'guinea-pig' ship for the atomic bomb tests at Bikini Atoll. Eyewitness accounts of the chase and sinking of *Bismarck* are on pp. 132-40.

'The loss of this splendid ship . . . to only one torpedo hit was, of course, the cause of great disappointment and the subject of searching inquiry'.
The end of HMS *Ark Royal*; the destroyer HMS *Legion* closing her to take off survivors. See pp. 148 and 153.

'God, she's going!': the battleship HMS *Barham* hit port side by three torpedoes fired from U-331. See p. 159.

'In all the war I never received a more direct shock'—Churchill's reaction to the news of the destruction of Force Z. Here, some of *Prince of Wales*' ship's company are being taken off by the destroyer *Express*. See pp. 164–73.

Operation Pedestal; Convoy to Malta, August 1942: the aircraft carrier HMS *Indomitable* on fire after receiving three bomb hits. Eyewitness accounts of the passage of the convoy are on pp. 228-37.

Aftermath of Dieppe: a captured German photograph of the beaches after the raid.

The shattered interior of a tank landing craft (*below*) after the Dieppe raid. These pictures add point to Marine Spencer's story on p. 252.

The destroyer HMS *Onslow*, bridge and funnel riddled with splinter holes, after her return from the Battle of the Barents Sea in which her CO, Captain Sherbrooke, won the VC. The action is described on p. 263 in a battle-poem by Alan Ross, who was an ordinary seaman in *Onslow* at the time.

A landing craft (rocket) in action. Early alarms and excursions of life in these craft are recounted on p. 284.

'The descendant of the Elizabethan fireship'—Captain Roskill's brilliant analogy for the midget submarine, or X-craft. Two outstanding X-craft commanders, Captain Godfrey Place and Lieutenant Commander Ian Fraser, describe the exploits for which they were awarded the VC: see p. 288 'The Midget Attack on *Tirpitz*', and p. 379 'The Attack on *Takao*'.

'The Happy Return': HMS *Wild Goose* being cheered into Gladstone Dock, Bootle, after Captain F. J. Walker's Second Escort Group had sunk six U-boats in one trip January/February 1944. Commander Wemyss, Walker's right-hand man, writes on p. 323.

The bleak beaches of Normandy. Denis Glover's account of what it was like to drive a landing craft ashore on 'Sword' Beach on D-Day is on p. 337.

A direct hit by a Kamikaze suicide bomber on the flight deck of HMS *Formidable* off Okinawa, May 1945. Eyewitness account of this incident on p. 370.

the hot boilers, would blow the ship open. And there was no assurance that another mountainous wave, such as shouldered *Reading* around midnight, might not hurl itself at us at any moment. All of us were near exhaustion. *Reading* had been hurt. The fo'c's'le storm-door was no longer there to stop the seas.

The overcast was thick and the night screamed violence. Dark-grey clouds sped by the ship's mast like frightened ghosts. The bow plunged and leaped as though it were a porpoise on a hook; the fo'c's'le was continually submerged in frothing sea-water. With only a pipe railing between them and the wild seas that lapped at their feet, Number One and a small party of sailors struggled with a collision mat on the fo'c's'le, trying to lash it in such a position as to close off the opening to the sea. Every moment they stood there carried the prospect of being spilled or hurled into the dark seas. We all breathed with relief when that job was over and we saw them hurrying away from that dangerous spot.

Scarcely had we forgotten this experience when a hush fell over the ocean, almost as if a wild gesticulating god of Discord had suddenly lifted his Wagnerian baton and called his fiendish fiddlers and doped perspiring percussives to an abrupt halt. The silence was so awesome that all on duty spoke in whispers.

For half an hour this weird silence reigned and then the baton came down with a bang and the elements about us went completely mad. It blew with all the fury of a great hurricane. The God of Winds let go with everything, and, below, Father Neptune stirred with all his might. Thick masses of ugly clouds, the colour of bats, whirled by, fleeing and pursued by what sounded like a cacophony of screaming vocalists, screeching cats, whining violins, blaring trumpets, and the howling of a mighty organ whose keys were hard pressed by crazed fingers. It was a task to hold on to one's senses. We peered into darkness, through strained unbelieving eyes, at a world in turmoil where nothing was static but our hopes. And each miserable dark hour so full of hardship and fright dragged on like an eternity. From moment to moment none of us knew whether we were of this world or on our way to the next; and in these god-forsaken latitudes the world was in darkness sixteen hours of the day. The ship's company was dazed and exhausted, and few were able to really sleep below.

Throughout the night SOS signals were heard from hundreds of miles away. Another destroyer, less fortunate than we, foundered with all hands aboard perishing. Still other ships vanished, but whether lost in the hurricane or subsequently sunk by U-boats will probably never be known.

Commander A. H. CHERRY OBE RNVR

★

SEASICKNESS

A rise . . . a fall . . . a long suspense,
A word just spoken . . . in the air.
A reel . . . a swerve . . . a time intense,
As eyes rest on uneaten fare.

A sigh . . . a gulp . . . a quick upheave,
A dash to parley with . . . a wave.
Too late! The deck does now receive
What I had fondly hoped to save.

O God! O Christ! How I blaspheme!
Your sea, your waves, your windy sky!
O man of earth! How I do scream
'Oh let me be. Oh, let me die.'

Of steel . . . of men . . . of gun and shell
Seasick I care for no such strength.
Give me the earth, a cool green dell.
I'll give you all the ocean's length.

What man . . . can stand . . . the bile so vile
Thick slimy coming from inside?
It pains . . . it strains . . . Oh, rasping file,
In regions of the unseen side!

I fling my soul to tide and wind,
God, do your worst with it . . . or give
Ease to my tummy full of wind;
Or let me die where fishes live.

Able Seaman RICHARD B. WRIGHT

★

HMS *WREN*

One of the 'W'-class destroyers had been named *Wren* just after the demobilisation of the 1917–19 WRNS, and although there was no indication that the name was intended as a compliment to the WRNS, the Association of Wrens claimed her as their own and provided boat badges and a silk ensign and other tokens of affection. This ship, with its many associations for ex-Wrens, was lost off Harwich in 1940. The Second Sea Lord, Admiral Little, suggested officially that the naming of a new ship *Wren* would be 'an encouragement to the WRNS, who were already doing excellent service', and, furthermore, proposed that the Director WRNS should launch the ship. Permission was obtained to allow Wrens to give towards the building of the ship, and a sum of over £4,000 was voluntarily subscribed, made up of very small sums. Representative parties of Wrens were allowed to come to the launching, and with large numbers from the nearby ports of Glasgow and Greenock it was a real WRNS day. Messrs Denny, the builders, gave a grand luncheon in pre-war style.

To launch a ship is an unforgettable experience, to feel her come alive, to move, to be released from captivity to her right element. And this was a very special ship; something took to sea with her of the love of British women for the service which has made their country's history.

The *Wren* was a sloop and although that sounds smaller than a modern destroyer, she was actually considerably bigger than her predecessor. She became one of the famous Second Escort Group under the late Captain F. J. Walker. On one of my happy visits on board, where I was always received like a queen and everyone felt that she was the Wrens' own ship, I was told by the then captain (Lieutenant-Commander S. J. Woods RNR) of the great reception given them when the group had come into Liverpool from one of their famous 'kills'. But the thing that had touched them most was when a squad of Wrens had marched along the quayside, eyes-righting proudly as they passed their name-ship.

Dame VERA LAUGHTON MATHEWS DBE

Throughout 1941 and 1942 the Mediterranean submarine flotillas (the 1st at Alexandria, the 8th at Gibraltar and the 10th at Malta) caused a steady attrition of Italian shipping, sinking 600,000 tons of merchant shipping and sinking or damaging a long list of major and minor warships. They continued to run supplies, personnel and mail into Malta at the height of that island's siege. Three outstanding submarine commanders were awarded the Victoria Cross: Lieutenant-Commander M. D. Wanklyn RN of HMS/M Upholder, *Commander J. W. Linton RN of HMS/M* Turbulent *(posthumously in 1943) and Commander A. C. C. Miers RN of HMS/M* Torbay. *Casualties were high: twenty-four submarines were lost, and at one time the survival chances of a submarine officer or man in the Mediterranean were put at 'less than even money'.*[1]

HMS/M Tempest *left Malta on 10th February 1942, for a patrol in the Gulf of Taranto. At 3 am on the 13th, while on the surface, she was jumped by the Italian torpedo-boat* Circe:[2]

She had seen us and was coming straight at us—to ram.

It was a crash-dive. It had to be. We went down steeply and heard the thumping of his engines. He was on us. My stomach went cold. Then I almost gasped with sudden intense relief as I heard the noise dying away again. He had missed us on the first pass.

Action always gave me an uneasy lurch in the pit of my stomach. I had it now all right. That destroyer was really going for us, no doubt about that. We were in for a very bad time.

It would be the first time for most of our green ship's company. Those kids must have had that sick feeling, that thumping heart I knew so well, but if they had they certainly did not show it as they went quietly and smoothly about their jobs like veterans. Of course, they didn't know what was coming. Being depth-charged is something which cannot be imagined. It is a terror which has to be experienced. Any minute now we were going to get it, and when we did it wouldn't be just the distant booming of a formal search. That Eyetie knew exactly where we were. There he is now—on top of us. My heart bumped as I watched the depth-gauge, sitting in my action station, at the after hydroplanes.

1. An officer who served in the 10th Flotilla, in conversation with the editor.

2. The Italian definition of 'torpedo-boat' was any destroyer of less than 1,000 tons.

The captain gave an order.

'One hundred and fifty feet.'

I turned the wheel. Rapidly we gained depth. I thought that first pattern will be keeping us company.

I had my eyes on the pointer. It was passing fifty feet. We'd never do it. . . . The dial shook and the pointer danced before my eyes. There was a tremendous, gathering surge of clanging thunder . . . seat, wheel, hands, brain, dials, deck, bulkhead, deckhead, everything shook like an earthquake shock as if every atom in the ship's company were splitting. Then it was dark, nearly all the lights gave out. Instruments were shattered, wheels locked, glass tinkled over the deck.

We were still going down. I watched the pointer . . . 150 . . . 155 . . . 160 . . . 165. . . . We were out of control.

We fought her, second cox'n Burns and I. The pointer reached 350 feet. There, at last, we steadied her and managed to bring her back to 150 feet.

Swiftly the damage reports came in. Nearly all the instruments and lights throughout the boat had been put out of action. The fore hydroplanes and hydrophones were damaged beyond repair. Worst of all, one of the propeller shafts had shifted in its housing. That accounted for the loud continuous knocking sound we could hear. We had had trouble with this shaft before leaving England and it had been put right. Now the depth-charging had thrown it out of true again.

The boat was trimmed at 150 feet and we maintained her level in the stop position with just the slightest movement of the motors or adjustment of the ballast. All ship's company not actually needed now were told to lie down at their stations and to move as little as possible so as to conserve the limited oxygen supply in the boat and reduce telltale noise to try to cheat his hydrophones.

That was the only 'evasive action' we could take now. Asdics and hydrophones were out of action, so we had no means of finding the bearing of our attacker. We didn't know where he was coming from next and we couldn't dodge what he was throwing at us. We just had to sit and take what was coming—until he finished us off for good and all. I began to get that this can't be happening to me feeling. So many times I had seen shipmates and chummy ships go out and never return—just, unbelievably, cease to exist, as if atomised into nothing. Failed to return from patrol. That was the official phrase. Wives and mothers sat at home and heard it over the BBC. Now our wives and mothers were going to hear it. . . . 'The Admiralty regret to announce that His Majesty's submarine *Tempest* has failed to return from patrol . . .' Now it was our turn.

But after the first pattern had done its worst my stomach settled down and we carried on as if all this were just a practice run. There were no more explosions for the moment. The moments lengthened and still we went free. After a little while the cook made some tea and cocoa, and this hot brew, with biscuits, was passed round the boat. It made us all feel a lot better, even though we could hear that destroyer's engines as he passed and re-passed above us, stalking us still, hour after hour.

But they dropped no more depth-charges. In fact by 7 am we were beginning to have hopes that they had really lost us when we heard engines very close overhead once more and then another series of shattering crashes as a pattern went off right alongside us. After that they came again and again, dropping pattern on pattern and all of them so close you could smell them. Dazed and shaken and scared, we hung on and hoped against hope. You couldn't tell where he was coming from until you actually heard him.

The master gyroscope was smashed and we had to rely on our magnetic compass. One oil-fuel bulkhead connection in the control-room was damaged, and oil fuel poured into the boat. The chief stoker, George Spowart, and his men got to it quickly and soon stopped the flood. The electrical artificer, John Winrow, slaved to put the gyro right, but it was past all hope of repair and we had to give it up. The fore hydroplanes were out of action and the boat was being controlled for depth by the after planes.

We were at the mercy of that destroyer. At regular intervals we heard her rumble over us. We could hear her Asdic 'pinging' us, the sound wave stinging our quivering steel flanks like an invisible whiplash, but never knew exactly where she was. Each time she turned and came back to try again. Each run did more damage than the last.

For a time the submarine was kept under perfect control. Then the ring main shorted on to the pressure hull, blowing the main fuses.

This put the ballast pumps out of action. This meant that the compensating tanks and auxiliary tanks had to be trimmed by using our compressed-air supply, when air was priceless to us. The boat was forced down willy-nilly to 500 feet completely out of control. I was helpless on the planes. There wasn't a thing I could do to stop her.

The position was so desperate that we had to bring her to rest finally by trimming her on the main ballast tanks. To lighten the boat these main ballast tanks had to be trimmed either by venting the air into them, or blowing water out by means of compressed air. This was a far from satisfactory method of trimming and we were particularly reluctant to resort to it because it was very noisy at a time when silence was vital to give us any chance of surviving at all.

This started us on our way up again and to check the rate of rise we had quickly to flood the main ballast tanks again. All the time the sudden extra noise was playing right into the hands of our attacker. With deadly regularity she passed overhead, each time laying her eggs. They burst all round us as we sat and shook in the semi-darkness, with only the secondary lighting flickering palely like candles guttering in a dark tomb and the ship lurching and wallowing between 100 and 500 feet and things breaking loose and crashing about us. *Tempest* was a strong boat and she was withstanding a pounding that would have completely shattered a less well-found ship, but nevertheless the strain was beginning to show in the state of her machinery and on the faces and movements of her crew.

We went on steering blindly at any old depth between 100 and 500 feet. Bulkhead fixtures and spare parts were torn from their housing, and hurled across the narrow spaces. The boat was continually either bow up or bow down, and the angle was so acute at times that the bubble in the fore-and-aft spirit-level would disappear completely.

In the engine-room heavy spares like the big breech-ends from the diesels, each weighing half a ton, were sliding dangerously up and down the steel deck at each plunge and lurch. It was quite impossible to stop them, much less secure them again.

To make matters worse we were carrying a big load of extra

spares for the submarines based at Alexandria—not to mention sack-loads of mail for the Fleet—and all these broke loose and started to smash about through the boat. All the time, as the relentless depth-charging went on, the always dim emergency lighting burned lower and lower until it was hardly more than a faint glow.

The position inside *Tempest* steadily worsened as more and more fittings were shaken loose. The earthings of the main electric cable against the hull increased the danger of fire and electrocution.

This hell went on until 10 am. Then, miraculously, unbelievably, there was a definite lull. We blinked, breathed again and looked around us to take stock of our position.

John Winrow, creeping through the submarine on the track of some electrical repair, accidentally kicked a bucket which clattered with a deafening noise along the deck.

'I'll have that man shot!' shouted the captain. It nearly made us jump out of our skins.

Then the attack began again. Again I thought this is not happening to me. I suppose many of us felt that. I know that no one, least of all the young submariners who had been civilians only a few months before, showed the slightest sign of panic or fear. They all behaved splendidly.

About 10.30 am the battery securing boards showed signs of lifting. A closer inspection showed that salt-water had got into the battery compartment and several containers, with sulphuric acid in them, were broken.

When salt-water and sulphuric acid mix they give off chlorine gas. That is the ultimate horror of all submariners.

The boat started to fill with it. One whole battery was flooded now. We had reached the end. The boat was just a pitch-dark, gas-filled shambles, flooding at the after end, with no instrument working except 'faithful Freddie' the magnetic compass. What use was a compass now? *Tempest* had nowhere to go any more, except to the bottom. At last, to save us from going with her, the captain decided to abandon ship.

Quietly the ship's company were told to put on the Davis escape gear. Without any fuss everybody buckled the gear on. Then the order was passed for everyone except men at key positions needed to maintain the trim of the boat to muster in the control-room.

Then the captain gave the order 'Abandon ship'.

Chief Petty Officer CHARLES ANSCOMB, *Tempest*'s coxswain

The submarine surfaced, and the twenty-three survivors of a ship's company of sixty-two were picked up by the Italians.

*

TWO POEMS

Spring 1942

Once as we were sitting by
The falling sun, the thickening air,
The chaplain came against the sky
And quietly took a vacant chair.

And under the tobacco smoke:
'Freedom' he said, and 'Good' and 'Duty'.
We stared, as though a savage spoke.
The scene took on a singular beauty.

And we made no reply to that
Obscure, remote communication,
But only stared at where the flat
Meadow dissolved in vegetation.

And thought: O sick, insatiable
And constant lust; O death, our future;
O revolution in the whole
Of human use of man and nature.

The Middle of a War

My photograph already looks historic.
The promising youthful face, the matelot's collar,
Say, 'This one is remembered for a lyric.
His place and period—nothing could be duller.'

Its position already indicated—
The son or brother in the album; pained
The expressions and the garments dated,
His fate so obviously preordained

The original turns away: as horrible thoughts
Loud fluttering aircraft slope above his head
At dusk. The ridiculous empires break like biscuits—
Ah, life has been abandoned by the boats—
Only the trodden island and the dead
Remain, and the once inestimable caskets.

Ordinary Seaman ROY FULLER

*

HMAS Perth *(Captain H. M. L. Waller RAN), Java Sea, 27th February 1942:*

THE LOWER STEERING POSITION

When John heard the captain's voice he was beginning to lose touch with reality. He was fighting an enemy all on his own. Standing by the ship's wheel and idly letting the spokes pass beneath one's fingers—this is many people's idea of what it is like to steer a ship. Under normal conditions, with a ship on course, it is indeed what happens. The ship was steered beautifully and precisely by 250-horsepower electric motors working in tandem on an hydraulic system, which had its powerful and infinitely sensitive fingers on the rudder cross-head with four great rams. Many times John had sat in the tiller flat watching this smooth, faultless interpretation of the captain's wishes being applied, through the rudder, to the complex fabric of the ship. The whole gunnery platform relied upon this so that it could come to bear on the enemy. He had heard the turning of the four propellers are high speed, and their turbulence roughly slapping the taut skin of the hull with a sound like a hundred distant depth-charges. But now he was 250 feet away from that vital compartment, connected to it only by two sets of thin copper tubing through which glycerine and water flowed. If these were shot away he would have to move to the after steering position, a small cabinet in the starboard forward corner of the steering engine flat. If the power went off he would have eight stokers laboriously to pump the great rams by hand.

In the lower steering position his crew was small. Besides himself, there was a leading seaman and an able seaman, both of whom he had trained to do the job as efficiently as himself, for at any moment the whole responsibility could fall on either of them. One wrong move at high speeds and in close order could bring complete disaster to the ship. Normally John was at the wheel, with the leading seaman on the port engine telegraph and revolution indicator, and the able seaman on the starboard engine telegraph. There was also a stoker petty officer to effect any mechanical change-overs required. But now they were desperate, and the usual order had gone by the board.

The enemy within the ship was heat-stroke, which, with the rushing of a steam train, irresistibly carries a man to oblivion. With the sounding of an action Alarm, all lower-deck ventilation is shut down so that any fires will starve for oxygen.

The spokes of the wheel were being wrenched and hurled around with such violence now that it looked as though they would be plucked out like carrots. The ship was being manœuvred under full helm, constantly changing engine speeds, the engines rung ahead or astern to turn her in an ever-tightening circle. This technique had been developed in the Mediterranean to evade dive-bombers. It had actually been used by Sir Philip Bowyer-Smythe, then captain, to avoid sticks of bombs which had already left the aircraft. This was all the more remarkable when it is remembered that *Perth*'s turning circle was one of the largest in the Navy. Much of the success was due to the engine-room's crew, whose uncanny and instantaneous co-ordination made the ship heel away and the engines pulse with a thrill of life through the whole ship.

'Starboard thirty-five!'

'Starboard thirty-five, sir!'

'Slow starboard. Full ahead port!'

'Slow starboard. Full ahead port, sir!'

'Thirty-five of starboard wheel on, sir. Starboard engine slow ahead, port engine full ahead, on and repeated, sir!'

'Ease to ten!'

'Ease to ten, sir!'

'Half ahead both engines!'

'Half ahead both engines, sir!'

'Ten degrees of starb'd wheel on. Both engines half ahead on and repeated, sir!'

'Midships!'

'Midships, sir!'

'Meet her! Steady on two-seven-o degrees!'

'Meet her! Steady on two-seven-o degrees, sir!'

'Course, two-seven-o degrees, sir!'

This was some of the dialogue for one simple manœuvre. Replies were gasped out as the wheel was hove around in great lunging movements so that one turn of the wheel, at a single lunge, put on five degrees of rudder. 'Hard over' is seven strenuous turns with the strong spring of the telemotor being compressed more at each turn. This meant that the helmsman had to heave around with a concerted swing of both shoulders: bending from the waist and carrying the movement down with the knees bent, then thrusting up again at the other side of the circle on tensed toes, which makes a compact ball of the muscles of the calves and a rigid line along the top of the thighs. It is a quick, smooth movement. With this abnormal manœuvring, the action of the helmsman is more like the weaving of a fighter around a punching bag—crouching, lunging, quick short sidesteps, arms jabbing strongly down, boring in then snapping up again. This goes on with sharp grunts and whistlings of sharply exhaled breaths.

No sooner would John report, 'Course, sir . . .' than, 'Port thirty-five! Slow port! Full ahead starboard!' would come down the voice-pipe. Over and over! Time after time! Urgent yet monotonous and measured, alterations as the ship snaked under the captain's hand.

But this, in itself, was not unprecedented. At the Battle of Crete they had sustained thirteen hours non-stop of concentrated dive-bombing from Hitler's 'yellow-nosed bastards', as they had referred to those special ME 110s and JU87BS he had called together for the job. And the next day they had endured a further seven-hour stretch for which, after 9 am, they had only a hundred rounds of four-inch ammunition left. Fatty, in the high-angle director, had received the order, 'Only fire when you see the whites of their eyes!' They had brought the ship's rifles (200 of them) on deck and ranged them round the ship in banks of fifty. Each man, with ten rounds in the magazine and one 'in the spout', had fired furiously as the attackers reached the bottom of their dives. The whole day had been spent in dodging bombs. John and his crew had managed it without relief; though they were fit, it had tired them. But then they had not had such heat to endure.

Now the air was foetid. It became impossible for the man at the wheel to handle it and answer the stream of orders as they came pouring down the voice-pipe. So one man now stood with his ear at the bell-mouth and his eyes on the helmsman, repeating the orders as he heard them, and calling back to the compass platform as they were executed. The man at the wheel did not waste a breath, and for the short periods they kept a course, he had his eyes fixed on the round face of the yellow-illuminated, tick-ticking gyro-compass card.

This card had become their guide now, in quite another way. The man steering watched it as if it were an enchanted moon. Sweat poured in streams over his body—continuous rivers of it running from under his arms, soaking the shorts which was all he wore. Suddenly he would feel his body generate a terrific heat, which rushed out of him: this radiation took the last ounce of energy with it. The yellow moon of the compass card whirled away from his eyes into an immense distance, leaving him spinning in blackness, blind and on the point of collapse.

As soon as the card started to rush away from him, he fell back against the bulkhead and the man on the voice-pipe, constantly on the look-out for this, stepped across, his hand falling on the wheel as the other man reeled away and groped blindly along the bulkhead to the door. Here, he called the third man back to the voice-pipe. One thing was saving them: by a freak of chance there was one punkah-louvre left running in the third auxiliary wireless office, just through the door from them. The man on the point of collapse would stagger into the office and lie flat on his back on a bench while the wireless ratings played a jet of cool life-saving air on his face. Above him the ships were manœuvring in close disorder, through smoke and gun-fire, at high speeds. John realised how much depended on his team instantaneously carrying out the orders. If that jet failed, or the man on the voice-pipe was slow in taking over from a fainting man . . .

At the peak of the action it was impossible for a man to last more than five minutes. Each turn was as hard as any boxing round. The stoker petty officer pulled them out by taking over the starboard telegraphs. Thus, in that important battle in which five nations fought desperately, there were spells during which a young able seaman, who at any minute might faint, held in his sweat-streaming hands the fate of a whole ship. He had not as many months in the Service as John had years, yet John had pride and confidence in him. Each of them in turn grunted, hove the wheel, sweated and gasped with painful lungs until that yellow moon spun away from him and he slumped against the bulkhead.

Chief Petty Officer RAY PARKIN RAN,
HMAS *Perth*'s Quartermaster

Perth *was sunk a few days later in the Battle of the Sunda Straits. With nine other* Perth *survivors, the author (a regular Royal Australian Navy rating—John in the text) made a fantastic voyage in the salvaged life-boat* Anzac *to Tjilatjap in southern Java but were there captured by the Japanese. He spent the rest of the war in Japanese POW camps and ultimately on the Burma–Siam railway. Captain 'Hec' Waller RAN, was perhaps the outstanding fighting RAN captain of the war; he was lost with* Perth.

*

In early 1942 intelligence reported that the new German battleship Tirpitz *had been completed and was getting restless. If she broke out into the Atlantic and then, like* Bismarck, *headed for France, there was only one dock on the western European seaboard which could take her—the* Normandie *graving dock in St Nazaire, at the mouth of the River Loire. On 3rd March the Chiefs of Staff Committee approved Operation 'Chariot', a fantastically daring scheme to crash the gates of the* Normandie *dock and blow them up.*

The explosive—twenty-four depth-charges with a time fuse—was carried in an ex-American destroyer HMS Campbeltown *(Lieutenant-Commander S. H. Beattie RN) which had been specially lightened to cross the sandbanks and had strengthened superstructure to protect personnel during the run in. Besides* Campbeltown, *the Chariot force consisted of MGB 314 (Lieutenant D. M. C. Curtis RNVR), carrying the Naval Force Commander and his staff; two escorting destroyers HMS* Atherstone *(Lieutenant-Commander R. F. Jenks RN) and HMS* Tynedale *(Lieutenant-Commander H. E. F. Tweedie RN); sixteen MLs, carrying Commandos under Lieutenant-Colonel A. C. Newman; and MTB 74 (Sub-Lieutenant R. C. M. V. Wynn RNVR) with delay-action torpedoes for use on the dock gates if* Campbeltown *failed. The force left Falmouth on 26th March and on the night of 27th/28th, led by MGB 314, they made*

THE ATTACK ON ST NAZAIRE

The weather, for our purposes, was perfect. The sky was completely overcast with low cloud; indeed, it was at times misty with a light drizzle, while the full moon above the clouds prevented the night from being too dark.

As the leading craft reached Les Morees Tower, however, the bright beam of a searchlight was suddenly switched on astern of the force. For a few breathless moments it swept up towards the last craft in the line, but was switched off without, apparently, having detected anything. Silhouetted against its beam we could see a vessel patrolling the entrance to the swept channel to the north-west.

So far this was excellent. We had not only reached a position one and three-quarter miles from our target undetected but had also, apparently, not encountered any minefields, booms, or other unexpected obstructions, and last, but not least, we had crossed the flats without any craft stranding. The warning had, however, evidently been given, as at 1.22 am all the searchlights on both banks were suddenly switched on, floodlighting the whole force. Every detail of every craft must have been clearly visible to the enemy. In anticipation of this, however, we had taken such precautions as we could; inadequate though they were, they helped. All the craft had been painted a dark colour, our dirtiest and most tattered ensigns were used, and the *Campbeltown*'s funnels had been cut on the slant, giving her a very good resemblance to the 'Mowe'-class torpedo-boats employed by the Germans on that coast.

Looking back at the force following us, however, it was difficult to imagine that there could be any successful deception. Each craft, with her silvery bow-wave, stood out clear and bright, and *Campbeltown*, rising conspicuously over the smaller craft, could be seen by her funnel smoke to be increasing speed. We were challenged from the shore, first by one of the coastal batteries and later from somewhere in the dockyard. It was for this moment that Leading Signalman Pike, who could send and receive German Morse, had been attached to my staff. The challenge was accompanied by sporadic flak, aimed indiscriminately at the force. It was 1.23 am, we were a mile and a half from our objective; ten minutes at that speed. How long could we bluff? Although we had successfully evaded the heavier batteries at the entrance, every minute still counted.

We did not know the correct reply to the challenge, but we instructed them to 'Wait' and then gave the call sign of one of the German torpedo-boats known to us. Without waiting for them to consider this, Pike embarked on a long plain-language signal. With an 'urgent' prefix, the gist of this was, 'Two craft, damaged by enemy action, request permission to proceed up harbour without delay.' Firing ceased. Without finishing the first message we made the operating signal to 'Wait' again. We had to reply to the second station. We were about to give them a similar message when we came under renewed fire from the north bank, heavier than the first but still, it seemed to us, hesitant. Using our brightest Aldis lamp, we made the international signal for ships or vessels being fired on by friendly forces. The firing ceased again. Another six minutes and *Campbeltown* would be home. Our bluffing had practically achieved its object. According to our information the enemy had no heavy batteries as far up as this and he was unlikely now to sink *Campbeltown*, though a lucky hit in her steering gear or on the bridge might still make her miss her mark. Information now available confirms the valuable part played by Pike in thus delaying the enemy's fire.

By 1.27 an increasing weight of fire directed on our force left little doubt that we had been identified as hostile. We had held our fire up to the last possible moment, and now was the time to let them have it. *Campbeltown* was the first to reply. For about five minutes the sight was staggering, both sides loosing off everything they had. The air was full of tracer; not sailing majestically into the heavens as must have been a familiar sight to many during air raids, but flying horizontally, and at close range.

At the moment of opening fire, we in MGB 314 were just coming up to a guard ship anchored in the river abreast the south entrance. In the glare of the searchlights we could see her clearly and her guns. At about 200 yards three well-aimed bursts of fire from our pom-pom silenced her. It was indeed an unfortunate day for that vessel, as she not only received bursts of fire from each craft in turn as they passed but finally provided an excellent target for their own shore batteries, who fired on her until she scuttled herself.

After about three or four minutes of this brisk action there was a perceptible slackening in the enemy's fire. This was a triumph for the many gun-layers in the coastal craft and in the *Campbeltown*. It was, at this stage, a straight fight between the carefully sited enemy flak emplacements ashore, enjoying all the protection which concrete could afford, and the gun-layers, handling the short-range weapons on the exposed decks of their small and lively craft. Only in the *Campbeltown* had it been possible to provide a reasonable amount of steel protection, and this was largely offset by her being the most conspicuous target in our force. To our advantage, on the other hand, we were the attackers and, by evading the batteries guarding the approaches, we had arrived off our objective, with a force mounting forty or more close-range cannon. With our craft steaming past the southern entrance to the port a big percentage of our armament could concentrate on each of the enemy emplacements in turn as they passed them, and, finally, on arrival at our selected points of attack, we could reasonably expect to outnumber them locally. For all this the enemy, with their heavily protected emplacements and heavier-calibre guns (20 mm, 40 mm, and 88 mm) had the advantage.

Our triumph, therefore, although it was short-lived, was a fine feat of arms for our guncrews and for those officers and gunners' mates who in many cases stood beside the guns to assist in directing the fire. The slackening in the enemy's fire, moreover, came at the precise moment when the *Campbeltown* had to aim for the lock gate.

MGB 314, increasing speed to keep ahead of *Campbeltown*, passed about 200 yards off the Old Mole and then sheered off to starboard while *Campbeltown* continued on round and in to her objective. She had increased to nineteen knots; there was a slight check as she cut the torpedo net and she hit the caisson of the lock with a crash. The exact time of impact was 1.34 am, four minutes after the intended time.

Captain ROBERT RYDER VC RN,
Naval Force Commander, Operation 'Chariot'

The author, Lieutenant-Colonel Newman, and Lieutenant-Commander Beattie were each awarded the Victoria Cross; posthumous VCs were awarded to Sergeant J. F. Durrant, Royal Engineers (attached Commandos) and to Able Seaman W. A. Savage of MGB 314 (and in recognition of the valour shown by so many others, unnamed, in MLs, MGBs, and MTBs).

Campbeltown *blew up at noon, killing a number of German officers inspecting her at the time, and totally wrecking the main lock gates. MTB 74s' torpedoes, fired into the Old Entrance gates, blew up a day later. These explosions and the loss of their officers caused the German troops to panic, and their final losses, inflicted on themselves, were greater than ours, which were eighty-five Navy and fifty-nine Commando killed or missing, of a total 'Chariot' strength of 630 (excluding the two escort destroyers).*

*

CAPTAIN CORTEZ

We no can see them, but I get my big gun straight in sun because I know they are there. I am all time working machine-gun, swinging it in figure of eight to throw cone of bullets where they must be. Then I hear noise them diving, but still no see. I tell my first officer, 'Wait. No fire yet.' He want to fire. I say, 'No. Noise get louder.' First one machine come one side us and drop bombs; then another come other side. His bombs fall only twenty yards away. Then third machine come straight. I see him, I say, 'Fire.' Gun go.

He almost over funnel when he turn, but pieces from his starboard wing drop off and fall on our deck. Beautiful! He go wobbling away, getting lower and lower.

In the bows my man is working another machine-gun when piece cannon-shell go through his thigh. 'Stick it,' I say, but poor fellow he presently faint and fall beside his gun. He all right in hospital now. I stop his bleeding with bottle peroxide hydrogen and put him sleep with bottle whisky.

From *Daily Mail* report

The speaker, a Spanish captain, was describing how he chipped pieces from the wing of one of three attacking ME 109s. He had just been congratulated by Admiral Cunningham on completing his twenty-fifth trip to Tobruk as master of a cargo steamer.

★

THE ROYAL MARINE BAND

In the centre of the room, ranged round a table large enough for a Lord Mayor's banquet to be served on it, sat the Marine band. In the old days travelling theatrical companies expected their players to do a double job, and take their places nightly in the orchestra preliminary to appearing on the stage; there would be advertisements in the theatrical papers for a 'heavy' who could 'double in brass'. Similarly, in *Artemis* the musicians had a double duty, and the provision of music was the less important. The time they spent rehearsing 'Colonel Bogey' and 'A Life on the Ocean Wave' was only the time that could be spared from rehearsals of a more exacting piece of teamwork. The machines all round them, the superhuman machines, even when the torpedo gunner's mate had supplied them with electricity and Chief Electrical Artificer Sands had tuned them to perfection, were still dependent upon human agency to interpret and implement their findings. Under the glass top of the table there were needles which moved steadily and needles which moved erratically, needles which crept and needles which jumped, and each needle was watched by a bandsman who had his own individual pointer under his control which had to keep pace with it, creep when it crept, jump when it jumped, utterly unpredictably. At the transmitting station table every item the Marine band played was unrehearsed and without score; the instrumentalists could never look ahead and find that some individuals among them had been allotted twenty bars' rest by the composer. There was no looking ahead, and each bandsman was obeying a different baton which might at any moment leap into activity and summon him to action.

At the head of the table, sitting on a higher chair which gave him a view over the whole expanse, sat the commissioned gunner, Mr Kaile, his telephone instrument clasped over his head, the other telephones within reach. In one sense, Mr Kaile was conductor of this mad hatter's orchestra. He had no control over what air should be played, nor when it should begin or end. He was rather in the position of a band leader who may find his instrumentalists suddenly striking up together at any moment without agreeing on the tune. He had to see that at least every instrument was in the same key and kept the same time, and, in accordance with the orders that came down from the bridge and from the gunnery lieutenant, and guided by the triple reports of the spotting officers, he was also expected—to continue the analogy—to swell or diminish the volume of sound as might be considered necessary; in other words, to send the range up or down the ladder, deflect to right or left, as the direct observance of the fall of the shells might dictate.

However perfect the machines, war in the last analysis is fought by men whose nerves must remain steady to direct the machines, whose courage must remain high when they as well as their machines are in danger, whose discipline and training must be such that they work together. Every improvement in the machines does not dispose of this problem, but only pushes it one remove further along. The Paleolithic man who first thought of setting his flint axe in a shaft instead of holding it clumsily in his hand still had to face and fight his enemy. Nelson's gunners had their ammunition brought to them by powder monkeys instead of by an automatic hydraulic hoist like the gunners in *Artemis*, but in either case the gunners had to stand by their guns to achieve anything.

So similarly round the table of the transmitting station it was necessary that there should be discipline and courage. Trembling hands could not keep those pointers steady, nor could minds distracted by fear be alert to follow the aimless wanderings of the guiding needles so that the guns above could continue to hurl forth their broadsides every ten seconds. Down here, far below the level of the sea, the men were comparatively protected from shell-fire, but not far below their feet was the outer skin of the ship, and around them were the bunkers of oil fuel. Mine or torpedo might strike there, engulfing them in flame or water. Other compartments of the ship might be holed, and the sea pour in as the ship sank slowly; in that case it would be their duty to remain at their posts to keep the guns firing to the last, while above them there were only the difficult iron ladders up which they might eventually climb to precarious life.

The Marine bandsmen were perfectly aware of all this—they were far too intelligent not to be. It was discipline which kept them at the table, it was even discipline which kept their hands steady and their heads clear. Intangible and indefinable, discipline might perhaps be more clearly understood by consideration of its opposites. Panic can seize a crowd or an individual, making men run for no known reason in search of no known objective; in panic men shake with fear, act without aim or purpose, hear nothing, see nothing. Disciplined men stay calm and steady, do their duty purposefully, and are attentive to orders and instructions. The one is a state of mind, just as is the other, and every state of mind grows out of the past. A myriad factors contribute to discipline—old habit, confidence in one's fellows, belief in the importance of one's duty. Roman discipline came to be based on fear of consequences; it was axiomatic in the Roman army that the soldier should fear his officers more than the enemy, and Frederick the Great used the same method with the Prussian Guard. An enthusiast will charge into danger, but, once stopped, he is likely to run away, and, running away, he is as hard to stop as when he is charging. Fear and enthusiasm are narrow and precarious bases for discipline. Perhaps the principal element in the Marines' discipline was pride—pride in themselves, pride in the duty entrusted to them, pride in the cause in which they fought, and pride in the Navy in which they served.

C. S. FORESTER, *The Ship*

*

The events described in The Ship *bear a strong resemblance to a very famous action on 22nd March 1942, in which Admiral Vian with a force of cruisers and destroyers defended a Malta convoy against a much more powerful Italian fleet in*

THE SECOND BATTLE OF SIRTE

I have always been blessed with excellent eyesight, and, with the help of a magnificent pair of Zeiss 'binoctars' bought in Malta years back on my way out to join *Ladybird*, I was determined to be one of the first to sight the Italian Fleet. After all, we had a reputation to keep up. 'I've discovered a strange fleet,' Captain Blackwood had signalled on the eve of Trafalgar, the frigate *Euryalus* being the first to sight the combined fleets coming out of Cadiz.

And it came off again. I say it with pride.

'Quick, Jones,' I called to the chief yeoman. 'Make to the flagship: "Smoke on the horizon bearing 350 degrees".' The time was 2.10 pm. The sea was reasonably calm with visibility maximum, but the wind was freshening.

Spotting ships hull down is not an easy matter. I swept the horizon again and again with my binoculars and found nothing beyond the smoke; then suddenly objects appeared.

'Three ships bearing 359 degrees,' I almost shouted in my excitement. Up went the signal flags, closely followed by a similar message from the destroyer *Legion*, but we were definitely first. The time was 2.17 pm.

'Captain speaking. The Italian Fleet is in sight. Masts and funnels of three big ships are clearly visible from here. Good luck, everyone!' The reaction to this broadcast, I was told afterwards, was encouraging in the extreme. Here was the Cockney at his best. 'Let 'em all come!' they said.

'Signal flying concentrate by divisions in readiness to fight a surface action,' reported the chief yeoman, and, as the flags came fluttering down. 'Executive signal.'

'Signal flying, sir, make smoke.'

Admiral Philip Vian led his striking force out at once towards the enemy, while we took up our appointed station astern of his flagship *Cleopatra*, *Penelope* paired off with *Dido*, and the Fleet destroyers broke up into divisions. *Carlisle* and the 'Hunt'-class destroyers kept close to the convoy, which had already been ordered to steer south towards the Gulf of Sirte. Great clouds of black funnel smoke, mixed with the pure white of smoke floats, billowed and spread, hiding our convoy from the enemy.

At 2.36 pm the Italian ships opened fire at a range of 27,000 yards and were recognised as two eight-inch cruisers, one six-inch cruiser, and some destroyers. Their shots fell short. The range was also too great for us, but as the two fleets were closing at fifty knots it was not long before *Cleopatra* and *Euryalus* were able to take on the two heavy cruisers. In the conditions prevailing it was impossible to observe our fall of shot, and no doubt it was the same for the enemy. A few of their eight-inch shells fell harmlessly about us, as well as bombs from high-level bombers that no one could see. The encounter lasted a few minutes, until the Italians broke off the action, turned northwards again and drew out of range.

'Check fire,' ordered the gunnery officer.

'Enemy driven off,' I shouted down the broadcasting system, the time being 3.35 pm.

Admiral Vian now led us back towards the convoy, which had been ordered to steer west again. In our absence they had been having an unpleasant time driving off wave after wave of dive-bombers, but had suffered no damage, thanks to the fine gunnery of *Carlisle* and her destroyers, and to the admirable handling of the merchant ships by their masters.

We had hardly reached the convoy before the whole show started up again.

'From *Zulu*, sir, "Enemy in sight bearing north: one battleship, cruisers and destroyers".' The time now was 4.37 pm.

'Stand by again,' I said into the loudspeaker. 'There's more to come!'

Admiral Vian led us out as before, first to the north to clear the convoy, then to the east to lay another smoke-screen, and then back to the west again, while the convoy with heavy heart turned south and increased to its maximum speed.

The enemy, as we know now, was in two groups at this stage, the nearer, about nine miles away, consisting of the two eight-inch and one six-inch cruisers and four destroyers we had met before, and the second group, at a distance of fifteen miles, comprising the modern battleship *Littorio* and four destroyers. We were in for something now, all right! I knew that Admiral Vian would never leave the convoy to its fate, so if needs be we would be fighting to the end.

In the next two hours the fate of our whole force was in the balance. With the powerful ships at his disposal the Italian admiral could easily have wiped us out, but he could not bring himself to enter the smoke-screen knowing that we were waiting for him on the other side. Instead he was content to try to work his way round to the westward, while we did our best to prevent him.

In one of the many brief encounters which followed, *Cleopatra* was hit on the bridge by a six-inch shell, but steamed on unaffected. Later, while our cruisers were searching for two Italian ships unaccounted for, Captain St J. A. Micklethwait in *Sikh*, with *Havock*, *Lively* and *Hero*, held off the enemy for half an hour in a most brilliantly fought action during which *Havock* was hit and stopped, but was later able to proceed.

Then, at 6.41 pm, the battleship *Littorio* spotted *Euryalus* through a gap in the smoke-screen. I saw flashes from her fifteen-inch guns rippling down her side as she fired a salvo at us—an unarmoured ship. An age seemed to pass before her shells arrived with a deafening crash, as they plunged into the water all round us, engulfing the ship in columns of water masthead high. We'd been straddled.

Poor Mollie! The thought of my wife left a widow tore through my mind as *Euryalus* shuddered and shook and then rocked so violently that I thought the topmast would come down, while fragments of shell screamed through the air to bury themselves in our ship's sides. But in a fraction of a second I was myself again.

'Starboard twenty!' I said down the voice-pipe, and to make double sure that the order was heard above the noise of battle I repeated it, 'Starboard twenty!' louder and clearer this time. I knew that the only way to save the ship was to alter the range before the next salvo arrived.

Again came the flash of guns and the seemingly endless time of flight while we knew that this might be the end of us, but luck was on our side, for the salvo passed harmlessly over and burst in the water beyond. Then *Cleopatra*, who had also been engaging the battleship, led round to port, and *Littorio* disappeared behind the smoke-screen—we could breathe freely again.

The situation at this stage appeared critical, but was finally turned to our advantage by a most determined torpedo attack at 6.45 pm by Captain A. L. Poland and his 14th Destroyer Flotilla, under cover of the guns of *Cleopatra* and *Euryalus*, in the face of which the Italians turned away, broke off the action, and disappeared in the fading light. The destroyers *Kingston* and *Lively* were damaged, but had the roles been reversed it is difficult to imagine that anything of either convoy or escort would have survived.

Captain ERIC BUSH DSO DSC RN,
Captain of HMS *Euryalus*

But despite Admiral Vian's success in the Gulf of Sirte, only about a quarter of that convoy's cargo was safely discharged in Malta: Breconshire *and* Clan Campbell *were sunk before reaching Malta,* Pampas *and* Talabot *were bombed while alongside. By midsummer 1942 the situation of the people and garrison of Malta was desperate. In June two more convoys were sailed: Operation 'Harpoon', with six merchant ships, from the west, and Operation 'Vigorous', with eleven ships, from the east. On the 15th, off Pantellaria, the 'Harpoon' convoy was menaced by the Italian VIIIth Division, under Vice-Admiral Alberto di Zara, comprising the cruisers* Eugenio di Savoia *and* Monte Cuccoli, *and five destroyers. While the convoy retired under a smoke screen by the 'Hunt'-class escorts, HMS* Bedouin *(Commander B. G. Scurfield RN) led the five Fleet destroyers towards the enemy. From a POW camp,* Bedouin's *captain wrote to his wife:*

'WE KNEW WHAT WE HAD TO DO'

This is what I had been training for for twenty-two years, and in nearly three years of war these were the first enemy ships I had seen. It was a great moment, but there was no time for musing. Up went the signals: 'Enemy in sight,' 'Steam for full speed,' 'Twenty-five knots,' and 'Form single line ahead,' and I led my five 'Fleets' up towards the enemy. It was a situation very much as we had envisaged and everyone knew what to do.

We had been on a course of 120 degrees and the enemy had been steering about 160 degrees, speed twenty-five knots and range twelve miles. As soon as they saw us turn towards them they altered course to about 130 degrees. Meanwhile the remainder of our force turned away to the southward under the smoke put up by the 'Hunts'.

I was in a fortunate position in many ways. I knew what we had to do and that the cost was not to be counted—the Italians must be driven off. It was no time for fancy manœuvres—it was to my mind merely a question of going bald-headed for the enemy and trying to do him as much harm as possible by gun and torpedo. Otherwise it was within his power to destroy us and then the convoy at his pleasure. I knew, too, that the other destroyers would follow me and so what I was about, whether they had signals from me or no. Finally, I knew that the ship was as ready for the test as we had been able to make her, and the result of our labours was now to be shown. I could do no more about it, except give Manners a target and do my best to avoid punishment for as long as possible.

The cruisers opened fire almost at once and the first salvos fell astern of the *Bedouin*. Their spread was good—too good perhaps at that range—and the shooting seemed to be unpleasantly accurate. Perhaps this is always the impression when one is the target! My attention was taken up by the time-honoured dodge of steering for the last splash. I had often heard of it being done and found it exhilarating. It worked, too, for some time. A little before 0630, Manners reckoned we were within range, so I told him to engage the leading destroyer, and we opened fire at 17,400 yards. Ten minutes later the enemy altered another twenty degrees away and we shifted our fire to the leading cruiser at 12,400 yards.

By this time we were starting to get hit. Tinny crashes succeeded one another to such a tune that I began to wonder how much the ship could stand. Though I did not realise it at the time, one of the first things to go was the mast, and with it the wireless. I knew the bridge had been hit; the compass repeater was shaken out of its gimbals and I had had water and paint flakes dashed at me, but the splendid *Bedouin* was forging ahead and closing the gap minute by minute, Montgomery was passing news to the plot and Moller was standing by to fire torpedoes—wounded himself and with his assistant lying dead beside him. Skinner, though I didn't know it, was lying at the back of the bridge mortally wounded in the throat; Yeoman Archer and most of the signalmen and 'rudolf' men on the flag-deck were either dead or wounded. All I knew was that the coxswain was calmly doing his job at the wheel and that the ship was responding splendidly. We appeared to be straddling the enemy and must have been hitting, but observation of fall of shot was difficult and it was not possible to allocate targets. That was the only signal I might with advantage have made.

At about 0650 the director was hit. The layer was killed outright and Parker, who was keeping the rate, mortally wounded; Manners and the sight-setter escaped unscathed and so did the cross-leveller, though he was blown clean out of the tower. The ship had received more punishment than I knew, and I felt in my bones that she would not be able to go much farther. So I told Moller to go down and fire the torpedoes from the tubes and when the range had come down to 5,000 yards—tracer was being fired at us by the enemy's close-range weapons—turned the ship to starboard. During the turn we were hit several times, but the torpedoes were fired when the sights came on. After swinging past the firing course the ship came to a standstill.

We scored no hits, I fear, nor did any of the others who fired torpedoes, but the enemy made a large alteration of course away from us and broke off the action. Soon afterwards he disappeared to the north-eastward. We were at least left masters of the battlefield, and the convoy had got a good start.

Commander B. G. SCURFIELD DSO OBE AM RN,
Captain of HMS *Bedouin*

Bedouin, *crippled and at a standstill, was taken in tow by HMS* Partridge, *but they were attacked and the tow was slipped.* Partridge was *approaching for a second tow when they were attacked again:* Bedouin *was sunk but* Partridge, *though badly damaged, reached Gibraltar three days later. In 1945, when the Germans were moving POWs away from the advancing Allied armies, a party of prisoners were bombed on the road by Allied aircraft. Commander Scurfield was killed.*

*

Meanwhile, the 'Vigorous' convoy were threatened by even more formidable opposition, including the battleships Vittorio Veneto *and* Littorio. *They suffered, in Admiral Vian's phrase, 'all known forms of attack' and were forced to return to Alexandria. Thus from the two convoys only two merchant ships from 'Harpoon' reached Malta, at the cost of the cruiser* Hermione, *the destroyers* Bedouin, Hasty, Airedale, *the Australian* Nestor *and the Polish* Kujawiak, *two minesweepers and six merchant vessels.*

The War Cabinet now decided that another convoy for Malta must be given first priority over every other naval commitment anywhere in the world. On the 10th of August fourteen merchant ships, among them the tanker Ohio, *headed eastward through the Straits of Gibraltar, escorted by a huge and powerful fleet: the battleships* Nelson *and* Rodney, *the aircraft carriers* Victorious, Indomitable *and* Eagle (*and* Furious, *with replacement Spitfires for Malta*), *the cruisers* Sirius, Phoebe, Charybdis, Kenya, Nigeria, Manchester *and* Cairo, *and thirty-two destroyers. One of* Indomitable*'s fighter pilots wrote an account of his flight above*

OPERATION PEDESTAL

The wind was chancy, and we were to be boosted off. I was in position on the catapult, engine running. The flight-deck engineer waggled the ailerons to draw my attention to something or other, and I looked out over the port side to see what he wanted. And, as I did so, I stared in shocked surprise beyond him to where *Eagle* was steaming level with us, half a mile away. For as I turned smoke and steam suddenly poured from her, she took on a heavy list to port, and the air shook with a series of muffled explosions.

Over the sound of the engine, I yelled: '*Eagle*'s been hit!'

Listing to port, she swung outwards in a slow, agonised circle, and in seven minutes turned abruptly over. For a few seconds longer her bottom remained visible; and then the trapped air in her hull escaped, and with a last gust of steam and bubbles she vanished. All that remained was the troubled water, a spreading stain of oil, and the clustered black dots of her ship's company.

There had hardly been time to assimilate the fact that she had been hit before she had capsized and sunk; and when I took off a few minutes later my mind was still numbed by what I had seen. It had come so completely without forewarning. Our thoughts had been focussed on the idea of air attack; we had never dreamed that a U-boat would slip through the screen of destroyers to attack with such chilling precision. It was as if, at any moment, our own ship might stagger and lurch and list, and our aircraft go slithering down the deck into the sea.

In the air we saw the whole fleet alter course, while the destroyers hounded back and forth, dropping depth-charges. The loss of *Eagle* had screwed up the tension by another full turn, and we flew our patrol with tingling nerves. And still the expected raids did not come.

The day wore on. At 2000 hours Brian and I were back on standby.

The sky was gaudy with the first high colours of sunset. In an hour and a half it would be dark, and readiness would be over for the day. We hung about on the flight-deck, Mae Wests on, helmets round our necks, gloves in sticky hands.

'Another forty minutes,' Brian said, 'and I should think we can call it a day.'

The Tannoy crackled. 'Scramble the Hurricanes. Scramble the Hurricanes!'

The fitters in the cockpits pressed the starter-buttons, and the four Merlins opened up with a blast of sound and a gust of blue smoke. As we scrambled up the wings, the crews hopped out the other side, fixing our straps with urgent fingers. Connect RT; switch on ten degrees of flap. Trim. Quick cockpit check. The ship was under full helm, racing up into wind—and we were off and climbing at full boost on a northerly vector to 20,000 feet, head swivelling. Down to 12,000; alter course; climb to 20,000 again. And there they were, a big formation of 88s below us. One after another we peeled off and went down after them. They broke formation as they saw us coming, and Brian and I picked one and went after him. He turned and dived away, and we stuffed the nose down, full bore, willing our aircraft to make up on him. At extreme range we gave him a long burst; bits came off and smoke poured out of one engine, and then he vanished into the thickening twilight. We hadn't a hope of catching him and making sure; already he had led us away from the convoy, and so, cursing our lack of speed, we re-formed, joined up with Steve and Paddy, the other members of the flight, and started to climb back to base.

The sight we saw took our breath away. The light was slowly dying, and the ships were no more than a pattern on the grey steel plate of the sea; but where we had left them sailing peaceably through the sunset, now they were enclosed in a sparkling net of tracer and bursting shells, a mesh of fire. Every gun in fleet and convoy was firing, and the darkling air was laced with threads and beads of flame.

For a time we hunted round the fringes of it, hoping to catch somebody coming out; but the light was going, and we were running short of petrol. We had already been in the air for an hour, most of it with the throttle wide open. There was no sign of the 88s which had started it all; and it was not clear at first what the ships were still firing at. Then we saw the tracer coming morsing up towards us, and one or two black puffs of smoke burst uncomfortably close. We moved round the fleet, and the bursts followed us; and the truth could no longer be disregarded. They were firing at anything that flew.

We pulled away out of range, and called up the ship and asked for instructions. Stewart Morris's voice was never calmer or more sweetly reasonable than at that moment.

'Stand by, Yellow Flight. Will pancake you as soon as possible.'

'If you'd stop shooting at us it would be a help,' Brian said, without eliciting a reply.

We closed the convoy again, to test their mood, and provoked another hail of gun-fire. We tried switching on navigation lights, which merely encouraged them to improve on their earlier efforts. Disheartened, we withdrew.

By now it was beginning to get dark, and in the gloom I lost the others. With the prospect of a night deck-landing at the end of it all, the situation was beginning to lose its attractions.

'Check fuel, Yellow Flight'; the urbanity of Stewart's voice gave one a sudden, sharp yearning to be back on the familiar deck. Worlds seemed to divide the dark cockpit and its glowing instruments from the dark air direction room, with its glowing screens, worlds of twilight sky and sea, as black now as well-water, and the spasmodic bursts of fire.

I tested the gauges of the three tanks, and found I had less than twenty gallons left, a bare half-hour's flying. On my own now, I throttled right back, cut the revs, went into fully weak mixture. It looked as if those eighteen gallons were going to have to last a long time.

Every now and then I approached the ships, still just visible below; and each time the guns opened up. At last, I dropped down to fifty feet, and ploughed slowly up and down between the screen and the convoy, waiting for a chance to find the ship, and hoping to find her into wind. From time to time one of the merchant ships on one side—they had thoughtfully been provided with four Bofors guns each against just such an opportunity—or the destroyers on the other side would spot me, and the red dots of their tracer would come drifting up at me. Once something bigger hit the water with a splash alongside, and I jerked away, frightened and angry. It was at about this point that my RT decided to pack up.

I was down to ten gallons, and began to go over in my mind the procedure for ditching, for if I wasn't shot down, and if I didn't find a deck to land on very soon, I should surely have to land in the sea. I jettisoned the hood and released my parachute harness and kept ducking the gusts of gun-fire, and came, all at once, to the sudden, stabbing realisation that this might be the end of me. Up to that exact instant, flying up and down between the dark lanes of ships, I hadn't thought of it like that. Now it hit me, as blindly bruising as hatred, as confusing as a blow. I didn't know how I was going to get back aboard: now, for the first time, it seemed highly probable that I should not, and I understood the implications. I didn't wholly accept them; there was still a loophole or two through which the mind went bravely peering, past the dead-end of the inimical night.

Automatically I checked the tanks. Five gallons. The time had come for desperate measures unless I was going to accept without an effort my own approaching death. I flew in low over the convoy, disregarding the squalls of fire, in search of a ship to land on. It was now 2130 hours, and quite dark, and the first one I chose turned out to have a funnel amidships. I sheered off hurriedly, and just managed to make out what looked like a carrier astern of the convoy. I made for it, dropping hook, wheels and flaps on the way. It was difficult to see what she was doing: then I caught the glimmer of her wake, and began my approach. There wasn't a light showing; but I could see by the wake that she was under helm. Would she be into wind in time?

I steadied into the approach, and a pair of lighted bats materialised on her deck and began mechanically to wave me round. I checked my petrol for the last time. All the tanks were reading '0'. There was a slight chance I might get down in one piece, even with the deck swinging: there was no chance of my getting round again. I continued my approach.

The batsman's signals were becoming a little feverish; but now I could see the deck, swerving away to starboard under me. It was my last chance. I crammed the nose down, cut the throttle, and with the last bit of extra speed, tried to kick the aircraft into a turn to match the ship's. She was swinging too fast. The wheels touched, and the skid wiped off the undercarriage and the aircraft hit the deck and slithering and screeching up towards the island on its belly. I hung on and waited. It stopped at last, just short of the island, on the centre-line—what was left of it.

For a fraction of a second I was too relieved to move. And then, out of the corner of my eye, I saw a tongue of blue flame flicker across the bottom of the cockpit, and I yanked the pin out of the straps and was over the side. An instant later the wreck went up in a haze of flame.

It seemed excessively ignorant to have to ask which ship I was in; and so I waited in the doorway into the island while the fire-crews doused the blaze, and Jumbo the crane lurched up and removed the bits.

'Did anyone see the pilot?' I heard close beside me.

'No. Did you?'

'I haven't seen him. Wasn't still in the cockpit, was he?'

'No.'

'Well, either he must have made a ruddy quick getaway, or the kite must have landed-on by itself.'

I didn't feel particularly like advertising myself, but I had to settle this.

'It's all right,' I said diffidently. 'I was the pilot.'

They both looked at me.

Lieutenant (A) HUGH POPHAM RNVR, of 880 Squadron

(*The author had actually landed on* Victorious.)

*

CONVOY JOB

Convoy the dead:
Those humble men who drown,
Dreaming of narrow streets, of alleys snug
In lamplight, love in a furrowed bed,
Pints in a Rose and Crown.

Escort the brave
Whose hearts, unsatisfied
With the kind stairs and tender hearths of love,
Are loyal to the cunning of the wave,
The sparse rule of the tide.

Fly over these,
Humble and brave, who sail
And trim the ships with very life; whose lives
Delineate the seas.
Patrol their deathless trail.

JOHN PUDNEY

*

HMS Eagle *(Captain L. D. Mackintosh RN) had been hit by four torpedoes from U-73. Although she sank so quickly, 930 of her company of 1,160 were saved, including the Exchange Telegraph correspondent:*

We scrambled up the ladder to the upper deck with the ship listing over terrifyingly to the port side on which we were. The sea, normally ten feet below the rails, was surging ominously a bare two feet below them. We made the quarterdeck and grabbed anything we could to haul ourselves up the steeply sloping deck to the starboard side. Clutching the bullet-proof casing enclosing the quarterdeck, I found myself next to a first lieutenant who was blowing up a lifebelt. I followed suit.

Looking round I saw the deck slanting more sharply than a gabled roof. Six-inch shells weighing over 100 lb. tore loose from their brackets and bumped down the cliff-like deck. Ratings on the port side saw them coming and flung themselves into the water to escape injury. Foolishly I asked the first lieutenant, 'Is she going?' He nodded. Several ratings, grasping the casing, clambered towards us. They fastened a stout rope to the deck. They slithered down into the thick oil welling out under the ship and coating the sea and drifted away. With perfect confidence in my lifebelt I did the same and let go.

I went under the wave but when I came to the surface I realised with horror that I had not put enough air into the lifebelt. My head was barely above water. With all the poor swimmer's dread of deep water I splashed and kicked clear of the ship. As I got free of the oil patch the sea became choppy and every wave washed clear over my head till I was dizzy. I gave myself up for lost.

No wreckage was near which I could grasp. Then as a wave lifted me I saw a glorious sight—a cork float twenty yards off with sailors clinging round it. I fought madly to reach it. Three times my head went under and then I saw the float a few feet away. I snatched despairingly but missed. Making another wild clutch, I felt my fingers grip.

Half a dozen ratings holding on tried to loosen the ropes to open the cork raft out. It was tied up like a round bundle. But the oil on their fingers made the task impossible. The water was quite warm, but I had difficulty in holding on firmly owing to my oil-smothered hands. Another rating swam up and caught hold too. He told us his leg was broken. We helped him to crawl on to the centre of the bundle. The waves broke over us. I pulled myself up and saw the *Eagle* 200 yards away, lying on her side. Down the great red expanse of the *Eagle*'s hull men like ants were sliding down into the sea.

Suddenly I felt a shock at the base of my spine. I knew it was a depth-charge from a destroyer hunting the U-boat responsible. 'She is going,' gasped one of the men. Then came a mighty rumbling as the sea poured relentlessly into the *Eagle*, forcing out the air. The water threshed over her in a fury of white foam and then subsided. She had gone.

ARTHUR THORPE, from Exchange Telegraph
From *Daily Telegraph*, 14th August/1942

The author was also a survivor from Ark Royal. *He was killed later in the war whilst on active service with the Royal Navy as a war correspondent.*

*

The next day, the 12th, HMS Ithuriel *forced the Italian U-boat* Cobalto *to the surface and rammed her with*

'A DELIGHTFUL CRUNCH'

Suddenly from the able seaman up on the rangefinder comes the report, 'Periscope green seventy.' Sure enough, broad on the starboard bow a slight feather can be seen in the water halfway between us and the aircraft carrier. I immediately give the following orders: 'Hard a starboard, twenty-four knots; make the alarm signal; depth-charges, ready, press the U-boat alarm.' We warn the aircraft carrier and other neighbouring ships by signal. The alarm bells ring loudly throughout the ship. Depth-charges are reported ready. The guns are ready to open fire. The boats are got ready in case required. Everything is ready. We're off. The periscope dips from sight, but we are heading towards him. Even if we don't kill we should give him something to think about. The Asdic has picked up the U-boat. That's fine; we're all set; let's hope we get him.

'Stand by depth-charges. Depth-charges, fire!' The able seaman standing by the firing levers pulls them, and after a few seconds the ship shudders as they explode violently astern of us. 'Quite a good attack I think, Sir,' says the RNVR sub-lieutenant, and everybody looks astern, hoping for some signs of wreckage to appear. I decide to carry out a second depth-charge attack and the ship is just turning when a roar goes up, 'There she is.' It was a successful attack, and the U-boat has come to the surface, but the job is not yet finished. Perhaps she will crash-dive and try to escape. We can take no chances. So, 'Full ahead both engines; prepare to ram.' The guns need no orders. They have already opened fire and the U-boat is getting seven bells knocked out of her. Some of the Italians start shouting and jumping overboard. I give the order 'Full speed astern' to take some speed off the ship and avoid damaging ourselves unnecessarily. After all, you don't need to use a hammer on a boiled egg, so to speak. We hit her abaft the conning tower and heel her right over. It is a delightful crunch.

Lieutenant-Commander D. H. MAITLAND-MAKGILL-CRICHTON DSO RN, Captain of the *Ithuriel*

*

SONG OF THE DYING GUNNER AA1

Oh mother my mouth is full of stars
As cartridges in the tray
My blood is a twin-branched scarlet tree
And it runs all runs away.

Oh Cooks to the Galley is sounded off
And the lads are down in the mess
But I lie done by the forrard gun
With a bullet in my breast.

Don't send me a parcel at Christmas time
Of socks and nutty and wine
And don't depend on a long weekend
By the Great Western Railway line.

Farewell Aggie Weston, the Barracks at Guz,
Hang my tiddley suit on the door
I'm sewn up neat in a canvas sheet
And I shan't be home no more.

Petty Officer CHARLES CAUSLEY

*

She had been uppermost in our thoughts from the moment we sailed, for she was a tanker carrying the most important and most dangerous cargo of all, and so very conspicuous from the air with her funnel right aft. Her name was *Ohio*, an American-built ship manned by a British crew, skippered by a very great man called Captain Mason. It was obvious that she would be a special target for the enemy and sure enough she was hit by a torpedo at the same time as we were.

She was forced to stop, and later, as we went up alongside in the *Ashanti*, another merchantman was blazing not far off. It was that night when things weren't looking too good. Admiral Burrough hailed her from the bridge. 'I've got to go on with the rest of the convoy. Make the shore route if you can and slip across to Malta. They need you badly.' The reply was instantaneous. 'Don't worry, sir, we'll do our best. Good luck.'

By next morning, by some superhuman effort, they had got the engines going and had caught us up in spite of having lost their compass and having to steer from aft. She then took station on our quarter and *Ohio*'s next bit of trouble was when a Stuka attacking us was hit fair and square and crashed right into her.

For the rest of the forenoon she was always picked out for special attention, and time and time again she completely disappeared amongst the clouds of water from bursting bombs. But again and again she came through. Then at last one hit her. She was set on fire, but after a terrific fight they managed to get the flames under control. Her engines had been partly wrecked, but she just managed to make two knots and plodded on. Destroyers left to look after her, but later she was hit again and her engines finally put out of action. Then they took her in tow, but the tow parted. During the night with the help of a minesweeper from Malta they got her a further twenty miles. All next day she was again continuously bombed and towing became impossible. But that night she reached Malta.

Admiral Burrough's last signal to *Ohio* was short and to the point: 'I'm proud to have met you.'

Commander ANTHONY KIMMINS OBE RN

Five of the fourteen merchant ships reached Malta. They included Ohio, *whose master, Captain D. W. Mason, was awarded the George Cross. In addition to* Eagle *and the nine merchant ships, the cruisers* Manchester *and* Cairo *and the destroyer* Foresight *were also lost during the passage of the 'Pedestal' Convoy.*

CHIEF PETTY OFFICER

He is older than the naval side of British history,
And sits
More permanent than the spider in the enormous wall.
His barefoot, coal-burning soul,
Expands, puffs like a toad, in the convict air
Of the Royal Naval Barracks at Devonport.

Here, in depot, is his stone Nirvana:
More real than the opium-pipes,
The uninteresting relics of Edwardian foreign-commission.
And, from his thick stone box,
He surveys with a prehistoric eye the hostilities-only ratings.

He has the face of the dinosaur
That sometimes stares from old Victorian naval photographs:
That of some elderly lieutenant
With boots and a celluloid Crippen-collar,
Brass buttons and cruel ambitious eyes of almond.

He was probably made a Freemason in Hong Kong.
He has a son (on War Work) in the Dockyard,
And an appalling daughter
In the WRNS.
He writes on your draft-chit,
Tobacco-permit or request-form
In a huge antique Borstal hand,
And pins notices on the board in the Chiefs' Mess
Requesting his messmates not to
Lay on the billiard table.
He is an anti-Semite and has somewhat reactionary views,
And reads the pictures in the daily news.

And when you return from the nervous Pacific
Where the seas
Shift like sheets of plate-glass in the dazzling morning;
Or when you return
Browner than Alexander, from Malta,
Where you have leaned over the side, in harbour,
And seen in the clear water
The salmon tins, wrecks and tiny explosions of crystal fish,
A whole war later
He will still be sitting under a pusser's clock
Waiting for tot-time,
His narrow forehead ruffled by the Jutland wind.

Petty Officer CHARLES CAUSLEY

*

A trawler skipper, with several enemy aircraft to his credit, was asked to explain his technique to ratings under gunnery instruction. His lecture was as follows:

'I sees an enemy aircraft ahead. It gets a bit closer, so I calls my mate Bill and says, "Enemy aircraft on the port bow, Bill. Get on the gun." So Bill gets on the gun. Then I says "Shoot the bugger down, Bill." And Bill shoots 'un down.'

*

When HMS *Edinburgh* was torpedoed in the Barents Sea while escorting convoy QP11 in May 1942, three '*Halcyon*'-class minesweepers put up a spirited fight against superior forces. The flag officer in command (Rear-Admiral S. S. Bonham-Carter, commanding the 18th Cruiser Squadron) had given orders that they should retire at full speed under a smoke-screen if attacked by surface craft. These orders never reached them. When *Edinburgh* was hit, instead of turning away they turned towards the enemy destroyers, 'Going in like three young terriers', as the admiral said, and firing whenever visibility permitted. Then, while one made a smoke-screen, the other two went alongside the sinking cruiser and took off the whole ship's company. Admiral Bonham-Carter was among the last to leave. As he stepped on to the sweeper's quarterdeck her commanding officer saluted.

'Everything correct, sir. Your flag is hoisted.'

The admiral looked upwards. Flying at the masthead was the Cross of St George, with two red balls in the upper and lower cantons. Its ragged edge suggested that it was a senior officer's pendant from which the tails had been cut, and the red balls looked as though they had been hastily daubed on with red paint. But there was no mistaking it for anything but a rear-admiral's flag.

From *His Majesty's Minesweepers*

*

FAMOUS LAST WORDS

'No mines there, we swept there yesterday.'
'They won't bother us, we're too small.'
'He won't have any bombs, he's going home.'
'It's only the engine-room fan.'

From a minesweeping flotilla's line book.

*

DESTROYERS IN THE ARCTIC

Camouflaged, they detach lengths of sea and sky
When they move; offset, speed and direction are a lie.

Everything is grey everywhere; ships, water, snow, faces.
Flanking the convoy, we rarely go through our paces:

But sometimes on tightening waves at night they wheel
Drawing white moons on strings from dripping keel.

Cold cases them, like ships in glass; they are formal,
Not real, except in adversity. Then, too, have to seem normal.

At dusk they intensify dusk, strung out, non-committal:
Waves spill from our wake, crepe paper magnetised by gun-metal.

They breathe silence, less solid than ghosts, ruminative
As the Arctic breaks up on their sides and they sieve

Moisture into mess-decks. Heat is cold-lined there,
Where we wait for a torpedo and lack air.

Repetitive of each other, imitating the sea's lift and fall,
On the wings of the convoy they indicate rehearsal.

Merchantmen move sideways, with the gait of crustaceans,
Round whom like eels escorts take up their stations.

Landfall, Murmansk; but starboard now a lead-coloured
Island, Jan Mayen. Days identical, hoisted like sails, blurred.

Counters moved on an Admiralty map, snow like confetti
Covers the real us. We dream we are counterfeits tied to our jetty

But cannot dream long; the sea curdles and sprawls,
Lavishly real, and merciless all else away from us falls.

Lieutenant ALAN ROSS RNVR

*

In what was perhaps the understatement of the war, PQ 17's convoy commodore, Commodore J. C. K. Dowding, described their passage as '. . . not *a successful convoy'. Thirty-six merchant ships set out from Reykjavik on 27th June 1942. Two returned early to Reykjavik, and, of the remainder, ten were sunk by U-boats and thirteen by aircraft. This account is written by the officer who was HMS* Keppel's *captain and leader of PQ17's close destroyer escort:*

'I AM READY AND WILLING TO GO BACK'

At 10.30 pm on 4th July, a quarter of a century ago, in broad, peaceful Arctic daylight, astonished eyes on the bridges of a well-formed convoy of thirty laden ships saw their six escorting destroyers form up, turn, and disappear with some distant cruisers over the horizon astern. In the next few days twenty-one of those helpless freighters felt the cold Arctic water close over them. Sir Winston Churchill called this one of the most melancholy naval episodes of the whole war. Stalin asked if the British Navy had any sense of glory.

I commanded that destroyer escort. It was I who led those destroyers away, and left those ships to their fate.

A few minutes previously I had written in my diary in the charthouse of HMS *Keppel* that the convoy, PQ 17, was going like a train, and if the ack-ack ammunition (which to date had been sprayed rather extravagantly) lasted out, I reckoned that we could get anywhere. Then suddenly, out of an ice-blue sky, PQ 17 was murdered by a single word, uttered some two thousand miles away.

The seventeenth convoy to Russia was born in a Quonset hut at Hvalfiord, Iceland, towards the end of June 1942. Skippers left their freighters groaning under the load of tanks and planes and came ashore to meet one another, their escort officers, and their next convoy problem. No merchant skipper who has sailed independently all his life likes the ocean round him turned into a parade ground, but they all listened politely to the old convoy sermon about funnel smoke, floating refuse, black-out. A wag added a crack about the danger of showing any dark in permanent daylight. A glance was spared for a poster stuck on the hut wall. It showed a few men clinging to some small wreckage in a lot of ocean. The caption: 'An extraordinary general meeting of the Stragglers' Club.'

From the escorter's angle there are three different Merchant Navy approaches to convoying, and at these conferences you can soon tell from the keen interest, the indulgence, or the yawn, what you are in for. We remembered the skipper who read a newspaper throughout; he lasted two days. But from the word go there was no doubt that this bunch was interested. They knew these Russian runs were by no means slices of cake. The terrible winter storms fought by their predecessors might have eased, but they were seamen, they knew jolly well that this floating town they were about to form would fill some twenty-five miles of non-stop visibility. They hadn't got to be told that enemy U-boats, planes, and warships would take full advantage of this.

They asked about the *Tirpitz*, the Big Bad Wolf. Yes, there was evidence that she and others were moving north. But four cruisers would be covering the convoy, and the Home Fleet would be in the background. The most formidable thing about the *Tirpitz*, they were reminded, was her threat. It seemed unlikely that Germany's last and greatest battleship would stick her neck out *Bismarck*-fashion. If Hitler ran out of battleships he would be running out of naval strategy. I added that my escort group had just had a couple of days at sea trying out some moves, in case she came our way. We believed that the timely use of smoke and torpedoes would trip anyone interested in the convoy-destruction business.

A day or two later, off the eastern coast of Iceland, PQ 17 became a formidable reality consisting of 33 merchantmen, 2 tankers, 3 rescue ships, 2 submarines, pegged round by 6 destroyers, 4 corvettes, 2 anti-aircraft ships, 3 minesweepers, 4 trawlers. Once formed, convoys, like any other community, have to get themselves organised. Apart from practising emergency manœuvres there are guns to try, barrage balloons to manipulate. Someone has a breakdown, who has a spare? Someone wants a doctor ('require some sort of medicine for some sort of rash'; 'have one hand with septic foot'). In a surprisingly short time it all sorts itself out; ships start keeping reasonable station; destroyers (fuel addicts one and all) drop into a smooth shuttle service to the tankers, the convoy gets into its stride.

Before long the first spread of U-boats were sighted and pounced on. It always pays to be generous with depth-charges to the early ones. Nobody was sunk on either side, but we learnt after the war that the reception we gave them changed their minds about attacking.

On the second afternoon we passed a convoy returning on an unexpectedly peaceful run from Murmansk. In return for one empty tanker we received an unprintable signal about the ladies of Murmansk, and Sam. Sam was a twin-engined Blom and Voss 138 'snooper'. As soon as he saw we had no carrier, he deserted his departing guests and settled down to circling our convoy just outside the range of our guns. It brought a chilly feeling knowing that from now on, visibility permitting, PQ 17 would be plotted on German operational wall maps as well as our own. At the same time his presence relaxed our restrictions on keeping radio silence, and it kept us on our toes. The distant drone of his engines was like the overture at a theatre. Any moment now the curtain would rise.

We were well past Jan Mayen Island when nine Heinkel torpedo planes appeared and circled warily round the horizon. Spirited shooting (especially from an American destroyer visiting our tanker from the covering cruiser force) made them hang back. They did not attack. When they had disappeared we glanced scornfully at Sam. Surely he could lay on something better than that. Suddenly the sunlight seemed to fade from his bat-like wings. He dimmed to a shape, a blurr, nothing. In as many seconds PQ 17 was wrapped in the protective comfort of a convoy's best friend, thick fog. However much those skippers had dreaded fog at sea in the past, now, with everyone going in the same direction at the same speed, it had its advantages. Sam became desperate. Twice he roared low over our heads. No one fired. We preferred to stay lost.

In the latitude we had reached by then day doesn't dawn, it just begins, as did the 166th anniversary of American Independence. The fog had lifted as quickly as it had come down and Sam had returned as I turned *Keppel* and steamed through the convoy. Fog may have its protective angle but it can play hell with a convoy's figure. The bold stand on, the cautious edge outwards, the timid drop back, formation goes to blazes. I wish I had an aerial photograph of what I saw then. Column leaders had kept their distance, ships in column their station. They were almost saying as I went by, 'Look, no radar.' It was a splendid sight.

But at 3 am we lost our first ship. A Heinkel dropped through a hole in the low cloud and an American freighter, carrying enough weapons to arm a battalion, caught a torpedo at point-blank range.

This did not deter the eleven remaining American ships from flying all the Stars and Stripes they could muster, a gesture which was repeated throughout the convoy. There was a definite feeling at sea-level that PQ 17 was toughening.

By noon all cloud had vanished, and the sun was shining in crystal-clear visibility when another American destroyer, this time *Wainwright*, joined us from the cruisers for some fuel. Like her predecessor she brought trouble, this time six He 115s. More excellent gunnery from the USN. Again no attack. During the fusillade I signalled to *Wainwright*'s skipper, Commander Moon, 'Was the original 4th July as noisy as this?' His reply, 'I wasn't there but I guess negative.'

Inside an hour twenty-five more torpedo planes were reported approaching. In they came, low, bravely led. Neither the leader's target nor the leader himself had a hope. The others wavered. In two minutes the convoy had gone from peace to Bedlam and back to peace, leaving the glassy sea scarred with three smoking ships and three orange bonfires which had recently been planes. I closed one of the wounded ships, a Russian tanker. She was under control, holed but happy, with a couple of lusty dames waving cheerfully from her bridge.

Once again, steaming back through the convoy was a tonic. Ships were still in station, looking prouder than ever. And, after all, why not? I had escorted larger and more valuable convoys (putting troop-carrying highest) before, but none that faced a bigger challenge. Here was a lesson that, whether we like it or not, we all respond to a challenge. True we had four more nightless days ahead, but we were well past the halfway mark without a single submarine attack, or anything very impressive from the Luftwaffe, and only four casualties. After that last air attack I think we all felt the enemy had realised that PQ 17 meant business, and that feeling did us good. I still feel entitled to that slightly boastful entry in my diary at this stage that I reckoned we could get anywhere, as long as the ammunition lasted.

There are two things I will always remember when I returned to the bridge. One, the breathless—mocking?—beauty of the Arctic peace with that odd-shaped chain of vivid emerald-green icebergs marking the southern edge of the pack ice. Two, the sudden appearance of a large bull seal just off our bow, who raised himself out of the water on his flippers to protest in a loud rusty belch at our intrusion into his realm. Then, for the third time, the peace was shattered. This time by signal.

The first of three high-priority radio messages from the Admiralty was addressed to the nearby cruisers. It ordered them to withdraw to the westward at high speed. The convoy might miss the comfort of their company, but not me. What escort commander wants an admiral breathing down his neck? The second, timed twelve minutes later, was addressed to me: 'Owing to threat from surface ships convoy is to disperse and proceed to Russian ports.'

Although these two signals bore personal addresses they were by no means private messages, and soon the convoy escorts could hear this alarm bell as clearly as I could, saying virtually that the *Tirpitz*, *Hipper* and *Scheer*, last heard of some 300 miles away, were suddenly on our doorstep. I well remember telling Admiral Tovey, Commander-in-Chief Home Fleet, a few days later in his flagship at Scapa Flow, that as we were now in the area where such an attack seemed most probable, I accepted the implication of these signals without question. Then, timed thirteen minutes later and carrying top priority, signal number three arrived: 'Convoy is to scatter'.

This one was lethal, it exploded in my hand. 'Scatter' is an order to ships in convoy to break formation, to separate as fast as they can, starring outwards from the convoy's centre. It is the final *sauve qui peut* direction from an escort commander in the presence of a superior enemy force, exhorting his concentrated flock to become a difficult, widely dispersed gunnery target as quickly as possible. It follows logically that, having given this order, the escort commander will then do his best to drive off, or at least distract, the enemy. I had never heard (and still haven't) of a convoy being scattered from afar. Once a convoy was scattered, I knew of no other method than a sheepdog's of re-forming it.

But at least the increasing urgency of these three signals, culminating in the order to scatter, cleared the air as far as I was concerned. No one in their right mind would scatter such a fine convoy and commit thirty valuable ships to the mercy of enemy planes and U-boats unless it was a lesser evil than confronting them with imminent extermination from an overpowering force of enemy warships. No enemy warships were in sight, but in my hand I held the assurance of the First Sea Lord that they soon would be.

Having made certain that the convoy commodore saw the situation as I did, my next instinctive step was to place myself and my destroyers under the orders of the cruiser admiral, still a few miles to the westward. There is no alternative to 'concentration of force' at moments like this. To the commodore I signalled, 'Sorry to leave you like this. Good luck. It looks like a bloody business.'

As we steamed through the convoy and down its wake for the last time, our guns, torpedo tubes, smoke-floats, and all, were being manned and checked, for there was no doubt in our minds that we were moving out to fight. My impression was that the fog-bank to the westward which the cruisers were approaching was probably where the enemy were hiding. Little did we know that the *Tirpitz* and her squadron were at anchor 300 miles away in a Norwegian fjord.

Into the fog-bank cruisers and destroyers plunged, jerking our minds from convoy-escorting to keeping station at high speed on a ghostly formation of shapes. But there was still room for conjecture on *Keppel*'s bridge. Was the enemy really hiding in this? Supposing he slipped past us on an opposite course? Were we trying to draw him on to the Fleet? Did our admiral, with his privileged radio link with the Admiralty, know more than we did? But on and on we sped; nothing happened. Our rapidly increasing distance from the convoy began to infuse unpleasant doubts. Was this situation getting unreal? Were we part of any plan at all? A mathematical fact, striking colder than the freezing Arctic fog, slowly registered that as far as our convoy was concerned we had passed the point of no return from the fuel angle. From then on, uncertainty nagged and grew, ending in a moment I am not likely to forget, when the first pitiable cry for help came limping through the gloom from a merchantman who was being attacked by U-boat and plane. Something had gone hopelessly wrong. A trust we believed in implicitly had let us down flat.

I signalled to the admiral that I was ready and willing to go back, but it was too late. That one word, that unforgivable, tragically misused order, was already busy transforming a perfectly good convoy into one of the most melancholy episodes in the whole war.

A lot of whitewash and criticism has followed in the wake of this disaster, with the whitewash mainly confined to the end of the story carrying the Top Brass. Historians, factual and fictional, still cash in by keeping this pot on the boil, but as one of the—few remaining—central figures I have never been able to see anything controversial about it. PQ 17 was just another splendid convoy, ploughing along with no claim whatever to history or fiction until those signals arrived from the Admiralty. The order given in the final signal either had to be obeyed or ignored. To my dying regret I obeyed it. Having done so, it triggered off a sequence of events which (as Admiral Tovey agreed later) were inevitable, by accepted naval procedure. Eleven ships reached Archangel. What the result would have been had the order to scatter not been given, no one knows. But with the *Tirpitz* and her consorts then almost regarded by the Germans as 'sacred cows', the result could hardly have been worse.

The responsibility for what actually did happen must therefore for ever rest on the shoulders of the man who gave that order, and his advisers.

Captain JACK BROOME DSC RN

*

The incident when all the American ships in PQ 17 changed their ensigns made a deep impression on another observer, a professional reporter taking passage in the anti-aircraft ship HMS Pozarica:

. . . It so happened that my arrival back on the bridge that morning coincided with an unexpected and unforgettable ceremony. When all the battles have subsided in one's consciousness, certain other things remain that give to the familiar Horace tag, *Dulce et decorum est*, a new and untarnished significance. And I am less shy to speak of the gesture of faith we witnessed in the dawn of that new day since it concerns another country from our own. At the same time, I must be honest and admit that at first sight all of us on the bridge viewed the gesture with dismay and bewilderment, as doubtless you would have done, suddenly having your attention drawn to the sight of the next ship in line . . . hauling down her flag. Moreover, it was that same Liberty ship, whose crew had danced and stamped with pleasure on the deck, hearing our music of welcome. How long ago was that? A week? A century? Inevitably, one had lost all sense of time: all we did know for certain, using the evidence of our eyes, was that our 'chummy' ship, as she had become, was now in the act of carrying out the ritual that can only mean one thing at sea. Surrender.

It was the yeoman, trained fine, who first saw the downward fluttering of their flag, out of the corner of his eye, and shouted out what was happening, his own face a mirror of disgust. 'The yellow muckers. They can't take it.' No one else made any comment. I think we were all too horrified. Surrendering because *one* of their number had been torpedoed the previous night? And surrendering to whom? It was preposterous, it wasn't happening . . . and then as the impossible explanations pursued one another round our minds, someone else shouted: 'Look.' In the place of the flag hauled down, torn by the wind, dirty and shabby, a new Stars and Stripes was being run up at the masthead, and the new one looked twice the size—in our relief—and also because it was clean and shiningly transparent.

Then my eyes travelling beyond, up and down the other columns, registered that all the other Liberty ships, whose numbers dominated the convoy, were carrying out the same manœuvre, a single united movement of such co-ordinated precision that you might have been witnessing a peacetime ceremony, much rehearsed, under ideal conditions. But what ceremony? Why this dawn particularly to choose to make such a parade of national faith? Strangely, it was one of the stooges, the look-out ratings on their swivel seats, three to one side of the bridge, three to the other, their faces in their Balaclavas without expression, eternally masked by the heavy binoculars glued to their eyes, who, in the end, solved the riddle. Instead of calling out, 'Aircraft bearing Green 070 . . .' he exclaimed excitedly, 'I've got it! I've got it!' And he put up his hand, like a small boy, in class. 'It's 4th July, sir. . . .' July the 4th? Then at last we all got it. *Their* Independence Day. Of course. And I remember thinking: they are much, much farther from home than we are: their ships don't possess any real armament like ours: for many of them, it will be their first voyage through hostile waters, and anyway, they've been at sea weeks longer than we have, with all the time, tension increasing. But still they remembered.

GODFREY WINN

On his return from Russia Mr Winn joined the Navy, becoming Ordinary Seaman Winn, G., Official No. J/X 377610.

*

QBB 255 was the designation of a huge enemy minefield in the Mediterranean which stretched from the Sicilian island of Marittimo across the Sicilian Straits to Cape Bon. In July 1942 HMS/M Unbroken, *of the 10th Submarine Flotilla, left Gibraltar for Malta—through the minefield:*

Our journey passed quietly until 4 am on 18th July when we dived to eighty feet south of Marittimo for the passage through QBB 255. I decided on a direct, bold route, suspended halfway between bottom and surface, that would take us straight through the minefield via Cape Granitola. The distance of the run was sixty miles—fifteen hours of it at four knots.

The thought of QBB 255 gave us all the jitters. The sense of helplessness. . . . The fact that you cannot hit back but are permanently on the defensive, listening, waiting, magnifying every jolt and movement. . . . You speak in whispers as though loudness of voice will, in some indeterminable way, add to the hazards, and you are reluctant to make any but the most necessary gestures or movements. It is a nerve-racking business.

Inside the minefield I had the mine-detecting unit—a refinement of the Asdic—switched on in an effort to plot the pattern of the mines and sail between them. A regrettable action. We plotted mines right enough—ahead, to starboard, to port, above, below—everywhere! Cryer's eyes popped from his head as he reported each new echo, and a few wild expressions and quivering lips were to be seen in the control-room. I found it difficult to overcome a tremendous temptation to alter course as the mines were reported, but common sense prevailed and we continued dead ahead. A submarine going through a minefield can be compared to a man walking through line upon line of soldiers with a ladder on his shoulder and his eyes shut. As he passes through one line he *may* hit a man in the line in front, but if he swings round he is *certain* to hit, not one, but half a dozen. So we kept to the straight and narrow.

Slowly, blindly, we crept forward, while the air thickened and our sweat-soaked clothes clung to our bodies, until, unable to bear any longer Cryer's maddening and demoralising reports, I ordered: 'Switch that bloody thing off and never switch it on again!'

The hours dragged past in uneasy, clock-ticking silence. We lapsed into a half-sleeping state of stiff-jointed, head-throbbing weariness, and it came as a shock to realise that it was nine-o'clock—we were through the minefield, and could surface.

Surface we did, and fresh air never smelled sweeter. I altered course to starboard for the sixty-mile run that would take us to our final hazard—the mine-blocked channel into Valetta.

We dived at the entrance of the channel as the new day opened a reluctant, bloodshot eye over the eastern horizon. The channel was sixteen miles long, shaped, roughly, in a semicircle, only half a mile wide at its broadest point, and beset by strong currents and tidal streams. To add to our difficulties, the big periscope was jammed in low power, and we could not obtain long-range fixes of position from the Malta coastline. As our orders were to surface at sunset one mile from the Castile Signal Station, we pressed on and hoped God was still with us.

After the exhausting fifteen hours in QBB 255 I was devoid of emotion towards this second minefield, and my mind was assailed with other, sadder thoughts—memories of friends and messmates of yesterday whose shattered bodies lay but a few fathoms below our hull. It is said that mourning is selfish—that you weep, not for the dead, but for your own loss. That may well be true, and my memories were a shroud of grief, for I had lost many good friends and noble companions among these tortured waters. . . .

Lieutenant-Commander ALASTAIR MARS DSO DSC and Bar RN
Captain of the *Unbroken*

Shortly before, the author had tried to insure his life for £1,000. The insurance company was willing, but the premium for £1,000 would be £500 per annum—actually more than the author's yearly pay.

*

Miss Maria Elizabeth Ferguson (known to her family as 'Johnnie') spent three weeks in an open life-boat after the Blue Star liner SS Avila Star *was torpedoed in the Atlantic on 5th July 1942. Afterwards she was awarded the British Empire Medal for her courage during this ordeal and she was also the first woman passenger ever to be awarded the Lloyd's Medal.*

BOATING, ANYONE?

By this time Johnnie had decided that if she could not be a ferry pilot she would become a boat's crew Wren. She had done a lot of boating back in the Argentine on some of the tremendous waterways. She had been used to yachts and motor-boats long before the *Avila Star* saga.

So she applied for the Wrens, specifying boat's crew. After the usual lapse of time she was summoned to a WRNS centre in one of the London suburbs. The authorities had all the details of her experiences to date.

A woman interviewing officer looked solemnly through these, then at Johnnie, and asked her slowly, 'But have you had any boating experience?'

'Yes,' said Johnnie simply.

JOHN FRAYN TURNER

*

During Operation 'Jubilee'—the Dieppe Raid on 19th August 1942—the Royal Marine Commando under Lieutenant-Colonel J. P. Phillipps were allocated a cutting-out expedition in Dieppe harbour. However, at 6.30 am on the 19th it was decided that the expedition had become impossible because of heavy enemy fire and the Royal Marine Commando were offered to Major-General J. H. Roberts, the Military Force Commander, as a reserve unit.

Because of smoke on the beaches and imperfect communications neither General Roberts nor Captain J. Hughes-Hallett RN, the Naval Force Commander, could obtain a clear picture of events on shore. At 8.17 am the signal was received in the headquarters ship HMS Calpe: *'White Beach under firm control.' General Roberts therefore decided to commit the Marines to that beach to reinforce the success.*

In fact, White Beach was not under any sort of control. Embarked in their assault craft, the Royal Marine Commando were heading for a holocaust:

DIEPPE

Five to six hundred yards from the beach, our craft still waddling gamely along under a hurricane of bullets and mortar bombs, the men all huddled under the protecting steel overhang, the colonel gave the order to stop.

'Put up a smoke-screen!' he called as the craft slowed down.

Smoke-bombs were ignited and tossed over the sides, where they floated and sent up first small columns and then great clouds of smoke. An inshore breeze blew the smoke in the faces of the Germans and hid us from them. But they had got the range and continued to pepper us through the fog with bullets, continued to lob mortar bombs all around us, and—it seems—got one of their six-inch guns bearing on us.

In the craft itself, because the breeze was carrying the smoke towards the shore, visibility was well nigh perfect. The colonel and adjutant left their places under the steel overhang and, standing in the middle of the craft, in the stern, proceeded to talk with the coxswain's mate, now in charge of the mechanism and steering, about what could be done to ensure the landing board would go down next time we touched the beach.

'It's a crazy business,' whispered the friendly corporal from 10 Platoon to me. 'We don't stand a bloody earthly of getting up that beach. Everything the Jerries were throwing at three or four thousand Canadians when they went in earlier on they've now got concentrated on us. It's bloody suicide!'

'Yeah!' breathed a man crouching near. 'Trust old blood-and-guts [the colonel] to try something like this. I reckon he volunteered for it!'

'That's about the weight of it,' agreed the corporal. 'Christ though'—and his eyes shone with an eager gleam—'if we *could* knock out the Casino and tobacco factory, and give the Canucks a chance to get through, we'd be the heroes of the day!'

'Yeah!' breathed a neighbour. 'We'd pinch the show if we did that!'

'I reckon all we're goin' to pinch today,' said another man, 'is a wooden overcoat. Or maybe a wet one!'

'Aw, cheer up man!' jollied the corporal. 'You can't live for ever anyway.'

'It's just one of them forlorn bloody hopes,' went on the dolorous one, 'and nobody can't kid me it ain't.'

This man was not a coward. He was notorious throughout the unit as a natural-born pessimist. We liked to have him about because we could always crack a joke at his expense. But not this time.

I am too hazy about anything in the engineering line to know quite what was going on in the stern about getting the landing gear in operation again, but that such an attempt was being made was clear enough. In addition to other moves we had to shift our hand gear and other heavy kit off cables that ran along the deck. Our kit—we were carrying with us boxes of demolition materials—might have had something to do with the jamming. I heard much talk about this later but I know too little of such matters to be able to form a worth-while opinion.

Came a heavier, more hideous, whining and screeching, a crack, a crash, a blinding flash, and the adjutant, clutching at his tin hat which had been knocked awry, stumbled in a huddle on the deck.

'Oh, my God!' he exclaimed as he fell.

A small part of the back of his head had been sheared off as if with a knife. As he lay crumpled on the deck his brains oozed bloodily into his tin hat.

A hole had been knocked in our bottom. Water began to flood in. The spare petrol tank had been burst open and petrol began to flow out and spread on top of the water. Men, wounded earlier on and wounded again now, began to struggle forward out of the mess. The colonel, himself wounded, glared about him, belligerent as ever, figuring what next to do.

It is a question what set the petrol alight. Some say a smoke-bomb, being lit at the time to be thrown overboard to keep our screen going, was knocked out of the man's hand by blast. Others say the flash from a bursting mortar bomb did it.

Anyway, the petrol ignited and a sea of flame formed on the enlarging area of water in the craft as she settled slowly down by the stern. All the stern was a sea of flame in a moment. And it spread forward menacingly, inch by inch, as more water poured through the hole in the bottom.

The wounded were dragging themselves along in this sea of flame towards the bows. The colonel, opening his mouth to give an order, suddenly clapped his hands over his belly and sank in agony to his knees in water and flame. He had stopped a cluster of machine-gun bullets in his stomach. His hair, his eyebrows, were singed away.

There was a surge of men from the forward end of the craft to help pull out the wounded from the flames. The colonel, right in the stern, on his knees and in agony, gestured his men to go back.

'Leave me, leave me!' he called through gritting teeth.'I'm done for. Look out for yourselves!'

And he crumpled up and lay half buried in water and with flames licking all over him.

A sick-bay tiffy, a navy man attached to us because the Marines have no separate medical service, tried to push into the flames with a hypodermic needle to ease and quicken the colonel's last moments. But the colonel, opening his eyes for a moment and looking our way, quietly, resignedly, waved the man back. He was dying with his boots on: dying terribly: dying without any show of fear, without any fuss: dying like the brave man he was.

The scene in the craft was now terrible beyond words. Flames, heat, men being pulled out of the flames and into the comparative safety of the forward part, men still lying in the water, flames licking over them. Men crowded together so that they could scarcely move. Men still huddled on one knee under the steel overhang craning their necks to see what was going on. Men looking questioningly into one another's eyes, and yet expecting no answer. And the water and flames advancing towards us.

I was myself on my feet. My left upper arm and shoulder were at once numb and burning. Something had caught me a clout. I did not know nor care.

'Christ Almighty, Nutty,' said I to a man named Nutman who stood near me, 'what the hell do we do now?'

An officer supplied the answer. He was one of the two officers left to us. Over the crashing and whining and woo-woo-whooshing of mortar bombs and shells, over the chatter and clatter of the bullets, he shouted:

'Every man do the best he can! Off kit and swim for it!'

Marine JAMES SPENCER

The author took off his kit and swam for it. He reached the shore and, like the other survivors from this landing craft, became a prisoner of war.

*

WE FOUGHT THEM IN GUNBOATS

The E-boat was lying two hundred yards to the eastward, black and silent. The first of the dawn was by this time taking effect. She was clearly silhouetted against the growing light in the eastern sky. The moment was exhilarating in the extreme.

'We must board!' I shouted.

So in the early glimmering light on that calm and peaceful sea we made our preparations. She was obviously hopelessly crippled: there was no fear of her suddenly departing. It was, therefore, worth taking what precautions we could. We got all our tommy-guns and revolvers, we arranged to approach one on either side, with Boffin to starboard, in such a way that we should not fire straight across the E-boat at each other. All guns were to be trained on and used to the full if she showed the slightest signs of fight. Boffin was to use his searchlight, one of the midshipmen who could speak German was to hail the enemy, calling upon them to surrender. Everything was understood.

'Start up.'

The order was given, the silence shattered. Slowly the gunboats closed on their prey, the engines throbbing, the guns trained, every man strung up with excitement. No sign from the E-boat. The light was making steadily, but it wasn't enough yet to see any details on the enemy's decks. Were we to get a withering blast at the last minute, or what were the Germans up to? Fifty yards, twenty-five yards. Still no sign.

'Do you surrender?' The midshipman's voice carried ringingly over the quiet sea. No answer.

This was passing strange. A brilliant finger of light shot out from Boffin's boat, played on the decks of the E-boat. A deserted shambles. Bullet-holes everywhere, gear lying about, no signs of life; at the yardarm of her diminutive mast the ugly German naval flag with the swastika and the iron cross hung lifeless in the still air.

Was it an ambush? Were there men hidden, guns trained, waiting until they could not miss, for one last desperate stand? It was impossible to tell in the grey dawn. The hard light and dark shadows thrown by the searchlight were no better.

'We'll come alongside port side,' to Head.

'Aye, aye, sir.'

'You will lead the boarding party. Shoot at sight if there is any opposition.'

The last orders were given, the last dispositions made. Slowly we edged alongside. 'Stop port.'

Head jumped for it while still a foot or two off. There was a crash of gun-fire.

'Christ, they were there after all!'

Then I realised it was our own gun, put together again now, ripping across the decks of the E-boat. Edwards had tripped over the firing stand where it had been shattered; in so doing he had pulled the trigger. The shells had gone perilously close in front of Head. He jumped aboard, made straight for the Nazi ensign, and lowered it forthwith. My boat was made fast alongside. Boffin's quickly joined her. At once we realised what had happened. It seemed incredible we had not guessed it before.

The German crew had been taken off by another E-boat. They had heard us coming while they were in the process of scuttling the boat, and had beaten a very hasty retreat.

Leaving a few hands on the gunboats, much to their chagrin and loudly sucking their teeth, the rest swarmed on board the E-boat. A motor mechanic was detailed to report on the engine-room and see if there was any chance of closing the sea-cocks.

Head, who had gone on to enter the wheelhouse, reported a destruction charge laid down the companion way from the wheelhouse, the charge at the foot of the ladder. Everyone was kept back. The midshipman and I approached the charge. There was a fuse-line leading down the ladder, with a peculiar wooden handle at the firing end. Had it been lit? Well, it must be a long fuse if it was; the Germans had left some fifteen minutes ago at least.

Then the midshipman saw on the handle in German: 'Remove handle to fire.' Without more ado he picked up the charge and threw it overboard. There are advantages in knowing the enemy tongue!

Meanwhile it was obvious we could not save the boat without help. The engine-room was full of water and diesel oil, the water-levels were rising fast in other compartments. It was impossible to get at the sea-cocks to close them. I sent a signal asking for towing assistance and a pump, inwardly doubting whether anything could arrive in time. It was exasperating.

'Bring them back alive' had been the orders, but heavy as she was with water, it was impossible to tow; we should merely have ruined our engines. Lacking a power pump there was no hope of keeping her afloat unless assistance arrived within the hour. I doubted if she would last longer.

The order was given to gut the boat. Sailors swarmed all over her, appearing from the hatches with arms full of equipment. Roberts removed all the W/T equipment, gunners took what guns they could detach and pans of ammunition. Charts, books, logs, compasses, searchlights, revolvers, even pictures of Hitler were bundled into the gunboats. Someone came up waving a long German sausage. They had found it all spread out, half eaten, on the mess-deck table for'ard: sausage, black bread, sauerkraut.

She began to settle by the stern. She was wallowing, very heavy, now. With men everywhere below, I had to consider very carefully how long I could hold on, at the same time trying to make a mental note of all the important features of the boat. A particularly unpleasant wallow accompanied by a downward lurch aft decided me. Smoke was coming from the smoke apparatus where the decks were awash, water was swishing through a large crack in the deck. Only forward was it possible to get below.

'Abandon the E-boat. Get back to your boats.'

The order was quickly though reluctantly obeyed. We let go and stood off fifty yards to watch her end. Only just in time! She was going rapidly by the stern. Her bows were lifting, lifting, until for a few moments she hung vertical, her stern underwater, her bows pointed upwards, as if in supplication to the sky. Then quickly she sank and disappeared from view. A cheer went up, but it was a feeble one. There is something awe-inspiring and a little saddening about the sight of any ship, however small, however hated, going down. It is so very irrevocable; in its setting of apparently limitless water, impressive.

I remember one day going to discuss tactics with the SOO. For some reason I had to wait in the Commander-in-Chief's secretary's office. I was idly turning over the pages of a 1938 edition of *Jane's Fighting Ships.*

Suddenly my attention was riveted. There before my incredulous eyes was an admirable photo of an E-boat exactly in every detail like the one we had captured a year before. The raised fore deck, the bridge, the four torpedoes, two of them reloads, the let-in torpedo tubes, the large after compass, the low-side rails, the smoke apparatus. I collected my scattered wits and read the paragraph beneath.

It was the advertisement of a German shipbuilding yard, proclaiming their wares and inviting all and sundry to come and buy! Here was the world's fastest diesel-driven torpedo-boat—thirty-six and a half knots! Exactly the speed we had arrived at after comparing notes with all who had taken part in E-boat hunts!

The whole thing seemed too fantastic. The reiterated instructions to bring one back alive at all costs; the intense interest in all the details we could guess at or find out; the continual bombardment of questions on every point, even as to whether the engines were diesels, carried on for weeks over Admiralty telephone lines; the tremendous discussions and controversies as to maximum speeds.

And here it was all laid out for us in *Jane's*. Come see, come buy!

The Admiralty could have bought as many E-boats as they wished, indeed were pressed to do so, but one short year before the outbreak of war.

Lieutenant-Commander ROBERT HICHENS
DSO and bar DSC and two bars RNVR

The author was the first RNVR officer to be given command of a gunboat. On 13th April 1943, after a minor engagement with the enemy had been broken off, he was killed by a last stray shell.

*

OPERATION 'TORCH': THE LANDINGS IN NORTH AFRICA

As darkness descended on the Rock on the evening of the 5th of November the invasion fleet approached the Straits.

No waters in all the wide oceans of the world, not even those which wash the shores of Britain herself, have played a greater part in her history, or seen more of her maritime renown than these, where the rolling waves of the Atlantic approach the constricting passage of the Pillars of Hercules. Here it was that in 1587 Sir Francis Drake raided Cadiz and 'singed the King of Spain's beard'; through these waters sailed the ships of Sir George Rooke to the capture of Gibraltar itself in 1704, those of Admiral Rodney which fought the Moonlight Battle and relieved the Rock in 1780, and Lord Howe's fleet which finally raised the three-year siege in 1782. Over there Boscawen led his battleships into Lagos Bay and, by destroying de la Clue's squadron, added one more laurel to those gathered all over the world by British seamen in 1759—the *annus mirabilis*. It was here that on St Valentine's Day, 1797, John Jervis, 'old heart of oak', to whom England owed so much in an earlier crisis which had shaken her maritime power to its foundations, gained the victory by which his name is still chiefly remembered—the victory which, as he said, was 'very essential to England at this moment'.

It was in these narrows that a young Captain Nelson, for once pursued instead of pursuing, backed his topsails in the face of a superior enemy to pick up his friend and lieutenant, with the remark, 'By God, I'll not lose Hardy.' Through these straits passed Nelson's ships which finally ran Brueys to ground in Aboukir Bay, and those which chased Villeneuve to the West Indies and back again; and it was here that, on a calm and misty morning in October 1805, he and Collingwood led their two lines of battleships down towards the widely stretched crescent of the combined French and Spanish fleets. It was in that bay near Cape Trafalgar, on that same afternoon, that a dying admiral urged that his victorious but shattered ships should be anchored at once, to meet the storm he felt approaching from the Atlantic.

Nobly, nobly Cape St Vincent to the North-West died away;
Sunset ran, one glorious blood-red reeking into Cadiz Bay;
Bluish mid the burning water, full in face Trafalgar lay;
In the dimmest North-East distance dawned Gibraltar grand and grey;
Here and here did England help me: how can I help England?—say.[1]

For the last two years and more Cunningham's, Somerville's and Syfret's ships had passed and re-passed through these same waters, escorting supplies from Egypt or Malta, holding off a superior enemy and harassing his own sea communications; and, throughout the defensive phase, they had again and again, at Taranto, Matapan, Sirte, Crete, Spartivento and in a hundred lesser fights, won fresh renown on the station where Nelson hoped for, and found, 'a bed of laurels'. It was they who had kept the torch burning, albeit sometimes dimly, through all the desperate days of 1940 and 1941. Now that same torch was to be fanned into full flame by the men of the troopships, landing craft, escort vessels and covering warships, commanded once again by Cunningham and sailing through those same historic waters on Operation 'Torch'. And, although none of them probably thought of the poet's rhetorical question, all of them now combined to answer it. For what they did marked the passing of the Defensive Phase. Captain S. W. ROSKILL DSC RN

*

The troops were given endless practice in going to their landing-craft stations, at first by daylight and then at night. In the intervals there was much knowledge to imbibe. An informative booklet on North Africa, its geography, history and its people, was given to each man. In it he would learn that he was going to a land populated largely by Ay-rabs, and that Arabs, so it seemed, were not like other people; the first 'hint on behaviour in North Africa' was: 'Do not monkey about with Mohammedan women'. The political advisers were full of bright ideas and strong convictions. They maintained that the French in North Africa had only to realise that Americans were landing to welcome them with open arms, and perhaps '*du vin*'.

1. Robert Browning, 'Home-thoughts, from the Sea'.

From the leading landing craft, therefore, an announcement would be made through a Stentorphone, explaining what it was all about. 'Comrades, do not shoot,' it started off, very sensibly, 'we are your friends'—and went on to explain why. So that it should not be thought that a de Gaullist was making the announcement, an officer was required with a bad French accent. He was found without prolonged search. He used to practise at unexpected moments over the ship's internal broadcast system, and the political people seemed to think that it would have much the same effect as Joshua's trumpet on the walls of Jericho. But whenever I heard his nasal, '*Ne tirez pas, ne tirez pas, nous sommes vos amis*,' I thought it far more likely to attract a terrific fire from Frenchmen maddened at having their language massacred. If this did not work, there was the Rocket. On bursting, this would unfurl an illuminated Stars and Stripes in the sky. It was reputed to have been left over from the New York World Fair and to have had the words 'Visit New York World Fair' cut off the bottom. If even that failed, then, said the political advisers, the boys might have to fight, although they did not think it likely. Just in case, however, the staff went on with the detailed preparation and instructions for every phase of the operation.

A cluster of lights shone out brilliantly away on the port bow, the lights of Mostaganem, so they were not expecting us; but on the starboard hand all was in darkness about Arzeu: not a glimmer of light came from the port itself, nor from any point round the bay, and we wondered that this might mean. Were they waiting for us and was this black-out a part of the preparations? However, a lighthouse was winking reassuringly, and we heard later that a practice black-out had been ordered at Arzeu that night, quite by chance.

Well, here we were five miles offshore—now for it. There was a whir and a tinkle of engine-room telegraphs on the bridge as the master rang down 'Stop engines'. The whisper of our tiny bow wave died away and the whole convoy lay stopped. The troops who had been waiting by their landing craft in perfect silence, and chewing gum so that one could smell the mint up on the bridge, quietly manned their craft. There was what seemed an appalling roar in the stillness as the landing-craft engines were started up and they were lowered into the water. They all got clear of the ship without any hitch, and lay off. A motor-launch appeared, flashed once with a shaded blue light, they formed up astern of her, and the first wave headed for the beaches.

... The first wave should be nearly in by now. We were expecting at any moment to be blinded by the sudden glare of searchlights, a ripple of tiny flashes along the shore, the crackle of musketry, the spurt of tracer. But not a light showed itself, and even an offshore puff of wind brought no sound—only the musty smell of land. The stars twinkled down on a sleeping coast. When would something happen, or was this just a dream?

Then a rocket soared up and we held our breath; but its trail of brick-red sparks ended suddenly in a burst of incandescent white light which curved slowly over and turned a dull red as it burnt itself out. It was the success rocket. We had landed, apparently unopposed. At this moment troops were landing at Algiers to the eastward and at Casablanca on the Atlantic coast.

For the first time in history military expeditions from two different continents had landed simultaneously upon a third.

Commander THOMAS WOODROOFFE RN
in the *Reina del Pacifico*

*

POMPHOLUGOPAPHLASMASIN

While providing anti-submarine protection for the Operation 'Torch' convoys off Algiers on 13th November 1942, the corvettes HMS *Lotus* and *Poppy* sank U-605. In his Report of Proceedings, *Lotus*'s captain (Lieutenant-Commander H. J. Hall DSO RNR)—evidently an unusually erudite officer—used the superbly onomatopoeic Greek word πομφολυγοπαφλασμασιν to describe 'underwater bubbling and boiling noises'. The word is from Aristophanes' *The Frogs*, lines 246–9, translated as:

'Or when fleeing the storm, we went
Down to the depths and our choral song
Wildly raised to a loud and long
Bubble-bursting accompaniment' (pompholugopaphlasmasin).

From *The War at Sea*

*

The year 1942 ended in the Arctic on a brilliant note. On 31st December Captain R. St V. Sherbrooke RN in HMS Onslow, *and four other destroyers, together with Force R (Rear-Admiral R. L. Burnett), with the cruisers HMS* Sheffield *(Captain A. W. Clarke RN) and* Jamaica *(Captain J. L. Storey RN)—successfully defended Convoy JW51B on its way to Russia against the pocket battleship* Lutzow, *the heavy cruiser* Hipper *and three destroyers. There was a poet serving in* Onslow *during that*

BATTLE OF THE BARENTS SEA

Herringbone waters, and the cold
Drifting south, narrowing
The escape routes, icing breeches;
A slow confetti of snow
Made bridal the gun teams,
Aiming awhile their dreams
At the blizzard of *Hipper*.
Who rounded, small flames
Pricking her, the stronger
Animal, able no longer
To stomach indignity
Firing broadsides on *Onslow*.

Onslow to *Obdurate*: Have been hit
Forward and in engine-room.
Onslow to *Obedient*: Captain (D) wounded,
Take over for time being.
Onslow to Rear-Admiral (Destroyers):
Am retiring on convoy making smoke screen.
Onslow to *Obedient*: Forward magazine
Flooded, fire in boiler-room.
Am proceeding to southward of convoy.

The lamp flicked out the messages.
While below, on port wave,
A leading telegraphist gave
Such information to Murmansk
As was necessary, repeating
To Force 'R' what was relevant.

And *Obedient* took over, *Onslow*
In flames retiring, relinquishing
Seniority, a private ship
Fighting her private battle.

'A' and 'B' guns unable to fire,
Radar destroyed, aerials ripped,
And, forward, the sea stripping
The mess-decks, spilling over tables,
Fire and water clinching like boxers
As the ship listed, sprawling them.
Tamblin, his earphones awry, like a laurel wreath
Slipped on a drunken god, gargled to death
In water with a noise of snoring.
Slip, slop, slip, slop, a boarding-house slattern
In carpet slippers answering
The door, a telegram from 5 Mess
Refusing to come home, Gone whoring
After a sleazy mermaid with tin fins,
Eyes rheumy with salt, shins
Barked on a stanchion, a pattern
Only too familiar, only this time
It was for good, not evil,
That the old devil
Was absent, and it was the sea
Slip-slopping, no woman, over his property,
Ditty box, Taxi case, bag and hammock,
Glazing his eyes under whose lids
Passed no parade of marriage,
But the sightless accountancy of one
Shocked out of debt, owing no one.

(Ammunition party hurled into attitudes
Of early morning after a wild night),
Smith going for'ard trod and stumbled
On Aistrop's belly, which for ever rumbled,
And now put him off balance,
Its last chance at assertion.

Passing buckets, not the buck,
From hand to hand, and heart to heart,
'X' and 'Y' doors clanging shut,
And merciful Arctic sliding at last
Its cold arms round the flames.
The human chain bent, passed,
Bent, passed, bent, passed,
Simmons forgetting his fibrositis
And Donkin, his four-eyes swept overboard,
Entered Heaven in a blur,
Which was as well, for little was left of him.

Mess traps banging, with a double issue
Of rum to all hands, ignorant
Now of the situation, apparent
Or real, but at all events
Warm, hearing steel shudder,
Noticing movements of rudder,
While smells of anaesthetic
Seeped for'ard, an Arctic
Stew was served of spuds
And corned dog, and the First
Lieutenant's voice coolly organised
What needed to be organised,
As if it was Sunday Divisions
And the Base Captain was coming aboard.

So *Onslow* rejoined in falling darkness,
Having aided the elements' cancellation
Of each other, fire and water
A litany henceforward for all
Who had use of litanies,
Her captain sightless in his sea cabin,
Having ordered the battle, wounded
As Ahab, and no less dogged.
Smythe, a C.W. candidate
With an eye to the future, smoothed
His beard, felt his neck
To confirm it was still there,

And ventured on deck,
Having a mind to recapitulate
The action, test the weather,
And generally nose out the future.

He saw, as he held to a ladder
For support (the angle of list
Being forty-five degrees), *Achates*
Laying smoke astern, though holed
Forward, once more straddled
By *Lutzow*, now up in support
Of *Hipper*; and slowly,
Northern Gem taking off survivors,
Doing the obsequies, she sank.

He saw, the convoy steaming sedate
As swans on a river, his own ship
Flying pennants of smoke,
Obedient and *Orwell* and *Obdurate*
To port, from time to time
Making sorties on a horizon
Of gunflash, returning to the rhyme
Of escort after passages of free verse.

And he learned soon how *Sheffield*
And *Jamaica*, surprising the enemy
On their disengaged side, had set fire
To *Lutzow*, and finding fine
On the bow a loafing enemy destroyer
Had incidentally removed it—
A salutary lesson, inflicted
With the minimum of effort
And a courteous lack of ostentation
Entirely in keeping
With the traditions of the Service.

Lieutenant ALAN ROSS RNVR

Captain Sherbrooke was awarded the Victoria Cross for this action.

★

In the same action HMS Achates *(Lieutenant-Commander A. H. T. Johns RN) faithfully lived up to her name with a long, self-sacrificing run to lay a smoke-screen protecting the convoy from the advancing heavy cruiser* Hipper:

FAITHFUL *ACHATES*

Four months ago I had my elbows on the bar of my own pub at Colchester. You see, I'm forty-eight, and up till then I'd imagined that this war was a bit beyond me. But in that old pub, first the Australians, then the Canadians, and then the Americans came roaring in. This one had been to the Middle East: that one to Persia —they'd all done something worth while. I got tired of this and suddenly I made up my mind to become the only bald-headed sailor in the Navy.

I must say I was rather proud when I passed A1, although I have lost my early streamline. In no time I was drafted to a training school. Within ten weeks came the great news—a ship. My highest hopes had been a patrol vessel until I suddenly knew I was drafted to the destroyer *Achates.*

Gosh—here was action! The vigorous down-to-the-bone life in the destroyer shrunk the last traces off me of twenty-five years of easy living. I should say 60 per cent of my shipmates in the *Achates* were about twenty-three years old. I kept my ears open for any remarks about 'grandpa'. I wasn't going to stand for that—although, as a matter of fact, I am one.

I have never been so excited as when *Achates* in a line of destroyers tore northwards all out to take charge of its convoy. That was life. It wasn't long belong we struck interference. Some big German stuff had manœuvred up near to us in the darkness and at 8.30 on the morning of 31st December the first salvos crashed out.

Our *Achates* was selected to make a smoke-screen to shield the convoy, and the enemy picked us out for his early fire. We must have been conspicuous. The German cruiser got us the first time. It'll show you how green I was. I said to our gunnery instructor, 'Was that our big gun?' He said, 'No, you mug, we've been hit.'

Later I was down in the TS (transmitting station to you). Then another crash blasted open the side of the hull. We tried to block the gap with a six-foot-wide bookcase but it fell right through.

By now it had occurred to most of us that it was time to seek pastures new, and we made for the deck. There was chaffing and singing going on to the last. A lot of us lay on the heeling hull until it was evident that the old *Achates* must go. Before the action, some of us had had a turkey put into the refrigerator to have for Christmas dinner when we got to Russia. One wag, just before the *Achates* rolled over, bawled out, 'What about our blankety turkey?'

Once you dived into the water you became numb in a few minutes. I thanked my lucky stars I'd been a competition swimmer. I had thought to rip off my duffle-coat and heavy gear, and now struck out for the rescue trawler about half a mile away. I wasn't doing very well and was getting very tired of it all when suddenly someone tore past me at knots, doing the trudgeon stroke. I thought, I can do that, too—and beat him to the trawler. I never saw my unknown rival again. I hope I meet him one day. He probably saved my life.

Ordinary Seaman TED CUTLER

*

A great deal has been said and written about the physical aspects of the war, but not nearly as much about the mental casualties:

NOW I KNOW

'Go on,' says the psychiatrist, 'tell me just what it was like.'

Words break themselves against the walls like angry bluebottles.

What was it like? The dive-bombers, subs, the Arctic strain and cold of long convoys to Russia.

I don't know now—I didn't know then. Then it was. I existed in the middle of that 'it' and the 'it' is at the back of the mind and the cause of all the trouble, I understand. The psychiatrist is going to reach out to the back of the mind. His long, ugly knuckled hands, sensuous on the polished wood of the table, will tickle memory like a trout in a stream. He will find out what it was like. Then he will tell me. Then I shall know.

It is not a question of forgetting, but a matter of knowing. You cannot know peace unless you have known war; that is the limitation of our minds. Yet I don't suppose the psychiatrist knows much about either, but he knows the devil of a lot about the mechanics of both. His mind is the answer to twice times two. His mind understands the answer three or five.

I am fascinated by his hands. I hate them. They are clean. Mine were clean once.

'Hold your hands out in front of you,' he says.

Like two branches touched by a soft wind they tremble under his gaze.

'Bit shaky, eh?'

Three words drop on the table. I do not trust him and I am suspicious of his sympathy.

Outside his door stands a queue. A line of shell-shocked matelots. Pilotless men whose personalities have been disintegrated by concussion and too many action stations. Men who do not understand why it is they cannot remember the simple, A, B, C of their lives or why they have—for them—a shameful tendency to burst into tears.

That queue outside will follow me, one by one, into the psychiatrist's cabin. To most of them he will say, 'A bit shaky, eh?' Some of them will answer with pathetic belligerence, 'I'm all right.' Those who say that are frequently given bromide three times a day.

Others will plead, will grovel and say, 'Don't send me back to sea again. Give us a spell on shore.' Some will be rated permanent shore service. Some will be given an immediate draft chit back to sea.

The psychiatrist knows. I hope to Christ he does know. But he hasn't been to sea, he hasn't seen a boy with head on the mess-table sobbing quietly after prolonged action and no sleep. He hasn't experienced the rough incomprehensible sympathy of men, without academic understanding. The sympathy of men who would laugh at the answer five to the question: 'What is twice times two?'

I gather the analysis (so-called, for there is not much time and there is that queue outside) is going well. Between us we are getting nearer to the 'it' at the back of my mind. I discover that I am not the person I imagined myself to be. I am someone quite different. But I don't care much. If it makes things any easier I'll be a schizophrenic.

Now the room is full of words. They swarm about the head, but none of them rest on the psychiatrist's hands. Their tiny feet creep up and down the back, in and around the armpits, into the corners of the eyes.

'You may smoke if you want to,' says the psychiatrist. 'Don't take any notice of my gold stripes. Talk to me as a friend.'

A friend, you bastard? What would you know of friendship? Living on top of men for two and a half years in the confined spaces of ships at sea has taught me something of friendship. It is not a situation you and I would support. For you're a phoney. You don't care. You just don't care.

There is that long queue outside your door. Are you going to be friends with all of them? You haven't the time. That queue is not men, but minds broken up. What friendship can you want with a broken mind?

A mind, then, like a red balloon. A mind rising and dipping between the edges of the air, turning, falling, blown, blustered—rolling over the hills of a high wind. Like a child's balloon broken from its string rising on the exhalation of a short-tempered day.

And the child still in the street, the balloon in the air, and the child crying. The child made suddenly big with loss and hurt.

This room has four white walls, four sharp corners, and the mind is bumped against the walls and caught in all the four corners. The psychiatrist's hands screech on the rubber of this red balloon. This foolish red balloon that wants to play tag round the oblique angles of the wind outside these four white walls.

Here is no air. Here is no wind. Here are two hands, a red balloon and a matelot holding a piece of broken string.

This matelot is determined not to cry. He is determined to behave like a man. Men don't cry; men behave like men. Men have tight lips, we understand. The wind blows very hard very suddenly. It shouts at the corners of the white room, at the corners of a cabin, a ship. . . .

'Clear lower deck!' The ship's company know what is coming. Jimmy the One is going to give us a pep-talk. Tons of flannel. In a few hours we shall be in the danger area. Subs and dive-bombers. So Jimmy the One is going to talk to the *men*.

He talks. What he says is neither inspiring nor particularly disquieting. We know what it will be like. We know the bold strokes that will be slashed on our canvas of living. We know pretty well how we shall react. That makes it hard. Some of us remember the last action stations.

Some of us dream about it. One 'man' has his wrist bandaged. He was not wounded in action. He just dreams the ship is going down and throws himself out of his hammock.

He is nineteen years old, with a complexion like milk. Before the war, in those extraordinary days we called peace, he was a chemist's assistant. Now he is a matelot. He writes regularly to his old woman and receives violet-coloured envelopes from his young lady. He is purity and kindness. He has fair hair and he is very popular on the mess-deck. Old three-badge able seamen offer him 'sippers' from their tots of rum and protect him from over-zealous killicks.

We wish he would not dream and fall out of his hammock. His name is Johnson. We call him our Blond Bombshell.

'Turn for'ard. Dismiss!'

Back in the mess acid comment mixes with freshly lighted cigarettes. Jimmy the One's pep-talk has not fooled us. We do not believe that it fooled him either. It's just part of the routine. Morale must not be allowed to flag. The spirit of the *men* must be kept high.

It comes. We knew it would come. Now we are glad. Anticipation has nagged at the nerves too long.

The concussion tears at the skin. Blast fills the head and chest with noise and sucks it out again. The body is more empty than before. The explosives are hard and savage. They bring bewilderment. The bewilderment goes. Then there is fear.

The flesh is soft. Bullets and shell splinters are vicious. You experience the nakedness of men who continue to exist when the civilised entities have ceased to be. Not thought, logic, intuition, nor strength nor anger can save you now. You are broken by the realisation that these things, of such high esteem in peace, are of little account in a dive-bomb attack.

Stand behind the gun. Hand up the 'ammo', fight, fight! Put your anger in the breech. But you are still blasted with the recoil and flash back. Your anger, your phoney wrath (the best antidote to fear), comes back at you and smashes the chest like a falling girder.

The bewilderment may keep you calm. Even the fear runs into the joints like hot glue, delaying the reflexes, delaying all save one. The instinct to duck when the dive-bombers scream over the mastheads like express trains with wings. The instinct to plunge deep back into the darkness of your primeval self. The passionate desire to get down into a hole, into the earth (only here is no earth), to take cover. Here is no earth; here is liquid emerald twenty degrees below zero.

The feet press into the deck, seeking resilience. Seeking earth which is known to you. No earth here, no earth. . . .

You would tear the deck like a dog after a rat. You would throw yourself flat and hide your head in your hands. You would cry for a woman's breast where you could lay your head. You might even think of your mother, for you would cry where once you had sucked life. Life that has brought you here where life and death compare their hideous notes.

Only you don't. You just turn your head from the blast and keep on handing up the shells. During the lulls you smoke endless cigarettes and Johnson is apologising because he has none. You give him half yours. He is embarrassed. He says:

'You can have my ration tomorrow, Lofty.'

You say:

'Sod that, chummie.'

You are glad he is with you. The Blond Bombshell. You look at the angle of his cheek and narrow your vision so that you can only see the curve of the delicate flesh. It might be the cheek of a woman.

You are cold and you are tired. You are bewildered again. You do not know about your manhood any more. The swagger is gone and you are very naked, but you do not blush because there are only men here. Men, men . . .

So now this matelot is determined not to cry. He will continue to behave like a man. He understands he is a man. He has been one of the 'men' for two and a half years. There should be no doubt about it.

But the child wants his balloon back. The broken string in his hands is bitter twine. It is lifeless. There is no gay red balloon pulling at its end. The balloon is just out of reach, hitting the ceiling with tiny noises and big echoes.

'Yes, yes, I understand. Come back next week. Report to the

sick-bay three times a day. They'll give you something to quiet you down.'

The psychiatrist smiles.

Outside the queue stand dejectedly.

'What did 'e say, Lofty?'

'It's all a lot of cock. Bloody wet, the questions they ask you.'

'He can give you your ticket, you know.'

'Who wants his ticket?'

'I don't. Not much, I don't.'

I say nothing. What can I say?

This went on for some time. Then one day the psychiatrist said:

'I think you'd be better off outside the Service. You've had rather a rough time. I shall recommend you be discharged.'

At the time I didn't feel much. Now, a year later, I am beginning to realise that I am no longer a matelot.

HUMPHREY KNIGHT

1943

In 1943 Wrens began to do duties as Naval Control Service boarding officers, boarding merchant ships in harbour, delivering sailing orders, explaining alterations of route, mustering confidential books, etc. Wrens were also DEMS boarding officers, responsible for checking the guns, ammunition and armament stores of defensively equipped merchant ships.

TO BE A BOARDING OFFICER

Below are some of the assets for a boarding officer offered by one to a friend in Officers' Appointments WRNS Headquarters 'in amusement but all the same very true':

(a) To have been a boat's crew, or some form of maintenance rating working on boats—so that they may know their way about easily and know all the terms of parts of a ship, etc.

(b) To have a complete lack of sense of modesty—we see wonderful sights of naked sailors every day as we go round the accommodation.

(c) To be more or less teetotal, to resist continuous offers of drinks.

(d) To be completely impervious to all insults, comments, and compliments from dockers to USA sailors.

(e) Not to mind having perpetually wet feet.

(f) To be more or less elastic and acrobatic and to have a good sense of balance—you should see the ladders and planks we have to climb and walk.

The writer adds that is 'a really heavenly job. I adore every minute of it, even when the snow is two feet thick on the ground.'

Dame VERA LAUGHTON MATHEWS DBE

*

Special prayers written for the service in Westminster Abbey on the fourth anniversary of the re-inauguration of the WRNS on 11th April 1943:

O Almighty Lord God, whose are the causes of righteousness on sea and land, the commander and defender of all that put their trust in thee: Bless thou and watch over these thy daughters in their stations of war, that they may serve with courage and constancy the

Navies of our Sovereign Lord, King George, the security of his peoples, and thine own eternal purposes of good; through Jesus Christ our Lord—Amen.

Almighty God, who art the protector of those who go down to the sea in ships, extend thy blessing we beseech thee, to the members of the Women's Royal Naval Service, who go forth to the help of their brethren of the Royal Navy. Inspire them with the splendour of their cause; strengthen their resolution and confirm their loyalties, so that with dauntless hearts and dedicated wills they may work together for the coming of peace and the glory of thy kingdom upon earth, through Jesus Christ our Lord—Amen.

It is believed that these prayers were written by a serving Wren officer who unfortunately remains unknown in spite of a great deal of research very kindly undertaken on the editor's behalf by the present Director, WRNS, Commandant Dame Margaret Drummond DBE, and her staff.

*

In the Atlantic the U-boat wolf-packs were heavily defeated in a series of great convoy battles during April and May 1943. In those two months the enemy lost from all causes a total of fifty-six U-boats (forty-one of them in May). One crucial battle was that fought around Convoy ONS 5 from 29th April to 6th May. Bad weather and continual U-boat activity made ONS 5's a long passage and by 3rd May the commander of the Escort Group (B7) in HMS Duncan *faced an appalling dilemma, which caused him to miss*

THE GOLDEN MOMENT

The convoy crawled on into heavy seas and in the *Duncan* we were rapidly reaching the point when we had only enough fuel left to make Newfoundland at economical speed. I had to decide whether to leave the convoy or to continue and to hope for an improvement in the weather. On the one hand, the enemy was still in touch, and I did not want to leave my group at such a time. On the other hand, the weather forecast was very bad indeed and I did not like the idea of running out of fuel altogether and having to be towed, possibly at a very inconvenient phase of the operation.

After much heart-searching I decided that the *Duncan* had to go.

The weather would not allow boat work, nor transfer by a jackstay, so I had to go with her. Command was therefore handed over to Lieutenant-Commander R. E. Sherwood RNR in the *Tay*, and we left at the best speed the weather would allow. After two days the wind shifted in our favour, we met an unexpected favourable current, and we managed to make St John's with 4 per cent fuel remaining. We were most depressed because we felt we left the group in the lurch and were thoroughly ashamed of ourselves, though there was really no one to blame except the staff who had decided in the 1920s the endurance of such destroyers.

The story of what happened after we left on the morning of 4th May is probably the most stirring of convoy history. That afternoon three destroyers of the support group had to follow our example owing to fuel shortage, leaving the escort painfully weak. By cracking our cyphers Doenitz's radio intelligence service had established the position of convoy SC 128, which was eastbound in the general area of ONS 5. By some chance of fate all the U-boats which were directed on to SC 128 missed it, but ONS 5 was again sighted by the middle man of a big group, and soon no less than thirty boats found themselves unexpectedly in a most favourable position for attack. On 5th May the weather moderated somewhat and the enemy attacked with much success. That night and again next day, 6th May, more attacks followed with further successes, despite a tough defence, and altogether eleven ships were sunk without the loss of any U-boats.

There were no aircraft available which could reach the convoy, and by dusk the position seemed desperate, for there were only five of the close escort and two destroyers of the support group, the *Offa* and *Oribi*, remaining with the convoy. All ships were worn out after many days of bad weather and a running fight which had already lasted more than a week. There were over thirty U-boats in firm contact and the first support group which had been sailing from Newfoundland to help, could not arrive until the next morning. All escorts were short of fuel and some of depth-charges as well. In the words of Captain D3, 'The convoy seemed doomed to certain annihilation.'

. . . Doenitz realised that it was essential to attack in force that night, for the convoy would soon be under the protection of the air 'umbrella' from Newfoundland. So he exhorted his U-boats to make this final attack 'with the utmost effort', and he even ordered them to remain on the surface when attacked by aircraft and fight it out with the gun, in order to avoid losing touch with the convoy.

By the intervention of providence the convoy entered fog at dusk, and by a combination of skill, luck, initiative and sheer guts, the pack was heavily defeated. The enemy made twenty-four attacks that night, all were driven off, and not one more ship was sunk. The U-boat casualties were very heavy and four were sunk and three more heavily damaged during the course of the night. Two of these were surprised on the surface in the fog and were rammed, and two others were sunk by depth-charges or 'hedgehog' attacks. In his report, *Tay* remarks, 'All ships showed dash and initiative. No ship required to be told what to do and signals were distinguished both by their brevity and their wit.'

All this time the *Pink* with her five ships was trundling steadily along astern. She had her troubles, but she got four of her charges into harbour and succeeded in sinking U-192.

Next morning, 6th May, the 1st Escort Group on its way to the convoy came upon some unsuspecting submarines and shook them severely, sinking one; and a Canso flying-boat of the Royal Canadian Air Force from Newfoundland also did some useful work and destroyed one.

At 9.15 am, 6th May, Doenitz called off both packs and ordered all boats to proceed to the eastward for replenishment. The convoy was still together and the longest and fiercest convoy action of the war had ended with a clear-cut victory. The passage from 'Oversay' to 'Westomp', where the local escort relieved us, took sixteen days, and the enemy had been in contact for ten of them.

German records recognise this battle as the turning point of the Atlantic war, and while I am very proud that ships of my group should take such a prominent part, I shall never cease to regret that I did not risk the weather and stay with them until the end.

This decision has haunted me ever since, It was entirely correct and based on common sense. I had been in the *Tay* with Sherwood during the last battle, and I knew that he could compete. My own ship was new to me, just out of refit, leaking badly, and I did not trust the fuel consumption figures. The weather forecast was shocking.

It is now clear that Doenitz had no intention of continuing the attack—though I did not know it at the time—and this is some balm to my wounded vanity. Yet the weather did improve and I would probably have been able to fuel. As we have seen, Doenitz attacked 'by mistake' and I had missed the 'golden moment' which comes but once in a lifetime.

Vice-Admiral Sir PETER GRETTON KCB DSO OBE DSC

ONS 5 lost thirteen ships, but the enemy lost seven U-boats sunk: 24th April, U-710, by aircraft of 206 Squadron Coastal Command; 4th May, U-630, by aircraft of 5 Squadron RCAF; 5th May, U-192, by HMS Pink, *and U-638, by HMS* Loosestrife; *6th May, U-125, by HMS Vidette, U-531, by HMS* Oribi, *and U-438, by HMS* Pelican.

*

After the North African landings the next obvious target was Sicily—so obvious that, as Churchill said, 'anybody but a damn fool would know *it is Sicily'. However, in the Admiralty an ingenious plan with the somewhat macabre code name Operation 'Mincemeat' was devised to hoodwink the German High Command that Sicily was only a cover target, the real objectives being Sardinia in the west and Greece in the east. The body of an unknown serviceman dressed as 'Major Martin', a Royal Marine officer on Mountbatten's staff, was dropped over the side from HMS/M* Seraph *(Lieutenant N. A. Jewell RN) off the south coast of Spain in such a position where it would surely drift inshore and come to the notice of the Spanish authorities. Major Martin's briefcase contained what purported to be vital secret documents outlining Allied plans for the future, among them a personal letter to General Alexander from General Archibald Nye (and actually written by him).*

To make Major Martin 'real' he was provided with all his private impedimenta—identity card, passes, theatre-ticket stubs, keys, money and personal letters, including two from his fictional 'fiancée', Pam:

LOVE FROM PAM

I had decided that the first of these should be written on my brother-in-law's notepaper, for I was sure that no German could resist the

'Englishness' of such an address as 'The Manor House, Ogbourne St George, Marlborough, Wiltshire'; this letter, dated 'Sunday 18th', ran as follows:

The Manor House,
Ogbourne St George,
Marlborough, Wiltshire
Telephone Ogbourne St George 242
Sunday, 18th

I do think dearest that seeing people like you off at railway stations is one of the poorer forms of sport. A train going out can leave a howling great gap in one's life and one has to try madly—and quite in vain—to fill it with all the things one used to enjoy a whole five weeks ago. That lovely golden day we spent together—oh! I know it has been said before, but if *only* time could sometimes stand still just for a *minute*—But that line of thought is too pointless. Pull your socks up, Pam, and don't be a silly little fool.

Your letter made me feel slightly better—but I shall get horribly conceited if you go on saying things like that about me—they're utterly unlike ME, as I'm afraid you'll soon find out. Here I am for the weekend in this divine place with Mummy and Jane being too sweet and understanding the whole time, bored beyond words and panting for Monday so that I can get back to the old grindstone again. What an idiotic waste!

Bill darling, do let me know as soon as you get fixed and can make some more plans, and don't *please* let them send you off into the blue the horrible way they do nowadays—now that we've found each other out of the whole world, I don't think I could bear it—

All my love,
PAM

It was followed by two sheets of plain paper, such as was used in Government offices for carbon copies; the letter was headed 'Office, Wednesday, 21st', and the writing, which started reasonably good, suddenly degenerated into a scrawl as the letter was hastily brought to an end when the writer's boss was heard returning. It ran:

Office.
Wednesday, 21st.

The Bloodhound has left his kennel for half an hour so here I am scribbling nonsense to you again. Your letter came this morning just as I was dashing out—madly late as usual! You do write such heavenly ones. But what are these horrible dark hints you're throwing out about being sent off somewhere—*of course* I won't say a word to anyone—I never do when you tell me things, but it's not abroad is it? Because I won't have it, I WON'T, tell them so from me. Darling, why did we go and meet in the middle of a war, such a silly thing for anybody to do—if it weren't for the war we might have been nearly married by now, going round together choosing curtains, etc. And I wouldn't be sitting in a dreary Government office typing idiotic minutes all day long—I *know* the futile sort of work I do doesn't make the war one minute shorter—

Dearest Bill, I'm so thrilled with my ring—scandalously extravagant—you know how I adore diamonds—I simply can't stop looking at it.

I'm going to a rather dreary dance tonight with Jock and Hazel, I think they've got some other man coming. You know what their friends always turn out to be like, he'll have the sweetest little Adam's apple and the shiniest bald head! How beastly and ungrateful of me, but it isn't really that—you know—don't you?

Look darling, I've got next Sunday and Monday off for Easter. I shall go home for it of course, *do* come too if you possibly can, or even if you can't get away from London I'll dash up and we'll have an evening of gaiety—(By the way Aunt Marian said to bring you to dinner next time I was up, but I think that might wait!)

Here comes the Bloodhound, masses of love and a kiss

from

PAM

Lieutenant-Commander EWEN MONTAGU OBE RNVR

After the war, captured records showed that the German High Command swallowed 'Mincemeat' whole.

*

The landings in Sicily in July 1943 saw the début of a new weapon, which went into action with a breath-taking display of pyrotechnics. Two officers concerned in its development tell of their early experiences in the

LANDING CRAFT (ROCKET)

We had no known gunnery rules to guide us in the behaviour of the new weapon. During the tests everybody was clad in asbestos suits. Now only one man remains above deck controlling the fire from the protection of something which looks like a telephone kiosk. We had a few casualties in those early days—one of them an army colonel collaborating with the Royal Navy. Although he was sheltering behind the flash screen, the back-flash found him and whipped off his moustache. All he suffered was a loss of dignity.

We had to load up with rockets at a North African base. The heat was terrific and the rockets so hot that the men had to handle them wearing gloves. The rockets were already fused ready for firing, but they were safe to handle so long as the temperature kept below 130 degrees. When the thermometer rose to 127 degrees a strange silence fell over the loading party, but they went on working as though no danger threatened. Fortunately the thermometer did not rise further and the job in due course was completed.

For the practise shoot preceding the Sicilian invasion a small island in the Mediterranean was chosen as a target. The only difficulty was presented by the sole occupants, an aged man and his wife who had never left the island and refused to do so when requested by the Navy. Compromise was reached when the couple transferred themselves and their possessions to the other side of the island—and stayed there until the completion of the shoot.

Lieutenant C. L. P. MOORE RNVR

We were all a little nervous as to how the craft were going to behave in actual battle. With thousands of our invasion troops already approaching the beaches as we went in to saturate with high explosive enemy territory only a few hundred yards ahead of them, we knew there was not the slightest margin for error. We were the happiest men in the Navy after the success of the Sicilian operations, and we went on with a new-found confidence to repeat the success at Reggio, Salerno, Anzio and the South of France.

Not only the enemy were surprised by the new weapon. One naval captain taking part in the Sicilian invasion was overheard to remark, 'Thank goodness they're here, but what are they?' After their first performance the rocket craft were a source of inspiration to the troops in subsequent landings. It became a much safer proposition for them to put foot on enemy soil after they had seen enemy defences blown to pieces by the rocket salvos.

A battery of 80 mm cannon concealed in a wood was giving our troops a great deal of trouble. We brought the rocket craft into position and poured our salvos into the trees. The effect was immediate. All opposition ceased and what few of the enemy survived could be seen scurrying like scared rabbits out of the wood. When a rocket craft goes into action all the ship's company, with the exception of the CO, who controls the firing mechanism from a protected position on the bridge, go below decks.

As the salvos are fired there is a deafening roar like that of an express train and a blinding sheet of red flame envelopes the steel deck. Sometimes it is not possible to see the rockets reach their target because of the overhanging cloak of smoke and the choking cordite fumes. The decks would get red-hot from the back-fire but for the automatic water spray. After a succession of salvos the decks are steaming—with boiling water.

Lieutenant-Commander C. W. T. BLACKMAN RNVR
From *War Illustrated*

★

PREMONITION

Sailors, like soldiers and airmen, are trained to display initiative and, when the need arises, to make instant decisions. I felt exasperated, therefore, that I, a commander in the Royal Navy and second-in-command of one of His Majesty's cruisers, could not make up my mind whether or not to press the buzzer; the buzzer which started with a push-button on the standard of the bridge pelorous and, if pressed, would end with a shattering cacophony, a few inches above the head of the captain, asleep on the bunk in his sea-cabin.

The date was 16th July 1943, and with one other cruiser and two destroyers we had spent a restless, sleepless night, patrolling off

Sicily to give protection, from the sea, to the northern flank of the Allied invasion forces and, God bless 'em, our own motor torpedo-boats had given us a good deal more cause for alarm than the enemy E-boats. The way those boys came in to attack, in spite of our urgent protestations on voice radio that we were their friends, indicated that the spirit of Nelson still lived in a lot of wooden heads. Luckily, there must have been one member of their crews who understood plain English as, in the nick of time, they broke off the attack and went off somewhere else to try and win their medals.

'Commander, I'm dead beat,' the captain said to me. 'It's beginning to get light now, and everything's quiet. Will you look out for about an hour while I get some sleep? When I come up, you can go and get your head down. Call me at once if you need me.'

The melodious swish of the bow wave, as we zigzagged at twenty-six knots, provided the right background music for the emergence of Mount Etna from the clouds and, with the exception of Sicily and a few seagulls, there wasn't a thing in sight. But I knew some calamity was about to occur. I cannot explain why, but I was positive that I ought to call the captain. I pressed the buzzer, hard.

'What is it, Commander?' the captain asked me, speaking through the voice-pipe.

'I don't know,' I replied weakly. 'Everything's quiet and there's nothing in sight, but I think you ought to come up on the bridge.'

As the captain reached the bridge, the explosion occurred; a sickening, shuddering explosion which stopped the ship, dead, from twenty-six knots. HMS *Cleopatra* listed over to starboard, while the screech of escaping steam drowned the noise of the men tumbling up on deck.

Captain HAROLD HOPKINS RN

★

The Italians were the most imaginative pioneers in the techniques of penetration of enemy harbours by underwater saboteurs. Italian 'human torpedoes' damaged the battleships Queen Elizabeth *and* Valiant *in Alexandria on 19th December 1941; human torpedoes, and swimmers trained in underwater sabotage, attacked Allied shipping in Gibraltar Bay and later in Algiers Bay on several occasions between 1940 and 1943.*

There were some notable exploits on the Allied side: the Norwegian Leif Larsen's sortie, carrying chariots under the fishing-boat Arthur *to Trondheim in October 1942; the penetration of Palermo harbour and sinking of the Italian light cruiser* Ulpio Traiano *by Lieutenant R. T. G. Greenland RNVR and Leading Signalman A. Ferrier on 3rd January 1943; the sinking of the cruiser* Bolzano *by the charioteers Sub-Lieutenant M. R. Causer RNVR and Able Seaman H. Smith at Spezia in June 1944; and Operation 'Heckle'—the destruction of the floating dock in Puddefjord, Bergen harbour, by X24 (Lieutenant H. P. Westmacott RN) on 11th September 1944. X24 was an example of a new and sophisticated weapon in this type of warfare:*

THE MIDGET SUBMARINE

Many times in history has a need arisen to strike at enemy warship squadrons or merchant ships ensconced within strongly defended harbours; and one frequently used method had been to force the harbours, and then send in fireships to wreak havoc among the enemy vessels. The midget submarine, or X-craft, whose development was therefore put in hand, can reasonably be regarded as the descendant of the Elizabethan fireship. They were fifty-one feet long and weighed about thirty-five tons; they could make six and a half knots on the surface, could dive to 300 feet, and propel themselves at five knots while submerged. Their operational range was limited by the endurance of their crews, which consisted of three officers and one engine-room artificer, all of whom were volunteers. After special training we believed that the crew might be able to live ten or even fourteen days in their craft, and cover 1,500 miles at four knots. Their only weapons consisted of two detachable charges, each containing two tons of explosive which could be dropped on the sea-bed under the target, and were then fired by clockwork time-fuses.

Captain S. W. ROSKILL DSC RN

Six X-craft were built and two crews—a 'passage' crew and an operational crew—were specially trained for each craft. Their obvious objectives were the German capital ships in Altenfjord. For this attack—Operation 'Source'—they were allocated targets: X5 (Lieutenant H. Henty-Creer

RNVR), X6 (Lieutenant D. Cameron RNR) and X7 (Lieutenant B. C. G. Place RN)—Tirpitz, *in Kaafjord; X9 and X10 (Lieutenant K. R. Hudspeth RANVR)*—Scharnhorst, *also in Kaafjord; X8*—Lutzow, *in Langefjord. The X-craft left their depot ship HMS* Bonaventure *in Loch Cairnbawn on 11th September 1943, and were towed by 'orthodox' submarines to their slipping points off the Norwegian coast. X9 (Sub-Lieutenant E. Kearon RNVR) was lost with all hands on passage, and X8 (Lieutenant B. M. McFarlane RAN) had to be scuttled because of defects. X7's captain describes*

THE MIDGET ATTACK ON *TIRPITZ*

On the evening of the 18th, although the weather left much to be desired, we decided to change crews. The actual change-over was satisfactory, but when *Stubborn* got under way again it seemed to me, on the casing of X7, that the tow was extremely long—it was, it had parted again. We only had two rope tows with us, so we were forced to use the last resort, a two-and-a-half-inch wire. It was no joke securing this in the sea conditions that prevailed, and Bill Whittam[1] and I—secured by lines to the boat against being washed overboard—spent three exhausting hours on the casing before X7 was finally in tow again. We were neither of us dry nor in good humour when we went below, but the orderliness within was a delight to be seen. One would hardly have known that three men had spent a week in this confined space, and the mechanical efficiency of the machinery was in keeping—the passage crew could not have done their job better.

The next day was a lazy one—on these occasions the human being seems to develop an almost infinite capacity for sleep, uncomfortable as his bed may be.

The only excitement before we slipped was Minerva. By that night, the 19th, we were within twenty miles of the slipping position and the weather had cleared completely. X7 was on the surface and charging to full capacity. Bill Whittam was keeping a lookout through the night periscope and the rest of us were having supper.

'*Stubborn*'s flashing and there is something bumping up against the bow,' he announced. I looked through the periscope. There was

1. Lieutenant L. B. Whittam RNVR.

something bumping against the bow, but I couldn't make out what.

'I'll go and have a look,' I said, and Bill went back to the periscope.

'You'd better hurry—it's a mine.'

I did. It was a German one, whose broken mooring had half-hitched itself round the tow and come to rest against X7's bow. I noticed it was painted green and black, that it was obviously freshly laid and that one horn had already been broken, but I didn't wait to examine it closely; keeping it off with my foot gingerly placed on its shell I loosed its mooring wire from the tow and breathed more deeply as it floated astern. When I got below I thought a tot wouldn't do us any harm, so we toasted the Geneva Convention and Minerva—the mine with the crumpled horn.

The night of the 20th was beautifully calm with only a gentle swell from the west. We slipped at 2000, exchanged a few comments on this and that with *Stubborn* and set a course for Stjernsund. During the night we saw one other X-craft, I think X5, but otherwise nothing. The internal exhaust pipe from the engine split just before dawn, so the fumes had to be extracted by the air compressor and X7 dived, rather later than had been intended, at 0145. At 0230 we came up to periscope depth and were able to identify the entrance to Stjernsund. (Times in this narrative are GMT—the sun rising at about 0200 and setting at 1900.)

The day, calm and peaceful, was spent mostly at ninety feet, coming to periscope depth to fix our position every hour or so. In Stjernsund the water was like a sheet of turquoise stained glass, the steep sides of the fjord luxurious in browns and greens emphasised by the bright sunlight and the Norwegian fishing-boats, picturesque enough for even the most blasé traveller. There were occasional patches of snow on the higher ground, but the water—clear as a mountain stream—did not appear to be very cold.

At 1230 we entered Altenfjord proper, where there was sufficient lop on the surface to allow us to raise the induction trunk and release the excess of pressure within the boat that five hours with the oxygen switched on had caused.

At 1945 we surfaced, and Whitley[1] immediately started to fit the spare for the broken section of the exhaust-pipe—regrettably without success; however, canvas bandages and spun yarn made the fracture

1. ERA W. M. Whitley

reasonably gas-tight and the charge was started about an hour after surfacing. The boat was cleaned up generally and empty tins, used protosorb and the used oxygen bottles were thrown overboard. Rafsbotm itself was the anchorage for German fleet auxiliaries, so the charge and the tidying up had to be stopped for short periods from time to time when small craft appeared to be heading our way and it was thought wiser to dive out of sight, but the weather was in our favour—overcast and enough wind to cover the noise of our engine. Not long after the charge had been started searchlights and starshell were seen to the northward, near the top of Altenfjord—at first it was feared that an X-craft had been located, but it was probably the *Scharnhorst* on night exercises. (She had been sighted anchored south of Arnoy Island when we went by that afternoon: a sitting target, but we were after larger fish.)

At 0100 on the 22nd the charge was stopped, the few engine fumes that had escaped extracted by the compressor, and X7 dived to make her way for the entrance of Kafjord.

Before 0400 the gap in the anti-submarine nets at the entrance had been located (it was over a hundred yards wide and had no way of shutting it) but we waited for a minesweeper to come out before entering—her ensign was the first I had seen worn by an enemy ship in commission. To avoid any close watch there might be at the entrance (the day was calm and clear with only a slight surface ruffle) X7 entered at forty feet, but on coming to periscope depth inside had to be taken down again immediately to avoid a small motor-boat. Somewhat uncertain of our position relative to the ships and net defences inside, X7 was brought up again as soon as seemed reasonable, but at thirty feet the boat ran into an anti-torpedo net—the water was clear enough to see it and it appeared as the most formidable-looking underwater defence I had seen. The wire of which it was constructed was thin, not more than an inch in circumference, but was meshed into squares less than six inches across and there seemed to be at least two such thicknesses, presenting a baffling jazz pattern to the observer. X7 was stuck, she did not 'fall out' when the motor was stopped, nor when slow astern speeds were tried. (High speeds were considered unwise lest the disturbance of the buoys on the surface betray our presence.) The internal tanks were flooded in the hope that the boat would 'fall out' with the increased weight but this had no effect and the pump was run to get back to normal trim. After ten minutes it was apparent that this pump was not sucking out any water. We tried the other pump, with almost laughable results—there was a single spark from the commutator casing of its motor but otherwise no movement. No. 2 main ballast was blown right out but X7 did not float out of the net. Finally, all main ballast tanks were blown, and the main motor run for two minutes full ahead and then put full astern, so that X7 could gather as much way as the slack in the nets would allow. She came clear—all main ballast tanks were vented but the boat did break surface before going to the bottom like a stone, more than half a ton heavy. We thought this escapade would be certain to invoke some attention even if we ourselves had not been seen. I felt they could not fail to notice the bubbles from the vented main ballast tanks.

We waited on the bottom for about twenty minutes to give the gyro a chance to steady (we had already been an hour in the net) then blew No. 2 main ballast tank gently—when it was right we still had not left the bottom and I noticed that a large wire (presumably a wire securing the nets we had recently been in) was across our periscope standard. However, a burst of full speed and a little air in 1 and 3 was enough to clear us, and we immediately left that unpleasant spot.

Trimming by air was not easy in these craft, but without pumps there was no choice. When we left the bottom this time we did, admittedly, break surface for a second or two, but subsequently Whittam managed it perfectly, using Q and 2 MB for bodily weight, and moving Aitken[1] (who, unfortunate individual, had no job during an attack).

At 0640, when X7 was close to the northward of a tanker of the *Altmark*-class, the *Tirpitz* was sighted for the first time at a range of about a mile.

My intention for the attack was to go deep at a range of 500 yards, pass under the anti-torpedo nets at seventy feet and run down the length of the target from bow to stern, letting go one charge under the bridge, the other well aft and altering to port to escape under the nets on the *Tirpitz*'s starboard side.

1. Sub-Lieutenant R. Aitken RNVR

At 0705 X7 was taken to seventy feet for the attack but stuck in the net instead of passing underneath. This time I had no intention of staying there. By similar tactics to those that extricated us before, but without breaking surface, we came out and tried again at ninety feet, this time getting more firmly stuck. On occasions when the craft is being navigated blind, it is extremely difficult to know one's position to within a hundred yards—in this case the *Tirpitz*, the nets and the shore were all within a circle of that diameter, and the gyro had again gone off the board with the excessive angles the boat had taken. Thus when X7 next came clear and started rising, the motor was stopped lest she run up the beach or on to the top of the nets and fall into enemy hands. When she broke surface I saw we were inside the close-net defences (how we got underneath I have no idea) about thirty yards from the *Tirpitz*'s port beam—'group up, full ahead, forty feet'.

We actually hit the target's side obliquely at twenty feet and slid underneath, swinging our fore-and-aft line to the line of her keel. The first charge was let go—as I estimated, under the *Tirpitz*'s bridge—and X7 was taken about 200 feet astern to drop the other charge under the after turrets. The time was 0720. It was just as we were letting go the second charge that we heard the first signs of enemy counter-attack—but, oddly enough, we were wrong in assuming they were meant for us.

In X7 we had to guess a course that we hoped would take us back to that lucky spot where we had got under the nets on our way in; but we were not lucky. We tried in many places within a few feet of the bottom, but in vain, and rapidly lost all sense of our exact position. The gyro was still chasing its tail and the magnetic compass could not be raised for fear it foul some wire or a portion of a net; we did use the course indicator (a form of compass that remains steady during alterations of course but does indicate true position) but the noise it made was most tiresome so we switched it off again.

The next three-quarters of an hour were very trying; exactly what track X7 made I have no idea, but we tried most places along the bottom of those nets, passing under the *Tirpitz* again more than once, and even breaking surface at times, but nowhere could we find a way out. We had to blow each time we got into the nets and the HP air was getting down to a dangerously low level—but bull-in-a-china-shop tactics were essential as our charges had been set with only an hour's delay—and those of others might go up at any time after eight o'clock. The small charges that were periodically dropped by the Germans were not likely to do us any harm and, when we were on the surface, no guns larger than light automatic weapons which caused no damage could be brought to bear—but we were sceptical about our chances against at least four tons of torpex exploding within a hundred yards. But the luck that had recently deserted us came back for a few minutes shortly after eight. We came to the surface—an original method, but we were halfway across before I realised what was happening. On the other side we dived to the bottom and at once started to get under way again to put as much distance as possible between us and the coming explosion. Sticking again in a net at sixty feet was the limit, as this confounded my estimate of our position relative to the nets. But we were not here long before the explosion came—a continuous roar that seemed to last whole minutes. The damage it caused X7 was really surprisingly small—depth-gauges, trimming bubble and some lights broken; considerable but not catastrophic leaks at most hull glands; the gyro spinning with almost the speed of its rotor—but the hull was still complete. An incidental effect of the explosion was to shake us out of the net, so we sat at the bottom to review our position. We had no pumps that would work; the HP air bottles were empty, but internal venting where possible had increased the air pressure within the boat and the compressor was still working. The leaks were not immediately dangerous, but, as we had no way of pumping them out, we could not afford to delay. So we set off again, aiming at taking advantage of the confusion to get a good check on our position (I was not really certain we were even out of the nets) and then lying up and refitting on the bottom in shallow water. Nos. 1 and 3 MB tanks had to be blown to get us off bottom and with air in these open-bottom tanks, depth-keeping was impossible—we could choose only between surface and bottom. Nor was I correct in thinking we would be able to fix our position when we were on the surface (it was provoking to see the *Tirpitz* still on the surface, but that was about all that could be seen). We did another of these hops to the surface and this time the night periscope was hit; as it was probable we had only enough air for one more surface and there was no chance of getting away, we decided to abandon ship. DSEA escape was considered, but we were not keen to risk depth-charges that were being dropped, so it was decided to try a surface surrender first. If firing did not stop at the showing of a white sweater, we could always try DSEA from the bottom after a delay to allow enemy activity to die down.

X7 was surfaced and I, gingerly, I must confess, opened the fore hatch just enough to allow the waving of a white sweater. Firing did immediately stop, so I came outside and waved the sweater more vigorously.

The Germans had put a battle-practice target some 500 yards off the starboard bow of the *Tirpitz*—probably an attempt to obscure other attacking craft's view of their target—and X7 hit this just after I came on the casing, with her extremely low bouyancy forward—one main ballast tank had presumably been hit—the curved side of this was sufficient to force the bow down so that water went into the wet-and-dry before I could shut the hatch. From Aitken's description this was probably not more than thirty gallons, but it was sufficient to send X7 to the bottom again—I was left on the battle-practice target.

From Aitken's description of subsequent events inside X7 it is clear that Whittam managed everything with great calm and skill. A DSEA escape was planned and a certain amount of wrecking of more secret machinery carried out. They waited more than an hour and then decided to make their escape. From this depth—120 feet—the oxygen in a DSEA set lasts very little time, so it is imperative that the boat is flooded as quickly as possible until the pressure within is the same as that outside and the hatches can be opened; also those escaping must breathe the air in the boat until the batteries are flooded and the air foul with gas. In this case the drill was perfect, but only one small hull valve could be opened for the flooding up—all others were tried and why they had jammed is impossible to say—perhaps the explosion was the cause. Thus it was that only Aitken managed to conserve his oxygen long enough for a successful escape—he gave the other two their emergency supply when they had already lost consciousness but they did not revive, and Aitken himself was picked up on the surface in a comatose condition.

I can only voice my disappointment that all my crew were not successful at this last hazard. When X7 went down I thought they would be, but perhaps we had already had more than our fair share of naturals. Whittam—six foot five of English public school with stories as tall as himself; Whitley—older than any of us, a gay lad whose father was waiting for him to take over his engineering works in the Midlands.

For my own part I felt ridiculous walking on to the quarterdeck of a Fleet flagship wearing vest, pants, sea-boot stockings and army boots size twelve. When I was told that I would be shot if I did not state where I had laid my mines (this much, at least, they now knew by surmise) I stated I was an English naval officer and as such demanded the courtesy entitled to my rank. (I didn't say what rank—I had a fleeting vision of Gabby, the town crier in Max Fleischer's cartoon of *Gulliver's Travels*, shouting, 'You can't do this to me, you can't do this to me—I've a wife and kids, millions of kids.')

Captain GODFREY PLACE VC DSC VM[1] RN

Charges from X6 and X7 exploded at 0800 on 22nd, damaging Tirpitz *so badly she was unable to move from her anchorage until April 1944; she was finally destroyed by RAF bombers at Tromso in November. Nothing definite was ever seen nor heard of X5 after the author's sighting on the evening of the 20th. X10's target* Scharnhorst *had left her anchorage; after many defects and delays, X10 eventually abandoned the operation and was picked up in tow by HMS/M* Stubborn *on 28th. The author and Cameron were both awarded the Victoria Cross.*

*

WINGS OF THE MORNING

If there was one branch of the Navy which truly came into its inheritance during the war 1939–45 it was the Fleet Air Arm. Between the wars the Fleet Air Arm was, to use the service phrase, buggered about by all and sundry. The war changed all that. The growth and importance of the Air Arm can be traced statistically, in the increase in the number of aircraft

1. Virtuti Militari, the Polish VC.

carriers: the Navy began the war with seven (if one includes Argus) *and ended it with more than fifty, of various types.*

FLAT-TOP

We were not very proud of her at first. It was difficult to think, looking at her ugly outline, that we should ever get to feel about her as men do feel about the ships they sail, live and fight in. For indeed, she hardly looked a ship at all.

Try to imagine a ship cut off along the line of her deck and covered by a rectangular box with a flat overlapping lid. You climbed up the gangway and entered the box by a hole in the side. There were no funnels or masts such as a ship ordinarily has and the smoke came belching untidily out from two tubular vents, one on each side under the lid. On the starboard side a little irregular house was perched. It bristled with an assortment of masts and gadgets and was known as 'the island'. It was all there was in the way of upper-works. It contained the bridge, chart-room, wheel-house and all that impressive nerve-centre of a ship that is usually forbidden to strangers and labelled: 'No Admittance. Ship's Officers and Crew Only.'

The lid which covered the whole ship from stem to stern was the flight-deck, a small ship-borne landing ground. Under it, inside the rectangular box which seemed to have been clamped upside down over the ship, was a great echoing space, the hangar deck, where the aeroplanes were stored and serviced. It was really a floating garage. It communicated with the flight-deck above by means of two lifts, one forward and one aft, each large enough to carry one aeroplane. And from the hangar you went down through narrow hatchways, as though into a luminous metallic underworld, into the living and working quarters in the hull of the true ship beneath.

No. She did not look like a real ship at all. When you climbed up the gangway and entered the hangar you did not feel the live spirit of her as you do when you step on to the quarterdeck of an old man-o'-war. You did not feel that this was an invincible old warrior with a soul compounded of the courage, faith, endurance and devotion of hundreds of men who had sailed in her. Nor had you the impression of streamlined efficiency, slick and deadly, which you might get in a warship of newer vintage. We did not feel that she could ever win our affection, so tinny and metallic, mechanical and soulless, was our flat-top.

But now we are not so sure.

Lieutenant-Commander (Sp) F. D. OMMANNEY RNVR

*

HMS *GLORY*

I was born on an Irish sea of eggs and porter,
I was born in Belfast, in the MacNeice country,
A child of Harland & Wolff in the iron forest,
My childbed a steel cradle slung from a gantry.

I remember the Queen's Road trams swarming with workers,
The lovely northern voices, the faces of the women,
The plane trees by the City Hall: an Alexanderplatz,
And the sailors coming off shore with silk stockings and linen.

I remember the jokes about sabotage and Dublin,
The noisy jungle of cranes and sheerlegs, the clangour,
The draft in February of a thousand matelots from Devonport,
Surveying anxiously my enormous flight-deck and hangar.

I remember the long vista of ships under the quiet mountain,
The signals from Belfast Castle, the usual panic and sea-fever
Before I slid superbly out on the green lough
Leaving the tiny cheering figures on the jetty for ever:

Turning my face from home to the Southern Cross,
A map of crackling stars, and the albatross.

Petty Officer CHARLES CAUSLEY

*

THE SQUADRON LINE-BOOK

At dawn the next day the Air Support Group signalled its good wishes to the commodore of the convoy and began its sweep to the southward.

The story of the sweep, which lasted five days, can perhaps be told best by quoting two pages verbatim from the squadron's 'line-book'.

'Line', of course, is short for 'line-shoot'—another word borrowed by the Fleet Air Arm from the RAF. A typical—perhaps, indeed, the original—line-shoot runs like this: 'There I was—on fire—upside down—nothing on the clock—and *still* climbing.' Somebody had the bright idea of perpetuating and immortalising the more extravagant 'lines' by recording them in a book. But soon the line-book became a sort of unofficial squadron diary as well, illustrated by drawings and leavened by a selection of the funniest cuttings from the Press. Almost every squadron now possesses such a record, and the book is a precious possession, a piece of contemporary history written by those who are making it.

The particular line-book belonging to the Swordfish squadron (with which the Seafires were amalgamated) was battered, torn, and in places almost illegible. It had accompanied the squadron across half the world, and it recorded impartially and at times ironically their triumphs and disasters during nearly three years of war. It was stained by sea-water; it was scorched by fire, having been rescued with difficulty when a dispersal hut was hit by an incendiary bomb at Malta. It had known the sand and the mud of the Western Desert, it had been evacuated from Crete, and saved from the torpedoed *Ark Royal.* Its value, in the eyes of the squadron, was greater than that of the *Codex Sinaiticus.*

It contained, in the first place, a list of every pilot, observer, and air gunner who had served in the squadron; in many cases with their photographs as well. There were more than 200 names. Opposite some of them were the initials 'POW'. Opposite many, many more was 'RIP'.

The rest of the book was filled with the squadron diary, dating from its formation in 1940, which told a story of Mediterranean war, of Crete, of Malta, and Libya, that has never been told on any printed page, nor can be told until the war is over. There were accounts of the squadron's battles and the squadron's parties; there were photographs of the squadron's more spectacular prangs; there were various versions of the squadron's unprintable songs. It was a curious hotchpotch in which blitz and popsies, bombs and beer, indeed, life and death, were treated with an equal lack of solemnity.

Here, then, are the two pages concerning the anti-submarine sweep after the Air Support Group left the convoy.

21st. Made a farewell signal to Porter, who was picked up by Smoky Joe and must now remain in Smoky Joe till it gets to Halifax. We said, 'Oh, Mr Porter, what shall I do, I meant to go to Birmingham and got carried on to Crewe.'

A/S patrols all day. Nothing to report, except that S. made a sighting report of a whale. He went down to look at it, and it spouted at him.

22nd. Very bad weather, and the biggest sea yet. No flying. Much poker.

23rd. Gale. At 1300 we picked up a distress message from a torpedoed ship fifty miles ahead of us. Captain (D) signalled us 'Can you fly in this weather?' To insure ourselves against any possible prangs we answered 'Not impossible but casualties and damage must be expected'. In the end we flew over one Swordfish to search for survivors. B. was pilot and W. observer, Leading Airman Sutton A. G. Ship was doing her rodeo act, she buried her fo'c's'le in the sea when they were taking off and they nearly had it. At 1420 W. reported by R/T a lot of wreckage and some survivors in rafts. Captain (D) sent off a sloop to try to pick them up. By this time it was blowing Force 7, and B. was ordered back to the ship. He made three shots at getting down and the fourth time he arrived, gedonk! A beautiful prang and nobody hurt, the Stringbag folded up like an old hen come to roost. We stripped her of her radios and various odds and ends and heaved her overboard. The sloop picked up the survivors, so it was a successful party on the whole, Stringbags being expendable. Weather continued too bad to hunt the submarine. At 1630 a poor misguided bird, which our tame ornithologist says is a phalarope, arrived on board. It was the only thing, except B., that landed-on today; and it made a better landing than B. so we fed it on crumbs.

24th. Phalarope took off at dawn, three Swordfish in company. Searched all day for the submarine which torpedoed the merchantman. At 1430 Captain (D) got a ping on his Asdic. Great scurryings to and fro by the sloops. Otherwise a blank day.

25th. Today, being Sunday, the better the day the better the deed, the ship got her first kill. F. in Miss Blandish on routine patrol just after dawn spotted a surfaced U-boat which apparently took some time to recover from its astonishment at meeting a single-engine biplane in mid-Atlantic. F. made his sighting report and attacked; at least we supposed he had attacked, for we heard some machine-gun fire on the R/T, then silence. F. did not answer any calls after that, we heard no more of him, and he is 'presumed shot down'.

Two Swordfish and one Seafire flew off at once (squadron commander and Seafire flight commander pinching this trip, of course, as they always do when there's anything worth having!). They found the submarine still on the surface, going round in aimless circles, having no doubt been damaged by F. before it shot him down. Squadron commander said on the R/T, 'Softly, softly, catchee monkey', and they cruised round for a minute or two just out of range. Then the Seafire went down and let him have it with m.g.s and cannon. The Swordfish saw strikes on the conning tower, and the gun crews tumbling off the deck. Then they attacked with D/CS. The explosions seemed to heave the submarine's bow right out of the water. After that it disappeared altogether for a few moments, then suddenly came up again stern first. The stern stuck up out of the white boiling sea like a sharp black rock. A beautiful sight. It sank very slowly, leaving a few survivors swimming about. These were later picked up by one of the sloops. They said the Seafire's first burst had killed their captain. Every time a coconut.

26th. Uneventful patrols all day, an anticlimax after yesterday. At 1700 we received orders to discontinue sweep and join a slow convoy homeward bound from Halifax.

Lieutenant-Commander (A) JOHN MOORE RNVR

*

AGAINST THE LIGHTNING

Silver in this transfigured light
above a world lost, unawake,
in a before-dawn sleep and smoke,
with wings not as of earth below,
drab, dope-flaked, too nearly real,

but masters of sun and air we wheel.
Arran is dark, dark
all the shadowed Clyde;
the small ships steal
still-groping, heavy-eyed
up channel.
Only the gaunt and sea-girt sentinel
of Ailsa Craig
toply demands the sun.
Above the haze,
stabbing the cloth of night,
her summit steals the dawn.
Bank westward—
lost the twilight of Kintyre—
and, far below,
the small flat leaf that is the carrier.
Wake-white the sea streams aft,
bow-waves arc out,
the deck still dark and inhospitable.
How far our present
swift Olympian splendour
from the realities of speed and height.
We turn and spiral
down to the dark again,
down for a second dawn.

Now I am one with this,
this, as I loose my straps,
turn off the switches, petrol, radio,
one with this facing wind,
with aircraft closely parked along the deck,
with this tower-tall, iron-grey, lopsided ship.
One with her steep sides' sweeping precipice,
with this array of guns,
the ringing of the warning lift-bells, this
great army of her complement.
A part of me,
this hurrying of aircraft fore and aft,

shouted instructions,
orders from the bridge:
and, as she turns, the sloping
mountain of her deck.

Under the flat, grey armoured deck,
the stuffy intricacies of a ship:
office and workshop,
hangar, galley, mess,
turret and engine-room,
linked, labyrinthine, by lit corridors,
away from sunshine, loud with dynamic hum,
fed air by shaft and fan.
Within the throb and chatter of her hull,
island-compact, surrounded by
the limited blue saucer of the sea,
lonely as cities built upon a hill,
life is patterned
in an unsure routine.

Lieutenant (A) HUGH POPHAM RNVR, HMS *Illustrious*

*

From 1940 until the end of the war the Department of Miscellaneous Weapon Development (DWDM, but better known as 'The Wheezers and Dodgers') under Commander Sir Charles Goodeve OBE, developed a variety of new weapons—some weird, some wonderful, some war-winners. Among their more spectacular undertakings, designed to breach the Atlantic Wall, was

THE GREAT PANJANDRUM

It consisted of two enormous steel wheels, each ten feet in diameter, with a tread about a foot wide. They were connected by a drum-like axle which could contain high explosive, and the monster would be propelled by a large number of slow-burning cordite rockets fitted round the circumference of each wheel.

The thing would be carried to the shore in a tank-landing craft. When the ramp went down the rockets would be ignited, and the monster would propel itself through the shallow water and up the beach to the wall like a giant catherine wheel, reaching a speed of perhaps sixty miles an hour by the time it struck the concrete bastion. There the steel wheels would collapse, and the drum of TNT would be hurled against the foot of the wall, where a mechanical device would set off the explosive.

Norway christened the monster 'Panjandrum'—'because the gunpowder ran out from its heels'[1]—and on 3rd August 1943, its construction began in great secrecy in a special hut at the Leytonstone works.

After some discussion the Great Panjandrum was taken to Westward Ho!, where at the head of the beach a great pebble ridge runs parallel to the sea, and on the morning of 7th September it was decided to launch the monster on its maiden run. First its central, explosive drum was filled with 4,000 pounds of dried sand. Then the rockets were clamped in position. As no one was quite certain how the Panjandrum would behave, only eighteen rockets were tried at the start, but even so it was an awe-inspiring sight.

Surrounded in clouds of smoke and flame, the Panjandrum thundered down the ramp of the landing craft, ploughed its way through the water, and set off up the beach. It kept a relatively straight course until two of the rockets on one side failed to ignite, causing it to swing to starboard, but Norway saw it was much underpowered, and it came to a standstill after covering 220 yards.

The rolling resistance on the sand seemed a great deal higher than they had expected, and without more rockets it was obvious that the Panjandrum would never reach a speed of 60 mph at the head of the beach.

The following day the Panjandrum was loaded into its landing-craft and taken round to Instow Beach, inside the Torridge estuary. With clouds of steam hissing around it, it negotiated 150 yards of water quite successfully, but just before it reached the target-marker on the beach a patch of uneven, loose sand slowed it up. Again some rockets failed, and it swerved aside, coming to rest after 406 yards. It was still far too slow and more stability was obviously needed.

1. '. . . and there were present the Picninnies, and the Joblillies and the Garyalies, and the grand Panjandrum himself . . . and they all fell to playing the game of catch as catch can, till the gunpowder ran out at the heels of their boots.' —SAMUEL FOOTE (1720–77).

Powered by more than seventy rockets on its third outing, the Panjandrum gave a sensational display. No sooner had it reached the water's edge than it swerved violently back towards the sea, heeling over until the wheel flanges caught in the sand. The Panjandrum lurched and overturned, the crash dislodging several of the rockets, which flew low over the beach in all directions, while others, still secured to the perimeter of the outer wheel, continued to explode under water, sending up fierce jets of steam.

The Wheezers and Dodgers realised that the experiments were becoming extremely dangerous, and the hazards were increased by the erratic behaviour of the rockets, which were not designed to withstand a lateral centrifugal force while burning. When the speed of the Panjandrum rose to over 50 mph it was common for one or two rockets to burst. This usually destroyed the attachment of adjacent rockets, which began darting all over the beach. These rockets were formidable pieces of ironmongery, each weighing some twenty pounds and burning for forty seconds with a thrust of forty pounds. When one broke away from the side of the Panjandrum it would scream across the sand in a series of hops at a height of only two or three feet, its progress lasting half a minute or more. A trial run was therefore a thing which had to be seen to be believed, the Panjandrum—a hurtling mass of smoke and flame—often careering straight for the spectators, or at the cine-operator, who usually thought he had chosen a safe position, while rockets which had burst free from the wheels flew in all directions.

When they next assembled at Westward Ho!, early in January 1944, the Panjandrum which they loaded into the LCT was almost a reversion to the original prototype in appearance, with just the two ten-foot wheels, the axle chamber (ballasted with two tons of sand), and no steering gear fitted. In the morning the Panjandrum was given a preliminary run with forty-eight rockets in position. Norway hoped for a speed of 65 mph but this time it mysteriously failed to reach even 50 mph over a measured 800 yards.

After lunch a resplendent gathering of admirals and generals made their way to the pebble ridge. There were a number of distinguished scientific observers present, too. Whitehall had come to pass judgement on the Great Panjandrum, and the Wheezers and Dodgers sensed that this trial would decide its fate.

First, two minefields were detonated to provide the craters which would be encountered on an enemy beach. Klemantaski, who was to photograph the run, chose a position about halfway up the course. As he got his cine equipment ready he was joined by several Brass Hats, and an Airedale dog, owned by an army officer and rejoicing in the name of Ammonal, which had somehow discovered what was afoot.

Far down on the beach lay the LCT. Through his binoculars Klemantaski could see the Panjandrum being brought to the head of the ramp. Then the signal was given, and Abel, crouched behind a wall of sandbags on the deck of the landing craft, pressed the firing key.

The Panjandrum made a slow, impressive start. As it began to move towards him it reminded Klemantaski of a photograph he had just seen of one of the new German rocket missiles leaving its launching platform.

In the first few yards the inevitable rocket burst from its clamps. Two more broke free, but now the Panjandrum was moving at a terrific speed. To Klemantaski, with his long experience of motor-racing, it seemed to be nearing a hundred miles an hour—a rushing inferno of smoke and fierce jets of fire.

At eighty yards the monster crossed one line of craters, and the shoreside wheel dipped ominously. At 120 yards the awed watchers realised it was out of control. The Panjandrum began to swing in a great curve to starboard. Hypnotised by the vast Frankenstein object roaring across the sand, Klemantaski continued to photograph it until it was heading straight for him. Then he sprang to his feet and ran for his life, following the VIPs as they flung themselves headlong down the far side of the pebble ridge into a mass of barbed wire.

'At any moment we expected the monster to come hurtling over the brow and crush us all to death.'

But the seconds passed and nothing happened. So they crawled back up the stony slope. From the crest of the ridge they saw an amazing sight.

The Great Panjandrum was in its death-throes. It had swung back to seaward and crashed over on its side in the sand. This smothered the rockets which were underneath, but the others continued to explode, wrenching and distorting the whole frame, until the remainder burst from their fittings and screamed off along the beach in every direction, some vainly pursued by the Airedale dog!

When the pyrotechnics were over, and the awestruck admirals, generals, and scientists descended cautiously to the beach, all that remained of the Great Panjandrum was a twisted and blackened mass of wreckage. Round it lapped the incoming tide.

Lieutenant-Commander GERALD PAWLE RNVR

*

The sinking of Scharnhorst *off the North Cape on Boxing Day, 1943, could be called the last battle of the dinosaurs; it was a straight fight between two capital ships, with no intervention from the air. On Christmas Day* Scharnhorst *left Altenfjord intending to attack the Arctic Convoy JW 55B, which had a close escort of fourteen destroyers under Captain J. A. McCoy RN in HMS* Onslow, *with Vice-Admiral R. L. Burnett and the cruisers HMS* Belfast *(Captain F. R. Parham RN), HMS* Sheffield *(Captain C. T. Addis RN) and HMS* Norfolk *(Captain D. K. Bain RN) in the deep field. Distant cover was provided by the battleship HMS* Duke of York *(Captain Hon. G. H. E. Russell RN) HMS* Jamaica *(Captain J. Hughes-Hallett RN) and four destroyers.*

These components of the scene were some distance apart, but, by well-judged breaking of radio silence and aided by some masterly shadowing and reporting by the cruisers, Admiral Fraser concentrated his forces and Duke of York *opened fire on* Scharnhorst *at 4.50 pm, to begin*

'A SLOGGING MATCH BETWEEN GIANTS'

The first shot was fired in star-shell by the *Duke of York*'s 5.25-inch turrets, and the report sounded dull and metallic to us. I raised my head from the binoculars and counted the seconds till one and then another burst into flickering light over the horizon. At first we could see nothing until one or two burst over to the right of the others, and, suddenly—there she was! A vague illuminated silhouette—the *Scharnhorst*. Almost as soon as she could be seen, there was a deafening crack and a spurt of flame as we fired our first full broadside of six-inch. The concussion momentarily deafened me, and my vision was blurred by the shaking of the director and the sudden flash out of the gloom. We could see the tracer shells coursing away like a swarm of bees bunched together, and could follow them as they curved gently down towards the target. Before they landed, the guns spoke again, and the sea was lighted for a brief second by the livid flash.

Then the *Duke of York* fired her fourteen-inch, and even to us, now a thousand yards astern, the noise and concussion was colossal, and the vivid spurt of flame lighted up the whole ship for an instant, leaving a great drift of cordite smoke hanging in the air. Her tracers rose quickly, and, in a bunch, sailed up to the highest point of their trajectory, and then curved down, down towards the target.

I think we had fired two or three broadsides before the reply came. Her first retaliation was by star-shell, probably from her 5.9s using relatively flashless cordite, as we did. From that distance the firing of these was quite invisible until the shells burst, two or three together, with intense white flares which hung in the air above us. In their light the sea was lit up as by the moon very brightly, and I remember thinking that we must have been visible for miles. I felt as if I had been stripped stark naked, and had to resist the natural urge to hide behind something away from the light, as if it would have mattered! After what seemed like an age her star-shell dimmed and guttered out in a shower of bright sparks, which fell down to the sea for all the world like stubbing out a pipe at night. Just as we had again been plunged into the comforting gloom I saw the angry white wink of her first eleven-inch broadside, and said half down the telephone and half to myself, 'She's fired'—not very comforting to those below, and not much better for me. Thank God we couldn't see her shells coming as we could see ours going. The waiting for their arrival was bad enough, but to see them coming all the way would have been far more grim. There was a vague flash off the port bow which I caught in the corner of my eye as I gazed through the binoculars, and then—crack, crack, crack, sharp like a giant whip, and the drone and whine of splinters passing somewhere near.

I don't know how much I was scared then—quite enough, anyway, though there was too much happening really to be properly frightened. The whizz of the shell splinters was the nastiest of all, as the director, with open face, was trained directly towards the enemy, and the clearance of my head above the binocular sight assumed, mentally, abnormal proportions. The trouble was, seated rigidly and surrounded by instruments and voice-pipe, I could only move enough to save one portion of my anatomy from temporary paralysis, to the subsequent detriment of another, even under normal cruising conditions, and now I felt an extreme urge for comforting protection!

Almost as soon as the first shells burst, the CP called up,—'Some shells landed pretty near us then, didn't they, sir? We felt 'em down here very plainly.' At that, any personal thought or introspection vanished from me, and I realised that it was up to me to say something comforting even to the point of obscuring the truth from those below who could neither see nor imagine much of what was happening. I replied in as much of a matter-of-fact voice as was available that I believed something had arrived somewhere near, but I wasn't very sure. These were the first proper words I had spoken since the action was joined, and it was personally reassuring to hear myself say something coolly and in a detached manner. Any further conversation was cut short by another six-inch broadside, and a few seconds later the same angry white wink on the horizon. This time I looked up and saw her shells burst for the first time, and in their light the splashes, mast-high, and unpleasantly near the *Duke of York*, who was steadily crashing away with her full broadsides. Vaguely I heard my communication number, crouched down on a seat, beside me, saying, 'All right, Geordie. All right, Geordie,' to his opposite number in the ADP.[1] The *Scharnhorst* was retiring, and we were increasing speed to twenty-eight knots, with a slight turn to port as we made off in pursuit behind the flagship.

For a short time no shot was fired, and I looked down to the for'ard turrets as they trained in unison, the guns in serried ranks raised threateningly, ready to fire again. We kept the director trained towards the enemy, altering the bearing against a change of course, and every minute or so the range was passed up to me, which I repeated for the benefit of the crew. It was steadily increasing. The flash and concussion of another broadside shook us again, but it no longer worried me. In fact it became rather a thrill eventually, and its power gave me a subtle exhilaration from a sense of our

1. Air Defence Platform.

might, although there still remained in the back of my mind the knowledge that the flash gave away our range and position to the *Scharnhorst* every time we fired. After a little the range increased, which rendered our six-inch rather out of it, and that, combined with the fact that our shell-splashes might have confused the flagship's spotting, made us cease fire temporarily, and we could follow the battle more closely. It was a slogging match between giants, appalling in their might and fury. Every time the *Duke of York* fired there came the vivid flicker of the *Scharnhorst*'s reply, the lazy flight of the fourteen-inch tracer, followed by the crack, crack of the eleven-inch reply in the sea, and the drone of splinters. At one period we were engaging her fine off our starboard bow, and both sides fired a succession of star-shell for the greater accuracy of their main armaments. I suddenly remembered my camera, and withdrew my gloves to fish it out of my oilskins. My fingers were wet and cold, and I fumbled wildly. Leaning to one side for a clearer view, I sighted it nicely just as about six star-shells were in the air, and took a long shot. As I released the catch to finish, 'A' and 'B' turrets fired again, and I whipped it up once more in an attempt to catch the tracers before they became too vague in the distance.

Suddenly the ship was bathed in light again as star-shell flared directly overhead, and simultaneously liquid deluged down over the director and streamed over my face. For a second there passed through my mind that it had come from a bursting shell—or some filthy chemical which might burn or disfigure. I passed my tongue over my lips and tasted the stuff. It had a queer tang. God—could it be . . .? and just as quickly it surged to my mind that it was no more harmful than plain salt sea-water! As I discovered some hours after the action, an eleven-inch shell had landed in the water starboard side and abreast of 'B' turret, only half the ship's breadth from our side. It sent up a column of water, which then collapsed all over the bridge and decks, and had, of course, drowned us as well.

Still the slogging match continued, flash for flash, round for round. Although the *Scharnhorst* was not firing at us directly, the shells were falling sometimes to miss the flagship and to come uncomfortably close to us. At one moment I thought the *Duke of York* was hit. Simultaneously with the burst of three eleven-inch close to her, a red glow blossomed from somewhere for'ard and lit up her entire bridge superstructure. However, it turned out to be the flash of her reply from 'A' turret, which was suffused in the billowing cordite smoke. This drifted back in acrid clouds, and was most unpleasant. We turned a few points to starboard at high speed, and I could again train the director on to the *Scharnhorst*'s flickering salvos. I tried to give a running commentary over the telephone to those below, but it must have been most disjointed.

'Boxing Day, bulletin number 30.' Again the cheerful voice of the first lieutenant. 'The destroyers are now going in to attack.' I confess to having completely forgotten about them up till then, but now I blessed their presence. There was a strange lull in the gun-fire. Everyone was on tiptoe, straining to catch the first signs of their attack. The familiar flash of eleven-inch again split the darkness, and a minute or so later an incredible and terrifying noise made me momentarily crouch down again. A whole salvo had passed clean over our heads, like the tearing of a huge corrugated cardboard box—an indescribable, devilish sound. 'Come on, Adolf, no more of that,' I prayed. Again the flicker in the distance, and again we waited for it to arrive. Nothing came. Again the flash, but followed this time by star-shell illuminating the horizon. Thank God, the destroyers must be in. We remained silent and sat back more comfortably.

Then the flagship turned, slowly at first, to port, and round we went farther and farther in her faint wake until our bows were directly towards the enemy. They were getting excited below. Dead ahead were the signs of a furious engagement. Star-shell flared high, guns flashed, red beads of pompom fire ran out in livid streams, each to fade in a small white burst. Strange bursts of high-angle fire spasmodically dotted the sky, and still we ploughed on steadily and silently, and our guns pointed mutely towards the flashes ready to crash out again.

No shell came near us for almost twenty minutes. We turned to starboard, the turrets following round so that both ships presented a full broadside. I think I yelled 'Stand by again!' over the telephones, but my words were drowned by the deafening crash of gun-fire. The tracer now appeared almost horizontal, so flat was the trajectory as they rushed like fireflies to converge at a point in the darkness.

Suddenly—a bright-red glow, and in it the enemy was to be

clearly seen for a brief moment. 'She's hit! My God, we've got her!' I was yelling like one possessed. We were cheering in the director. All over the ship a cheer went up, audible above the gun-fire. I had risen half standing in my seat as the wild thrill took hold of me. Again the dull glow, and in its light the sea was alive with shell-splashes from an outpouring of shells. Great columns of water stood out clearly in the brief instant of light, and I could see smoke hanging above her. I was mad with excitement until I realised that my ravings must be an incoherent babble of enthusiasm to those below as the telephones were still hanging round my head. I straightened my tin hat, sat down, and told them as calmly as I could that we could see that our shells had set her on fire, and that both the *Duke of York* and ourselves were hitting, and hitting hard.

She must have been a hell on earth. The fourteen-inch from the flagship were hitting or rocketing off from a ricochet on the sea. I had no coherent thought. The sudden knowledge that we were beating her to a standstill had gone to my head. My crew were just as bad. Nothing seemed to matter. Great flashes rent the night, and the sound of gun-fire was continuous, and yet the *Scharnhorst* replied, but only occasionally now. She was engaging the destroyers with what armament she had. We were keeping the director trained dead on her, and none of us noticed that our course had altered. The blaze and concussion of our gun-fire seemed to grow, and, as in a dream, I heard someone shout, 'The back of the director's blown in, sir.' A second later something hit me in the back, and lay there heavy and inanimate. I looked round and saw that indeed it had been blown in. The hinges had given under the blast of our turrets, and left a gaping rectangular space through which the wind and spray whistled. It occurred to me quickly that another broadside would go off any moment, and the flash come in on our unprotected backs, and so we trained on to the beam just in time. The next broadside left us dazed, but what did we care! I crawled out of my seat and crouched at the side, gripping on to a strut to steady myself for the next. 'A' and 'B' turrets were trained until the muzzle gave our director a minimum of clearance, and the shells could be passing only a few feet away from us. We clung to anything, and gazed intent on the target as the blast and flash of our broadside shook the director like a can. It was terrific.

Then faintly, but growing more loud and clear as we ceased firing, came the pipe—'Boxing Day, bulletin number 38. Commander-in-Chief ordered *Jamaica* to go in and finish her off with torpedoes.' A moment later, divorced at last from the comfort of the flagship's heavy guns, we turned, in a sweep of spray, bows on again towards where we had last seen the *Scharnhorst*'s flash. We were alone.

How alone we felt! The tumult and the noise had died, leaving almost a hush—the hush of expectancy. All I could hear was the wind and the sea, and into the quiet came the return of foreboding and tension. Everyone was thinking—what lies ahead? When last seen the *Scharnhorst* was still firing. Had she any eleven-inch yet able to bear on us? As we closed what sudden crash of gun-fire might envelop us? God, how much nearer? A sudden large flash ahead. Wait!—no, nothing arrived near us. Still firing at the destroyers, perhaps. 'Stand by, four-inch, port side,' came the order down a voice-pipe.

I was galvanised into action. 'Train round, train round. Stop. No, a little more. There she is! Guns follow director. Enemy in sight. No deflection. You've got the range, haven't you? O.K. Stand by, then.' It had come. At last we were going to open fire, and I was controlling. I was cool now, and desperately grim in concentration. I mustn't lose this chance. We were turning, turning to starboard, and again came the flicker of gun-fire right in front of us, but much more vivid and far nearer. I caught sight of a red blob, then another, which rose in front and then curved down, and it seemed to come straight for us. No, it had gone over. Again everything blurred, and was shaken as one six-inch broadside and then another was fired—straight into her. We couldn't miss at that range—3,000 yards. I could smell the sweetish smell of burning. It must be the *Scharnhorst*. I yelled above the din for permission to open fire. We waited and waited for an answer, but none came. They probably never received it on the bridge. And then we turned away and ceased firing. My four-inch hadn't even opened up, and we were bitterly disappointed.

Star-shell from nowhere burst over our heads, bathing the whole ship in light. Surely she will open up now. We were naked, illuminated in every detail. But nothing came. No shot was fired at us, and once more everything was plunged in darkness. At 3,500 yards we turned a full half-circle, so that our starboard side was presented, and we on the port side could sit back and try to imagine what was happening. Another burst of fire and more flashes. Then we turned away and made off. There was no noise now. What had happened? Nobody seemed to know. What had become of the torpedoes? As I was trying to find out from the ADP, two distinct underwater explosions, deep and dull, made the ship quiver slightly. 'Those were our "fish" hitting!' came the cry. Still there was no noise of firing. We stood up in the director and looked around. Nothing in sight. Ten minutes passed and nothing happened. Hardly a sound could be heard above the wind and the sea. We asked the ADP if they could see anything, and they told us that there was one solitary searchlight burning on the starboard side, sweeping the sea, over which could be seen a vague pall of smoke. Minutes dragged by. What was happening? Where was everyone?

'Boxing Day, bulletin number 43,' came the pipe, and, in scarcely suppressed excitement, 'The *Scharnhorst* has been sunk. Destroyers are picking up survivors.'

Lieutenant B. B. RAMSDEN, Royal Marines, in HMS *Jamaica*

It is estimated that Scharnhorst *sustained a probable total of thirteen fourteen-inch shell-hits, a dozen eight-inch and six-inch hits from the cruisers, and eleven torpedo hits before sinking. Thirty-six survivors were picked up from a ship's company of nearly 2,000.*

*

A SHIP OF THE LINE

His Majesty's ship of the line *Indomitable* was a ship to warm the heart of man or boy.

She was a ship whose glistening quarterdeck even Captain Horatio Hornblower RN himself would have been proud to tread, and I doubt whether even so stern a martinet as he could have faulted spar, stay, brace, reef or halyard in the billowing pyramid of white sail.

She was a two-decker of ninety guns; their muzzles grinned

wickedly through black-and-white-check gun-ports, twenty-four-pounders on the main and lower decks, quarterdeck carronades, and bow and stern chasers. From topgallant to main-deck she measured a full forty-five inches, and she hung between the two stone stoves in the centre of the barrack.

Over 2,000 wooden pegs had been used in the building of the ship, for there was not a nail in her, and from the day when Jim Abernethy traced the first lines of her keel on a piece of Canadian Red Cross packing case to the day when he bent the ensign to the gaff and the admiral's broad pennant to the maintop, four and a half months had passed, four and a half months of single-minded unremitting care and craftsmanship.

Everybody in the barrack had taken a personal interest in her construction, and everybody agreed that Abernethy had done a magnificent job.

No one, in fact, not even the most carping critic, could suggest an improvement or find anything that was skimped or omitted. Diminutive cutter and whaler swung snugly in the davits. Binnacle and helm had fittings of burnished brass, made from the slides and buckles of a service haversack. The main-deck lifted out, and you could see little cabins built around the guns with collapsible bulkheads so that between-decks could be cleared for action. The mullioned windows of the admiral's cabin were made out of tiny lozenges of green-and-blue cellophane, and his dining-table hung on chains from the ceiling bulkhead.

The finish of each of the ninety guns was a never-ending source of admiration. Each gun was complete with its tangent sights, training hand-spike, gun-truck, and relieving tackle. There were kegs of powder in the magazines and the lockers were full of shot.

Many arguments raged about the price she would have fetched in a Bond Street or Fifth Avenue shop window, for she had the rightness and completeness of a great work of art, and to examine her detail and its relation to the main design was an aesthetic pleasure all could share.

For Abernethy's ship was the only thing of beauty in the long squalid room. It was an emblem of the mind's escape, the triumph of spirit over environment, and during the long winter evenings, when men huddled in greatcoats and blankets round the stoves and the smoke eddied and wreathed between them, the *Indomitable* seemed to ride upon it and become alive, as if in action, and was the symbol of men's dreams and hopes.

Lieutenant GUY MORGAN RNVR Marlag Nord

The author, who wrote Albert RN, *was captured by the Germans in a partisan fishing-boat off the Dalmatian island of Lussin on 13th November 1943, and, because of his wounds, was repatriated via Sweden on 9th September 1944. The description of the model ship is from a tragic story: in the winter of 1943 HMS* Indomitable *was burned by the POWs to boil a kettle for tea.*

*

NAVAL BASE

Waiting in the bar for the war to end—
Those who for the second time saw it begin
And, charting the future, watched death crawling
Like a lizard over the lidless eyes of the sun
And the leprous face of the coast being eaten
Away by the sea—the glass shows them now
The face and features that they find appalling.
Reflections on launches move across the mirror,
Destroyers and corvettes swinging round buoys, sweepers
At anchor—but here the voyages begin and end,
Gin-time stories which they hear, like keepers
Of lightships, as they wait for news of friends—
The same routine, continuing the war until it ends.

Lieutenant ALAN ROSS RNVR

1944

The author, now a well-known actor, was in command of HM Landing Craft (Flak) No. 16 during the landings at

ANZIO, ANZIO, ANZIO

We were to land troops, etc., at the small watering-place of Anzio, which was a popular holiday resort for Romans, being only twenty miles distant from the capital. The invasion was intended to relieve pressure on the Cassino front and render Rome immediately accessible. It all looked fine on paper, and for once I did not see quite as much cause for alarm as usual. The Americans were joining us, and with the close proximity of Naples, with its airfields and supplies, it appeared on the surface to hold every hope of success.

We sailed on a moonless but beautiful night on the 20th of January 1944, in sublime ignorance of the ordeal ahead of us. Priest's customary eve-of-invasion *bon mot* concerned two islands we passed to port on our way.

'Do those islands belong to us, sir?' he asked.

I had not thought of it before, and although I replied in the affirmative, I realised that time alone would tell. However, they were to prove the least of our worries.

At dawn on the 22nd we lay a mile and a half off the coast. The rocket ships had already done their fabulous stuff, and through the smoke the landing craft were weaving their way in to the beaches. It was an astounding morning, because there was little or no sign of enemy activity: we could see, farther up the coast, spasmodic shelling of minesweepers near the port of Rome, but our sector was subdued and unsensational. I recall very few enemy aircraft the first day, and we hugged ourselves with delight. It was plain that the enemy had been taken by surprise, and we fondly imagined that our troops were by now requisitioning the Colosseum for T. Trinder. It was not until later that we learned that, instead of pressing on, the troops had been ordered to entrench themselves strongly to avoid another possible Salerno. I am not enough of a strategist or tactician to discuss the rights and wrongs of this policy, and nothing could be easier than criticism even from an unsafe distance, but when I heard several weeks later that we had advanced just the three miles I was flabbergasted. But we had surprised the enemy and now it was their turn to surprise us.

I had the flotilla officer with me, which always hampered my movements, and meant there was less to eat in the wardroom, two results which irritated me. Yet on the 22nd of January I was in such a good temper that nothing worried me, and I waved cheerfully to my LCT chums as they passed us in an endless stream. We had stationed ourselves about a thousand yards from the shore, where we had a splendid view of the proceedings. At dusk there were several red warnings, but nothing of serious import occurred. At 0300 the following morning we were told to carry out anti-E-boat patrol, which I did without the foggiest notion of what we would do if we saw one except go into reverse screaming for help.

The day was uneventful, but at first signs of nightfall there was a severe dive-bombing attack on two destroyers a mile or so out to sea. A direct hit was scored on one and the ship sank in a few seconds. It gives me a certain twinge of pride to record that we shot down one of the bastards who had done it. It was a Dornier 217, and this time I made no mistake in my claim, as I noted every small detail, and their Lordships acknowledged our kill. That night we carried out our anti-E-boat patrol as if we were the latest cruiser.

On the 24th of January we were instructed to accompany some Liberty ships to the other side of the harbour, and at noon we anchored close to the port entrance. It was at this time that the flotilla officer said he would look after the ship if I would like to have a lie-down. I had had very little sleep since sailing and accepted his offer with alacrity. There was a light breeze, and I asked him to let me know if anything funny happened. Our senses of humour must have been strangely divergent, as when I reappeared on the bridge four hours later we were chugging slowly past Nettuno, a couple of miles from our starting position. I told them to pull in the anchor, which did not astonish me by its non-appearance. Loss of this commodity always presaged disaster at hand, and this occasion was no exception. I moved to a slightly more sheltered spot and dropped my spare anchor. This held for twenty-four hours, when I noticed that we were once more dragging.

At 2330 on the 25th our tribulations started. All the familiar storm signs were starting, the hissing through the mast, the frenzied movement on the top of the sea and the sickening feeling at the pit of my stomach. But worse was in store: on starting up engines

Sandy reported that the port engine was useless and I could only have the other for the time being. This was a real problem, since it meant that I could not turn to starboard, as there was an onshore wind. The engine which was operating had a strong bias to port, and even with the wheel hard over the other way it made no difference. However, I managed to clear the harbour, but I could not make my way to the open sea; craft other than those with stores, etc., on board had been forbidden to use the port for shelter, and the elaborate instructions detailed at length in the operation orders were quite impracticable. We were slowly being carried over to the southern sector, where enemy interference had just started to become tiresome. Shells were reaching the beaches and the ships lying offshore, and I suddenly saw an LST go up in flames. As we were drifting towards her, our position was desperate. I knew that a heavily ammunitioned ship like ours would only need a burning fragment to touch something off, and yet, however I manœuvred, I simply could not turn the craft. Within 200 yards of the burning hulk I said in a soft voice: 'Please, God, make her turn to starboard.' I said it three times, and then yelled down the voice-pipe: 'Hard to starboard, emergency full speed starboard engine.' I rang the bell to the engine-room, which informed Sandy of conditions, and against every rule of navigation, engineering and nature HM LCF 16 turned to starboard and a few hours later the other engine started . . . a definite lull took me back to within 500 yards of the port, a position which we were to maintain almost continuously for the worst fortnight in my life, although I suppose it is too soon to come to that conclusion. We were to be closed up for twenty hours out of the twenty-four, and were hardly ever in a position to warrant opening fire; we were to come into close contact with the whole bag of the enemy's more ingenious tricks, and our nerves were to be stretched to twanging point. There were the rocket bombs, and although they were aimed at bigger game (a brand-new battleship was an early success), there was something terrifying about the way they turned and twisted in their flight. There were the midget submarines which crept up in the night, and E-boats perpetually on the warpath. But worst of all were the acoustic mines which low-flying aircraft used to drop in the area at dusk. These only went off when a number of ships had already gone safely over them: they tried to drop them in the main channel, but there were numerous outlying bosh-shots. The channel itself was swept every morning before the LSTs and LCTs were permitted into the harbour, but where we were stationed was either not swept at all or swept later in the day. I had a feverish time trying to choose between taking the anchor up and going to a swept area, or staying put and hoping that as we swung round with the tide we would not touch them off. We saw two go up within a hundred yards, and both contacting craft had astonishing escapes with their crews. The first was an RAF rescue launch which was going at top speed and got past before the mine exploded. The other was a DUKW which got away with only its stern blown off. We watched the two incidents with awe in our gaze, but had the common sense to lower the dinghy for the fish which littered the scenes of the explosions.

I took to the bottle in desperation, but I do not think it affected me either for better or worse. I stayed on the bridge permanently and made terrible jokes into the microphone. On the radio from the Port Wave station would come the information that eighty Junkers were approaching the harbour. 'Oh,' I would mutter into the mike, 'I can only see seventy-nine.' Or, 'I think that's a Handley Page,' as the latest type of enemy aircraft sped by, dropping *billet-doux* as she went. I hope never to recapture the fears that passed through my mind during these crucial days. I like to think now that the fear of giving way in front of the lads overruled my personal terror. But the sheer physical fatigue caused by constant watchfulness was almost insufferable. I am told that there were innumerable cases of desertion from duty both ashore and afloat during this operation, but the medical authorities said that the circumstances were exceptional when direst penalties were threatened. I know I was several times within an ace of complete breakdown, but I was saved by two things: the faith that the boys expressed in their faces and the fantastic example set by the LCTs. On the thirteenth morning LCF 10 (our salvagee from Salerno) hove in sight, and she must have been staggered by the warmth of her reception. I cruelly broke the facts of life to her and practically waltzed the ship into the channel home. Our relief sent us a signal as we departed, about her relief, and I made a mental note that under no circumstances would it be us.

Lieutenant-Commander PETER BULL DSC RNVR

Nevertheless, LCF 16 did return to Anzio and eventually spent longer off those beaches than any other ship of her complement. The author was awarded a DSC—a fact of which he first became aware after the war when he read about it in his old school magazine.

*

Just as in the beginning the U-boats had their aces, so as the Battle of the Atlantic progressed the escorts evolved their own maestroes—notably that formidable man Captain F. J. Walker CB, DSO and three bars, RN in HMS Starling. *He and his Second Escort Group developed the technique of hunting and killing U-boats to a high art form. Second Escort Group left Liverpool at the end of January 1944 and killed*

SIX IN ONE TRIP

1. U-592. 31st JANUARY

The U-boat was abaft my beam when I started to turn towards her, and the noise of a number of ship's propellers in her hydrophones must have drowned the sound of my ship's increase of speed at the start of the attack. At any rate she made no move to get out of the way, nor did she get off her torpedoes in a hurry as I came charging in, and it looked as though the attack was unexpected up to the last moment. Then I imagine there came a cry from the U-boat's hydrophone operator of: 'Propellers . . . Fast . . . Loud . . . Getting louder!' and a '*Himmel*' from the captain as he swung his periscope round and caught sight of us coming. He acted fast and in time, for he dodged my pattern of depth-charges all right. His mind, however, was no longer occupied with thoughts of attacking and sinking anyone, which meant that we had achieved our first objective. His next intention, to get safely away out of all this, could be dealt with in the manner we liked best, in slow time.

My chief fear during the run in to attack was that I should get there too late to put the enemy off his stroke. The Asdic contact was grand, and the attack more or less ran itself, but try as I could to stop them, those big ships would come on. Of course, the whole thing was very quickly over, though it seemed to take ages at the time, and the depth-charges produced an immediate response. With delight I saw the carriers turn and present their sterns, which meant that even if torpedoes had been fired they would now miss. With fresh heart we were now free to proceed with the second part of the programme.

There is not much more to tell. Conditions were very good indeed, and the enemy proved strangely docile after his early show of spirit. We regained our contact after the attack and had it confirmed, first by the *Magpie* and then by the Boss in the *Starling*. The *Magpie* had a go, but missed and was told to rejoin the screen. The Boss then ordered an 'Extra Special' and charges rained down. Debris and oil appeared in sufficient quantity, and that was the end of the hunt.

2. U–762. 8th FEBRUARY

The weather held wonderfully fine, and the night of 9th February was clear and moonlit. My ship was out in the deep field on the convoy's port bow when a shout from the port look-out drew the officer of the watch's attention to a U-boat on the surface. It was a nice bit of work, as the enemy was fully a mile and a half away, with little but the conning tower showing, and I am glad to say that the lookout, Able Seaman J. G. Wall, was decorated for it.

We turned towards her at once, but before I had got to the bridge, or the guns had opened fire, she dived. The Asdic team, however, did their stuff and it was not long before we had contact, had told the Boss about it, and had been ordered to hang on until he could team up as usual. The U-boat made no use of speed or violent manœuvre to shake us off, while, since we knew that she had a long way to go before she became a danger to the convoy, we kept quiet as well. The two ships approached one another in this leisurely manner on opposite courses until it was clear that the U-boat would pass more or less directly underneath the ship. I do not suppose the U-boat realised that she had been spotted before diving, nor, apparently, did she hear anything on her hydrophones, as her next action caught us completely by surprise and made me feel extremely foolish. She put up her periscope not more than twenty yards from the ship. The look-out saw it and let out a yell: I followed his pointing arm and there it was in the moonlight, a good two feet of it. The U-boat captain evidently intended to have a good look round, and I trust he was even more surprised at what he saw than we were.

My first reaction was to go full ahead and drop a pattern: a really good shot with the port thrower would score a bull on that periscope. I had hardly got out the orders to the engines, and the depth-charge party had only started to take action, when I looked in the water alongside and realised we could never make it. We might damage the U-boat, but we could certainly never get enough way on the ship to avoid blowing our own stern off. She was too close for the four-inch guns, and the only action was the result of some quick thinking on the part of the men stationed at the close range weapons. Ordinary Seaman R. W. Gates on one Oerlikon got off a pan of ammunition, and I think the stripped Lewis-gun got off some rounds; at any rate tracer hopped all round that periscope, we thought we saw sparks fly from it, we hoped the fellow at the other end got an eye-bath, and then it disappeared.

Having persuaded the depth-charge party not, repeat NOT, to fire, we tried to withdraw to a more convenient range to collect ourselves, and continue to carry out the Boss's orders, but found that the enemy had made up his mind to beat it in exactly the same direction. We simply could not get away from him, and the situation seemed to be getting out of hand when order was restored by the arrival of the *Woodpecker*. She had been told to join in the hunt as well, and had beaten the *Starling* to it. When she had got contact there were two of us on the job and matters could proceed properly. She ran in for the first attack, dropped her charges, and the contact disappeared. Up came the *Starling*, and was directed to the spot. 'Come over here,' signalled Captain Walker to Commander Pryse, 'and look at the mess you have made.' I circled round the two of them while they examined her handiwork, and then we dispersed to our stations again.

3. U-734. 9th FEBRUARY

That action finished at about 1 am. Not long after 4 am I was once more flying up to the bridge to learn that Able Seaman J. D. Hunt, on radar watch, had detected another U-boat on the surface. The sequence of events was the same as before; she dived before we could get the guns off, we got Asdic contact, told the world and were told by the Boss that he was coming. I knew, however, that this time he was a good way off and would be a couple of hours reaching me. Hang on as I would, but be stared at through a periscope twice in one night was more than anyone could stand, and so I determined to have a smack at this one right away. We might lose contact in the commotion, but we should just have to pick it up again if we missed, and anyway it would keep her quiet until we could attend to her properly. It worked out according to this plan. The pattern produced no evidence of damage, but we picked up the trail after our attack and followed it without trouble as the U-boat made no real effort to shake us off. The Boss turned up at 6.30 am and between us we put in two 'Extra Specials'. The first one winged her, and after that she left a trail of oil wherever she went; the second one got her. Again we got debris, but no survivors.

4. U-238. 9th FEBRUARY

As soon as the Boss was satisfied, we were on our way again to a fresh 'incident'. From snatches of intercepted signals we gathered that the *Kite* had picked up another U-boat at about the same time as our second, which, with the *Magpie* to help, she had been hammering ever since. This enemy had proved a tougher and more wily opponent than the other two, so that all their patience and perseverance had not managed to hurt her much, although she had not succeeded in getting away and losing herself either. We sped along at a brisk pace to the scene of this struggle, a matter of thirty miles away, and on arrival I was put on patrol to keep the ring, while the Boss mixed it with the others in the middle. After all the drama of the night this was a welcome spell of quiet, though it was good to see our leader going at it with undiminished vigour. There was some hard slogging still for him to do, with this agile customer sidestepping attack after attack. The *Kite* had to be pulled out of the struggle to join me as ring-keeper because she was practically out of depth-charges. Then, at last, the end came. Our scientists ashore may not have been best pleased at the way in which it was done, but that is a technical joke not worth telling here. Sufficient to say that the *Magpie* was duly blooded, and the Group's third victim within fifteen hours was safely gathered in.

5. U-424. 11th FEBRUARY

It was just before midnight on the following night, as we reached the end of our beat, that we found one, and once again my ship was in luck. The moment was an awkward one, as the Group was engaged in the manœuvre of changing the direction of search, which meant that we were not in a formation to keep clear of one another. I told the rest what I had found, and our new senior officer tried to confirm the contact, at first without success. Still under the influence of what I can only describe as a 'Won't be stared at through periscopes' complex, I then made to attack, and went through a hair-raising time, as I had to break off and stop the ship to avoid a colleague, and then re-start the attack from only 400 yards range. The explosion of the pattern lifted the stern of the ship, but she still held together, and the instruments still worked so the battle could proceed. Conditions for some reason were not as good as usual, and an uncomfortable time followed while we lost and regained and lost contact again while trying to follow the U-boat, which was snaking freely. The *Woodpecker* got contact firmly, though she was not sure that she had a genuine submarine echo, and only attacked it for luck, without result. They then lost it altogether, and it looked as though this whole operation would turn out a frost until Wilkinson, promoted to leading seaman, and his Asdic team, announced a firm contact at last, well clear of consorts. It was astern and at long range, which sounded on the face of it unlikely, but Leading Seaman Wilkinson was so confident that I begged to be excused, and went back after it. It got better as we got closer, until we were not only sure that we had got hold of the real thing, but knew enough about it to attack. The proper thing would have been to wait for a colleague to confirm, but this groping around, dot and carry one business was tiring people out without getting anywhere, and so in we went. We lost contact again on the way in, but were determined to have a bang, and completed the attack. After that we waited.

There was no contact, but instead we were rewarded with sounds. First of all I was told my listeners could hear a noise as though someone was hitting a bit of metal with a hammer. That went on intermittently for some minutes, and then there followed a sharp crack: two more bangs like muffled explosions came next, and then silence.

We had heard of what the submariners call 'breaking up noises', which came from a ship as she sinks after disappearing from view. It seemed fair to assume that what we had been listening to were breaking up noises from a U-boat, and, since other ships present had also heard them, and none of us now had a contact, it was decided not to hunt further, but to patrol around this spot until daylight and see if any evidence could be found then. We told the Boss what we had done, and gathered from his reply that he was hastening back, having replenished his stock of depth-charges, and would give us his verdict when he had seen the evidence.

The investigation at dawn was rather disappointing. There were patches of oil, of which we picked up samples for analysis, since the light diesel oil that the submarines use is different from the oil burnt in ship's boilers, and there was some wooden debris painted grey, but of a nondescript character that might have come from any kind of vessel. The Boss turned up about ten o'clock and was justifiably unconvinced, but I was so insistent with my story of the bangs that he gave us the benefit of the doubt, and decreed that we would all go away and return before dark, when he would give us his decision. We formed up and away we went. It was a long and tiresome day, and I, for one, got my head down all the afternoon to make the time pass. At 5 pm we were back, and what a sight met our eyes this time. An oil patch covered several square miles of sea, in the middle of which floated a convincing quantity of debris. 'The U-boat is sunk,' signalled the *Starling*, 'you may splice the main brace.'

6. U–264. 19th FEBRUARY

At daybreak the convoy was clear of attack, but it was tolerably certain that the discomfited U-boats would be found not far astern of the convoy, and so that was where Captain Walker took the Group to look for them. We started the search at 9 am and by 11 am the *Woodpecker* had 'found'. She had plenty of depth-charges left, and so she and the *Starling* hunted while the rest of us kept the ring. It was a long hunt this time, of great interest to the people in the middle, but dull for the rest of us until the climax came. A series of attacks had damaged the U-boat until her leaks got beyond the capacity of her crew to keep under. She was getting heavier and heavier and nothing further could be done, so her captain decided to abandon ship. He used the last of his high-pressure air to get to the surface, the crew got out and the submarine sank at once. We got off some shots when she broke surface, but soon realised it was a waste of ammunition and ceased fire. The whole crew was picked up.

*

THE HAPPY RETURN

We . . . were informed by Sir Max Horton that on our return home to Liverpool he intended that we should be cheered into harbour. And what a welcome they gave us. We steamed up the channel into the Mersey in line ahead and turned left in succession to enter the lock leading into Gladstone Dock, and there was the crowd. Rows and rows of our comrades from the escort ships were there together with the captain and ship's company of the battleship *King George V*, which was in dock nearby, masses of Wrens (who were making as much noise as all the rest put together), merchant sailors, crews from Allied ships and dock workers. To lead the cheer party stood Captain G. N. Brewer on a dais, himself not long returned from a career of violence at sea that included one of the longest and most savage battles fought round a convoy in the course of the whole war. He was now in command of our base, he had strung up a hoist of flags which read: 'Johnny Walker Still Going Strong', and he conducted the cheers that greeted each of us as we took our turn to berth.

Commander D. E. G. WEMYSS DSO DSC RN
Captain of HMS *Wild Goose* and later leader of
Second Escort Group

Unhappily, Captain Brewer's signal was not fulfilled. On 9th July 1944 Captain Walker died of a stroke brought on by heavy strain and overwork. Admiral Sir Max Horton, Commander-in-Chief Western Approaches, read the epitaph at the funeral service in Liverpool Cathedral. '. . . Not dust nor the light weight of a stone, but all the sea of the Western Approaches shall be his tomb. His spirit returns unto God who gave it.' Captain Walker's body was buried at sea from the destroyer HMS Hesperus. *By chance there were two huge convoys in the Mersey at the time. Their crews stood bareheaded and silent as* Hesperus, *colours at half-mast, passed them on her way to sea.*

*

ORDER OF THE DAY: 31st MAY 1944

It is to be our privilege to take part in the greatest amphibious operation in history—a necessary preliminary to the opening of the Western Front in Europe which, in conjunction with the great Russian advance, will crush the fighting power of Germany.

This is the opportunity which we have long awaited and which must be seized and pursued with relentless determination: the hopes and prayers of the free world and of the enslaved peoples of Europe will be with us and we cannot fail them.

Our task in conjunction with the Merchant Navies of the United Nations and supported by the Allied Air Forces, is to carry the Allied Expeditionary Force to the Continent, to establish it there in a secure bridgehead and to build it up and maintain it at a rate which will outmatch that of the enemy.

Let no one underestimate the magnitude of this task.

The Germans are desperate and will resist fiercely until we outmanœuvre and outfight them, which we can and will do. To every one of you will be given the opportunity to show by his determination and resource that dauntless spirit of resolution which individually strengthens and inspires and which, collectively, is irresistible.

I count on every man to do his utmost to ensure the success of this great enterprise which is the climax of the European war.

Good luck to you all and Godspeed.

Admiral Sir BERTRAM H. RAMSAY KCB KBE MVO
Commander-in-Chief, Allied Naval Expeditionary Force

*

OPENING GAMBIT

One mile off the coast of France a periscope broke the surface of the water. Thirty feet below, crouching in the cramped control-room of the X23, Lieutenant George Honour[1] pushed his cap back. 'Well, gentlemen,' he recalls saying, 'let's take a look-see.'

1. Lieutenant G. B. Honour DSC RNVR

Cushioning one eye against the rubber-cupped eye-piece, he slowly pivoted the periscope around, and as the distorting shimmer of water disappeared from the lens the blurred image before him straightened out and became the sleepy resort town of Ouistreham near the mouth of the Orne. They were so close in and his view was so magnified that Honour could see smoke rising from chimneys and in the far distance a plane that had just taken off from Carpiquet Airport near Caen. He could also see the enemy. Fascinated, he watched German troops calmly working among the anti-invasion obstacles on the sandy beaches that stretched away on either side.

It was a great moment for the twenty-six-year old Royal Naval Reserve lieutenant. Standing back from the periscope, he said to Lieutenant Lionel Lyne, the navigation expert in charge of the operation, 'Take a look, Thin—we're almost bang on the target.'

The X23's mission was a particularly hazardous one. Twenty minutes before H-Hour, the midget sub and her sister ship, the X20[1] —some twenty miles farther down the coast, opposite the little village of Le Hamel—would boldly come to the surface to act as navigation markers, clearly defining the extreme limits of the British-Canadian assault zone: three beaches that had been given the code-names Sword, Juno and Gold.

The plan they were to follow was involved and elaborate. An automatic radio beacon capable of sending out a continuous signal was to be switched on the moment they surfaced. At the same time sonar apparatus would automatically broadcast sound waves through the water which could be picked up by underwater listening devices. The fleet carrying British and Canadian troops would home in on either or both of the signals.

Each midget also carried an eighteen-foot telescopic mast to which was attached a small but powerful searchlight that could send out a flashing beam capable of being seen more than five miles away. If the light showed green, it would mean that the subs were on target; if not, the light would be red.

As additional navigation aids, the plan called for each midget to launch a moored rubber dinghy with a man in it and allow it to drift a certain distance towards shore. The dinghies had been fitted

1. Commanding Officer, Lieutenant K. R. Hudspeth DSC and two bars, RANVR

with searchlights which would be operated by their crewmen. By taking bearings on the lights of the midgets and their drifting dinghies, approaching ships would be able to pinpoint the exact positions of the three assault beaches.

Nothing had been forgotten, not even the danger that the little sub might be run over by some lumbering landing craft. As protection the X23 would be clearly marked by a large yellow flag. The point had not escaped Honour that the flag would also make them a fine target for the Germans. Notwithstanding, he planned to fly a second flag, a large white navy 'battle duster'. Honour and his crew were prepared to risk enemy shell-fire, but they were taking no chances on being rammed and sunk.

At the periscope Lieutenant Lyne took a series of bearings. He quickly identified several landmarks: the Ouistreham lighthouse, the town church, and the spires of two others in the villages of Langrune and St Aubin sur Mer a few miles away. Honour had been right. They were almost 'bang on the target', barely three-quarters of a mile from their plotted position.

Honour was relieved to be this close. It had been a long, harrowing trip. They had covered the ninety miles from Portsmouth in a little under two days, and much of that time they had travelled through minefields. Now they would get into position and then drop to the bottom. Operation 'Gambit' was off to a good start. Secretly he wished that some other code name had been chosen. Although he was not superstitious, on looking up the meaning of the word the young skipper had been shocked to discover that 'gambit' meant 'throwing away the opening pawns'.

CORNELIUS RYAN

The landings were postponed one day because of the weather and X23 and X20 spent nearly three days submerged off the Normandy coast. But at 5 am on 6th June their logs read: 'Commenced flashing green light.'

D-Day . . .

. . . FIRST, THE MINESWEEPERS

By sundown our little flotilla of sweepers was hurrying south-east for the rendezvous from which the whole invasion fleet would head for France. From far away downwind on our port side came the steady drone of hundreds and hundreds of landing craft heading in the same direction, white water flashing from their blunt bows in the last of the daylight.

That night we fixed bayonets on the ship's rifles.

We were perhaps a little disturbed as we sailed toward Normandy. Only a fool wouldn't be. We'd be right out in front, sweeping a path for the armada that followed. With the dragging weight of a sweep out astern, our manœuvrability would be almost nil. Thus would we meet the Luftwaffe, out in force to protect the Atlantic West Wall since surely the easiest time to stop us would be before we got a footing on the land.

No one spoke about it, but every one of us expected bombs, torpedoes, gun-fire, mines, E-boats, destroyers, secret weapons of new and horrible types, and gas. Besides our ordinary respirators we were issued with transparent visors against liquid gas. Each was good for only fifteen minutes. Then you tore it off and put on a fresh one—very quickly.

Fellows went about quietly making their own arrangements for the coming fray. Silently they adjusted the bands of their tin hats, checked their identification tags, made sure their life-jacket flash-light worked, and tied their most precious possessions in a small bag at the waist. One lad was practically draped in razor-sharp sheath knives. 'Figurin' on some hand-to-hand fightin'?' I asked. 'You never know,' he answered vaguely.

The boys were very keen on the new RCN life-jackets. We were practically living in them now. They'd been issued on board the 'Tribal' destroyer *Athabaskan* just before she went out on her last patrol, and they saved many lives then. We liked them and were preparing to float around in them indefinitely as survivors.

Choice edibles the fellows had been hoarding in their lockers now came to light. Nothing could have shown more clearly what they thought was ahead than the way in which they now brought out these tidbits from home and insisted that we eat them—right away, while we still could! No use going into the water on an empty stomach! Even the canteen manager began to have doubts, and let us buy all the chocolate bars we wanted. It was a regular Belshazzar's feast.

I'd never seen ratings taking things so seriously. They tested the escape hatch in the mess-deck to see that it worked, and the ladder to be sure it came free easily. One of the 'Killicks' checked and double-checked the 'bottom line' that ran around the bow to take a collision mat in case we got holed. At night, without any orders whatsoever, guys went round checking up on the ship's black-out, so no chink of light showed to a prowling E-boat. I even went and hacked off my lovely beard, after reading in an old newspaper how bearded survivors from the torpedoed frigate *Valleyfield* nearly choked to death in fuel oil!

All next day there were vapour trails overhead from passing aircraft. They could be enemy planes just as easily as ours, for all we knew, and the look-outs were supposed to report each trail they saw. If a man off watch and passing the time of day on deck spotted one of these trails before the nearby look-out did, he gave his shipmate a terrific blast for not keeping his eyes open. 'I'm not going to swim just because of you,' he nattered.

We hadn't started our sweep yet, but it would be fairly simple. The ships, all twelve, would take up a sort of arrowhead formation. The leading ship would then put out a sweep on both sides, and the next ship behind her on each flank would put out a sweep in the direction of that flank. With each ship keeping her bow inside the end of the next ahead's sweep, we'd clear a wide channel and no one would hit anything. At least that was the theory!

Just in case anyone's wondering about it, I suppose I should add that there were two small Yankee MLs to sweep ahead of the flotilla and so protect the leading ship. The senior officer in the MLs, so we learned, was the man who'd spirited General MacArthur away from the Philippines.

Next morning we were having breakfast in the mess-deck as usual. The sweep had been out since three o'clock, but everything was quiet, even the conversation. 'I've got my money and my liquor permit wrapped up in oiled silk. . . What for? Your permit'll be no good in France. . . . I'll bet those Limies in the next sweeper will be out scrubbing down the fo'c's'le even with mines comin' up. . . . Pass the butter, you clown. . . . Get that life-jacket out of my way, will you, so a guy can drink his coffee? . . . Don't throw that tin away: I'm gonna use it for water to cool my Oerlikon barrel. . . . Wonder what kind of headlines this'll make back home? . . . BOOM! BOOM!

The whole ship shook like a piece of sheet tin. There was a dead silence in the mess. Then it came again and much louder than before, BOOM! This time everything on the table leaped into the air. A voice yelled down through the for'ard hatchway: 'Hello, below! In case you're interested, we're cuttin' mines out here.' As if we didn't know!

Well, we rose from that table as one man. The first bloke took off with the coffee-pot in one hand, his plate in the other, and his mouth so full of toast he couldn't speak. Another chap came flying out of the washroom in such a hurry he left his false teeth behind and had to go back for them. In about three seconds we were out of the mess-deck, and had taken all the breakfast with us. We closed the door and dogged it down tight. That extra bulkhead would help a lot if we hit anything.

The last mine had blown the end off our sweep, and we were delayed getting a new one rigged. We didn't care much about the mines we cut, but those cut by the ship ahead might come up right in front of us. 'Now,' said the captain, 'all eyes ahead.' He needn't have worried: fully half the ship's company was watching intently already.

Oddly enough, no more mines were detonated that day. Several were cut by the ships ahead of us, and we tried to set them off by gun-fire. They looked clean, as if they hadn't been down long. We opened up at them with all our small arms, but couldn't hit the horns. Then, as their outer casings became pierced with bullets, they filled and sank. One that popped up much too close for comfort had us pretty excited until it turned out to be an old bucket dropped overboard by HMCS *Vegreville* up ahead.

We were heading in straight for France now. Owing to bad weather in the Channel, there'd been a twenty-four hour postponement shortly after the start, but this didn't worry anyone except the cook. He had won the ship's five-pound sweep on the date of D-Day, and now he had to hand the money over to the leading writer.

As our flotilla swept a channel, trawlers put down spar buoys to mark the path. The buoys carried flags for daylight and dim blue-green lights for night. Far astern, but closing on us, we could now see a jumbled mass of invasion ships, their balloons mere black dots against the grey sky. On either side of them idled destroyers, PT boats, and cruisers.

By the middle of the afternoon one spearhead of the armada was right behind us. The landings were set to begin early the following morning. Besides the infantry and tank-carrying vessels, there were ocean-going tugs, landing craft towing barges laden with more landing craft, barges with heavy guns, and raft-like somethings barely awash with people walking about on them. There were also the rocket ships, looking like a direct steal from *Popular Science* or *Amazing Stories.*

In the early evening we were still roughly forty miles off the French coast. Everyone planned to spend the night on deck. The galley would make cocoa and sandwiches for us. The men were all much too curious to sleep when they came off watch. They were scared stiff they might miss something absolutely terrific.

We hadn't met any opposition at all so far. We couldn't understand it. Why hadn't there been any German planes? Lordy! Maybe they were waiting to trap us close in by the coast. We all knew what had happened off the shores of Greece and Crete.

But whatever the Germans did about the invasion fleet, obviously we'd catch it first, and the boys kept chattering contentedly about the awful time we'd be having in just a few hours. They weren't exactly measuring themselves mentally for harp and halo, rather just groping for a few quotable last words. The situation was growing more tense by the minute and they frankly revelled in it.

Of course, even the impending clash didn't keep us from nattering about the liver we had for supper. And surely that couldn't be Canadian bacon! But I wasn't complaining. At least I was back in a ship that had toilet tissue. Paper was so scarce in England that every tiny sheet of the roll I'd had to steal from the POS heads in the *Duke of York* was stamped 'Government Property'! I thought we were invading very comfortably.

Lieutenant WILLIAM H. PUGSLEY RCNVR
in HMCS *Georgian*

Then . . .

IT WAS D-DAY

The flotilla made a grand sight, steaming down to the open sea, threading its way in line ahead through the massed transports, crowded with men and vehicles that lay at anchor in the land-locked roadstead. In the grey evening could be smelt and felt the fresh tang of the Channel in one of its boisterous, threatening moods. The Commandos on deck looked round at the unfamiliar scene, at the waters they had exercised in so often. They were cheerful but restrained. There was the island, there the spit. The mainland lay on the quarter, misty, indistinct, in the smoky setting sun. For many it would be the last sight of England.

I must close up a little. On this of all occasions our station-keeping must be perfect. *Steady on the stern of the next ahead, Cox'n.* What's that hoist? Good, the flotilla officer wants more revs. Let's do the thing in style; might be our last gesture. The unknown morrow lies over our bows. They're cheering us from the transports. 'Give 'em hell!' I expect we all feel how few we are, how small and very much alone. Being cheered makes one feel heroic in a grand and desperate way. We assault early, but the transports will be there soon enough. We're all in this.

Now's the time for our signature tune over the loudhailer. *Switch on, signalman.* Impudent and cheerful. But what's that? The pipes. Damn it, that's the brigadier's own piper on the fo'c's'le of the flotilla leader. The pipes are best. Mine sounds strident, flauntingly casual about the prospect of death, too flamboyant a gesture—but the pipes, the pipes are striking, fittest music for the fight. *Number One, why isn't that man wearing a lifebelt? Does he think this is a bloody picnic?*

Pray now for luck. The colonel and all these Commandos, battle-skilled and tough, putting themselves irrevocably into the hands of an amateur sailor. Well, I'll land these troops if it's the last thing I ever do—probably will be—I'll fight this ship till the guns fall off. Land them, if the whole crew lies dead on the deck. Oh, don't indulge in such silly private dramatics with yourself! *I say, Number One, ask the Middy to organise some cocoa.*

'Look here, you chaps,' said the flotilla officer at that last briefing, 'we won't let the Commandos down. We know these troops, we've trained with them, and we think a hell of a lot of them. We can't and won't let them down. We've only got two things to do. First, find the place over there, then put them ashore at all costs. What if we don't find exactly the right place? Don't start looking for it; land the troops at all costs.'

Port look-out! Keep your eyes open for a light on the port bow. By my reckoning it should have showed up by now. *Cox'n, how's your head?* South twenty east. And I estimate it should be south eleven east. But we can't steer to within ten degrees in this sea. All the same, don't want to end up in Le Havre—we'd look damn' silly making an invasion by ourselves. Where in the hell are all those buoys? I haven't seen one yet, and by dead reckoning we've passed at least four. But how can you find buoys, or even lay them, in a sea like this? What a night—dark and wet, with just the sort of sea that makes the old tub wallow like a lovesick hippopotamus. All right for sailors, but I'm thinking about the troops. A lot sick already and half the rest in a stupor. They'll need their strength tomorrow, every ounce of it. I wish to hell I felt certain, absolutely certain, of our exact position. We're too much to the east. They said to avoid easting, emphatically. Wonder if I ought to signal up the line. No, Rupert knows what he's doing, though I wouldn't allow so much for wind myself. Funny, I thought there'd be lots of traffic about, and we haven't seen a single thing. Of course, we land pretty early, and are faster than most.

My God! Just these twelve small ships, and all these precious lives, alone in mid-Channel. Query, are lives precious in wartime? Yes, until they can be thrown away for their planned objective. *Hello, Colonel, come up on the bridge.* I wonder how he feels. *How are we getting on? Oh, fine, sir. Right up to time. We'll hit the run-in position in approximately three hours twenty minutes.* Either that or Le Havre harbour boom. Wacko, Rupert's spotted a dan buoy and altered course. That's better, south five east. *You see, sir, everything weighed off! Buoys laid to mark every channel—can't go wrong! No, the RNVR hasn't done badly in this war. Do you know, there isn't a single RN officer with us. Navigation? That's no worry—it's your seasick troops I'm worried about.* Yes, south five east, that allows for too much easting, and brings us back to my mean course of south eleven east. Navigating all of us to death, that's what I may be doing. To hell, I'm getting my head down for a while now Number One's been called. *Hello, Fitz. Good sleep? Course south five east, position about thirty miles from the run-in. Don't close up too much in this sea. Call me in two hours' time—till then for nothing less than an enemy destroyer!*

Reluctant dawn drew up the curtain on a grey and heaving sea, turning fantasies to spray-drenched reality. Far ahead gun-fire rumbled and rolled, and the flashes were echoed faintly on the low cloud. Overhead through it swift squadrons raced southward. Dan buoys appeared, floating soddenly, their marker flags drowned and bedraggled. The deck of the next ahead plunged wetly through the seas; the next astern, who cheerily signalled Good bloody morning, yawed and rolled on its course. The flotilla drove steadily on. One or two Commandos, who had elected to sleep on deck all night, damply unrolled themselves, sat up, and shivered with the cold. This was the awaited dawn, fatal or glorious, heralded by guns.

Those flashes come from battle-wagons. Too deliberate a fire, too deep a roar, for anything smaller. *Bearing red one five? Very good, look-out.* Yes, there she is, and another beyond her. We're not a mile to the east, if they're in their bombardment positions. There they go again, now wait for the sound to reach us. Something mighty reassuring about battle-wagons. War elephants of the fleet, unhurried and packing a wallop. Destroyers rush about, guns barking like frenzied sheep-dogs. And cruisers slide swiftly, specialists in pretty shooting, the accurate placing of sweet salvos. But the battle-wagon—her great guns swing up in a silent arc. Then woof! with a sheet of flame that hides the ship she's hurled a packet of one-ton bricks at something out of sight. Then she stops to think for a while, and the ginger smoke rolls lazily away. Woof! again. The first for your concrete wall; now for your bathroom window. *Colonel, I once saw a sixteen-inch gun blow a perfect and gigantic smoke ring. I half expected the gun to waggle with pleasure, but it took absolutely no notice.*

Now what's Rupert altering away westward for? Ah, yes, run-in position. *Yes, look-out, I see them.* There they are, huddled together on the skyline, a lot of ships, too. Lowering position for the assault craft, just like putting perambulators off a bus. *What's that, Colonel? Call you when we sight the beach—you know just what it looks like? Yes, sir, I'll do that. It'll be at least an hour yet.* This is where the old heart goes thump, thump in that heavy way. One more hour of uncertainty in which the chill finger of foreboding lays itself across my brow. Hm, line for a tragedy king. *How d'you feel, Middy? Myself, I wouldn't be elsewhere for a thousand quid. Well, not for a hundred anyway.* It's a comforting show of ships. We're not alone any more. Eight miles from them to the enemy, and just listen to the gun-fire. All the mad dogs of hell barking over a bone on the beach, the invisible beach; and the shattering roll of the bombs. These ships are all too close together, if they're under fire themselves. *There's a wreck, port look-out, only her bows showing. Why the hell didn't you report it?*

Those assault carrier ships look like wolves meditating the attack. Some of their craft will have gone in by now. Small targets, but desperate business in this running surf. Some, maybe many, will be lost, but the rest will swarm on like sea-lice. We ignore this friendly company of ships, and go straight on. Perhaps the admiral there will note with approval that we are dead on time. Our job is by ourselves, a vital job, a king-pin job in the involved machinery of this invasion. *Well, Cox'n, you're a lucky man. Not everyone gets paid for taking a trip to the Continent! What? You'd sooner go to Blackpool?* Visibility is poor. At what distance will we sight that flat and fatal coast? In good time, I hope, to make any necessary alteration of course. Past the lowering position now, and off into the unknown. Nobody takes any notice. We'll show them. *Number One, old boy, we are altering to south seventeen west. Eight miles to go, and the revs up to 1,400.* Good old ship, she runs her sweetest at 1,400, and still 600 in reserve. *No, Middy, the gunners may not, repeat not, open fire if they see a submarine. Nor at anything else unless they're told. It is considered bad form to shoot down Spitfires.* This is exhilarating, this is exultantly fine. Never felt more aware, more full of life—if it weren't for that unpleasant tight feeling round the heart.

What did I say to Frank when we toasted ourselves the other day after those few drinks? Steer for the sound of the guns! Very dramatic, but the guns happen to be all round us, and all ours as far as I can make out. Hello, splashes. Not all ours then. That destroyer is firing as if it's had a fit, yes, and someone's been badly knocked about over there. Can't worry, it's a good gamble. We get hit or we don't get hit. Shell-fire you can't do anything about, but damned if I can feel happy about machine-guns on the beach. Here I am, conning a shipload of 104 hefty Commandos, fifteen seamen and two officers of my own, running on a time-table towards terror. And there are 4,000 gallons of high-octane petrol under my deck. Wonder how they feel in the engine-room where they can't even see what's going on, just trust in me and hope like hell. I shall light another pipe.

The silhouettes and scale models in the intelligence room looked like toys out of an expensive nursery. It was all there—the canal entrance, the scattered town along the shore, the church spire, the château by the wood, the pill-box, trench, strong-point, emplacement, emplacement, emplacement. Stretching seaward over the flat tidal beach the rows of posts, stakes, spikes and mines bristling like a hedgehog. 'Your parking beach,' said the naval intelligence officer, 'is 800 yards long. Its limit on the east is this modern villa by the road, on the west these two distinctive steep-roofed houses. To the west it doesn't matter much—you may get in the way of others, but land anywhere if you must. But to the east, not one yard beyond your limit.' He smiled cheerfully. 'Not that any of these buildings are likely to be standing by the time the Navy and the RAF have got going. All you can expect is smoke and fire and haze and maybe a helpful pile of rubble.' He spoke perfect English for a Frenchman, and knew so much he might have been on that beach for the past few months. He probably had.

There it is, the flat, sleeping coast, charged with peril. Ships, warships, lie all round us. Their guns are going all the time. I like the way they've comfortably dropped their hooks as if they've come to settle down. *Disappointing from a tourist's point of view, Number One*—why must I give way to this affectation of flippancy?—*but call the colonel: he wants to view the promised land.* How good our ships look. Small, but purposeful. They were built for this hour. There's a signal hoist—how many have I watched from that same yard-arm? —division, church, order zero: assume arrowhead formation when executived. There's Jack astern looking at me through his glasses just as I look at him through mine. *I'll* be very funny indeed and raise my cap with extravagant politeness!

That's surely the château, Colonel, through the smoke. A cable to starboard of it is our limit. Can you see the modern villa? Not there. That should be it, sir, that white ruin, what do you think? Good, bang on the right beach. We've been steering a lot more west than seventeen too. Good old Rupert, good old all of us! Not far to go, and anywhere in the 800 yards to the west of the ruin. Any minute; every ship for itself.

Now eyes for everything, eyes for nothing. The beach looms close, maybe a mile. There are people running up and down it. There are fires, and the bursting of shells. Yes, and wrecked landing craft everywhere, a flurry of propellers in the savage surf and among those wicked obstructions. Beach-clearance parties, I expect, bloody heroes, every one. Special craft stooging quietly in, some of them on fire, though. Diesel fuel burns black. That vicious destroyer to port is irritating me, but the colonel doesn't seem to mind. He's cool but I bet he's worried. Curious how all these soldiers dislike an assault by water. I'd hate to dash out of foxholes at machine-guns. Damn him, I can pretend I'm cool, too. *It's the noisiest gun—starboard ten!—it's the noisiest gun in the Navy, that four point seven—Midships, Cox'n!* What a cool, disinterested reply he makes. Colonel, you make me grin. I like your nerve.

We are on those bristling stakes. They stretch before us in rows. The mines on them look as big as planets. And those graze-nose shells pointing towards us on some of them look like beer bottles. Oh, God, I *would* be blown up on a mine like a beer bottle! Now for speed and skill and concentration. Whang, here it comes—those whizzing ones will be mortars—and the stuff is falling all round us. Can't avoid them, but the mines and collisions I can avoid. Speed, more speed. Put them off by speed, weave in and out of these bloody spikes, avoid the mines, avoid our friends, avoid the wrecked craft and vehicles in the rising water, and *get these troops ashore*. Good, the Commando officers have their men ready and waiting, crouched along the decks. Number One is for'ard with his ramp parties ready. Everything is working as we've exercised it for so long. Oh, hell, this new tin hat is far too big for me—I'll shake it off my head out of fright if I'm not careful. *Port twenty. Midships. Starboard ten.* That was a near one. Nearly hit it. But we won't, we can't, slow down. *Midships. Port ten, port fifteen, port twenty.* We're going to hit it, we're going to hit it! A beer-bottle, I knew it. *Ease to ten. Midships!* Not bows on, though. We'll strike to starboard on the beam. One, two, three, four, five. . . . Huh, nothing's happened. Must be luck for me in beer bottles after all. Now for the next lot of obstructions.

Don't jump, you fool. It was near, but you're not hit. Straddled. All right, keep on. And here's where I go in, that little bit of clear beach. *Port ten. Midships. Starboard five.* Wish the swell weren't throwing us about so much. Let's be in first, as a glorious gesture, then no one will know how frightened we really were. Tommy always said when coaching us, If you hang around on the outside of the scrum you'll get hurt—go in! *Sorry to give you so much work, Cox'n.* That'll rock him, and I'll light up my pipe, too. What does he say? Nae bother at all, sir, and I'm still sticking to my pipe, am I? Can't even the enemy take the bounce out of this, Cox'n? *You're not being familiar, I hope, Cox'n?* I mustn't grin. What? Not bloody likely? Anyhow, he's a cocky bastard and cheerful. A shell may kill us both any minute.

Slow ahead together. Slow down to steady the ship, point her as you want her, then half ahead together and on to the beach with a gathering rush. Put her ashore and be damned! She's touched down. One more good shove ahead to wedge her firm. *Out ramps!*

Smooth work, Fitz, oh, smooth as clockwork. *Now off you go! Good luck, Commandos, go like hell! Next meeting—Brighton!* How efficiently, how quickly, they run down the accustomed ramps, not a man hit that I can see, and there they go splashing through a hundred yards of water, up over more of the flat beach than that, and out of sight among the deadly dunes. The colonel turns to wave, and is gone with them. They ignore beach fire. They have their objective and they are going for it, the best troops we can produce. God be with them.

Rupert's decks were clear before ours after all, there he is to port.

And now here's Woodie beside me to starboard. And Chris and Jack grounded on my port quarter. Good work, oh, good for us! *Number One, in ramps! Come on, get those bloody ramps IN!* None of the crew hit yet that I can see. Let's get out quick. Any of our craft hit? Yes, there's Les—seems to be on fire aft, but quite unperturbed. And Chris has a lot of confusion on his fo'c's'le. Casualties. How can I get out with him across my stern? *Middy, take the depth aft.*

Christ, that's too near! Don't want to be killed now. Mortar, fifteen yards. Little bits rattling against the bridge. And a nasty concentration on the beach. How slowly men spin before they fall. Some look surprised as they die. Oh, come on, Chris! Who's that damn' fool opening up with a machine-gun past my bridge? Minor craft astern, I suppose. As if there isn't enough to put up with. No! It's coming from ashore! *Port gunner! Tall building bearing red one five, red one five. Fire!* Hah, quick-triggered, that boy, oh, and lovely shooting: a stream of tracer from both guns hose-piping on every window. Don't you take us on with a machine-gun, Jerry. You'll get hot porridge back. No return fire, anyway. Hope we got the bastard.

Right. *Half astern together.* We're off. Must avoid incoming craft as well as dodge those stakes. Damn, she never would steer coming astern. We hit that one. Never mind, the mines are all set on the seaward side. Turn short round. *That's that, Fitz. Now we'll take a look round. I say! Those aren't chance shots. They're stalking us out to sea!* Splash to starboard, splash to port, ahead, astern. Now I'm in a rage, full of exultation, fear, contempt, intoxication with the hour and the day. Does that damned Jerry think he can hit us going out when he couldn't hit us coming in? Wasting time on an empty ship when the beach is full of targets! Of course, he just might. . . . Good shooting, oh, very nice. But now I've landed my troops it's ME you're taking on. *Cox'n, steer for that last burst.* Bet he can't put one on the same spot twice.

Hell! What an explosion! And, my God, it's one of ours! *Fitz, who is it, who is it?* Must have been hit in the tanks. God, oh God, poor bastards! *No, we're too far away. Others are going in.* There won't be a man alive when the smoke clears. But they landed their troops at all costs. At all costs. And blown up coming off. Who's that over there, bows up and sinking? Stan. I can read his number.

Abandoned, I think. *Signalman, call her up. Take a look, Number One. I think she's abandoned. Yes?* This area is warming up. Surely the fire is faster and better than it was? Jerry is a stubborn bastard. The landing has been made, and the others are coming in wave upon wave. Now, why the hell must he keep on firing at me?

On the beaches the opposition intensified in many places some hours after the initial assault. The Germans went to earth to fight, using cunning where force had failed. Guns and mortars ranged the landing areas with precision, the sniping was deadly and persistent. But still the assault went on, till the shallow water was crammed with twisted metal wreckage, blazing vehicles and disabled craft. Still the assault went on, and the troops were put ashore with the inevitability of the rising tide that covered the beach obstructions and made navigation more perilous than before.

Who's that hailing us? Yes, that infantry landing craft. Full of troops. She's been hit. Listing badly. Sinking, I should say. *LCI(L), LCI (L), I am coming alongside. That's right, Number One, all the fenders you've got. We'll get a bashing in this swell. Give the lines plenty of scope.* Holed on the waterline, she is. I think she'll last, though. Don't like these shells falling round, but it's worse for the pongos, and them still seasick. *Bad luck, chum! But we'll run the ferry service. All aboard for Margate!* Damn silly to shout such rubbish, but it may sound confident. Hell, I don't want to go into that bloody beach again.

Come on, lads, help them aboard, and ALL their equipment. Now, wait for it, there, wait till she rolls towards you, THEN jump. This is going to take time. Horrible being hove to under fire. Honest, I'm in a worse funk than the first time. Because of that gun that seems told off to get us. Surely it will be easier on the beaches by now. *Casualties? Sure, we'll take them for you. Number One, Cox'n, get them aboard and do what you can. Hello, Major, now where can I take you? Oh, I know where it is: nothing's a trouble.* Bad luck being smashed up before they've landed, but what a load—twice as many as we should take. One hit and this crowded deck will look like a butcher's shop. Troops don't know the craft either. Slow getting on means slower getting off. And all that equipment! Commandos move fast because they're light. Well, in we go again. *Cox'n, steady on the gap between those two buildings ashore. See them? Right.*

This is being under fire in real earnest. Or am I more nervous than I was? We'll pick our way between the bursts, swerving nicely, duck when we hear a mortar, and keep our fingers crossed. *Starboard ten. Midships.* Nearly didn't see that sunk tank or whatever it was. Too many new fires on that beach, and small-arms shooting, too. Hope it's us cleaning up. *Yes, Major, that's it ahead. We've been surf-riding round here all morning. The beach is ours all right. It's just like home to half the army now.*

Good old Fitz. He's standing by to beach as if we were running a London bus. And the crew were lounging as if they'd been under fire for weeks. Showing off in front of these pongos—good. Don't expect they've been through it before, and they're seasick as well. Ah, another row of obstructions. There should be more like these, totally submerged. Horrible to be wrecked now. But take a chance —I'm going in here, and going in fast.

Out ramps! And there goes one right overboard. Preventer stay gone. *All right, you troops, now get off on the other one. Take it easy, but get off, and DON'T leave your equipment behind you.* Nothing to do but wait. And there are more explosions, beach mines, bodies, going up. Men and machines tossed in the air. And that mortar is killing people. Too damned near, and the tank beyond our bows blazing like hell.

Oh, for Pete's sake, why must this big landing craft come in so close to me? His kedge-wire will be hard to miss, and if I go to port I may crash on the wreck there. *Come on, troops, get OFF! Throw that equipment down to them, you, for'ard. No, NOT in the water.* The men are coming off this next craft. And on to a mine, not twenty yards from our bows. Here's another mortar. *Duck!* Hell, right on her fo'c's'le. If she hadn't come so close we would have stopped that one. Oh, I don't like this at all. *Number One, are those troops getting off?*

Off at last! And still not hit, by some good luck, except for the rattle of fragments on the deck. Some of our troops hit, though. Silly bastards, they should have got up that beach and away, instead of milling around. Now out to sea, Harry Flatters. *See any more of our craft, signalman?* Thank God. I've had enough of this for a while. after how many mathematical probabilities does one run into a shell while trying to dodge them? *Two thousand revs, Cox'n, steer north fifteen east.* We must rendezvous. Heaven knows what's happened to the flotilla. *I say, Number One, we're two miles out and still being shelled. Persistent sods, aren't they?*

So it is. That's Joe's craft. What's he going as far out as this and sinking, too? He can't last long—screws out of the water and blowing down on the uncleared mines. *Starboard ten. We'd better close him.* Now what earthly good do those stupid Jerries think they're doing by trying to shell a sinking ship? *Flash him, signalman, Will take you off.* Okay, Joe, we're coming. *No, Fitz, he's past towing. Too far gone. We won't be any too soon.*

Hiyah, Joe! I'm coming alongside. Got all your crew there? Under-water damage, I guess. Yes, there's a bloody great hole midships. Silly those propellers look sticking uselessly out of the water. *What's that, Joe? Told you to beach yourself in shallow water? Eh? You said you would if you were a bloody Spitfire?* Good old Joe. Perhaps I'm jumpy, but I'm not putting out lines. She looks as if she'll nose-dive any minute. Crash alongside, and get them over. We may still stop a packet. *All aboard?* Yes, she's lurching now. Poor Joe. Nobody wants to see a ship go down, let alone his own. *Well, Joe, if that's Jerry's Atlantic Wall I don't think much of it. What? Just shows you can't trust no bastard, does it?* Good old Joe, that's right in character.

Number One, we will now get to seaward out of here, and find the rest. Issue rum to everybody. And, my God, I'll have a tot myself!

Lieutenant-Commander DENIS GLOVER DSC RNZNVR

The author was in command of HM LCI(S) No. 516 in a convoy of LCI(S) under Commander Rupert Curtis RNVR which took Lord Lovat's Commando Brigade to the assault at Ouistreham on D-Day. He was awarded his DSC for his work that day.

*

The D-Day armada included some of the strangest warships—for instance the

LANDING BARGE (KITCHEN)

We found her amid a huddle of ships on a Normandy beach when the tide was out—a queer, top-heavy-looking craft surmounted by a battery of galley chimneys. At some time in her career she had been a Thames lighter. But now, equipped with twin rudders, twin screws and engines which will drive her through the water at twelve knots, she is the Sailor's Joy. Officially this strange craft is one of ten LBKs—landing barges, kitchen—which are providing hot meals for the men in hundreds of small craft which are helping to ferry supplies from the ships to the Normandy beaches.

The mud exposed hereabouts at low tide does not always smell pleasantly, but this afternoon the LBK is baking bread for 600 men. Mud or no mud, this spot smells good to one who knows hard compo biscuits. The CO, wearing a white pullover and flannel trousers, was walking round his craft. He was critically examining the work of his crew, who were giving the hull a new coat of white paint. The Commanding Officer is Midshipman J. S. McIntyre RNVR, of Berwick-on-Tweed. He is nineteen and very proud of his first command.

'This is definitely an occasion for painting ship,' he said. 'We have a reputation to maintain; already we have been recommended for our accounts, for the cleanliness of the ship and the high standard of the food we serve. Our complement is twenty-five men, including thirteen cooks, nine seamen, and three stokers. Until recently we supplied every day and in all weathers hot meals for 500 to 700 men. Now we are baking 1,000 lb of bread a day. Our last dinner was served to 600 men. On the menu were roast pork, cabbage and baked potatoes, followed by fruit and custard. Among the craft we supply are LCMs, LCV(P)s and supply and repair barges. That is a considerable achievement for thirteen cooks, among them men who until recently were a miner, a bricklayer and a factory hand.'

The CO invited us on board. We found a ship spotlessly clean, a floating kitchen in which was installed the most up-to-date equipment, including oil-fired ranges, automatic potato-peelers and refrigerators. Pots and pans were polished until they shone. In a rack on the starboard side were scores of golden loaves, still warm from the ovens. The chief cook, Petty Officer R. F. White, of Shepperton, Surrey, has had immense experience in field bakeries and kitchens. He took part in the African landing and was later in the Sicily operations. He appreciates the splendid work of his present shipmates.

'Except for two leading cooks, I do not believe any of them had been afloat before D-Day,' he said. 'The weather then was so bad that we lost both rudders and had to turn back. All but five of the crew were seasick for we were rolling until the decks were awash.' The landing barge kitchen is one of the most popular ships in the armada off the Normandy coast. On a calm night, when ships come alongside, more than 120 craft have called for the insulated canisters of steaming meat and vegetables, and safari jars of soup, coffee, or tea. In rough weather the squadron leaders organise the distribution of food to their own craft. The kitchen is always busy, for it must be prepared to supply hot meals at any time.

'During the gale, when we were dragging our anchors nearly to the beach, and we were constantly being shelled by enemy batteries, the cooking still went on,' said Petty Officer White. 'We had many near misses. One shell dropped five yards away and peppered the meat safe with shrapnel. We are a lucky ship. There were no casualties. During all that time we victualled the Army, or anyone who came on board. These ships are fitted to carry about a week's supply of food for 800 men.' Petty Officer White is particularly proud of one fact. During the whole of one month—June—corned beef was issued for only one supper, and then it was disguised as cottage pie.

From *War Illustrated*

*

THE NELSON TOUCH IN CHANGI GAOL

Last Armistice Day there were fifty survivors from HMAS *Perth* in this camp, passing through from Java. They only moved up to Burma a week ago. A few were left behind, sick. One of them told us this story:

'The brigadier had organised a march-past for Armistice Day. Somehow the Japs allowed it. We thought it was a funny thing to celebrate in the middle of a war in the middle of a prison camp. Anyway . . . the Navy decided if it was on, we would be in it. We were a bit scruffy and some of us were barefooters. Most of our boots flapped a bit. Our bits of Dutch uniforms didn't fit too well, either. But we got under way at last, the gunner in charge. We put on a real Gunnery School show. When we formed up at the head of the column, there were screams from everywhere. "Get to the tail of the column!" But not the gunner! No, sir! He said, "I've been twenty-five years Navy and I know where we belong—we are Senior Service." He quoted King's Rules and Admiralty Instructions. They tried to talk him out of it. He just stood there, they *couldn't* shift him. I thought, "By golly! We'll have to keep our yard-arms clear after this!"

'So we led the whole mob. When we got abreast the saluting base the Gunner roars, "Eyes-ss . . . *right*!" and he snaps up to a real tiddley salute. On we go—eyes right, arms straight and swinging up, and all that. We would show them how to march. When all at once there's a cry like a wounded bull from the brig. "Who *is* that man giving *me* the Japanese salute? *Report to me at once!*" Well, the Gunner doesn't bat an eyelid. He wheels us round the base, stands us at ease, and waits. At last, after they have all marched past, His Nibs comes over to us. You should have heard the blast he dished out to the Gunner! He finished up with something like, "Explain yourself, sir!" The Gunner stands to attention like a wooden dummy, pusser-like. He looks straight ahead and says, "Sir, I have been twenty-five years in the Royal Navy. I gave you the salute of the British Navy—I am sorry you should know the Japanese salute better than ours." Well, that did start something! The brigadier said he *knew* the Gunner had given him the Japanese salute—he had *seen* him. Don't deny it! The Gunner maintained it was the only one he had used for the last twenty-five years. Eventually some of the army officers convinced the brigadier that there was no difference between the two salutes.

'Anyway . . . that's what happened. . . . You wouldn't read about it, would you?'

Chief Petty Officer RAY PARKIN RAN

Of a total ship's company of 682, only 229 survivors from HMAS Perth *went home to Australia in 1945. The remainder died during the battles of the Java Sea and Sunda Straits, or on the Burma–Siam railway.*

*

THE NEED TO ESCAPE

All through our captivity I had believed that everyone who could should escape. In innumerable arguments mine was one of the tongues that never failed to lash the protagonists of the non-escape theory. As time went on and those arguments recurred, it became increasingly difficult for me to speak convincingly, for two and a half years was a long time to hold a view without proving my sincerity. Still, there had to be a reasonable chance of success, and no such chance had come.

Now was the time to put my theories to the test, the time to take the plunge from which there could be no return. Once started on my way the end must be either freedom or death. Doubts assailed me. Why take the risk? It would be so easy to sit back and wait for the end of the war, and certainly no one would cast any blame. Those fences looked extremely difficult, and the Japanese had nasty habits with swords and bayonets. Death at their hands would be horrible.

Then visions of the future would drift into my thoughts, and it seemed that an accusing spirit hovered over my shoulder, pointing a scornful finger. 'You were afraid; your conscience was clear on every point, the way was open, and you were afraid to take the risk.'

It was true. Given the right weather conditions there was nothing now to keep me in camp except fear of the consequence of failure. Therefore there was only one course open. If I failed I would be dead; but if I failed to try, that accusing devil would haunt my every waking moment, and I could never again look men clearly in the eyes. No; fear of my own soul was more powerful than any other. My mind was made up and at peace; I was determined to go.

Lieutenant-Commander R. B. GOODWIN OBE RNZNVR

The author was the only prisoner of war to make a successful escape from Hong Kong. He went over the Shamsuipo Camp wire on the night of 16th/17th July 1944 and swam to the mainland of China, travelling overland to Kunming. He arrived back home in New Zealand in November.

*

In 1944 the submarine flotillas which had borne the heat and burden of the day in the Mediterranean moved to the Indian Ocean and thence to the Far East. At 0708 on 17th July 1944 HMS/M Telemachus *was at periscope depth in the Malacca Straits in position 156 degrees One Fathom Bank Light seven miles. Her captain tells the story of*

A COLLECTED SHOT

I saw a sea mirror-calm, metal-still. The fingers of mist half dispersed were moving in the morning sun. My heart tightened as out of a curl of fog there burst a large Japanese U-boat. She was going top speed for home on the surface.

This was the Joker. The card you abandoned the rest of the pack to get.

For twenty minutes I watched with my eyes glued to the eye-pieces. There she sped. Only four miles away. Thinking herself safe. All set for Singapore—dreaming of the lights and lemonade! Strangely I could sense the mood of the captain. He was placed in a narrow channel with no room to zigzag, but batting along full of confidence, relying on his speed and the mist to keep him secure.

His look-outs would, of course, be top-line, alert. But although frightened of their captain all the crew must be thinking of the fun they were going to have in Singapore. They would be country boys with superb eyesight, unlike the Japanese student class, but the brains behind the eyes would not be concentrating on every ripple, on what might be a small black stick showing for a minute in the glistening water of this superbly lovely morning. Their thoughts seemed transmitted to me through the sunshine. How often had I raced back on the last lap just as they!

I reckoned that U-boat would pass about three-quarters of a mile off me. For a moment I contemplated speeding up to close a little, but any telltale swirl in the early stages of the attack might give us away and cause the target to dive or zig. It seemed better to get collected and keep an accurate estimate of his course and speed with the crew settled down at their action stations and the trim perfect.

Through the periscope I could not pick out any escort vessels but there might be several hidden by patches of mist. It was so still I could see flies floating on the water. In these vital moments the captain of a submarine has to keep an almost psychic relationship with the leading stoker who works the hydraulic control lever of the periscope rams. As the huge brass cylinder weighing several tons comes out of its well the captain squats down, seizes the handles in both hands, presses his face to the eye-pieces. His knees straighten as the periscope ascends and by the briefest order or even the moving of a finger he dictates the control of the height of that tip showing above the water.

I concentrated on the U-boat with tiny popping-up looks. We had to estimate her speed and course very exactly for a certain hit. The course was pretty easy to work out, for she could not leave that narrow channel. Estimations of her speed could be helped by looking up intelligence reports. The third officer crouched beside me with his pile of reference books.

'What is the best speed of Jap big-class submarines?'

His fingers, probably shaking with anxiety, found it fast.

'Nineteen knots,' he replied.

We had plotted this U-boat on the chart at twenty knots, but I thought she would travel slower after a long patrol because her bottom must be fouled by marine growth. I gave her eighteen knots—it was tricky to pop up the periscope now but I risked it for one more glance.

Nearer and nearer she came. Everything was ready in *Telemachus*. The gauges showed we kept a steady thirty-two feet below the surface and I heard eager confident voices reporting the torpedo tubes ready. Something in me recorded with pleasure that my crew did not have the depth-charge-shocked tightness of earlier days.

I longed to poke the periscope higher up to examine the U-boat's bow wave and thus obtain a check on her speed, but I dared not. Above all, we must not be spotted. But when you cannot see a bow wave the target appears to move slow and I itched to reduce the estimate of her eighteen knots. Within *Telemachus* the whole action was so silent that it had a dream-like quality. Although I had done all this before it seemed strange. The tubes were ready. The crew at diving stations. Twenty minutes of careful, often-rehearsed work And now all was ready for a collected shot.

As the U-boat approached to within a mile and reached the firing point beam-on, *Telemachus* hung steady beneath the water.

There was a moment's silence in the submarine. You could hear men breathing while they waited the order. 'Stand by to fire numbers one, two, three, four, five, six tubes.'

By each tube a pin is pulled. A valve opened.

'*Fire one! Fire two! Fire three . . .*'

As the torpedoes shot out at regular intervals I realised that the unbelievable was happening to us. Johnnie Pope, the competent first lieutenant, couldn't hold our submarine under water. Something had gone wrong. *Telemachus* was rising inexorably to the surface.

Periscope down, we strove by flooding, speeding up and putting planes to 'Hard adive' to keep her under water. The seconds of torpedo running time ticked by. Seventy. Eighty. Ninety. *Ninety-two.* As *Telemachus* clove the surface with her top hamper a shattering explosion rent the sea dead on the range running time.

One of our torpedoes had hit.

At the same instant the flooding of our forward tank coupled with speeding up enabled us to regain control and our submarine dived down into the sea. I shot up the periscope as we sank. Swirling water blotted out all view and we had to hope wild hopes that the U-boat had been done to death. One torpedo hit is enough to sink a submarine but the explosion *might* have been something else. Could the U-boat be waiting for us to surface in order to torpedo us in turn?

I longed to be able to tell my men we had got her but I *knew* I was right not to surface and look for an oil patch or debris. Our intelligence found out later that she had sunk with all hands.

Commander WILLIAM KING DSO and bar DSC RN

The target was I-166, a large U-boat of the Kaigun-class. The loss of trim after firing was caused by Telemachus *being loaded with torpedoes carrying a heavier war-head than before; the ship's company were not informed, and therefore did not adjust the amount of compensating water for each torpedo fired.*

*

Later, in September, HMS/M Storm *was on patrol off the islands of the Mergui Archipelago in southern Burma. The Japanese were passing convoys of small ships along the coast from the Pakchan River northwards to the town of Mergui. After one bold but unsuccessful attack on a convoy,* Storm*'s captain decided not to waste any more torpedoes on these small ships. Instead, he chose what is, for a submarine, a much more hazardous method*

SURFACE AND GUN ATTACK

It was not until half past nine that morning that we saw the head of the convoy emerging from the inner channel exactly where I had expected. As on the previous day, it was a long time—about an hour and a half—before the slow-moving ships reached our position. In the intervals of watching them through the periscope I studied the chart and memorised the general shape of the sea's bottom so that I had a fairly accurate mental picture of the shoal dangers. I knew that once the action started there would be no opportunity of precise fixing and that this would be another case of navigating by eye.

Beyond deciding to let all the ships pass me before surfacing, hoping thus to minimise the chances of a massed ramming attack, I still could not make up my mind what tactics to adopt. Submarines had never been designed for this sort of work, and I had a strong foreboding that the odds were weighted too heavily against us. But we could not sit tamely there and watch them pass unharmed. We must *do* something.

Once again I had to contend with a sea that was as unruffled as a sheet of polished glass. It was desperate work trying to keep track of the movements of so many ships with only split-second observations through the periscope. The two escorts seemed very much aware that they were approaching a danger point, for they were moving in a rapid and continuous zigzag on the seaward beam of the convoy. However, although they passed within about 200 yards of us, they did not spot the periscope, and when the second of them was well past us we were abeam of the last coaster of the column. Now, if ever, was the moment for gun action.

When I gave the order to surface it was the first time I had ever done so without knowing exactly what I meant to do when I got to the top. Climbing the ladder to the bridge on the heels of the gun's crew, I was in a blue funk and full of a premonition of disaster.

Yet as soon as I reached the bridge and stood in the sunshine under the blue sky all my apprehensions were miraculously swept away. Every one of our guns opened fire at once without a hitch and continued firing for the next thirty-six minutes without any of the stoppages which had sometimes let us down in the past. Action, once joined, produced its own stimulus to the brain; our tactics were adapted every moment to meet the changing situation, and we were never at a loss.

1117 Opened fire at the rear ship at a range of 2,000 yards, obtaining seven or eight fairly destructive hits. She turned away and limped towards the shore. We then attacked and stopped the ship ahead of her, but both the escorts were now racing towards us, firing their machine-guns. Turned to port to bring them both on to the starboard bow, and directed the fire of all our guns on to them. In turn they were each hit and stopped by several direct hits from the three-inch. This part of the action was most exciting, the range eventually closing to 400 yards. The enemy were very brave, and we were lucky not to suffer any casualties. Both these escorts were carrying a score or so of Japanese, presumably troops. One of them released a depth-charge (or it may have been shot over the side) when it was 500 yards away, and it went off on the bottom causing the submarine to heel slightly to starboard for a moment. One of the escorts got out of control, and eventually drove herself under, still with way on. The other remained afloat and was sunk later when things calmed down.

In the meantime, a small vessel had been sighted approaching from the northward at great speed. This looked too much like a motor torpedo-boat to be healthy, so it was the next target to be engaged. At the same time a constant-helm zigzag was maintained. Several near-misses were seen before the torpedo-boat, at a range of about 3,000 yards, turned and fired two stern torpedoes. The tracks passed about 100 yards astern of us. One definite direct hit was scored on this MTB as she was retiring, at a range of about 4,000 yards, and she took little further interest in the proceedings. I think our shooting had put her off quite effectively.

Before this, some vessel had opened up with a pompom. We traced the firing to a small ship not previously sighted which lay stopped about 4,000 yards away, and began to get uncomfortably accurate. Fortunately this fellow, probably a motor gunboat, obtained only one direct hit, which struck *Storm*'s bridge casing below the Oerlikon and caused no casualties. Neither the motor torpedo-boat nor the gunboat had been previously seen through the periscope, and it is considered that they came out from Mergui to meet the convoy.

All this time, also, there was a perpetual whine of machine-gun bullets, but it was difficult to see exactly which ships were firing. They caused no casualties. It was now decided to finish off the coaster which had been stopped earlier (the second target engaged) and also the other escort. These both sank after a few short-range waterline shots. Meanwhile, the first coaster we had attacked and severely damaged appeared to have beached herself; later, however, she seemed to be still under way and may have succeeded in proceeding with the remainder. Fire was now directed at a coaster which had stopped about 4,000 yards away. Two direct hits were obtained, and his bridge demolished.

But by this time we had fired over 150 rounds of three-inch and the barrel was so heated that the next round jammed. Moreover, the remainder of the convoy was getting out of range, we had exhausted all our pans of Oerlikon and Vickers ammunition, and I was getting anxious about the navigation. I decided to call it a day, as the situation did not justify the risk of running the submarine aground.

1153 Broke off the action and retired westward on the surface, passing through the gap north of Bentinck Island. There seemed no point in remaining in the vicinity.

The net result of the action was: Two escorts and one coaster sunk, two coasters damaged, one torpedo-boat hit. Also, the last clue to the inshore convoy route had been uncovered. An interesting point was that all the survivors seen in the water were apparently Japanese. Not a single Malay or Burman was among them, though these had been plentiful in the coasters sunk on the previous patrol.

I was staggered, and profoundly thankful, that we had survived those thirty-six minutes without a single casualty. There was great elation throughout the boat at our success. The gun's crew were no doubt regaling their messmates below with vivid descriptions of the action; they had enjoyed themselves, and were only too disappointed when the engagement was broken off. Inspired by the grim determination of Taylor, the gun-layer, they had done very well, quite unperturbed by the machine-gun fire coming at us from all directions; even Greenway, now back in the gun's crew as breach-worker, was unshaken by any memories of his previous wounding in somewhat similar circumstances. My highest admiration went to Richard Blake, who as gunnery control officer had been faced with unusually rapid decisions—for my constant shifts of target, and the wild zigzag forced on us by the threat of torpedoes from the MTB had demanded frequent and immediate corrections to range and deflection. In spite of these difficulties he had remained cool, patient and accurate. At the end both he and I were hoarse from shouting our orders above the inferno of noise. For several hours afterwards we were partially deaf, and I think it must have been on this occasion that Blake suffered the damage to his eardrums which led, five years after the end of the war, to his being invalided out of the service.

Needless to say, all this noise inspired Stoke Rooke to one of his longest and most glorious epics, which ran as a serial in many subsequent issues of *Good Evening*. Neater, perhaps, was the crop of clerihews produced by another contributor:

> He takes the cake
> Does Lieutenant 'Whaley' Blake.
> He's just as accurate, though himself no boaster,
> At shooting stars or an enemy coaster.
>
> 'Captain Kettle' Taylor[1]
> Is a most belligerent sailor,
> At the sight of his gun every Nippo and Hun
> Turns considerably paler.
>
> A Jap, not so quick as
> His pals, didn't know that a Vickers
> Was death in the hands of a Hewetson—
> But he knew it soon!

1. Taylor was so nicknamed on account of the red beard he wore at this time.

Now Brown (AA3),
A quiet enough fellow is he,
But in the midst of a good hurly-burly can
Make a big noise with his Oerlikon.

Out of the original nine ships we had sunk three and damaged two. It was better than I had hoped for when we surfaced, but I could not help remembering that if I had been quicker in the uptake on the previous day we should probably have taken a heavier toll and might even have sunk the entire convoy.

Commander EDWARD YOUNG DSO DSC RNVR

The author was the first RNVR officer to command a submarine during the war.

*

20th November 1944

From Commodore Western Isles (Admiral Sir Gilbert Stephenson) to Commander-in-Chief Western Approaches (Admiral Sir Max Horton):

HMS CLOVER THE THOUSANDTH VESSEL TO BE WORKED UP AT TOBERMORY SAILED AT 2200 TODAY.

From Commander-in-Chief Western Approaches:

HEARTY CONGRATULATIONS ON THE THOUSANDTH VESSEL. THE UNIQUE METHODS OF TRAINING EMPLOYED AND HIGH STANDARDS YOU HAVE SET HAVE BEEN OF THE UTMOST VALUE IN DEFEATING THE U-BOAT AND PRESERVING THE OLD TRADITIONS. HELEN OF TROY'S ACHIEVEMENT WAS NO GREATER ALTHOUGH GAINED WITH CONSIDERABLY LESS EFFORT.

From Commodore Western Isles:

YOUR REFERENCE TO HELEN OF TROY. MAY I SAY THAT YOU ARE THE FIRST OF MY FRIENDS TO APPRECIATE MY FACE VALUE.

From *Max Horton and the Western Approaches*

1945

THE SURRENDER OF THE U-BOATS

Admiral Sir Max Horton (Commander-in-Chief, Western Approaches) formally took the surrender of a token force of eight U-boats at 2 pm on 14th May at Lisahally, near Londonderry.

The day turned out to be foul with a south-westerly gale, low visibility and a cloud base of about 200 feet. However, he took off from Liverpool in his Dominie aircraft. The pilot said that he had a most objectionable journey, and had to do a steep banking turn to avoid the cliffs at Larne. After arrival, the weather improved to a 'pleasant afternoon'.

The U-boats had been escorted from Loch Alsh, where their torpedoes and two-thirds of their crews had been removed. As the sinister black forms crept slowly up the Foyle, a surge of emotion swept through the crowds who lined the banks. Some cheered and some wept. The people of Londonderry, that vital outpost of the Western Approaches, had reason to know the portent of the great event, and their hearts went out to the men of the Allied navies who had brought it about. The White Ensign flew triumphantly in each boat, and they were led by the British destroyer HMS *Hesperus*, Commander R. A. Currie DSC RN. The Canadian frigate *Thetford Mines* and the USS *Paine* assisted them to their berths. On the jetty the Prime Minister of Northern Ireland stood beside the Commander-in-Chief in front of a parade of seamen of the Londonderry Command, most of whom were seeing for the first time the faces of the men they had mercilessly hunted in the grim years of war. The German crews were mostly very young men. Some were sullen and many were arrogant. Simpson[1] was struck by the length of their hair which in some cases, he says, was like a female 'bob'. An officer of Horton's staff says that the morale of the commanding officers was unbroken. They were convinced that Hitler had died in action, and their first question was: 'When do we start fighting the Russians?' One or two of them firmly believed that war with Russia was imminent, and had retained their confidential books and secret equipment to be ready to continue the war facing east.

Rear-Admiral W. S. CHALMERS CBE DSC

1. Captain G. W. G. Simpson RN

It is said that you must set a thief to catch a thief. Doenitz was a formidable and wily opponent, but Horton, an ex-submariner himself, beat him fair and square.

*

Meanwhile, almost ignored by the British press and public, the naval war in the Far East was moving towards its climax. On 22nd November 1944 Admiral Sir Bruce Fraser hoisted his flag as Commander-in-Chief of the British Pacific Fleet, then assembling in Ceylon and including a task force of four Fleet aircraft carriers: Illustrious, Indomitable, Indefatigable *and* Victorious *under the command of Rear-Admiral Sir Philip Vian. In December the BPF began its passage to Fremantle, Australia, and on the way carried out a strike against the oil refinery at Belawan Deli in north-eastern Sumatra. This was a rehearsal for a much greater undertaking. The Fleet Air Arm had come a long way since Esmonde and his six Swordfish: at dawn on the 24th January 1945 forty-three Avenger bombers with a fighter escort of eighty-nine Corsairs and Hellcats took off to attack the largest oil refineries in South-East Asia, in southern Sumatra. The spare, professionally critical prose of the Air Co-ordinator's report very well describes the Fleet Air Arm strikes at*

PALEMBANG

The formation of both the strike and escort was exceptionally good. For reasons unknown one Avenger from *Indefatigable*'s squadron started to straggle. I have a photograph of this and have sent it to the squadron in the hope that it will teach them what not to do.

At 0738 we passed over Matapoera at 7,500 feet and observed three landing strips. Details of these have been reported separately. At 0803 the strike reached 12,000 feet. This was only twelve minutes before the attack and I do not consider soon enough. From the escort point of view, we want the strike at its top height a minimum of fifty miles from the target. This distance, allowing an average speed of 160 knots and a descent from 12,000 to 8,000 feet, would only take nineteen minutes.

About twenty miles from the target the Strike Leader requested the Fireflies (*Indefatigable*) to go ahead and strafe the balloons which could be seen flying in the target area at about 3,000 feet. Unfortunately, owing to delays in the carrier, the aircraft still had not joined the main strike. I judged their time of joining to be 0806 and almost immediately afterwards they went ahead to strafe their special target. I do not think they heard the request for the balloons to be strafed.

At about 0808 the enemy AA defences opened fire whilst the strike was still out of range, indicating that they had had warning of our approach.

Almost immediately afterwards the escort was engaged by an estimated twenty-five Tojo fighters, although I myself only counted about twelve at the time. Their initial height was 13,000–15,000 feet.

There seemed to be a rather long delay after the enemy had opened fire until the first bombs fell (about six minutes). When surprise has obviously not been achieved, as in this case, the time interval must be cut down to a minimum and the bombing become more concentrated.

I did not see the Fireflies attack, but the first group of bombs to fall struck several oil tanks with the inevitable result; it seemed that all subsequent attacks had the same effect. The target of No. 1 Wing (*Indomitable* and *Victorious*) appeared well hit. No. 2 Wing (*Illustrious* and *Indefatigable*) appeared to have destroyed only half of theirs. During this period, when not engaged with enemy fighters or occupied in avoiding predicted flak, I was able to secure a series of oblique photographs of the bombing. When I finally left the target area (about 0823), the Avengers were just about to leave the rendezvous and I did not see them again.

Throughout the attack the enemy had just sufficient fighters to saturate the escort. Enemy pilots showed as much contempt for Japanese heavy AA as we did, and fights were raging all over the target area. It was almost funny to see the aircraft scrapping and all the while the AA bursting at all heights up to 15,000 feet. As far as I know no one was lost by this fire and very few damaged.

The presence of three or four twin-engined aircraft seemed to indicate some air-ground control of AA or fighters. No noticeable difference was observed after three of these twin-engined aircraft had been shot down.

R/T discipline during this air battle was good. No report was received from Force X-Ray. An immense column of black smoke to the north-west of the target indicated their passage, but when I left they still had not arrived at Talangbetoetoe. Thus, although they achieved very excellent results, they were too late to be of any material help to the strike.

Once again the withdrawal was insufficiently protected by the escort. The Fireflies appeared to be the only aircraft there and they were unable to prevent several attacks by fighters taking place. There is no doubt more of the escort could have got there and discipline on this point must be tightened. At 0825 the enemy fighters appear to have been ordered off, as no further attacks developed after this time and the escort quickly formed up on the strike. In my attempt to rejoin the formation, my flight became engaged with four Tojos of which I shot down two and the remaining two in my flight damaged one each.

Return was without incident. The top cover (*Victorious*) dispersed two Tojos which were attempting to shadow the formation. The fleet was several miles to the north of her advertised position. Attempts to home by beacon, as usual, failed. The reason for this continued failure of the beacon is not clearly understood. A very large number of aviators report failure each time with a lucky one or two reporting success. At any rate this matter needs most careful attention. At 0928 the group broke up for landing which was carried out speedily and with skill.

I think this has been one of the better strikes the Fleet Air Arm has ever accomplished.

There was some initial confusion in the operation orders since most places in South Sumatra appear to have more than one name.

Maps were good and briefing excellent. Despite the unwelcome appearance of enemy fighters, balloons and intense AA the Avengers wrote off a good 60 per cent of their targets and, now we know the form, succeeding strikes should be better still.

On the 29th, forty-six Avengers carried out a second strike:

At 0718 the Strike Leader commenced his left-hand circuit of the fleet. All units were ready for him, and joined up promptly. At 0729 the complete strike was all formed up and on the east side of the fleet, ready to take departure. Alas, the Strike Leader once again, for no known reason, made a 360 degree orbit. I decided against breaking R/T silence, which was my error. Anyway, the flagship came up and ordered departure to be taken, but it was too late. The result of this extra, unnecessary, circuit was:

(a) The strike departed at 0734 (four minutes late).
(b) Three Avenger squadrons were hopelessly out of position.
(c) The fighter escort was all jumbled up, which, with the poor weather conditions obtaining, made aviation in the area extremely hazardous.

I think the time allowed, i.e. forty minutes before collection and fifty minutes before departure, could be reduced. The Strike Leader should collect thirty minutes after take off and depart ten minutes later. At 0733 I observed an aircrew being picked up by a destroyer: it seemed a little early in the day to start losing aircraft.

At 0740 the strike commenced climbing and the escort took up position. An accurate landfall was made at 0752 at 5,500 feet. Formations had by now all closed up and the escort was very tidily in position. I lost sight of the fleet at about ten miles owing to masses of low cumulus. But over the land, conditions were much improved. There was thin 10/10th at about 14,000 feet and over the eastern plain of Sumatra 10/10th cloud, 500 feet thick, covering large areas. In fact, the weather could not have been more ideal.

On passing over Lake Ranau, one Avenger commenced straggling and soon after turned for base. I reported this to *Indomitable* but got no reply. The climb was continued over the mountains to 7,500 feet. The formation of the strike and escort was very good. The weather, however, got worse and I had some doubts whether we would be able to see the target. As the top cover was being forced down by cloud, requests were passed to the Strike Leader to fly lower. But he continued to climb to 10,000 feet and caused embarrassment to the escort above him.

The journey to the target was otherwise uneventful. At 0830 I shifted to R/T Channel C and heard Forces X-Ray and Yoke at work. They were on their targets about fifteen minutes before we struck and by the sound of things they were far too late. Most of their reports were of bandits airborne.

At 0835 the vexed question of balloons cropped up and the Escort Leader, much to the relief of the bombers, decided to use the Fireflies for this work. At 0840 the target could be seen, fortunately quite clear of clouds. The balloons were about 4,000 feet. All fires from the previous raid on Pladjoe were out. Shortly after, the Fireflies reported 'Out lights', the bombers deployed according to plan and I moved ahead to observe the target.

Almost immediately the heavy AA opened up on the Fireflies. Several groups of about ten rounds were observed extremely accurate for height and range, but, fortunately, out for bearing. My flight also attracted the attention of the gunners, but they were completely unable to cope with gentle evasion. All this drew quite a bit of the AA away from the bombers. But just after the deployment, several enemy fighters were seen diving down on them. I observed no reaction by the top or middle cover. The plan for guarding individual squadrons by sections of the escort appeared in most cases to be a failure. Both squadrons of No. 1 Wing received the unwelcome attentions of Jap fighters which did not cease until they commenced to bomb. During this period no protection was afforded by our own fighters. I believe No. 2 Wing were more fortunate. About three balloons were destroyed, but I don't think they were worth the attention the Fireflies gave them.

I commenced photographing at 0850 as the first bombs fell. From visual observation, some targets were severely hit and the photographs have confirmed this. Bombing by No. 1 Wing was truly impressive. By the time No. 2 Wing commenced bombing, it was getting a bit difficult to see. The first squadron of that wing (*Illustrious*) set off some oil tanks in the vicinity and certainly were very close to their target. Some of the last aircraft to bomb obviously could not observe their correct target and so, quite rightly, chose another. One stick was seen to burst along the wharves. It seemed a pity that so many aircraft were put on to one small target whilst Pladjoe was completely clear and could have been bombed accurately.

About three minutes after the last aircraft bombed I finished photographing. I then climbed from 6,000 feet to 10,000 in order to take vertical-line overlap photographs as the flak had died down. I soon had to change my mind as a Tojo was coming for us. In shooting this one down, we descended to O feet and, attracted by the gunfire, an Oscar came along, and by 0905 he, too, was dead.

During this time the radio was giving me an interesting picture of a long stream of Avengers dribbling out of the target area to the rendezvous, thirty miles away. It was evident some of them could not find it. Nor could I from 7,000 feet, even though I searched for some time. During this period there was quite a vicious air battle of which I can give no detail.

The return was without opposition of any kind. There seemed to be a little confusion as to who was going to escort the stragglers. Formation on the return was good and the escort in position. I climbed to 10,000 feet and swept the area astern of the formation but no enemy aircraft attempted to shadow. After the strike had crossed the coast I examined Lake Ranau for any survivors but saw none. I then proceeded to the submarine rendezvous[1] for the air-crews forced down and took oblique photographs of all the river mouths in the bay in question.

R/T discipline up till now had been 100 per cent improved. But crossing the coast seemed to be the signal for complete radio chaos. Primarily the Avengers giving their damaged friends extracts from pilot's handling notes. It is about time everybody knew their emergency drill without having to talk about it.

I found it extremely difficult to get a word in edgeways in order to report my return which was independent of the main strike and might have been mistaken for a raid. I could get no reply from *Indomitable* and eventually had to pass the message on Channel C to *Victorious*.

Break up and landing requires no comment from me.

'Meridian' One and Two have been the most interesting and successful operations I know of. In both cases we succeeded in our object and I would like to praise the determination of the Avenger pilots who bombed so accurately in the face of maximum discouragement.

The fighter escort proved itself against the most serious air opposition it has so far met.

Major R. C. HAY, Royal Marines, Air Co-ordinator,
HMS *Victorious*

From Supplement to *London Gazette*, 5th April 1951

1. A Walrus aircraft on Lake Ranau and a submarine in position off the Sumatran coast were ready to provide a 'get-you-home' shuttle service for aviators in reduced circumstances.

'Meridian' One and Two were indeed successful operations. The two Palembang refineries at Pladjoe and Soengei Gerong, together capable of producing three-quarters of Japan's aviation fuel requirements, were put completely out of action for two months and remained at much reduced capacity for the rest of the war.

*

During the last year of the war in the Far East, the Japanese introduced a new weapon, born of desperation. The first Allied warship to suffer it was HMAS Australia, *while supporting the landings on Leyte in October 1944. On 4th May 1945, during the Okinawa campaign, it was HMS* Formidable*'s turn to experience the 'Divine Wind', or*

KAMIKAZE

Suddenly, without any warning, there was the fierce 'whoosh' of an aircraft passing very fast and low overhead, and I looked up in time to see a fighter plane climbing away on the starboard bow, having crossed the deck from port at about fifty feet. I was thinking casually what a stupid thing it was to do and, at the present juncture, how lucky he was not to have been shot at, when the starboard bow Oerlikons opened up with a stream of tracer. The plane banked steeply. I saw the red blobs of its Japanese markings. Pompoms joined the Oerlikons and it flew down the starboard side of the ship, the focus of a huge cone of converging tracer. I thought he was certain to 'buy it' and stood watching until he passed behind the island. The noise of the close-range weapons drowned the engines of the taxi-ing aircraft.

Then the Jap came into sight again from behind the island, banking hard to close the ship over the starboard quarter. He was still apparently unharmed and now, out astern, the target of fewer guns; for fewer could be brought to bear at that angle, a fact he probably knew. His silhouette changed to a thin line with a bulge in the middle and he seemed to hang in the air as he dived for the ship.

I had waited long enough and ran about fifteen yards forward to a hatch, down which I jumped in the company of a rather fat leading seaman. As we hit the deck an immense crash shook the ship. I gave it a second or two to subside, during which the light from above changed to bright orange, and ran up again.

It was a grim sight. A fire was blazing among wreckage close under the bridge, flames reached up the side of the island and clouds of black smoke billowed far above the ship. Much of the smoke came from the fires on deck but as much seemed to be issuing from the funnel and this for the moment gave the impression of damage deep below decks. The bridge windows seemed to gape like eye-sockets and much of the superstructure was blackened. The deck was littered with debris, much of it on fire, and there was not a soul to be seen.

Men soon poured up from the side of the deck and the work began. The main fire was very fierce and occasional machine-gun bullets 'cooked-off'. The smell of fire mingled with the indescribably disgusting smell of the foam-compound. Subsidiary fires in the tow-motor park, fire-fighting headquarters (!) and elsewhere were attacked by hand extinguishers. Unburnt aircraft were pushed clear, casualties were carried below, and after about half an hour everything was under control. Additional hands and foam-compound arrived from below and large pieces of smouldering wreckage were ditched by crane.

The Kamikaze which hit us had carried a 500 lb. bomb and it is thought the pilot released it just before he struck.

A slice of bomb about 1 ft by 9 in by 4 in went straight downwards and came to rest in a fuel tank. On its way it buckled a hangar fire curtain and penetrated an emergency steam pipe which filled the centre boiler-room with steam; one or two valves had to be turned very promptly before that space was left to the scalding steam. It was this large and persistent splinter which was responsible for the volumes of black smoke and the thin white streamer of steam from the funnel, and for the reduction of our speed to eighteen knots. The work of filling the hole with steel plate and rapid-hardening cement and of making one aircraft carrier work by hand tackle began, and the repair of damaged electrical, radar and signalling equipment was put in hand. By 1700 these and machinery repairs were to be so far advanced that the captain could tell his admiral that we were capable of twenty-four knots and of landing-on our aircraft.

When one considers the appearance of the deck immediately after the incident our casualties seemed comparatively light. Two officers and six men were killed and six officers and forty-one men wounded.

One Avenger—its pilot and the petty officer directing it died of their wounds later—blew up with the Kamikaze and seven other aircraft on deck were completely burnt out. Other aircraft on deck were damaged. All the small tractors were destroyed and aircraft thereafter had to be moved by man- and jeep-power.

The fact that the Japanese pilot coldly decided his aim was not good enough and went round again points to a high standard of training among suicide pilots. This fellow dealt with himself very thoroughly, too, for he scattered his pieces all over the place. The wrist-watch found far away on one of his hands had stopped and the gunnery officer was at one stage seen poking pieces of him off the funnel with a long stick.

From *A Formidable Commission*

From *Formidable*, after this incident, to the flagship *Indomitable* (Admiral Vian):

LITTLE YELLOW BASTARD.

From *Indomitable*:

ARE YOU REFERRING TO ME.

From *Make a Signal*

★

The Royal Navy's brilliant destroyer tradition, enhanced by Cossack, Hardy, Glowworm, Acasta, Kelly, Bedouin, Onslow, Achates *and scores of others, was upheld to the very end of the war. On the night of 15th/16th May 1945 the 15,000-ton Japanese heavy cruiser* Haguro *(ten eight-inch and eight five-inch guns, sixteen 'Long Lance' torpedo tubes) was intercepted, brought to action and sunk in the Malacca Straits by the 26th Destroyer Flotilla, commanded by Captain (later Admiral Sir Manley) Power CBE DSO RN in HMS* Saumarez:

'IT WAS QUITE SIMPLE: WE WERE TO SINK HER'

Twenty minutes before first light on 15th May I was called, as usual, for dawn action stations. As I rolled off my camp bed on the fo'c's'le and stumbled aft along the catwalks to the twin Bofors mounting amidships, I guessed that this time something unusual was brewing. *Saumarez* was driving through the night at twenty-seven knots, and the whole ship shook and rattled like an express train.

The flotilla had refuelled and reammunitioned in Trincomalee on 9th May, dead tired after the seaborne assault and capture of Rangoon. On 10th May we were ordered to sea again, and sailed in company with the *Queen Elizabeth*, that superb French battleship *Richelieu*, four cruisers, four aircraft carriers and nine other destroyers.

The Fleet was bound on an anti-shipping sweep in the Andaman Sea, to prevent Japanese attempts to reinforce or evacuate their garrisons in the Andaman Islands.

By midnight on 15th May we were south of the Nicobar/Sumatra Channel. At 0217 the 26th Destroyer Flotilla was detached to sweep eastwards round the northern tip of Sumatra. Our target was a force of escorted merchant ships off Diamond Point.

My usually sleepy guns' crew—a mixed bunch of stokers, seamen and supply ratings, but all experienced and expert gunners—were eager and excited when we heard on the armament broadcast that we were off on our own.

Dawn action stations over, I left the duty crew closed up, power on the stabilised mounting, guns trained into the eye of the sun—we kept up the up-sun guard for the whole flotilla—and went below to take over as duty cypher officer.

At 1000 the alarm rattlers hurried us back to action stations; air attack was expected from Japanese airfields in Sumatra. We did not realise at the time that we were to remain closed up for another sixteen hours. Back at my gun, I settled down in my deck-chair—not to enjoy the sun, but to stare round its rim through darkened binoculars, searching for the black speck of a diving bomber. Every fifteen minutes I would change places with the layer on the gun, to rest my eyes and my sunburned face.

Meanwhile the flotilla swept on eastwards in close order at twenty-seven knots. The sun was blazing, sea milk-smooth and visibility extreme. A following wind added to our sweaty discomfort.

In the operations room Captain Power had received a signal from the Commander-in-Chief ordering him to abandon the sweep and rejoin the main Fleet. This was an unwelcome surprise, because our aircraft were still reporting worthwhile targets in the area. Believing (rightly) that the recall signal had been originated without knowledge of the local situation, and would soon be cancelled, and remembering the famous paragraph in the Fighting Instructions which dissuades any captain from prematurely relinquishing touch with the enemy, my captain ignored the order, and we stood on the east. Seventy minutes later an aircraft reconnaissance report was received—one heavy cruiser and one destroyer 130 miles ahead and to the east-north-east of us, steaming towards Penang.

All doubts dispelled, the flotilla settled down to intercept the enemy—if we could.

At the Bofors gun the prospect of action was greeted with a cheer and the usual ribald sailor's comment on most things Japanese.

At first I felt the familiar eager excitement taking hold of me, but as the hours passed the full appreciation of our prospects began to sink in.

We were all well-blooded and expert in action against aircraft, shore batteries and ships of our own size, but a heavy cruiser was something beyond our experience. We knew that if we met her in daylight our chances would be slim indeed: with her great speed and overwhelming gun power she could destroy the flotilla piecemeal long before we could get close enough to retaliate. My excitement, mounting all the time, became more strongly tinged with apprehension.

As the heat increased and the day wore on, the men around me—no doubt for the same reasons—fell silent, pale and sweating in their jungle-green action dress.

At noon we were still storming eastwards, but now the flotilla was spread in line abreast, five miles apart, cracking along at near maximum speed.

Food that day was welcome. I can still remember the taste and feel of bully beef, tepid from a sunwarmed can, eaten with the fingers, and washed down with tinned apricots, fruit and juice and all running stickily down my chin. The heat, the strain of searching the sky and distant horizon for signs of the enemy, the rattle and shake of the ship herself, began to have an effect on us all. Most of the men dozed around the gun, spreading their anti-flash gear over the deck to protect themselves from burning on the hot steel: only the layer, the trainer and I remained fully alert throughout that long day.

In our operations room it was now clear that the enemy ships, unaware of our presence, were holding course for Penang. We were cutting across like a rugby full-back, going for the corner flag, where it seemed we might intercept them. The *Richelieu* and the *Cumberland* were hurrying to our support, but they were still a hundred miles astern. We felt a long way out on our limb.

My captain's intentions at this juncture were to stand on to the Malay coast south of Penang, and then sweep back westwards across the Malacca Strait. If we met the enemy in daylight we were to hold off at extreme range and entice or drive her westwards to annihilation under *Richelieu*'s guns. If we met her at night—it was quite simple: we were to sink her.

At dusk we were still holding our course and speed, now spread out four miles apart in line abreast. Heavy rain squalls and lightning began to shorten the visibility and the effectiveness of our radar. The enemy was seventy miles to the north of us, still unsuspecting, still making for Penang.

I seized the opportunity to send my guns' crew, one by one, to shift into clean clothing. The gunner relieved me for a spell while I too went below to change. In a moment of schoolboyish bravado I reappeared, immaculate, clad in full white uniform. At least this gave my guns' crew something to laugh about, and curiously I felt better for it.

At 2245 *Venus* reported an enemy contact bearing 045 degrees at the phenomenal range of 68,000 yards. *Venus*, incredulous, held the contact down to 46,000 yards, when it was certainly identified as *Haguro*. At this point the flotilla swung round to the north, still in line abreast, speed reduced to twenty knots: the enemy appeared to be walking right into the trap.

At 2347 *Haguro*'s range was down to 38,000 yards. Three minutes after midnight *Saumarez* got her first radar contact—enemy dead ahead, range 28,000 yards. Immediately the whole flotilla reversed course to due south, reducing speed to twelve knots to allow the enemy to penetrate deeper into the trap. By this time the five destroyers were well strung out in a great half-circle, from north-west through south to east, and *Haguro*, now alarmed, began zig-zagging violently, still steaming south at twenty knots, well inside the net.

At 0050 all seemed set for a simultaneous attack by all ships, planned to be executed at 0100. The flotilla turned north, thus putting *Haguro* dead ahead of *Saumarez*, range 12,000 yards closing at the rate of over forty knots.

Suddenly, at 0054, *Haguro* altered right round to starboard and fled to north-west, increasing speed to thirty knots. Captain Power faced with a sudden transition from a bow attack to a stern chase, increased to thirty knots in pursuit.

After that things began to happen very quickly indeed.

At 0105 *Haguro* reversed course again to the south-east, now placing herself fine on *Saumarez*'s port bow, closing at sixty knots, range 6,000 yards. At the same moment, her attendant destroyer[1] was sighted on our starboard bow, crossing from starboard to port. I could see her bow wave gleaming in the lightning flashes as she first appeared, 3,000 yards away. Our forward guns engaged, hitting with the second salvo. *Saumarez* heeled violently to port, shuddering under full helm as she turned to starboard to pass under the enemy's stern—indeed it was a very near miss.

The next few moments were confused but exciting. The enemy destroyer reappeared under our port bow, and as she passed close down our port side at more than fifty knots relative speed, the Bofors raked her from stem to stern.

Above the growl and groan of the stabilised mounting, always level in spite of the heel and slew of the ship, I heard my layer yelling wordlessly as he depressed the gun and stamped on the pedal: then the shells streamed out in a hosepipe sweep, the tracers hitting along her whole length—no ricochets on this soft target.

All this time I had been conscious that the familiar crack of our 4.7s and the thump-thump-thump of my own guns were being blotted out by a gigantic hammering storm of tremendous noise, drowning all speech and sense. *Haguro* was firing on us, point-blank, with her main armament, opening with a full ten-gun broadside.

At this moment I had forgotten her existence, and could not comprehend why great waterfalls of water were erupting before

1. The destroyer was the *Kamikaze*.

and behind me. *Haguro*'s salvos were pitching close aboard, short and over, and the tons of water thrown up were swamping the upper deck so that our position was awash up to the lids of the ready-use lockers.

All this took but a minute or two, when *Saumarez* heeled far over to starboard (beyond the maximum depression of the gun) as we slewed to port. The Bofors stopped firing, and I glimpsed the high, shining wet side of *Haguro* herself, lit by intermittent lightning flashes and our rocket flares.

As *Saumarez* swung further to port, closing *Haguro* at thirty knots, a tremendous crack and a roar like the end of the world overwhelmed us; all our guns stopped firing.

An unnerving silence fell: all power was off and communications dead. Deaf, wet and confused I looked forward and saw that the upper half of our funnel—thirty feet away—had disappeared. The remnant was belching out a towering eruption of steam and smoke. The silence was not silence, but the total deafness caused by the tearing shriek of escaping superheated steam. Beneath my feet the deck tilted even more to starboard as our turn to port tightened, and looking down on to the iron deck a few feet below me I saw (but could not hear) all eight torpedoes leap, one by one, from their tubes, trained to starboard.

Slowly *Saumarez* came upright, and slowly she appeared to be coming to a halt. We were no longer under fire, our guns were silent, and the enemy had vanished. The uncanny stillness persisted; only the steam still roared out.

I looked astern, and saw three golden explosions split the blackness. *Haguro* was hit.

The time was 0115. We had been in close action exactly ten minutes.

While *Saumarez* was limping slowly northwards, temporarily out of action and control, the rest of the flotilla, assuming we had been sunk, closed in for the kill.

At 0114 *Verulam* got her torpedoes away from fine on *Haguro*'s bow at 2,000 yards. Her salvo and ours arrived on target a minute later. At 0125 *Venus* closed to 2,500 yards on the enemy's starboard side and scored one torpedo hit: two minutes later two torpedoes from *Virago* stopped *Haguro* dead in the water; on 0151 *Vigilant*, hindered until now by the movements of her sister ships, closed in to 1,800 yards and scored one hit. At 0202 the end came when *Venus* fired her last two torpedoes at 1,200 yards.

Haguro sank at 0209, hit by nine torpedoes and having been under heavy close-range fire from the flotilla's guns for nearly an hour.

Meanwhile in *Saumarez* power, light and communications were quickly restored. We turned south, summoned the rest of the flotilla and set course to the east.

Our damage was unbelievably light. *Haguro*'s eight-inch guns had fired nearly sixty shells at *Saumarez* alone, at point-blank range, and many more five-inch and lesser stuff. One eight-inch shell had nicked our fo'c's'le, our main aerial and the top of the funnel had been shot away, and one five-inch shell had severed the main steam-pipe in our boiler-room, killing two men and burning three more.

The rest of our flotilla had no casualties or damage.

The enemy destroyer, badly shot up, reached sanctuary in Penang.

At 1220 on 16th May the flotilla rejoined the main fleet and set course for Trincomalee, 1,500 miles away.

Commander DENIS CALNAN RN
Captain (D)'s Secretary, in HMS *Saumarez*

This was the Royal Navy's last major surface gun and torpedo action in World War II. It was a jewel of an action, which was widely taught and demonstrated in Tactical Schools and Staff Colleges for years after the war. Incredibly, no full account of it appears to have been published; the author's report was specially commissioned for this anthology.

*

The depot ship HMS Bonaventure *(Captain W. R. Fell RN) arrived in Victoria harbour, Labuan, in July 1945 with six XE-craft—improved versions of the midget submarines which attacked* Tirpitz. *Although at first it seemed that no operational use would be found for them, these craft distinguished themselves in several memorable exploits before the war ended: XE4 (Lieutenant M. H. Shean RANVR) cut submarine telegraph cable at Cap St Jacques, Saigon, on 31st July, and XE5 (Lieutenant H. P. Westmacott RN) did the same in Lamma Channel, off Hong Kong, on*

1st August. Meanwhile XE1 (Lieutenant J. E. Smart RNVR) and XE3 (Lieutenant I. E. Fraser RNR) attacked shipping in Singapore harbour. XE3's target was the 9,850-ton cruiser Takao, *which had been lying in shallow water in the Johore Straits since being damaged by USS/M* Darter *in the Battle of Leyte Gulf in October 1944. XE3 was towed to the entrance of the straits by HMS/M* Stygian *and, on 31st July, made*

THE ATTACK ON *TAKAO*

Excitement was betrayed in my voice. 'There she is!' I cried.

At that part of the strait where the *Takao* lay the water is shallow, with depths shown on Admiralty charts of from eleven to seventeen feet; but there is a depression in the sea-bed, which amounts to a hole, 500 feet across, 1,500 feet long, and some five feet deeper than the water around. The *Takao* lay across this depression so that the first hundred feet of her length, beginning at her bow, lay in water which dropped to less than three feet at low tide; and the same conditions occurred at her stern. It was proposed that I should pass over this shallow patch and down into the hole where I was expected to manœuvre my boat under the ship. As I have already said, I had made it clear that I thought this feat impossible.

'Stand by for a bearing, ship's ahead, now,' I ordered. Then I translated the bearing into a true bearing and laid it on the chart. The attack had started.

From that moment, until I was back on board the *Stygian*, all fear left me.

I felt only that nervous tautness that comes so often in moments of stress. I let each of the others have a quick look at the *Takao* through the periscope, and then we were ready.

It was eight minutes to two when I finally decided that the position of XE3 was right enough for us to start the actual run in. By this time the sun was high in the heavens, the sea was as placid as a Scottish loch early on a summer's day, and visibility, both above and under the water, was excellent.

Looking through the attack periscope, I could see distinctly the tall outlines of cranes in the dockyard lying behind the *Takao*, and the barrack buildings and numerous small boats making their way back and forth from the vessels anchored in midstream. I could see a small destroyer escort, and, tied up between the buoys, a ship of

7,000 or 8,000 tons, which, for a moment, I thought might be worthwhile attacking, should we get away from the *Takao* quickly. I also saw the mooring buoys of battleships lying in the channel, and always looming up I could see the *Takao* as she came closer and closer. Her three for'ard turrets stood out distinctly like Olympic winners on a rostrum, the centre one above the other two, and all three close together. The guns in 'C' turret pointed aft, unlike any other cruiser constructed at that time. Her massive bridgework was easily discernible, with the thick black-topped funnel raking astern of it. I could see the second funnel, smaller, and somewhat insignificant, stuck vertically upwards between the two tripod trellis-work masts, and on 'B' and 'X' turrets a sort of tripod framework.

From her vertical bow with the acutely curved top, stretched two anchor cables, gently rising and falling in the slowly ebbing tide. I could see the gangway on her starboard side, and, just above, a derrick used for hoisting in aircraft. I saw no aircraft.

When, during a spell on the run in, I glanced through the night periscope, I was disturbed to find that I could see both ends of XE3 quite distinctly, showing that the underwater visibility was ten feet or more. I reconciled myself to this disadvantage by thinking that I would at least be able to keep an eye on Magennis[1] as he attached the limpet mines.

Later on, at eight minutes past two, the range was 2,000 yards, one mile away, about thirty degrees on our port bow.

'Four hundred and fifty revolutions, steer 218 degrees, stand by to start the attack.'

'Course 218 degrees. All ready to start the attack,' came the reply.

'Start the attack,' I ordered.

Magennis started the stop-watch, and we prepared ourselves.

'Up periscope.'

Magennis pressed the switch, the motor whirred.

'Whoa!'

The motor stopped.

'Bearing right ahead, range two degrees on her funnel—down periscope.'

Magennis changed the degrees into yards by means of the slide rule.

1. Leading Seaman J. Magennis.

'Length 1,600 yards, sir,' he called.

I did not answer; there was no need to. Each of us was sweating profusely, and energy and air had to be reserved. In any case, we were doing now the thing that we had practised time and time again when stationed in the Scottish lochs and when lying off the coast of Australia.

The only sounds in the boat were the whirr of the main motor, the hiss of escaping oxygen from the cylinder in the engine-room, and an occasional scraping sound of steel on steel in the well-greased bearings when the hydroplane wheel was turned. Ten feet, forty feet. 'Up periscope', range, 'Down periscope'. So it went on until the range had narrowed to 400 yards.

'Up periscope, stand by for a last look round.'

Click! Down went the handles: I fixed my eye to the eye-piece for the hundredth time, slowly swinging to port.

'Ah, there she is, range eight degrees.'

Slowly I swung the periscope round to starboard.

'Flood "Q", down periscope, quick, thirty feet. Bloody hell! There's a boat full of Japs going ashore; she's only about forty or fifty feet away on the starboard bow. God, I hope they didn't see us!'

So close had they been that I could make out their faces quite distinctly, and even had time to notice that one of them was trailing his hand in the water. The boat, painted white, stood out clearly against the camouflaged background of the cruiser. Similar to the cutters used in the Royal Navy for taking liberty men ashore, she was packed with sailors. The helmsman stood aft, his sailor's coat and ribbon gently lifting in the breeze caused by the boat's headway. She was so close that it seemed that her bow waves almost broke over our periscope. I could see the lips of the men moving as they chatted away on the journey ashore. They should have seen us. I do not know why they did not.

'Thirty feet, sir.'

My mind re-focused.

'All right, Magennis, the range is 200 yards, we should touch bottom in a moment.'

To Smith:[1] 'Keep her as slow as you can.'

1. Sub-Lieutenant W. J. L. Smith RNZNVR

Followed anxious silence, then a jar and the noise of gravel scraping along the keel as we touched bottom. Reid[1] had to fight hard to keep her on course as we scraped and dragged our way across the bank at depths of only fifteen feet, which meant our upper deck was only ten feet below the surface.

Watching through the night periscope, I could see the surface of the water like a wrinkled window-pane above our heads, until it gradually darkened as we came into the shadow of the great ship. Something scraped down our starboard side, and then, with a reverberating crash, we hit the *Takao* a glancing blow, which stopped us. I thought we had made enough noise to awaken the dead, and I was worried in case someone above might have felt the jar.

'Stop the motor! I wonder where the hell we are?' I said. I could see nothing through the periscope to give me a clear indication of our position in relation to the enemy ship, only her dark shadow on our starboard side. Obviously I was not underneath it, as the depth on the gauge was only thirteen feet.

I began to fear that we might be much too far forward, that the ominous-sounding scraping along our side had been made by an anchor cable at the target's bows.

'We seem to be too far for'ard,' I reported. 'We'll alter course to 190 degrees and try to run down her side. Port thirty half ahead, group down.'

The motor hummed into life again, but we did not budge.

'Group up half ahead,' I called, and we tried many other movements. The motor hummed even faster, the propeller threshed, but still no sign of movement. We were jammed, and, looking back on this afterwards, I am inclined to think that as the *Takao* veered in the tideway, the slackening cable came to rest on us. Then it lifted as she veered away again, or else we were jammed for the same reason under the curve of her hull at this point. It was only after some really powerful motor movements in both directions, and ten minutes of severe strain, that we finally broke loose and dragged our way across the shingly bottom to the deeper channel.

I had attacked from too fine an angle on the bow, and after running out again I altered course and steered for a position more on the *Takao*'s beam, which would mean a longer run over the shallow

1. ERA C. Reid.

bank, but I decided the risk was worth it if I were to hit the ship amidships.

At three minutes past three we were ready again, a thousand yards away. Once more we started the run-in for the attack. This time we were successful. We slid easily across the bank with the gauge at one time registering only thirteen feet, and then, blackness, as we slid into the hole and under the keel of the *Takao*. It was just as I had practised it so many times before, and I was surprised how easy it was.

The depth gauge began to indicate deeper water, fifteen feet, eighteen feet, twenty feet, and then a greying of the night periscope and upper viewing window.

'Stop the motor.'

Then blackness in the night periscope and upper viewing window.

'Full astern.'

The bottom of the *Takao* showed dimly, and then suddenly it was distinct, encrusted with thick heavy layers of weed as it fell sharply to her keel.

'Stop the motor!'

The hull stopped sliding overhead. We were under her.

We were resting on the bottom with the hull of the *Takao* only a foot above our heads. I wondered if we would be able to go straight through.

'Come and have a look at this,' I called to the crew, and they left their positions to come and see the encrusted bottom of our prize.

'What a dirty bastard!' said one of them; and I couldn't have agreed more. It would have been nice to have gone out and written my name on the years and years of growth on the keel, but time was passing, and the need for haste cut short our conversations. We were anxious to be away. The *Takao* held no interest for us, other than the need to blow her up.

'Raise the antennae,' I called.

Smith operated the lever and the two antennae came up hydraulically from their stowage positions on either side of the bow.

'It doesn't matter about the after one,' I told Smith, 'there's no point in trying to raise it.'

The after antennae, unlike the two for'ard ones, was raised by hand, and sometimes it was an awful struggle, particularly after several days at sea, to get it up, and in any case it would not have been effective owing to the sharp slope of the ship down to her keel.

Magennis was ready: he must have been stewing in his rubber suit, and I thought, momentarily forgetting the dangers, how pleasant it would be for him to get out into the cool water. He strapped on his breathing apparatus. The only instruction I could give him was to place all six limpets in the container as quickly as possible and not to make a noise. I fitted in the Perspex window, patted him on the shoulder, and into the escape compartment he went. Reid closed the door on him; the valves were opened and shut, and the pumps started. Looking through the observation window into the wet-and-dry compartment, I could see Magennis breathing steadily into the bag as the water rose around him, and then I moved over to the night periscope again, with its larger field of vision and higher magnification. I could see along the keel of the *Takao* for some fifteen yards in either direction, and it was like looking into a dark cave with XE3 lying across the centre of the sunlit entrance. I swung around on the periscope so that the keel of the enemy lay against our upper deck, just for'ard of the periscope bracket, and as the bottom rose away sloping from the keel at a fairly sharp angle the antennae stuck up from the bow like an ant's feelers. They were not resting on the *Takao*'s bottom. Huge lumps and clusters of seaweed hung down like festoons and Christmas decorations, and the faint sunlight danced between them.

Inside the boat we waited patiently. Suddenly, almost as though we hadn't expected it, the pumps stopped and the wheels controlling the valves began to move, as if controlled by a hidden power, as indeed in a sense they were. Reid again moved across from his seat by the wheel to help Magennis to shut them off, and looking through my only means of communication with the diver now that he was outside, I saw the lever which operated the clip on the hatch swing round in an arc of 120 degrees. A few bubbles of free air escaped and gyrated to the surface, wobbling and stretching as they floated through the tangled weed. I saw there was not enough room between us and the *Takao*'s bottom for the hatch to rise fully, but, fortunately, it opened enough for Magennis to squeeze through as his hands gripped the sides of the hatch: and he was safely out. He looked all right, safe and confident, and he gave the 'thumbs-up sign. I noticed a slight leak from the join between his oxygen cylinder and the reducing valve on his breathing set. It wasn't really big enough to cause concern, but I imagine that to Magennis it must have seemed like a full-scale submarine venting its air. He shut the lid and disappeared over the side, and we settled down nervously to await his return.

We counted the limpets as he bumped them out of the containers and moved them one by one along the starboard side, and occasionally I caught a glimpse of him as he worked away under that hull above. Six limpets he took—three towards the for'ard end and three towards the after end. In all, the total time taken was somewhere round about thirty minutes. To me it seemed like thirty days. I cursed every little sound he made, for every little sound was magnified a thousand times by my nerves. It was a long wait. I couldn't remember if we talked or kept silent through it. I think and hope we were pretty calm superficially.

The inside of the boat was like a boiler, but we had to keep quiet. I dared not start the fan or motor. We had simply to sit still and drink tin after tin of orange juice from the Freon container.

The tide was still falling. Although the rise and fall in the Johore Strait is only eight feet, this was more than sufficient to allow the cruiser to sit on us in the shallow hole beneath her hull. High water had been at 1200 zero hour for the attack, and it was now nearly four hours later. I was very anxious to get away. Magennis still seemed to be an age, and just when I could hardly contain myself a moment longer, he appeared on the hatch. He gave the 'thumbs-up' sign again and in he jumped. I saw the lid shut and the clip go home. He was back, and now at last we could go.

Quickly, we started to release the side cargoes. The fuses on the port charge, four tons of amatol, had, like the 200 lb. limpets, already been set to detonate in six hours' time, so that it was only necessary for us to unscrew the small wheel which started the mechanism, and then to unscrew the larger wheel which released the charge. The first ten turns of this wheel opened a kingston in the charge to allow water to enter the compartment, previously filled by air, and rendered the charge negatively buoyant. The last turn released the charge itself, which should have fallen away and rested on the bottom. In order to relish the full pleasure of placing four tons of high explosive under a Japanese ship, the three of us took it in turns to operate the wheels as Magennis was draining down his compartment. The port charge fell away—we heard it bump down our side, but we hung on for Magennis to re-enter the craft before finally letting the starboard limpet-carrier go. As a result of this delay, it became too heavy and would not release or slide away. Such an emergency had already been thought of by the designers of XE-craft, and an additional wheel had been provided. This operated a pusher to push the side cargo off, and between us we wound the wheel out to its limit, but with no effect. The bottom of the cargo swung out from the ship's side, but the top was still held fast. By now I felt sure that the pins at the top were holding, but I thought to myself that the movement of the craft might shake it loose. We certainly couldn't make headway very far with two tons of dead weight fast to our side.

In the meantime Magennis reported that he had found it very difficult getting the limpets into position; the work of attaching them successfully had exhausted him. I could well imagine his feelings, as, out on the lonely water with only the sound of his own breathing to accompany him, he struggled and fought, first of all to clear an area of the bottom so that the magnetic hold-fasts could be fitted against the bare plate of the ship's hull. With his diving knife he had cut away the thick weed waving like the feelers of an octopus above his head, too tough to pull away, and all the time a slow leak from his breathing set. After clearing away the weed he had to tackle the encrustation of barnacles and other shell-fish attached to the bottom. These had to be chipped off as silently as possible. The limpets themselves, clumsily designed (they were big awkward jobs to drag through the water, all angles and projections, and they caught and tangled in the weeds), had to be attached. Unfortunately, owing to the positive buoyancy of the charge itself and the angular bottom of the *Takao*, there was a tendency for the charges to break loose from the magnetic hold-fasts, which, for reasons unknown, had become very feeble, and to run up towards the surface, with Magennis chasing after them to bring them back into position in two groups of three charges. In each group he had secured the limpets some fifty to sixty feet apart—three away along the cavern to our starboard side, and three along the cavern on either side of the keel, so that they could not dislodge and slide off on to the bottom. He had set the firing mechanism working, but in his exhausted state had become unable to remove three of the counter-mining pins, which ensure that should one limpet blow up the rest will follow immediately, even if the clocks have been wound for the set delay.

The counter-mining device, which was lethal after twenty minutes, also ensured that any diver sent down by the Japanese to render the mines safe, or to remove them, would blow himself to eternity should he give the charges the slightest blow.

Looking back on the limpet-placing part of the operation, I see how wonderfully well Magennis did his work. He was the first frogman to work against an enemy from a midget submarine in the manner designed: he was the first and only frogman during the whole X-craft operations ever to leave a boat under an enemy ship and to attach limpet mines: in fact, he was the only frogman to operate from an X-craft in harbour against enemy shipping.

Perhaps I had, in some undetectable way, made him aware of my own nervousness. The limpets should not have been less than sixty feet apart for successful working, but although we should, perhaps, have moved them away a bit further, it was too late now; a final effort had now to be made to get clear of the harbour.

'Group up, half ahead—let's get to hell out of this hole!'

I gave the order with a feeling of relief.

'Main motor, half ahead, sir,' from Smith. 'May I start the fan, sir?'

'Yes, start the fan.'

Magennis began to take off his breathing set and hood.

'What is the course, sir?' asked good, calm, cheerful Reid.

'Two hundred degrees,' I answered. 'Let me know if you have any trouble keeping her on.'

I moved over to the sounding machine and switched it on, and then back to the night periscope to watch as we moved out under the vast hull which was slowly settling down upon us with the fall of the tide, and through which we hoped our charges would blow a hole big enough to sink her for good.

But although the motor had been running for several seconds there was no sign of movement.

'Full ahead,' I ordered.

Still no movement!

'Stop, full astern, group up.'

Glancing at Smith, I sincerely hoped I was not becoming hysterical. I felt certain that the *Takao* must have settled down on us, thus preventing any movement whatsoever. We couldn't go astern as the *Takao*'s keel was lower than the rear periscope standard. We must go ahead if we could go anywhere at all.

'Stop, full ahead, group up, lift the red, stop.'

This gave us maximum power, the motors whirred and we could hear the propeller thrusting hard against the water, but it was useless. We seemed to be well and truly stuck, and for a moment I thought of hanging on until half an hour before the charge was due to go off and then abandoning the ship. After all, I consoled myself, it was only 200 yards or so from the shore, and we might be able to hide in the swamps and forests until Singapore fell into British hands again. Our flags and emblems were going to come in useful after all!

We tried pumping the water aft and then for'ard, out and then in, and finally we even partially blew No. 2 main ballast tank to try to shake loose from what looked like being XE3's watery grave. I was in despair. Sweat poured into my eyes. But still that black menacing shape stood overhead. Then suddenly, with a final effort, she began to move.

'Ship's head swinging to starboard, can't control her.'

Once again Reid's quiet voice calmed my turmoil. We began to move slowly ahead, the flooded charge dragging like a broken wing on our starboard side. The black roof slid astern, and fresh pure welcome sunlight streamed through the water into my upturned eyes.

We had a bow angle on some five degrees, and slowly the needle of my depth gauge moved in an anti-clockwise direction until it steadied at seventeen feet. The weight on our right swung the ship's head round until we were parallel to the side of the *Takao*, and I reckoned some thirty feet away on her port side.

'Stop the motor, we'll have to try to release the cargo. It'll have to be very carefully done as we're only a few yards away.' I explained.

Magennis was still sweating away in his suit, and I felt he had done enough to make the operation a success. As Reid had little or no experience of underwater swimming in the frogmen gear, and

Smith wasn't particularly good at this either, I considered that it was justifiable for me to take the risk of leaving the boat for a few moments, even if I was the commanding officer. Should anything happen, I had enough confidence in Smith to know that he could get her out to rejoin the *Stygian*.

'Come out of the way, Magennis, I'll go out and release it myself. Get me the spare set from the battery compartment.'

'I'll be all right in a minute, sir,' said Magennis, 'just let me get my wind.'

What a wonderful lad he was! He said this with a most hurt expression on his face, quite obviously meaning that since he was the diver it was up to him to do the diving. And so we sat quietly for five minutes, and when he was ready I replaced his hood and perspex face. 'Thanks,' he said, and into the wet-and-dry compartment he went for the second time.

The wheels spun, the pumps started and the water began to rise. Reid had equipped Magennis with an elephant-size spanner, and as the lid of the hatch opened, I saw this come through the opening immediately behind a mass of air bubbles, followed by Magennis. Once again I wondered what he was thinking about only thirty feet away from a Japanese cruiser in seventeen feet of clear water, his only weapon being a spanner. The bubbles released from opening the hatch were quite enough to cause me a great deal of worry. Had anybody been looking over the side of the *Takao*—perhaps a seaman gazing idly into the water with his thoughts away at home in Yokohama, Nagasaki, or somewhere like that—he must have seen us. The water was as clear as glass, and Magennis in his green diving suit was sending out a steady stream of bubbles from the reducing valve of his set.

Inside the boat it was as quiet as death: none of us spoke. I could hear the ship's chronometer ticking away, the anxious seconds interrupted by an occasional clank as Magennis used his spanner. It took some five minutes to release the cargo—five of the most anxious minutes of my life. Watching through the periscope, I could see the position of both securing pins at which he should have been working, but for some reason or other he was out of sight. I bit my fingers, swore and cursed at him, swore and cursed at the captain and all the staff on board *Bonaventure* who had planned this operation, at the British Admiralty, and finally at myself for ever having been so stupid as to volunteer for this life, and, having volunteered, for being so stupid as to work hard enough to get myself this particular operation. I wished myself anywhere except lying on the bottom of Singapore harbour.

I don't know what Reid or Smith thought of this little display, but as far as I know they never mentioned my temporary lapse.

I had told Magennis to make no noise, but his hammering and bashing, in what I thought to be really the wrong place, was loud enough to alarm the whole Japanese Navy.

'What the bloody hell is that bloody fool doing?' I asked no one in particular. 'Why the hell doesn't he come on top of the charge? Why didn't I go out myself?' Then I saw Magennis for a moment, and at the same time the cargo came away and we were free. He gave me the 'thumbs-up' sign for the third and last time and slid feet first into the wet-and-dry compartment and closed the lid. Wheels turned, pumps started and down came the water.

Right, I thought. Then:

'Starboard twenty steer 090 degrees half ahead group up,' I ordered all in one breath.

'Aye, aye, sir.'

'Twelve hundred revolutions.'

'Aye, aye, sir.'

'O.K.,' I said. 'Home, James, and don't spare the horses.'

I think we all managed a smile at that moment.

Lieutenant-Commander IAN FRASER VC DSC RNR

The author and Leading Seaman J. Magennis were both awarded the Victoria Cross. In the same operation XE1's target was the cruiser Myoko, *some two miles further in the straits; XE1 was delayed by Japanese patrol boats and, time running out, added her charges to XE3's burden already under* Takao. *Both craft returned safely to Brunei Bay on 4th August.*

*

THE SURRENDER OF HONG KONG

As we arrived off the coast of China we were still completely in the dark as to what attitude the Jap troops were adopting, and whether they were obeying the Emperor's instructions to lay down their arms. We also had very little information as to the position of minefields.

Admiral Harcourt decided to lie off the coast for a time while efforts were made to get in touch with the Japs by radio. At last the following message was received:

'To any British man o' war. From Hong Kong, Japan. To the Chief of the Communications Corps of the British Squadron off Hong Kong from Y. Kawato, lieutenant, the Chief of the Communications Corps of the Japanese Army.

'One: Congratulations for the commencement of the wireless communication between your squadron and our corps.

'Two: Our location is Two Three Seven Queen Mary Road, Kowloon.

'Three: We want to know the name and rank of you, the name of the ship and the location of it.

'Four: We hope that the friendly and smoothly communication should be continued between us for ever.'

This was followed almost immediately by a request to send an aircraft to Kai-Tak aerodrome to bring off a Jap envoy and Commander Craven, the senior British naval prisoner. Douglas Craven, a term-mate of mine at Osborne and Dartmouth, had made a special name for himself in the Navy as a brilliant amateur jockey, and in the past had always had difficulty in keeping his weight down, but as he stepped out on to the flight-deck of the *Indomitable*, almost straight from a long stretch of solitary confinement, he could have ridden as bottom weight anywhere. But in spite of being so weak, he braced his shoulders and saluted just as smartly as if he had been on parade at the gunnery school. Here was the moment he must have prayed for again and again during those interminable minutes, days, nights, weeks, months and years, but he never said a word of all that. He was back on the job, a staff officer with important information regarding future events. As I followed those two matchsticks of legs up the ladder to the admiral's sea-cabin there was something about the polish which he had given to what was left of his shoes that made me proud to belong to the same Service.

Later that evening—after Craven had finished his discussions with the admiral—I took him down to the wardroom. This was the moment, I felt sure, when he would explode with pent-up relief. He could have what he liked—beer, whisky, gin—he only had to say the word. I searched eagerly for the look of excitement in his eyes, but it was too early yet. They seemed unable to focus. They were still numbed by countless hours of staring at a blank wall only a few feet away. He politely accepted a glass of beer, but the noise and crowded room were obviously too much for him. I was just about to take him away to a quieter spot when a New Zealander—the one man who had escaped from the prison camp where Douglas Craven had been senior naval officer—came in.

There was something almost uncanny about the way those two shook hands and looked into each other's eyes.

'We never heard, of course,' said Craven, 'but I was always certain you'd get through.'

Goodwin didn't answer for a moment.

'My one worry was reprisals. I heard a rumour that you'd been executed.'

I crept quietly away. It seemed the most offensive form of eavesdropping, as if one were listening in to two men who belonged to another world.

Commander ANTHONY KIMMINS OBE RN

*

From Commander-in-Chief Fifth Fleet to Fifth Fleet Pacific: THE WAR WITH JAPAN WILL END AT 1200 ON 15th AUGUST. IT IS LIKELY THAT KAMIKAZES WILL ATTACK THE FLEET AFTER THIS TIME AS A FINAL FLING. ANY EX-ENEMY AIRCRAFT ATTACKING THE FLEET IS TO BE SHOT DOWN IN A FRIENDLY MANNER.

From *Make a Signal*

*

On the 27th August, when Admiral Rawlings's flagship anchored at the entrance to Tokyo Bay the snow-capped cone of Fujiyama, the sacred mountain of Japan, stood out exceptionally clearly against the western sky; and, as evening drew on, the watchers on the quarterdeck of the *King George V* saw the red orb of the sun go down right into the middle of the volcano's crater. Rarely, if ever, can a heavenly body have appeared to act with such appropriate symbolism.

Captain S. W. ROSKILL DSC RN

*

RETURN TO ENGLAND

Hush now the raucous voice, the chattering face,
breathe deep the scented valley's ascending peace,
    and stand erect, a tree,
feeling through feet grown roots and hands like leaves
that singing sap which powers our million lives.

After the sour dust of Sicilian roads,
the rocked fields and the rank malarial reeds,
    where, stripped by death and Time,
starred skeletons of gliders with torn wings
stare—in a day grown prehistoric things:

after the leprous stone of Malta's caves
beneath the festering cactus whose sun carves
    no respite for the eyes:
after Algiers where the sirocco crawls
to paralyse the will and the brain reels;

after the orange whirlwind blown from Ras el Ma
to silt the gates of Fez; after Rabat
    where the rich saunter
staring with insolent eyes at the strange fighter;
after the long fret of sea; after Gibraltar—

to see from the easy train the first slim wood
misted by autumn sun and the hedged road,
    to watch quietly
the harrow pattern with care the Devon field
and the sheep crowd silent in the safe fold;

to hear again the rooks chatter at evening,
etching with lines of flight the day's ending,
    and the last wind mourn
the departed swallows, while a skylark strings
its bubbled music through the curlew's songs,

We who were born of England, who are bound forever,
being of her strange earth, to be her lover;
    whose precious dead
walk, still erect, in her flowers and speak to us
in her rivers' murmur and her rains' kiss—

it is not for those who defile her, the slum captains,
the headline bankers, the spinners of captions,
    the millionaires—
it is not for these that we fight, but, rather,
to save from these our mother, our father,
her earth, our dead, her past, our future,
    who are her heirs.

Lieutenant RICHARD GOODMAN RNVR

*

OFF BRIGHTON PIER

I saw him, a squat man with red hair,
Grown into sideburns, fishing off Brighton pier;
Suddenly he bent, and in a lumpy bag
Rummaged for bait, letting his line dangle,
And I noticed the stiffness of his leg
That thrust out, like a tripod, at an angle.
Then I remembered: the sideburns, that gloss
Of slicked-down ginger on a skin like candy floss.
He was there, not having moved, as last,
On a windless night, leaning against the mast,
I saw him, groping a bag for numbers.
And the date was the 17th of September,
Fifteen years back, and we were playing Tombola
During the last Dog, someone beginning to holler

'Here you are' for a full card, and I remember
He'd just called 'Seven and six, she was worth it',
When—without contacts or warning—we were hit.
Some got away with it, a few bought it.
And I recall now, when they carried him ashore,
Fishing gear, lashed to his hammock, wishing
Him luck, and his faint smile, more
To himself than to me, when he saluted
From the stretcher, and, cadging a fag,
Cracked, 'I'm quids in, it's only one leg,
They'll pension me off to go fishing.'

Lieutenant ALAN ROSS RNVR

*

THE VOYAGE BACK

It was the time of voyaging back. It was the time, now, at last.
We had come to the end of the days and night we went patrolling
The wastes of ocean. We'll not retrace our wake, all that is past;
The slat-bleached struggling ship, the frozen spray in the rigging,
Like filigree icing, and the sight of the seamen's wind-scored faces
As they hump the shells, with blue-red hands, to the taut, whitened,
Intractable single-whip tackle while the ship plunges and races,
Shudders and slips to the slash of the waves, and the stomach feels tightened
In a gritty, queasy contraction, and the smell from the galley
Swims in the head, and the staler stench of tobacco smoke stains
Fingers and mouth. To watch no more for the green break of light that stilly
Creeps out of the spume to etch again the twisted convoy lanes,
And later the stretched out stragglers hove up from the pallid mouth
Of a snowing dawn. To feel, to know, to touch this no more,
To say it is done, for a few years at least, makes the heart want to shout
With the joy of relief for the flesh that was flayed by the raw
Wracking winds from the south and the west. Praise God, it was the last, last time;
We were just about at the end of the rope, waking or sleeping,

We dreamed of the plunge and the rise and the endless wind and
the rime
Of the needling frost that ate its way into eyes and ears and brain.
No wonder I saw a young seaman his face puckered and weeping
As we ran in the lee of the land back to port and he felt the rain
Falling quietly down from a sky that stood still, out of a peace
That spelled home, gentleness, love. His tears were only the tears
of release.

R. C. M. HOWARD
Far East, August 1945

*

DEMOBILISATION LEAVE

I have seen the white tiger,
Imagination,
In the Douanier Rousseau forest:
Isosceles leaves and a waterfall of compasses.
And although I am writing in Cornwall, in winter,
And the rain is coming in from the moor,
Trincomali, ah, Trincomali!
The Technicolor market, the monkeys and chickens,
The painted boats at Vegetable Jetty,
The rattling lizard and the bored crow
In the burning graveyard:
Here lies David Kelly, Naval Stores Officer,
Died of the Fever,
1816.

O the drums and the pythons and the trick of the mango tree,
The warrior Buddha with the brandished sword,
The rosewood elephants and the porcupine cigarette boxes.
O the fire opal, zircon and water sapphire,
And the warm beer and peanuts in the P.O.s' canteen.
The Chinese cafés, and the rickshaw boys
Grinning and gambling by the fish-market.
The rings from Kandy and the black ivory elephants
Crossing the eternal bridge for the mantelshelves
Of thousands and thousands of sailors.

And the carrier and her exhausted planes
Lying in the oily harbour,
Hands to bathe
And the liberty-boats
Buzzing over the water.
O the sickly lime-juice at Elephant House
And the cooking that looks of the West
But tastes, O tastes of the East.

And they say:
'You must be fed up with your leave,
Fifty-six days is a long time,
You'll start work before it's over—
You'll be tired of nothing to do,
Nothing to think of,
Nothing to write about,
Yes: you'll go back to the office
Soon.'

CHARLES CAUSLEY

*

EPILOGUE

And so, not long after the last U-boat had raised its evil, dripping hull to the surface and hoisted the black flag of surrender, and the last Japanese warship had been pounded into unrecognisable disintegration, quiet descended once more upon the seas and oceans. For nearly six years they had been torn by plunging shells and bombs, sundered by rending mines and charges in the depths, and furrowed by the tearing tracks of deadly torpedoes. The sea had mercifully engulfed the wrecks of hundreds of shattered and burning ships; it had covered and concealed the last agonies of thousands upon thousands of seamen of many races and nations; and in the end it had provided the road on which the Allied armies had been carried to their final victories.

Now the mines were swept and the channel marks replaced, the lighthouses blinked again into the darkness to guide the home-bound ship; wireless signals and radar beams flashed to the assistance of seamen of all nations; and they travelled through the days and nights of their passages without the anxious uncertainty, so long experienced as to have become instinctive, whether there would be another sunrise for them, or another dusk.

What of the merchant ships themselves? They—liners and coasters, tankers and dry cargo ships, tugs and fishing vessels—were soon in dockyard berths gladly stripping off their nondescript wartime grey, and decking themselves out again in the proud colours of their companies. House flags, forbidden emblems for so long, were re-hoisted, and distinctive funnel markings, familiar only to the older hands, began to reappear. Deadlights over the portholes were hooked back or permanently unshipped, blackout screens to the bridge and engine-room ladders were torn down and thankfully burnt. The liners cleared themselves of the tiered steel bunks of their troopship days and restored their luxurious cabin and saloon furnishings; the fishing craft got rid of their minesweeping tackle, and replaced it with the more welcome trawls and drift-nets; guns and ammunition were landed wherever and whenever they could be got rid of, and the encircling girdles of the degaussing cables quickly followed. Before many months had passed the ships were all once more ploughing the seas 'on their lawful occasions', navigation lights now burning brightly, portholes blazing and music often sounding across the water. Their wireless sets are no longer clamped down against all telltale transmissions, and listening only for the remote voice of warning or the sudden call of another ship's distress; but instead freely send and receive weather signals, cargo instructions, or merely the interchanged greetings of happy mortals; the quarter-master steers easily by the light of a full bright binnacle, after so many months and years of eye strain over a dimmed compass card; and the look-out, though still at his post, no longer watches for enemies lying in ambush. Down in the engine and boiler-rooms the great machines throb and hum, while the engineers go about their work, no longer conscious that the fifty-foot vertical steel ladder above them is their only means of escape when the water rushes in; and the watches change with the knowledge that during their eight hours off duty there will be no sudden calls to man the guns or to rescue another ship's survivors.

At first it all seemed strange, and men even looked to the habitual stowages for their lifebelts when they awoke; but soon older customs reasserted themselves and more recent urgencies were forgotten. Most of the ships proudly preserved some token of their wartime service by way of battle honours. Passenger liners left untouched a small section of the teak guardrails on which soldiers had carved their names, their home towns, or a message to a distant sweetheart. On the main stairway of a cross-Channel steamer one may see a lettered plaque baldly stating 'Dunkirk 1940; Normandy 1944'; while a great liner may unemotionally record that she was at the fall of Singapore, the seizure of Madagascar and the landings at Algiers; that she sailed in so many WS convoys, and in all carried so many tens of thousands of soldiers to such and such distant theatres of war. But probably few of the passengers even notice these modest emblems, and fewer still realise anything of the romance and endurance which lie behind the simple statements. When the ships themselves disappear so will the plaques, and then their stories will live only in old men's memories—and in books.

And the warships? A few, and the newer ones, were soon beginning to recommission with Royal Navy crews in place of the wartime mixture of long-service men, reservists and 'hostilities only' ratings; and before long their clean White Ensigns, burnished brasswork and white-scrubbed ladders were to be seen once more on their accustomed foreign stations. Some were given or lent to the Commonwealth countries, who realised that now they must bear an adult's share of the burden so long borne by their exhausted mother country; others were transferred to Allied nations whose navies had almost ceased to exist during the years of enemy occupation; yet others were very gradually taken in hand in British yards for conversion and modernisation; and a few were sold to small nations on the look-out for armament bargains in the great demobilisation reduction sales. But many, very many, were considered too old or too worn out for further service. For them there could only be the undeserved indignity of the shipbreakers' yards—a process made all the more welcome to a harassed and empty Treasury by the prevailing high price of scrap metals. Truly we are an unsentimental, commercially minded race. Not one of those thousands of ships which kept the life-line open has been preserved to posterity's wonder and instruction, and to the education of the youth of Britain.

Yet by no means all found comparatively quick and merciful oblivion in the breakers' yards. A watchful and experienced Admiralty knew that those that were not too worn-out or too old might yet be needed again, in a sudden emergency which gave no time to build. And so, before many months had passed, the creeks and estuaries of Britain's rivers began to receive groups of salt-rimed, rust-stained little ships—corvettes and destroyers, sloops, minesweepers and frigates. Their fragile and valuable equipment removed or protected by sealed 'cocoons', funnel covers laced on, and gun tampions driven hard home. Moored bow and stern they could not even swing to the tides they had known so well, but as the ripples ebbed and flowed could only gently nudge each other, and pass through the group the mumbling mutters of their memories. This one, the leader, had carried a famous Escort Group Commander, and with him on the bridge had fought through convoy after convoy; her depth-charge racks and throwers had loosed death on many a lurking U-boat, detected by the relentless probing of the Asdic in her bottom; her sisters had screened the battleships in the chase of the *Bismarck*, the sinking of the *Scharnhorst*, and at Matapan; they had returned from Dunkirk's beaches and Grecian harbours loaded down with exhausted soldiers; they had escorted the troopships and covered the landing craft in many combined operations. That one, a minesweeper, had swept the great ships of the main fleet in and out of harbour countless times; the sloop next door had run the straggling east coast convoys up and down the narrow channels from Thames to Forth for six long years, protecting them all the time from mines, bombs and torpedoes. The flat-bottomed craft across the bay had seen the first landings in Africa, then Sicilian beaches and Salerno's struggle; and finally the great Normandy invasion. That group of motor-launches was for sale and will soon be tied up as houseboats in rivers, far upstream from the harbours they had patrolled and defended. Few passers-by or seaside holiday makers who saw the ships could guess their memories. To them they were only a bunch of useless encumbrances on the tideway.

But what of the warship crews who had manned and fought them? These can still be found or identified, though the seeker has got to know the touch and the look of what he seeks, or he will seek in vain. Ask the liner quartermaster, as he spins the ship's wheel, in which of them he served; walk aft and watch the able seaman setting out the passengers' chairs. The way he wears his cap betrays him, and in the little 'caboosh' where he keeps the tools of his new trade there are some telltale tokens of a former one. The railway porter who seized a civilian's suitcase, took one glance at its owner and said, 'We served together in *Ramillies*'; the young veterinary surgeon who tied a cow's halter with a bowline, and so marked himself for the Volunteer Reservist he had been; the lighthouse keeper, polishing his powerful lenses; the grey-haired pensioner tending the flowers of his village garden near the sea; the stocky figure sauntering along a seaport street in a rather too well-worn bluejacket; the coastguard, telescope in hand; and often the small shop- or inn-keeper too. All are identifiable—if you know the type; and they are the men who knew intimately the rusting hulks in the river creeks, and who served those relentless grey mistresses, grumbling as lovers do, yet always returning to them. They are the men whose loyalty, endurance and patience did most to bring the cargo ships home and take the troopships out; whose ribald humour could never be suppressed by danger or discomfort or the worst that fate, the weather or the enemy could do to them. Now they are scattered far and wide; but they have not forgotten. Occasionally they still gather for an evening's talk in White Ensign clubs, or visit ships in Navy Week, to see what sort of a job the youngsters are making of it. One who had served for nearly forty years recently said he 'would go back on one meal a day'. Another, who had been chief gunner's mate of the famous *Warspite*, watched the knackers tearing at her hulk on the rock-bound Cornish coast, and told his old commander what he felt. Others, from distant dominions as well as the nearby fields and valleys of England, like still to keep in touch with 'old ships'. There is an antipodean ship's company which has its own club, and, on each anniversary of an action in which their ship was damaged, remembers their English one-time captain. The sense of comradeship, hardened in the furnace of war, has not left them. But they are a tiny minority, and have lived on into an age when numbers and votes, pressure groups and self-seekers, sensation and scandal drown the small voice of those who served selflessly and faithfully.

True, one does not see in the streets the mutilated seamen whose condition aroused an earlier generation's shocked compassion and led to the foundation of Greenwich Hospital. A more highly developed social conscience now provides pensions and medical care for the maimed. Yet it may be that those who fought on, above and beneath the sea, yet feel arise in their minds the old questioning doubts which have so long troubled men of understanding in maritime affairs. Will the new generation of their countrymen be ready to pay the certain price of true security for Britain?

Captain S. W. ROSKILL DSC RN

Index

NOTE: You may notice that the spelling of a few surnames differs in this index from the spelling in the text ('Illustrious' Fight For Life, and Kelly, contain a few examples). I have left the writer's spelling as it is in the text, but have used the Navy List spelling in this index.

Smith, W. J. L., S/Lt. RNZNVR: in XE3 attack on *Takao*, 381
Snapper, HMS: 55
Somerville, Admiral Sir James: F.O. Force H, exchange of signals with Cunningham, 86, 91, 144
Spain, Nancy, 2nd Officer WRNS: extract from *Thank You, Nelson* (Hutchinson, 1948), 62–3
Spencer, James, Marine: 'Dieppe', from *The Awkward Marine* (Longmans Green, 1948), 252–5
Spowart, G., Ch. Sto.: in *Tempest*, 206
Stammers, H. J., Temp. Surg. Lt. RNVR: of *Acasta*, 42n.
Stanning, G. H., Lt. (S) RN: of *Hardy*, takes command, 31
Starling, HMS: 2nd Escort Group, 323–9
Steele, W. R., Pay Cdr. RN: of *Ark Royal*, 148
Stephenson, Admiral Sir Gilbert: Commodore Western Isles, 359
Stopes, Dr Marie Carmichael: elegy for HMS *Cossack*, 'Instead of Tears' (published by Count Potocki of Montalk, 1942), 143–4
Storey, J. L., Capt. RN: i/c *Jamaica*, Barents Sea, 263
Storm, HMS: gun attack on Japanese convoy, 354–9
Strait Malakka: alias *Kormoran*, 155
Stuart, HMAS: at Matapan, 114
Stubborn, HMS: 288
Sturdy, Michael, Lt. RN: of *Kelly*, killed, 122
Stygian, HMS: 379
Suffolk, HMS: sights *Bismarck*, 133–4
Sun IV, tug: at Dunkirk, 44, 47
Sydney, HMAS: sinks *Bartolomeo Colleoni*, 159; loss of, 155–9
Syfret, Sir E. N., V.-A.: 260

Tacoma, tender to *Graf Spee*: 18
Tairoa: sunk by *Graf Spee*, 13
Takao, Japanese cruiser: attacked by XE-craft, 379–90
Talabot: bombed in Malta, 225
Taranto: attack on, 86–91
Tay, HMS: convoy battle ONS 5, 279, 280
Taylor, Alfred, R.-A.: 46
Taylor, W. T., Ldg. Sea.: in *Storm*, 358
Telemachus, HMS: sinks I-166, 352–4
Tempest, HMS: loss of, 204–9
Tennant, William, Capt. RN: i/c *Repulse*, 169, 172
Thames, tug: tows *Ark Royal*, 151, 154
Thetford Mines, HMCS: 363
Thomas, Ldg. Sto.: in *Ark Royal*, 154
Thompson, Pte.: Crete, 132
Thompson, Lt. RNVR: 825 Sq. attack on *Scharnhorst*, *Gneisenau*, 184
Thorpe, Arthur, Exchange Telegraph correspondent: extract on the loss of *Eagle*, from *Daily Telegraph*, 14th August, 1942, 234–5
Times, The: 56, 85; extract from leader of 14th February, 1942, 179
Timperson, Ord. Sea.: of *Broke*, 109
Tipping, A.B.: of *Peterel*, 163
Tirpitz, German battleship: 214; threat to PQ 17, 242, 245; attacked by X-craft, 288–95; sunk by RAF, 295
Tollesbury: at Dunkirk, 46
Tooley, George, *Maid of Orleans*; at Dunkirk, 48
Torbay, HMS: 204
Torch, Operation: 259–62
Tovey, Admiral Sir John: C.-in-C., Home Fleet, *Bismarck*, 140; PQ 17, 245
Tower, Ian, Capt. RN: at Le Havre, 50
Trotter, Wilfred: at Dunkirk, 46
Tuck, G. S., Cdr. RN: in *Illustrious*, 96
Turbulent, HMS: 204
Turner, Bradwell, Lt.-Cdr. RN: boards *Altmark*, 26
Turner, C. E., S/Lt. RNVR: of *Campeador V*, 56
Tweedie, H. E. F., Lt.-Cdr. RN: i/c *Tynedale*, at St Nazaire, 215
Tynedale, HMS: at St Nazaire, 215

U-boats (German): U-29, sinks *Courageous*, 6; U-30, sinks *Athenia*, 5; U-39, attacks *Ark Royal*, and sunk, 6; U-47, sunk by *Wolverine*, 101; U-64, sunk in 2nd Narvik, 33; U-73, sinks *Eagle*, 233; U-81, sinks *Ark Royal*, 147; U-99, sunk by *Walker*, 101–5; U-100, sunk by *Vanoc* and *Walker*, 101, 105; U-125, sunk by *Vidette*, 281; U-192, sunk by *Pink*, 280–1; U-238, sunk by *Kite*, *Magpie* and *Starling*, 326; U-264, sunk by *Woodpecker* and *Starling*, 328–9; U-331, sinks *Barham*, 162; U-424, sunk by *Wild Goose* and *Woodpecker*, 326–8; U-438, sunk by *Pelican*, 281; U-531, sunk by *Oribi*, 281; U-592, sunk by *Starling*, *Wild Goose* and *Magpie*, 323–4; U-605, sunk by *Lotus* and *Poppy*, 262; U-630, sunk by aircraft of No. 5 Sq. RCAF, 281; U-638, sunk by *Loosestrife*, 281; U-710, sunk by aircraft of 206 Sq. Coastal Command, 281; U-734, sunk by *Wild Goose* and *Starling*, 325–6; U-762, sunk by *Woodpecker* and *Wild Goose*, 324–5; surrender of, 363

Also available from Vintage

FREEDOM'S BATTLE VOLUME II

The War in the Air 1939–45

Edited by Gavin Lyall

From the brilliant summer nonchalance of 1940 to the grim, anonymous exhaustion of the bomber crews delivering the infernos of Hamburg and Dresden. All the great dramas of the air war are here, described by the men in the British and Commonwealth Air Forces who did the fighting. We accompany them in the desperate days of the fall of France; during the Battle of Britain; throughout the agony of Bomber Command; over the high seas, Malta, the desert battles and in the struggle with Japan.

This is the second volume in the unique *Freedom's Battle* trilogy, which provides intensely vivid accounts of war at sea, in the air and on land. Far better than any single narrative, the extracts build up a complete picture of the War as it was experienced by the men and women who actually took part in it.

'Comprehensive, skilfully edited and eminently readable'
Sunday Times

'A wonderful selection'
Yorkshire Post

'It presents a faithful and graphic series of pictures linked by the briefest and clearest summaries . . . Well balanced and comprehensive'
Times Literary Supplement

VINTAGE BOOKS
London

Also available from Vintage

FREEDOM'S BATTLE VOLUME III

The War on Land 1939–45

Edited by Ronald Lewin

'This anthology is . . . a distillation of what the fighters put down at the time or in retrospect to tell others (or perhaps convince themselves) what it was all about. Here are the words of the wise, the witty, the nonchalant, the devil-may-care: the poets and the prodigals.' From the Editor's Foreword

On land, the Second World War provided an infinite variety of experience, often under stresses as great as human beings have endured. Reactions are correspondingly various – from the comic to the appalled.

Here are the testimonies of those who fought in all the great campaigns – in Europe, Africa and the Far East. Here too are the words of prisoners, partisans, saboteurs and soldiers in private armies.

This is the third volume in the unique *Freedom's Battle* trilogy, which provides intensely vivid accounts of war at sea, in the air and on land. Far better than any single narrative, the extracts build up a complete picture of the War as it was experienced by the men and women who actually fought in it.

THE FREEDOM'S BATTLE TRILOGY

ALSO AVAILABLE FROM VINTAGE